APOLOGETICS

"If I were asked to list the top three books that have had the greatest impact on me as a Christian thinker, John Frame's *Apologetics to the Glory of God* would undoubtedly be one of them. It brought about a paradigm shift—one might even say a 'Copernican revolution'—in my understanding not only of apologetics but of all other intellectual endeavors as a Christian. Ever since then, it has been the first book I recommend to those looking for an introduction to Christian apologetics, and it is required reading in my apologetics classes. I'm therefore delighted to recommend this updated and expanded twentieth-anniversary edition, which incorporates additional material by Dr. Frame, as well as many helpful annotations by Joseph Torres. *Soli Deo Gloria!*"

—**James N. Anderson**, Associate Professor of Theology and Philosophy, Reformed Theological Seminary, Charlotte

"This book is as vital as when it first appeared. John Frame manages to tackle the most difficult problems facing a Christian who endeavors to defend the faith: the nature of evil, world religions, the use of evidences, and much more. And he does so with grace, theological acumen, and an enviable straightforwardness—rare for apologists who are at home with the principal philosophical issues of the day. Extraordinarily profitable volume from a veteran Christian thinker."

—**William Edgar**, Professor of Apologetics, Westminster Theological Seminary

"Over the last several decades, few books have been as helpful to so many for so long as *Apologetics to the Glory of God* by John Frame. I eagerly welcome the twentieth-anniversary edition of this important book. As apologetics takes on an even greater significance for every believer, I can only hope that the influence and impact of this book will spread far beyond even its original publication. This is a book that, twenty years after its initial publication, is even more timely—and that is a rare achievement."

—**R. Albert Mohler Jr.**, President, Southern Baptist Theological Seminary

"For decades, John Frame has given himself to the church, to his students, and to meticulous thinking and the rigorous study of the Bible. He winsomely, patiently, and persuasively contends for the gospel, and brings together a rare blend of big-picture thinking, levelheaded reflection, biblical fidelity, a love for the gospel and the church, and the ability to write with care and clarity."

—**John Piper**, Chancellor, Bethlehem College and Seminary; Founder and Teacher, www.desiringGod.org

APOLOGETICS

A JUSTIFICATION OF CHRISTIAN BELIEF

JOHN M. FRAME

Edited by
JOSEPH E. TORRES

P&R
PUBLISHING
P.O. BOX 817 • PHILLIPSBURG • NEW JERSEY 08865-0817

Unless otherwise indicated, Scripture quotations are from The Holy Bible, English Standard Version, copyright © 2007 by Crossway Bibles, a division of Good News Publishers. Used by permission. All rights reserved.

Scripture quotations marked (NIV) are from the HOLY BIBLE, NEW INTERNATIONAL VERSION®. NIV®. Copyright © 1973, 1978, 1984 by International Bible Society. Used by permission of Zondervan Publishing House. All rights reserved.

Scripture quotations marked (NASB) are taken from the New American Standard Bible®, copyright © 1960, 1962, 1963, 1968, 1971, 1972, 1973, 1975, 1977, 1995 by The Lockman Foundation. Used by permission.

Italics within Scripture quotations indicate emphasis added.

Portions of this work were originally published in John M. Frame's *Cornelius Van Til: An Analysis of His Thought* (P&R Publishing, 1995), *The Doctrine of God* (P&R Publishing, 2002), and *Speaking the Truth in Love*, edited by John J. Hughes (P&R Publishing, 2009). They have been edited and revised for this volume.

Some material in chapter four appears in a similar form in John M. Frame, "Transcendental Arguments," in W. C. Campbell-Jack and Gavin J. McGrath, eds., *New Dictionary of Christian Apologetics*, consulting ed. C. Stephen Evans (Downers Grove, IL: InterVarsity Press, 2006), 716–17. Used by permission of the publisher.

Printed in the United States of America

Library of Congress Cataloging-in-Publicaion Data

Frame, John M., 1939-
 [Apologetics to the glory of God]
 Apologetics : a justification of Christian belief / John M. Frame ; edited by Joseph E. Torres. -- Second edition.
     pages cm
 Revision of: Apologetics to the Glory of God. 1994.
 Includes bibliographical references and indexes.
 ISBN 978-1-59638-938-0 (pbk.) -- ISBN 978-1-59639-939-7 (ePub) -- ISBN 978-1-59638-940-3 (Mobi)
 1. Apologetics. I. Torres, Joseph E., editor. II. Title.
 BT1103.F73 2015
 239--dc23
                    2014047572

To all my students,

from whom I have learned much

CONTENTS

FOREWORD

This second, expanded edition of John Frame's book on apologetics is a vital and welcome contribution, because apologetics continues to be an important area for us to think through. It is important not only for people who are especially interested in evangelism and apologetics, but for every Christian believer. In many prestigious institutions in the West, hostility to Christianity has increased. The need for wise presentation and defense of the Christian faith has therefore also increased. I commend this book to the attention of Christians everywhere because it helps us to live as Christians, in accord with what God did to renew us when he brought us to know Christ and to bow to him as Lord.

What more should be said? I will briefly underline a few salient points that Frame's book expounds at length.

Being a Disciple

The Bible has instructions and insights that affect every area of life, including apologetics. Our conduct is not the basis for our salvation, but is influenced by our salvation. The Bible indicates that God brings salvation to those who trust in Jesus. This salvation is a gift of God's grace, not something that we earn or deserve on the basis of achievement. We do not try to transform ourselves in order to be saved. Rather, God saves us by reaching out to us in our state of sin and alienation from him. But then any person who is saved is also transformed by the power of God.

Romans 12:1–2 illustrates this principle. The preceding chapters, in Romans 1–11, reflect on the meaning of salvation. Then, as an implication of salvation, Romans 12:1–2 exhorts believers to be renewed in their minds:

> I appeal to you *therefore*, brothers, by the mercies of God, to present your
> bodies as a living sacrifice, holy and acceptable to God, which is your

spiritual worship. Do not be conformed to this world, but *be transformed by the renewal of your mind*, that by testing you may discern what is the will of God, what is good and acceptable and perfect.

A Christian believer is not supposed to just lie still, relax, and enjoy the salvation already given to him. He is to be active in serving the Lord, like an athlete or a farmer working hard (1 Cor. 9:24–26; 2 Tim. 2:5–6). Jesus says, "If you love me, you will *keep my commandments*" (John 14:15).

To put it another way, "You are not your own, for you were bought with a price. So glorify God in your body" (1 Cor. 6:19–20). A person who truly trusts in Christ has given up every other loyalty in order to be loyal to Christ alone. He has become a disciple of Christ:

> If anyone comes to me and does not hate his own father and mother and wife and children and brothers and sisters, yes, and *even his own life*, he cannot be my disciple. Whoever does not bear his own cross and come after me cannot be my disciple. (Luke 14:26–27)

A true disciple is never "off duty." He is always a disciple. He is a disciple in the actions of his body, and a disciple also in the actions of his mind—a renewed mind. Consequently, he is a disciple in every word that he utters in an apologetic discussion.

Being a Disciple in Apologetics

So discipleship has implications for apologetics. If Sue is a Christian believer, she must remain a believer and act like a believer when she is in discussions with non-Christians. She cannot pretend to be religiously neutral when she evaluates religious or philosophical claims, or discusses miracles, or discusses who Jesus Christ is, or discusses the basis for moral standards. She cannot be neutral because God has already given her truth in Jesus Christ. She ought not to betray what God has given.

Of course, she must grow in knowing Christ. But she already has some fundamental answers. And God intends that she should use these answers. She knows that Jesus is indeed the Son of God, not just a prophet, not just a religious teacher. She knows that the miracles of Christ described in the Gospels are real, just as Christ is real. She knows that God's standards for morality, such as he gives in the Ten Commandments, are expressions of true moral standards, not just relative cultural preferences. In these and many other ways, she is thinking and evaluating issues in a different way from non-Christians. In the words of Scripture, she is committed to "destroy arguments and every lofty opinion raised against the knowledge of God, and [to] take every thought captive to obey Christ" (2 Cor. 10:5). Her supreme loyalty is to Christ. And that loyalty gets exercised in her thinking, as well as in her bodily actions.

Christian apologetics is concerned with how Sue should present her faith positively to unbelievers, in order to invite them to Christ. But apologetics especially focuses on how Sue should defend her faith when others bring objections:

> But in your hearts honor Christ the Lord as holy, always being prepared to *make a defense* to anyone who asks you for a reason for the hope that is in you; yet do it with gentleness and respect, having a good conscience, so that, when you are slandered, those who revile your good behavior in Christ may be put to shame. (1 Peter 3:15–16)

Sue's defense of the faith should be in harmony with regarding "Christ the Lord as holy" in her heart.

The Lure of "Religious Neutrality"

Many people are tempted to picture a discussion in apologetics as a religiously neutral search for truth. Everyone supposedly starts off uncommitted and is trying to find out whether God exists, and which of the world religions might be true. According to this way of thinking, it is most important that everyone should be "unbiased." But the Bible indicates that this picture is completely unrealistic. It contradicts the actual situation in which we live. The actual situation is that some people have been saved by the grace of God in Christ, while others are still lost.

Not all ways lead to God. Christ is the only way to God:

> I am the way, and the truth, and the life. No one comes to the Father except through me. (John 14:6)

> And there is salvation in no one else, for there is no other name under heaven given among men by which we must be saved. (Acts 4:12)

The Old Testament radically rejects the worship of false gods, such as was common in the nations around Israel. Likewise, the New Testament radically rejects other proposals for how to be saved. This rejection is not religiously neutral. But it is the truth. Christian believers have come to know the truth, and they cannot pretend to be "unbiased" in the way that a non-Christian expects them to be. Sue is already a disciple; she is already committed. And that commitment is deep. To a non-Christian, this looks "biased."

Moreover, the Bible indicates that non-Christians already know God, the true God who made the whole world:

> For what can be known about God is plain to them, because God has shown it to them. For his invisible attributes, namely, his eternal power and divine nature, have been clearly perceived, ever since the creation of the world, in the things that have been made. So they are without excuse. For although *they knew God*, they did not honor him as God or give thanks to him, but they became futile in their thinking, and their foolish hearts were darkened. (Rom. 1:19–21)

The worship of idols is not an innocent practice, but a reaction in which a non-Christian uses idols to replace the worship of God, who is already known:

> Claiming to be wise, they became fools, and exchanged the glory of the immortal God *for images* resembling mortal man and birds and animals and creeping things. (Rom. 1:22–23)

In short, non-Christians are biased by a commitment *against God*.

So what picture of apologetics is right? Are some people wandering around among religious possibilities in a neutral way? Or is everyone already "biased"? And if everyone is already biased, are all biases created equal? Or is there a pronounced difference between knowing the truth in Christ and not knowing it?

> Whoever is not with me is *against me*, and whoever does not gather with me scatters. (Matt. 12:30)

Here is one area where loyalty to Christ matters. If we are loyal to him with our minds, we must think through apologetics in a way that rejects the idea of neutrality and accepts the Bible's own description of the nature of the situation. Such renewed thinking is what John Frame undertakes in his book.

Working on the Basis of Prior Commitment

Such an approach has been called *presuppositional* apologetics. Why? Because we who are believers in Christ are already presupposing our loyalty to Christ and the truth about Christ presented in the Bible. The involvement of presuppositions is not an intellectual game. It is not just an exercise in logic, in which someone proposes, "Let us explore in a disinterested way where various presuppositions lead." It is a requirement for Christian discipleship. A disciple, as we have observed, is *committed.* John Frame prefers the label *basic commitments* to *presuppositions* for this reason. The whole person is involved. No one is religiously neutral.

And not just *any* presuppositions will do. It matters in a crucial way whether we are following Christ or Buddha or Joseph Smith or Immanuel Kant. Knowing the truth in Christ leads to growing knowledge of the truth. Substituting a counterfeit for the truth leads to confusion (Prov. 4:18–19).

One of the common objections to presuppositional apologetics is that it represents an argument in a circle. "And so," the objector says, "it has no real power to persuade anyone who is not already persuaded." Frame handles this objection at greater length in his book.[1] But I may say a brief word here: this picture of the "circle" of presuppositional apologetics is a misunderstanding.

On the one hand, every person has a *kind* of circle, in that no one is religiously neutral. If our loyalty to Christ leads us to submitting to his teaching in the Bible, we move in a kind of circle in which the teaching of the Bible functions as our standard for sifting claims. The teaching in the Bible profoundly influences our beliefs. Among those beliefs is belief in Christ, which the Bible confirms. Analogously, people with *other basic commitments*—to reason or to pleasure—have their beliefs influenced by their commitments. We ought to acknowledge the existence of these circles, rather than try to ignore them. Given that the circles exist, we can still present evidence and arguments, just as the apostles did in their sermons in Acts, and just as the Old Testament prophets did when they called on people to turn back from idols to the living God.

In fact, the whole world offers evidence for God, as Romans 1:18–23 indicates. God is continually presenting people with the truth about himself, both through general revelation in nature and through special revelation in Scripture. Scripture in particular is designed to present the gospel, and the gospel "is the power of God for salvation to everyone who believes, to

---

1. Note also Joseph E. Torres's Appendix D.

the Jew first and also to the Greek" (Rom. 1:16). The gospel leads to people's salvation. It *does* persuade people (Acts 17:4, 12; 28:24). Through the gospel, the Holy Spirit changes people and brings them to faith. Through the power of the Holy Spirit, people have their spiritual eyes opened and come to acknowledge the evidence.

In the process, God makes himself known as One who is distinct from all the false gods. Jesus makes himself known as One who is the way and the truth (John 14:6), distinct from all other false ways and counterfeit truths. Not all religious commitments are "equal."

Each one of us who has become a believer has made a transition from darkness to light. Each of us has *changed* the circle of belief. Somehow, through the illumination of the Holy Spirit, we woke up to what was true all along, namely, that God the Father of Jesus Christ is the true God and there is no other. We rejected former religious commitments—commitment to a traditional form of false religion, or commitment to atheism or agnosticism, or commitment to the worship of money or pleasure, or some other modern form of ultimate allegiance. When we rejected former religious commitments, we did not become neutral in religion. We came to Christ. Without Christ and the working of his truth and his power, we never would have made the transition.

Religious neutrality is a mirage. It is a mirage that never existed in our life. And so why should we pretend in apologetics that it is an ideal that an unbeliever should emulate, or that we ourselves should temporarily emulate for the sake of dialogue? It is disloyalty to Christ to pretend that the desire for neutrality is a good thing. Once again, "whoever is not with me is against me" (Matt. 12:30).

The Centrality of the Bible in Human Living

The Bible's picture of proper human living is radically different from the world's picture, and the difference occurs already at a very basic level, namely, over the question of the independence of human thinking and the independence of human decision-making. Let us approach the question of independence by considering how the Bible describes the place that verbal communication from God plays in human living.

God created man "in the image of God," according to Genesis 1:26–27. He did not create man to live in isolation, but to live in personal communion with God himself. We can appreciate this communion when we see the contrast between the situation before the fall of Adam into sin and the situation afterward. Afterward, Adam and Eve tried to hide (Gen. 3:8–10). They were afraid to stand in God's presence. God was "walking in the garden," according to Genesis 3:8, so that if they had not sinned they could have walked with him.

One aspect of this personal communion between God and man is communication in language. Before the fall into sin, God instructed man concerning his role (Gen. 1:28–30) and his obligations with respect to the tree of knowledge (2:16–17). Immediately after the fall, God continued to speak to Adam and Eve (3:9–19). He gave words of judgment indicating some of the penalties for their sin. But he also gave a word of comfort: he promised to send the offspring of the woman to triumph over the serpent, that is, over Satan (3:15).

It is evident even from this early narrative that God intended his verbal communications with mankind to play a crucial role. Verbal communication was one aspect of personal communion between God and man. Through his words God also gave guidance and direction in both general and specific ways. At the general level, God indicated that human beings were to "be fruitful and multiply and fill the earth and subdue it" (Gen. 1:28). God also gave specific instructions about not eating the fruit from the tree of the knowledge of good and evil (2:17). When he created man, God never intended that man should find his way in the world just by using his mind and observing the trees and the soil around him. God spoke. God instructed. And because it was God who spoke, he spoke with absolute authority, the authority of the Creator. This speech was designed to govern everything else in human life.

We see the same theme of the centrality of God's instruction later on. God's instruction was central for Noah, when God commanded Noah to build the ark (Gen. 6:13–22). It was central for Abram, when God commanded him to leave Ur of the Chaldeans (Gen. 12:1–4).

God's word also played a central, guiding role in the life of Israel under Moses:

> Now this is the commandment, the statutes and the rules that the LORD your God commanded me to teach you, that *you may do them* in the land to which you are going over, to possess it, that you may fear the LORD your God, you and your son and your son's son, by *keeping all his statutes and his commandments*, which I command you, all the days of your life, and *that your days may be long.* Hear therefore, O Israel, and *be careful to do them,* that it may go well with you, and that you may multiply greatly, as

the Lord, the God of your fathers, has promised you, in a land flowing with milk and honey.

Hear, O Israel: The Lord our God, the Lord is one. You shall love the Lord your God with all your heart and with all your soul and with all your might. And these words that I command you today shall be on your heart. (Deut. 6:1–6)

The instructions of God must be continually on the lips of parents, in order that the children may learn:

You shall teach them [God's words] diligently to your children, and shall talk of them when you sit in your house, and when you walk by the way, and when you lie down, and when you rise. You shall bind them as a sign on your hand, and they shall be as frontlets between your eyes. You shall write them on the doorposts of your house and on your gates. (Deut. 6:7–9)

The responsibilities placed on Israel are similar to the responsibilities that a Christian disciple has in our day. The Christian disciple is never off duty. He is a disciple in all circumstances because Christ is his Master in all circumstances. Christ is Lord in all of life. Similarly, Israel was responsible for hearing and keeping God's commandments in all circumstances: "when you sit in your house, and when you walk by the way, and when you lie down, and when you rise" (Deut. 6:7). Discipleship involves listening to God's instruction. And we are not only to listen, but to obey—to *keep* God's commandments.

The same theme reoccurs with Joshua:

Only be strong and very courageous, being careful to *do according to all the law* that Moses my servant commanded you. *Do not turn from it* to the right hand or to the left, that you may have good success wherever you go. This Book of the Law shall not depart from your mouth, but you shall meditate on it day and night, so that you may be *careful to do according to all that is written* in it. For then you will make your way prosperous, and then you will have good success. (Josh. 1:7–8)

And we find it in Judges:

And you shall make no covenant with the inhabitants of this land; you shall break down their altars. But you have *not obeyed my voice.* (Judg. 2:2)

The northern kingdom of Israel was taken into exile because the people failed to listen to God's voice:

> Yet the LORD warned Israel and Judah by *every prophet and every seer,* saying, "Turn from your evil ways and *keep my commandments and my statutes,* in accordance with all the Law that I commanded your fathers, and that I sent to you by my servants the prophets."
> But *they would not listen,* but were stubborn, as their fathers had been, who did not believe in the LORD their God. They *despised his statutes and his covenant* that he made with their fathers and *the warnings* that he gave them. They went after false idols and became false, and they followed the nations that were around them, concerning whom the LORD had *commanded* them that they should not do like them. And they abandoned *all the commandments* of the LORD their God, and made for themselves metal images of two calves; and they made an Asherah and worshiped all the host of heaven and served Baal. And they burned their sons and their daughters as offerings and used divination and omens and sold themselves to do evil in the sight of the LORD, provoking him to anger. Therefore the LORD was very angry with Israel and removed them out of his sight. None was left but the tribe of Judah only. (2 Kings 17:13–18)

The same happened to the southern kingdom:

> The LORD, the God of their fathers, sent persistently to them by *his messengers,* because he had compassion on his people and on his dwelling place. But they kept mocking the messengers of God, *despising his words* and scoffing at his prophets, until the wrath of the LORD rose against his people, until there was no remedy. (2 Chron. 36:15–16)

We hear the same theme from Jesus himself:

> Everyone then who *hears these words of mine and does them* will be like a wise man who built his house on the rock. And the rain fell, and the floods came, and the winds blew and beat on that house, but it did not fall, because it had been founded on the rock. And everyone who hears these words of mine and *does not do them* will be like a foolish man who built his house on the sand. And the rain fell, and the floods came, and the winds blew and beat against that house, and it fell, and great was the fall of it. (Matt. 7:24–27)

Jesus asks us pointedly to keep his commandments:

If you love me, you will *keep my commandments.* (John 14:15)

Some of the passages focus on God's "commandments" and his "statutes." But these commandments do not come as just an isolated list of rules, which would be independent of God. God speaks them. And he speaks them in contexts in which he gives himself to us and instructs us. Everything that God gives us in Scripture helps to guide how we understand the parts that contain specific commandments. All of God's speech serves to guide us. In our day, we have a completed canon of Scripture. And all of that canon functions to guide us.

We considered earlier what it means to be a disciple of Christ. It means submitting to his teaching. And we find among his teachings affirmations of the divine authority of the Old Testament (Matt. 5:17–19; 19:4; John 10:35).[2] So we infer that we must receive the Old Testament as God's Word and submit to its claims. Since the New Testament apostles are commissioned by Christ, they have his authority, and we submit to New Testament teaching as well.

In sum, God does not leave us to our own thoughts. He guides us by speaking to us. Today he speaks through the completed canon of Scripture. He intends that his words should have a central role in guiding the whole of life. God created human beings in the beginning with this process of verbal communication already in view. We were created by God to have continual communication with him. We falsify what we are as creatures when we attempt to just "work out the truth" independently.

The Disastrous Fruit of Independence

The Bible also includes some instances of human beings' attempting the alternative strategy of working independently of God. The history of the alternative starts in the garden of Eden. Adam and Eve decided to make up their minds for themselves in their thinking about the fruit of the tree of the knowledge of good and evil. That step involved rebelling against God, ceasing to trust him, and rebelling against and despising the good words of direction that God gave. The history continued in the wilderness, where the people were determined to appoint a new leader instead of Moses and return to Egypt (Num. 14:3–4). Later they decided to go up on their own initiative and take the land from the Canaanites (14:40, 44). This kind

2. See John Murray, "The Attestation of Scripture," in *The Infallible Word* (Philadelphia: Presbyterian and Reformed, 1946), 1–54.

of behavior represents the desire to be *autonomous*, to make up one's one mind regardless of what God says.

The pattern continues in modern universities. With few exceptions, the overall atmosphere for university learning is an atmosphere of autonomy. That atmosphere is mostly assumed, rather than being discussed or questioned. Followers of Christ submit to his teaching. Most other people in the university setting prefer to submit to no one. They think that their approach is obviously right, and they despise genuine Christian faith. They think that Bible-believing Christians are naive or dogmatic or both.

Here we have a modern polarization between Christians, who submit to the teaching of God in the Bible, and non-Christians, who do not. This polarization echoes the polarization in Scripture itself between the desire for autonomy and the desire to serve God faithfully. Adam and Eve in their first sin desired autonomy. In the wilderness the Israelites in their desire for autonomy proposed to appoint a new leader and return to Egypt. By contrast, faithful saints listen to God's instruction.

It follows that modern universities are not religiously neutral, though they pretend to be. The atmosphere of autonomy represents a form of deep rebellion against God. Most participants in a university are committed to following their own way, and in so doing they are also committed to rejecting God's way.

But is the commitment of non-Christians really this bad? Some people might claim that non-Christians are merely ignorant of the truth, not actively committed to resisting God's way and God's instruction. It is true that some people on the face of the earth have never heard about the Bible or the description that the Bible gives of the true God, or the message of salvation in Christ that the Bible contains. But even these people are not neutral. According to Romans 1:18–23, they have general revelation and a knowledge of the true God. They suppress this knowledge.

But the participants in a modern university in the West are typically much worse off. They aspire to be educated. They aspire to search for truth or to search for a wise way to live. And unless their education is peculiarly defective, they will know at least bits—maybe highly distorted bits—about the nature of Christian faith and the Bible. And because of their commitment to autonomy, they have already determined to reject the transcendent claims that come from Christianity.

Someone might still want to argue in their favor, by pointing out that what they know is only a grievous distortion, and so they have an excuse. Yes, there are many distorted understandings. And here is where questions about apologetics strategy begin. If the problem is only that they do not know what the Bible claims and what genuine Christians believe, communication from a Christian can take the form of a simple presentation of the gospel. What will be the reaction? God might use the gospel to draw a person to faith. The gospel has divine power (Rom. 1:16) and may overcome all objections.

But does a simple presentation of the gospel always lead to a response in faith? No. Why not? Often modern people are not even curious about the gospel. They are convinced secularists. They are already committed to another way of life. But even if they are curious, their curiosity is mixed with resistance. The gospel is not pleasing to people who are in rebellion against God and are determined to continue in rebellion (1 Cor. 1:18–31).

Questions of apologetics arise, then, when Christian proclamation meets resistance and objections. And the resistance and objections do not come from nowhere. They are energized not merely by the general love of autonomy, but often by pride and comfort that the individual participant at a university feels because of the alleged superiority of the principle of autonomy and the knowledge claims of the university. The alleged superiority of the university contrasts with the alleged ignorance and primitive thought of Bible-believing Christianity.

I focus on the university setting because the atmosphere of autonomy is so strong and so obvious. It is the basic assumption about how to conduct discussion about any point at issue. But of course the universities influence everything else. The powerful people in business, education, media, and politics are usually university-educated. So the polarization between Bible-believing Christians and nearly everyone else characterizes most portions of Western societies.

In all this, my point is that Christians and non-Christians do not think alike and do not make the same assumptions. They have different assumptions in particular about the role of the Bible and the role of "making up one's own mind" and running one's own life. The Bible itself contains many examples of the difference. We must reckon with this difference when we prepare for apologetic discussion.

Points for Apologetic Discussion

So how will we conduct an apologetic discussion with an unbeliever? Will we undertake to present evidence for the resurrection of Christ? Of course. But how will we do it? Will we do it without any attention to what people think are the *standards* for evaluating evidence? Then we run the danger that unbelieving hearers will never analyze what might be mistaken in their idea of appropriate standards.

There is plenty of evidence for the resurrection, as Paul indicates in 1 Corinthians 15:3–8. But evidence gets interpreted against a background of assumptions. Paul interprets the evidence against the background of the Old Testament, as he indicates by the phrase "in accordance with the Scriptures," twice repeated (1 Cor. 15:3–4). By contrast, a modern unbeliever might interpret the testimonies of 1 Corinthians 15:3–8 and elsewhere against a background that includes the assumption that science has shown that miracles are impossible. This assumption has a firm place in an unbeliever's mind partly because the commitment to autonomy in thought contributes to a manner of thinking in which human insights become ultimate godlike claims rather than approximations. A regularity perceived by science is viewed as truth, rather than an approximation that might have exceptions because God can work exceptionally. So we are wise if we tackle the ways in which modern assumptions differ from the Christian view.

How else might we try to persuade an unbeliever? Will we present an argument for the existence of God, perhaps the argument for a first cause? Well, God is the first cause (Gen. 1:1). But how will an unbeliever understand such an argument? Typically, his commitment to autonomy leads him to treat all causes on a level. And that kind of understanding leads not to the God of the Bible, but to one more cause on the same level with the causes involving the interaction of two created things. One billiard ball hits another. Can we trace the causes of the billiard balls back into the past? Even if there is a first cause, it gets demoted by autonomous thinking to one cause among many. It is one billiard ball among many.

We need to challenge the underlying assumptions. Otherwise, the claims from the Bible tend to get distorted and rejected as they are filtered and misunderstood through the lens of antibiblical assumptions—a non-Christian worldview.

So we undertake to analyze the assumptions and commitments that belong to unbelief and that energize objections to the gospel. When we consider typical intellectual objections within the Western world, we find at least three vulnerabilities among these assumptions.

First, we find irony. Non-Christians think of Christian faith as ignorant and dogmatic. But ironically, they have ignorance and dogmatism of their own. The typical inhabitant of the university system looks down on Christianity in the midst of considerable ignorance concerning its actual claims, and in the midst of massive ignorance about the roots of his own notions. He feels comfortable affirming autonomy and rejecting Christianity, not because he has analyzed or checked out his commitments, but because everyone around him has similar notions. He has just accepted an atmosphere. And he is ignorant that this is what has happened. Having accepted the atmosphere, he holds it dogmatically. He is afraid of losing social position if he asks prying questions about it. He is influenced by pride and by fear. His reactions display not only ignorance but sin.

Second, some people might have thought through autonomy and might reject Christian faith in a much more informed way. But they, too, have the foundations of their lives on sand. For example, they have no firm foundation for moral judgments. If God does not exist, moral standards evaporate into personal or social preferences. The attempt to pronounce judgments about the alleged ignorance and dogmatism of a Christian evaporates into the will to exercise power, according to which a person projects his subjective preferences onto others. Similarly, knowledge might evaporate into skepticism as a person wonders how he can know that his mental apparatus is properly in tune with the world. The moral standards for knowledge itself disappear, and with them standards for evaluating what claims to be knowledge.

Third, the non-Christian secretly depends on God and his good gifts, day by day, in issues of morality and knowledge and other spheres.

All three of these vulnerabilities represent possible starting points for apologetic discussion. Frame's book helps us forward in the process.

The Pervasiveness of General Revelation

Let us consider a bit more the third vulnerability, concerning secret dependence on God. A robust doctrine of general revelation helps apologetics because it enhances appreciation of human dependence on God and the human knowledge of God that unbelievers are engaged in suppressing. In his book *Introduction to Systematic Theology*,[3] Cornelius Van Til took care to work out a robust appreciation of general revelation, before discussing special revelation and Scripture. He saw that our thinking about general revelation makes a difference. In particular, Romans 1:18–23 makes a difference, by its claim that creation reveals God and that human beings consequently know God.

---

3. Cornelius Van Til, *An Introduction to Systematic Theology: Prolegomena and the Doctrines of Revelation, Scripture, and God*, ed. William Edgar, 2nd ed. (Phillipsburg, NJ: P&R Publishing, 2007).

A non-Christian in the West typically assumes that reality consists in facts that do not clearly reveal God. If a Christian concedes this assumption, or if he *appears* to concede it by never challenging it, the special claims of Scripture soon lose plausibility. A divine voice in Scripture does not fit into a world where God is allegedly absent. The resurrection of Christ also loses plausibility. A special miraculous act in which God raises his Son from the dead makes no sense in a world of mere "facts," where God is effectively absent. If the non-Christian gains the alleged "right" to interpret the world autonomously, he will also interpret Scripture autonomously, and conclude that it is merely human. He will interpret the resurrection autonomously, and conclude that it is a mythic story. Or even if he admits that it happened, it remains a strange exception without meaning. He might say, "Strange things sometimes happen. Who knows what they mean?" Suppression of general revelation, if conceded, leads to suppression of special revelation.

On the other hand, a robust understanding of general revelation helps to unveil ways in which the knowledge of God is suppressed in unbelief. Non-Christians depend on God and simultaneously corrupt their knowledge of God in their situation of dependence. Frame unpacks the dependencies.

In the providence of God I, too, have tried to make a contribution. My work has not focused primarily on the challenges involved in direct apologetic dialogue and confrontation with unbelievers; rather, I have focused on positive appreciation of the nature of general revelation. In the process, I have come to appreciate more deeply that every nook and cranny of science and scientific law, every nook and cranny of language, every bit of personal relationships, every piece in the area of logic—each testifies to its source in God, whom we continually meet.

God made human beings themselves for the purpose of enjoying his glory: "Man's chief end is to glorify God, and to enjoy him forever" (Westminster Shorter Catechism Answer 1). The phrase in the original title of Frame's book, *To the Glory of God*, is apt. We are called by God to praise his glory as he reveals himself through science and language and relationships and so on. In general revelation as well as in special revelation, God the Father reveals his glorious character through the radiance of God the Son in the power of the Holy Spirit. We were created to perceive and receive this glory. We depend on him at every point. And if, when we look around us, we evade and suppress this revelation, we deny not only the reality concerning what we see, but our own selves.

Discipleship Again

We return to the beginning. What is needed is discipleship to Christ. Of course we need to be calling to discipleship those who are caught in the prison of unbelief and darkness. But we also need to grow as disciples ourselves. Serious discipleship leads to understanding God and the world. And understanding bears fruit in apologetics. Every piece of food and every moral issue are potential starting points for apologetic discussion, because every apple testifies to its source in God. In the end, Frame's book expounds discipleship in the arena of apologetics. To do so is also to expound the glory of God—it is to write apologetics to the glory of God.

> Vern S. Poythress
> Professor of New Testament Interpretation
> Westminster Theological Seminary
> Philadelphia

PREFACE TO THE SECOND EDITION

I am delighted to see this new edition of my book. It is an anniversary celebration; the original book was published in 1994, and this one now appears twenty years later. During that period I have done more writing in apologetics, and I am very thankful to the editor, Joe Torres, for adding that material to this book, with his own editorial notes. Joe has been a good friend and correspondent for maybe ten years, has worked with me as a teaching and research assistant, and who understands my apologetic approach as well as anyone else in the world.

Another who shares this level of understanding is my longtime friend and colleague Vern Poythress. Many thanks to Vern for his illuminating Foreword to this book. He introduces the apologetic issues by a careful account of the biblical history of redemption. I hope the reader will conclude that everything in the book is rooted in the Bible's account of creation, fall, and salvation through Jesus Christ.

Besides Joe and Vern, I would like to thank all of those who have worked to bring out this second edition of my book. John J. Hughes, as in many previous books of mine, has managed the publishing process. Karen Magnuson has done here an excellent job in copyediting. Tim Muether has developed the indices. And we all agree that without God's grace we could do nothing.

My prayer for this book is that it will motivate believers to take the gospel to the streets, even to the world, without fear. Among Christian apologists there are "not many . . . [who] were wise according to worldly standards" (1 Cor. 1:26), but those worldly standards themselves are foolishness in God's estimation. So we should expect apologists faithful to the Lord to "destroy arguments and every lofty opinion raised against the knowledge of God, and take every thought captive to obey Christ" (2 Cor. 10:5). May God use this book to help believers to present the gospel with such power.

John Frame

PREFACE TO THE FIRST EDITION

As the title indicates, this book is an "introduction" rather than a comprehensive system of apologetics. But it is intended for people who can do college-level reading and are serious about resolving issues of some difficulty.

Those who want or need a more comprehensive, philosophical background for considering the issues of apologetics should peruse my *Doctrine of the Knowledge of God*.[1] That is a somewhat larger study, presenting the general theory of knowledge that underlies this introduction to apologetics. Many of the points made in this book are discussed there at greater length. The epistemology developed in that book is applied in the present volume to specific apologetic issues. This book will, I trust, be more suitable as a textbook in apologetics.

In good conscience I can describe this volume as "Reformed" apologetics and as belonging to that special kind of Reformed apologetics developed by Cornelius Van Til. I do not necessarily agree with every sentence Van Til wrote; indeed, some Van Tillians will describe this work as "revisionist." But I believe that Van Til's approach is still the best foundation for Christian apologetics at the present time. Although I will refer to Van Til from time to time, however, it will not be my goal in this book to explain Van Til or to show the precise relationships between his ideas and mine. That will come later, God willing. I am preparing another book, which will attempt to comprehensively analyze and evaluate Van Til's work. (I am praying that it will be published in or before 1995, the one hundredth anniversary of his birth.)[2] That book will show more adequately than I can here why I continue to follow, and occasionally depart from, the Van Tillian model.

I do not particularly like the term *presuppositional* as a description of Van Til's apologetics or my own, although it is often used in this way.

---

1. Phillipsburg, NJ: P&R Publishing, 1987.
2. This book was published as *Cornelius Van Til: An Analysis of His Thought* (Phillipsburg, NJ: P&R Publishing, 1995).

Presuppositions are often contrasted with evidences, so that to call a system presuppositional tends to convey the message that that system recognizes the importance of presuppositions but despises evidences. Gordon Clark used the term of himself, and rightly so, because he had a very skeptical view of what could be known through human sense-experience, and thus a skeptical view of what is usually called *evidence*. He believed that the term *knowledge* should be reserved only for what we learn from Scripture. Van Til, however, did not have such a skeptical view of sense-experience, did not believe that knowledge was restricted to the Bible in that way, and was not inclined to reject the use of evidence. Thus, the term *presuppositional*, used in that sense, is not an adequate description of Van Til's position or mine. Others, such as (I believe) John Gerstner, misunderstand Van Til's use of the term. They stress the *pre* in *presupposition* and thus take it that a presupposition is something that one believes *before* (temporally) one believes anything else. This is wrong. The *pre* should be understood mainly as an indicator of eminence (e.g., *pre*eminence), not temporal priority. (Yet there is a sense in which the Christian presupposition—i.e., the knowledge of the truth that even unbelievers have while dishonoring it—is temporally prior: it is present from the beginning of life.) Still others equate *presupposition* with *hypothesis* or assume it to be an arbitrary, groundless supposition. (On Van Til's view, presuppositions are grounded in divine revelation and are categorical, not hypothetical.) With such confusions abroad, I am reluctant to use the term at all! Still, I don't want to quibble over words, and the term has become a standard label for all those who understand that there is no religious neutrality in thought and knowledge. So I will occasionally use that label of myself and Van Til, by way of accommodation, and also to emphasize what we share with Clark and others: the rejection of neutrality.[3]

But why another introduction to apologetics? Well, Van Til's work is still valuable, but it has always been in need of translation into more easily understood language. I think also that it needs some revision, as I have indicated, lest its weaknesses obscure its tremendously important insights. And apart from the writings of Van Til, few if any introductions to apologetics go to Scripture itself to ask in some detail concerning the norms for apologetics. I hope this book will fill that gap.

One weakness in Van Til's own writings is the lack of specific arguments.[4] Van Til always said that there was an "absolutely certain argument"

---

3. This paragraph has been added to the original preface to clarify the term *presuppositional*.

4. I will occasionally use the term *argument* in this book, although it is sometimes misunderstood. By it I do not mean a hostile encounter, as the term is sometimes used in ordinary

for Christianity, but he rarely produced an example, except in the barest outline form. I am somewhat less inclined to make the claim of an "absolutely certain argument," for reasons that appear within. But this book does include some specific examples of reasoning, which the reader is free to criticize or emulate.

Although this book is a bit heavy on theoretical matters, I realize that the Reformed apologist has a responsibility to speak in ordinary language. Chapter 10 is one step in that direction, although in the final analysis others may be better suited than I to do this kind of popularization. At any rate, if the reader is unsure about his aptitude for or interest in the theoretical portion of this book, he might still find chapter 10 helpful, and I suggest that he read that chapter first.

Besides Van Til, I am indebted to a great many other people who have, in one way or another, contributed to these thoughts and their publication here. I would like to give special thanks to McIlwain Memorial Presbyterian Church of Pensacola, Florida, for inviting me to lecture at their Pensacola Theological Institute in August 1990. The institute audiences gave me some good feedback and encouragement, motivating me to develop the material (here greatly expanded) for publication.

I am also indebted to a number of friends who read the first draft of this book and gave me much encouragement and many suggestions. Jim Scott did a fine job in editing the manuscript for publication. Special thanks go to Derke Bergsma, Bill Edgar, Thom Notaro, Scott Oliphint, Jim Jordan, and R. C. Sproul, who contributed many helpful ideas concerning both the broad structure of the book and many of its details. I could not accept all of their suggestions (indeed, some of them contradicted others!), but I have taken all of them seriously, and that process of self-critical thought has been invaluable. I trust that this book will, in turn, stimulate others to respond to the apologetic challenge for the love of God and the fulfillment of Jesus' Great Commission.

---

language. Nor do I mean an arid, purposeless discussion of abstract or theoretical issues—the concept that some people connect with the word. Rather, I use it in the logical sense: an argument is simply a group of premises that, the arguer claims, imply a conclusion. So understood, the term is roughly synonymous with *reasoning*, which, for example, Paul did, according to Acts 17:2; 18:4, 19; 24:25. People sometimes advise Christian witnesses not to argue. That advice may be good if we take *argument* in the sense of a hostile confrontation (but see the section "Dangers" in chapter 1). It may also be good if *argument* refers to a mere debate over abstract issues unrelated to sin and salvation. But in the logical sense, argument is quite unavoidable. Every sermon, every Bible study, and every witness to Christ seeks to warrant a conclusion (faith, repentance, obedience) and thus has an argumentative aspect.

INTRODUCTION

Why release a second edition of John Frame's *Apologetics to the Glory of God* (hereafter *AGG*)? *AGG* has served as an introduction to Christian apologetics from a presuppositional or "Van Tillian" perspective for twenty years. So it would appear that the book had a good run and that it's time to look to other resources to instruct budding apologists. It's been available for two decades. Isn't that enough? Truth be told, this rerelease of *AGG* is long overdue. The card-carrying *Framean* thinker that I am, I suggest three reasons why: *AGG*'s biblical perspective on the discipline of apologetics, the constant need to clarify what Van Tillian (or presuppositional) apologetics really is (and is not), and a new generation of readers.

A Biblical Perspective on Apologetics

Like any other discipline, apologetics lacks a uniform definition. The standard that's largely been adopted is "the defense of the faith," but overlapping definitions abound. Apologetics has been defined as "that branch of Christian theology which seeks to provide a rational justification for the truth claims of the Christian faith,"[1] "developing one's authentic self so as to present one's faith as helpfully as possible to one's neighbor,"[2] the demonstration "that Christianity is reasonable and thus (a) to assure Christians that their faith is not idiotic and (b) to clear away the obstacles and objections that keep nonbelievers from considering the arguments and evidence for the truth of Christianity,"[3] "the discipline that deals with a rational

---

1. William Lane Craig, *Reasonable Faith: Christian Truth and Apologetics*, 3rd ed. (Wheaton, IL: Crossway, 2008), 15.

2. John G. Stackhouse Jr., *Humble Apologetics: Defending the Faith Today* (New York: Oxford University Press, 2002), xvii.

3. James W. Sire, "On Being a Fool for Christ and an Idiot for Nobody," in *Christian Apologetics in the Postmodern World*, ed. Timothy R. Phillips and Dennis L. Okholm (Downers Grove, IL: InterVarsity Press, 1995), 110–11.

defense of Christian faith,"[4] "the task of defending and commending the truthfulness of the gospel of Jesus Christ in a Christlike, context-sensitive and audience-specific manner,"[5] and finally "the business of engaging the worldviews of the day intelligently and thus bearing witness to Christ with credibility."[6] Of course, each of these definitions of apologetics is helpful. As Frame reminds us, a word can have more than one useful definition. And Frame himself presents two complementary definitions. In *DKG* he argued that apologetics is little more than *the application of Scripture to unbelief*,[7] and on the first page of the first edition of *AGG* he defined apologetics as "the discipline that teaches Christians how to give a reason for their hope." These definitions are simultaneously simple and profound. Their simplicity provides an umbrella to cover all branches of Christian apologetics. Let's elaborate on this profundity.

Apologetics is giving a reason for our hope. This definition jumps right off the page from the charter verse of Christian apologetics (1 Peter 3:15). Apologetics is simply obedience to the command of Peter—no more, no less. When we define apologetics in terms of obedience, Scripture maintains its unique status as the final court of apologetic appeal. But apologetics is also *application of Scripture* to unbelief. The unregenerate heart desires a god that it can handle with a revelation that it finds palatable. The Christian defender is not free to water down the faith to suit the tastes of rebels. The unbeliever may be without excuse with regard to God's existence and moral requirements (Rom. 1:18–32), but the apologist is likewise without excuse with regard to the truth that he or she must uphold and defend. God has revealed himself and requires his people to serve as kingdom heralds. A proper grasp of Scripture, its teachings, and their interconnections is paramount to its robust and God-glorifying application to unbelief.

Finally, apologetics is also application of Scripture *to unbelief*. Unbelief is no respecter of persons. Both Christians and non-Christians wrestle with doubt and suspicion. A biblical apologetic targets unbelief wherever it may be found, strengthening the faith of Christians and calling unbelievers to repentance and faith in Christ.

---

4. Norman L. Geisler, *Baker Encyclopedia of Christian Apologetics* (Grand Rapids: Baker Academic, 1999), 37.

5. James K. Beilby, *Thinking about Christian Apologetics: What It Is and Why We Do It* (Downers Grove, IL: InterVarsity Press, 2011), 30.

6. Michael Goheen and Craig Bartholomew, *Living at the Crossroads: An Introduction to Christian Worldview* (Grand Rapids: Baker Academic, 2008), 29.

7. *DKG*, 87.

The Constant Need for Clarification

While Frame's definition of apologetics is clear enough, his methodology hasn't always been properly grasped. Misunderstandings of Reformed apologetics linger. Many of the most basic tenets of a presuppositional apologetic are misunderstood, caricatured, dismissed, or maligned. In March 2012, Paul Copan contributed an article on the blog of the Gospel Coalition titled "Questioning Presuppositionalism," in which he shared several concerns. His objections, in his own words, are as follows:

- First, it engages in question-begging—assuming what one wants to prove.
- Second, Christians share common ground with unbelievers, who are likewise made in God's image, which is not erased by the fall.
- Third, some (not all) presuppositionalists seem inconsistent about natural theology.
- Fourth, it is important to distinguish between the confident ground of our knowledge of God and the highly probable public case for the Christian faith.[8]

Unfortunately, all of Copan's concerns were based on easily avoidable misunderstandings. While responses to his concerns are parceled out throughout this second edition of *AGG*, a quick response to the first two objections might be handy.[9] First, not all circularity is created equal. Presuppositionalists admit to a kind of circularity, but reject others. In these pages you will find Frame's expanded and revised discussion of circularity as well as Appendix D, "Between Scylla and Charybdis: Presuppositionalism, Circular Reasoning, and the Charge of Fideism," which I wrote in response to this objection. Second, no Van Tillian to my knowledge has ever claimed that the *imago Dei* was lost in the fall. To the contrary, twenty years ago—in the first edition of *AGG*—Frame stated that "Orthodox Calvinists . . . recall that God made man in his image—an image that is marred by sin, but not destroyed. [Cornelius] Van Til argues that part of that image is knowledge of God, which, though repressed (Rom. 1), still exists at some level of his

---

8. Paul Copan, "Questioning Presuppositionalism" (March 12, 2012), http://thegospelcoalition .org/blogs/tgc/2012/03/12/questioning-presuppositionalism/.

9. For my own response to Copan's piece, see "Presuppositionalism and Circularity . . . Again?" (March 15, 2012), http://apolojet.wordpress.com/2012/03/15/presuppositionalism-and -circularity-again/.

thinking. That is the point of contact to which the apologist appeals."[10] My prayer for this second edition is that God will use it to help to foster both genuine understanding of presuppositionalism and, following from this understanding, forward-moving dialogue with those brothers and sisters in Christ who do not accept its distinctive emphases.

A New Audience

Both the rise of Reformed theology among younger evangelicals and the renewed interest of "gospel-centeredness" have rightly placed a high emphasis on Scripture. With this focus, people are looking to know what the Bible says on everything from gay marriage, questions of medical ethics, parenting, and unifying themes of Scripture to how to present and defend Christianity against its cultured (and uncultured) despisers. Young, Restless, and Reformed Christians want to know what Scripture says about apologetics and epistemology. Without the least hint of self-serving arrogance, it can be said that the Reformed tradition has been known for its intellectual prowess. Often this has been a boon for the movement, but not too infrequently it has sucked the vitality out of many a living faith. The sinful heart knows all too well how to distort any good thing. But under the instruction of Scripture, a humble recognition of man's fallibility and moral frailty, and the rigors that come from combining the two to meet the challenges of unbelief, what do we get? My answer: you get the essential tenets of Frame's approach to apologetics. If adherents to the New Calvinist movement are looking for a seasoned guide to direct their journey for an apologetic that magnifies the sovereignty and the glory of God, they have to look no further than John Frame.

About This Edition

A word about the expansions in this twentieth-anniversary edition is in order. Numerous editorial decisions were made to make a great book even better. Here I should mention my sources. This work includes the integration of both previously published and unpublished material. As an introduction, the original *AGG* sketched the general contours of Frame's approach to apologetics. Such an overview brings with it a challenge—namely, the occasional lack of specificity. A paradigmatic example will help here: In *AGG* Frame argues against Van Til's contention that

10. *AGG*, 83.

transcendental arguments are necessarily distinct from arguments of a more traditional kind. Some justification is made in *AGG*, but a fuller argument is found elsewhere (*CVT, STL*). The second edition includes these expansions. Sections from *DG* on miracle, evolution, and the problem of evil have also been integrated into the relevant units of this expanded work. John was also gracious enough to provide unpublished material for this project, providing helpful nuance and further clarifications on his original formulations.[11]

The inclusion of new content also required some shifting around of material. Some originally relegated to a footnote has been elevated to the main text, and on the rare occasion that the inclusion of material altered the flow of an argument, material originally found in the main text has been moved to a footnote. Chapter 7 (the first of two on the problem of evil) has been restructured to fit with Frame's perspectival approach offered first in *DG* and then again in *ST*. Another feature of this edition is the inclusion of annotations. The bulk of Frame's literary output was produced in the days following *AGG*. This material includes detailed discussions on a variety of topics, such as ethics, apologetics, the doctrines of God and revelation, and philosophy. Some of his formulations have been revised, expanded, or clarified in this edition. It would serve readers well to see how Frame's approach to apologetics is not only the application of Scripture to unbelief, but also the outworking of his overall biblically informed worldview. So cross-references to fuller discussions of related issues in his other works have been included here. Frame's discussion on miracles and their apologetic value (taken from *DG*) has also been included in order to make the book more comprehensive. Appendix C is a real online correspondence with an atheist. Unlike the fictional—and therefore idealized—dialogue provided by Frame in chapter 10, this discussion takes steps both backward and forward. Overall, I am convinced that it is helpful to provide an example of *one possible way* to apply the material found in this book. Unless noted otherwise, all biblical quotations in the main body of this new edition have been updated to the ESV.

Finally, this work is unique not only in that it updates, revises, and expands original material, but also in that I have provided a running commentary throughout the footnotes. My goal was to highlight the

---

11. Some of this material is found in Frame's contributions to Steven B. Cowan, ed., *Five Views on Apologetics* (Grand Rapids: Zondervan, 2000), and Gavin McGrath, W. C. Campbell-Jack, and C. Stephen Evans, eds., *The New Dictionary of Christian Apologetics* (Downers Grove, IL: InterVarsity Press, 2006).

subtlety of Frame's approach when needed. Sometimes he reformulates a traditional argument without saying so, and the reader may risk missing the subtlety of his thought. I've also included a few summarizing charts to aid student comprehension. References to Cornelius Van Til's *Defense of the Faith* and *Introduction to Systematic Theology* have been updated to match the most recent editions of those works, except in the appendices.[12]

There are many to thank for their encouragement on this project. Sarah Flashing (writer and speaker at sarahflashing.com) was my cheerleader from the initial stages of this project to the very end. This newer edition might never have gotten off the ground without her helpful feedback and suggestions. My brother David has been my sounding board for years on all things philosophical and apologetic. He's always pressed me to move beyond the simple recitation of material to critical analysis. A heartfelt thanks to Dr. James Anderson, Associate Professor of Theology and Philosophy at Reformed Theological Seminary in Charlotte, North Carolina. James graciously agreed to review the manuscript and to critically interact with it. His suggestions and analysis have certainly improved this book and helped to catch many defects to which I was previously blind. I take full responsibility for those that remain! A special word of thanks is due to my wife, Jessica. This past year has thrown quite a bit at us both, the greatest challenge (and blessing!) of which was the birth of our first child, Jenesis Eden Torres. The responsibilities that come along with parenthood are great, but God's grace toward us during this time has been even greater. This year, Jessica has become my hero all over again. She balances the multiple responsibilities that come along with marriage and motherhood in a way that evidences God's grace and frankly boggles my mind. She's been the guardian of my writing and editing schedule, and truly is my Barnabas (in this case, *daughter* of encouragement).

Finally, a special word of thanks is due to John Frame. His committing this project to my care has been both an honor that words can hardly express and daunting beyond belief. But with that trust comes a relationship. Over the course of a decade, John has challenged and encouraged me to think God's thoughts after him. I am not only thankful for Frame

---

12. Cornelius Van Til, *The Defense of the Faith*, ed. K. Scott Oliphint, 4th ed. (Phillipsburg, NJ: P&R Publishing, 2008); Cornelius Van Til, *An Introduction to Systematic Theology: Prolegomena and the Doctrine of Revelation, Scripture, and God*, ed. William Edgar, 2nd ed. (Phillipsburg, NJ: P&R Publishing, 2007).

the academician, but also thankful to God for John the redeemed sinner and godly saint. I had the privilege not only of studying and working with him but also of worshiping alongside him at Covenant Presbyterian Church in Oviedo, Florida. He is a devoted churchman, a loving father and husband, and a godly example of Christlike humility. I am a better man for knowing him.

Joseph E. Torres
Thanksgiving 2013

ABBREVIATIONS

AGG	John M. Frame, *Apologetics to the Glory of God: An Introduction* (Phillipsburg, NJ: P&R Publishing, 1994)
CVT	John M. Frame, *Cornelius Van Til: An Analysis of His Thought* (Phillipsburg, NJ: P&R Publishing, 1995)
DCL	John M. Frame, *The Doctrine of the Christian Life* (Phillipsburg, NJ: P&R Publishing, 2008)
DG	John M. Frame, *The Doctrine of God* (Phillipsburg, NJ: P&R Publishing, 2002)
DKG	John M. Frame, *The Doctrine of the Knowledge of God* (Phillipsburg, NJ: Presbyterian and Reformed, 1987)
DWG	John M. Frame, *The Doctrine of the Word of God* (Phillipsburg, NJ: P&R Publishing, 2010)
ESV	English Standard Version
KJV	King James Version
NASB	New American Standard Bible
NIV	New International Version
NOG	John M. Frame, *No Other God* (Phillipsburg, NJ: P&R Publishing, 2001)
ST	John M. Frame, *Systematic Theology* (Phillipsburg, NJ: P&R Publishing, 2013)
STL	John J. Hughes, ed., *Speaking the Truth in Love: The Theology of John M. Frame* (Phillipsburg, NJ: P&R Publishing, 2009)
TAG	Transcendental argument for the existence of God
TANG	Transcendental argument for the nonexistence of God

1

APOLOGETICS: THE BASICS

In 1 Peter 3:15–16, the apostle exhorts his readers:

> But in your hearts honor Christ the Lord as holy, always being prepared to make a defense to anyone who asks you for a reason for the hope that is in you; yet do it with gentleness and respect, having a good conscience, so that, when you are slandered, those who revile your good behavior in Christ may be put to shame.

Definitions

Christian apologetics (which has nothing to do with "apologizing") seeks to serve God and the church by helping believers to carry out the mandate of 1 Peter 3:15–16. We may define it as *the discipline that teaches Christians how to give a reason for their hope.*[1]

I believe that we can distinguish three aspects of apologetics, which we will discuss in detail in later chapters:

1. *Apologetics as proof*: presenting a rational basis for faith or "proving Christianity to be true." Jesus and the apostles often offered evidence to people who had difficulty believing that the gospel was true. Note John

---

1. In *DKG*, which relates apologetics to other forms of human knowledge, I define apologetics as "the application of Scripture to unbelief" (p. 87). That shows that apologetics is part of Christian theology, which I define in general as "the application of Scripture." The definition given in the present volume arises from 1 Peter 3:15–16 and focuses on the person of the apologist rather than on the discipline of apologetics in the abstract, but in my view it is logically equivalent to the definition in *DKG*. The "reason for our hope" is precisely the certitude of God's Word, as we will see. (Notice, by the way, how a word may have more than one useful definition.)

14:11; 20:24–31; 1 Cor. 15:1–11. Believers themselves sometimes doubt, and at that point apologetics becomes useful for them even apart from its role in dialogue with unbelievers. That is to say, apologetics confronts unbelief in the believer as well as in the unbeliever.[2]

2. *Apologetics as defense*: answering the objections of unbelief. Paul describes his mission as "defending and confirming the gospel" (Phil. 1:7 NIV; cf. v. 16). *Confirming* may refer to number 1 above, but *defending* is more specifically focused on giving answers to objections. Much of Paul's writing in the New Testament is apologetic in this sense. Think of how many times he responds to imaginary (or real) objectors in his letter to the Romans. Think of how often Jesus deals with the objections of religious leaders in the Gospel of John.

3. *Apologetics as offense*: attacking the foolishness of unbelieving thought (Ps. 14:1; 1 Cor. 1:18–2:16). In view of the importance of number 2, it is not surprising that some will define apologetics as "the defense of the faith."[3] But that definition can be misleading. God calls his people not only to answer the objections of unbelievers, but also to go on the attack against falsehood. Paul says, "We destroy arguments and every lofty opinion raised against the knowledge of God, and take every thought captive to obey Christ" (2 Cor. 10:5). Non-Christian thinking is "folly" (ESV), or "foolishness" (NIV), according to Scripture (1 Cor. 1:18–2:16; 3:18–23), and one function of apologetics is to expose that foolishness for what it is.

These three types of apologetics are perspectivally related.[4] That is to say, each one, done fully and rightly, includes the other two, so that each is a way of looking at (i.e., a perspective on) the whole apologetic enterprise. To give a full account of the rationale of belief (no. 1), one must vindicate that rationale against the objections (no. 2) and alternatives (no. 3) advanced by unbelievers. Similarly, a full account of number 2 will include numbers 1 and 3, and a full account of number 3 will involve numbers 1 and 2.[5] So in a way, the three forms of apologetics are equivalent. But it is good for us nevertheless to distinguish these perspectives, for they certainly represent genuinely different emphases that complement and strengthen one another. For example, an argument for the existence of God (perspective no. 1) that

---

2. Note what the father of a demon-possessed child says to Jesus: "I believe; help my unbelief!" (Mark 9:24).

3. For Cornelius Van Til's major exposition of his apologetics, see K. Scott Oliphint, ed., *The Defense of the Faith*, 4th ed. (Phillipsburg, NJ: P&R Publishing, 2008). But his apologetics is certainly less "defensive" and more "offensive" than most others.

4. There are many such relationships in Scripture; see *DKG* for more examples.

5. So Van Til might well have argued that by "defense of the faith" he intended to include positive evidence for Christianity and attacks on the inadequacies of unbelief.

takes no account of unbelievers' objections to such arguments (no. 2) or to the ways in which unbelievers satisfy themselves with alternative worldviews (no. 3) will to that extent be a weakened argument. So it is often useful in apologetics to ask whether an argument of type 1 can be improved by some supplemental argumentation of type 2, 3, or both.[6]

Presuppositions

Our theme verse, 1 Peter 3:15, begins by telling us, "In your hearts honor Christ the Lord as holy." The apologist must be a believer in Christ, committed to the lordship of Christ (cf. Rom. 10:9; 1 Cor. 12:3; Phil. 2:11).[7] Once we have made the distinction between God's Word and the imaginations of our own hearts (Gen. 6:5), God calls us to live according to the former. God's Word is true (therefore dependable), though every human authority may lie (Rom. 3:4). If we adopt the Word of God as our ultimate commitment, our ultimate standard, our ultimate criterion of truth and falsity, God's Word then becomes our "presupposition." That is to say, since we use it to evaluate all other beliefs, we must regard it as more certain than any other beliefs.

Noah had no empirical evidence that the world would be destroyed by a flood, only the evidence of the word of God; but by grace he believed God (Gen. 6:8, 22; Heb. 11:7). Others heard that word, but rejected it (2 Peter 2:5), doubtless often with laughter. Abraham believed God, even though the apparent empirical evidence contradicted God's word. God said that he and Sarah would have a son, even though both were well into old age (Gen. 18:10–15). Sarah laughed, but Paul commends Abraham's unwavering faith in God's word despite the temptation to disbelieve (Rom. 4:20ff.).

The New Testament commends those who believe even without empirical signs (John 20:29), and it condemns those who refuse to believe without such signs (Matt. 12:39; 16:1ff.; 1 Cor. 1:22). There is a difference between walking by faith and walking by sight (2 Cor. 5:7; Heb. 11). The world says, "Seeing is believing"; Jesus says, "If you believed you would see the glory of

---

6. For students of my three perspectives in *DKG*, constructive apologetics is normative, offensive apologetics is situational, and defensive apologetics is existential. You figure it out!

7. *DKG* includes quite a bit of reflection on the centrality of Jesus' lordship in Scripture, Christian theology, and the Christian life. In the light of this central and pervasive biblical teaching, recent assertions that one can be a believer without trusting Jesus as Lord must be rejected as not only wrong but wrongheaded. On the other hand, this teaching must not be confused with perfectionism. The sincere confession that Jesus is Lord marks the beginning, indeed the essence, of the Christian's testimony, but the young Christian only gradually and progressively comes to understand and act on the full implications of Jesus' lordship.

God" (John 11:40). Our apologetic approach is firmly rooted in our commitment to Christ's covenant lordship.[8] Some theologians present apologetics as if it were almost an exception to this commitment. They tell us that when we argue with unbelievers, we should not argue on the basis of criteria or standards derived from the Bible. To argue that way, they say, would be biased. We should rather present to the unbeliever an unbiased argument, one that makes no religious assumptions pro or con, one that is neutral. We should, on this view, use criteria and standards that the unbeliever himself can accept. So logic, facts, experience, reason, and such become the sources of truth. Divine revelation, especially Scripture, is systematically excluded.[9]

This argument might appear to be simple common sense: since God and Scripture are precisely the matters in question, we obviously must not make assumptions about them in our argument. That would be circular thinking. It would also put an end to evangelism, for if we demand that the unbeliever assume God's existence and the authority of Scripture in order to enter the debate, he will never consent. Communication between believer and unbeliever will be impossible. Therefore, we must avoid making any such demands and seek to argue on a neutral basis. We may even boast to the unbeliever that our argument presupposes only the criteria that he himself readily accepts (whether logic, fact, consistency, or whatever).

This sort of apologetic is sometimes called the traditional or classical method,[10] because it claims many advocates down through church history, particularly the second-century apologists (Justin Martyr, Athenagoras, Theophilus, and Aristides), the great thirteenth-century thinker Thomas Aquinas and his many followers down to the present day, Joseph Butler (d. 1752) and his followers, and indeed the great majority of apologists in our own time.

---

8. See *DKG*, 1–49, esp. 45. "Lord" in Scripture refers to the head of a covenant relationship. In that relationship, the Lord dictates to his covenant servants the way they are to live and promises them blessings for obedience and curses for disobedience. He also tells them of the blessings that he has already given to them—his "unmerited favor," or grace, which is to motivate their obedience. Without words of grace, law, and promise, there is no lordship. To recognize the Lord is to believe and obey his words above the words of anyone else. And to obey the Lord's words in that way is to accept them as one's ultimate presupposition.

9. On the role of natural revelation, see the section "*Sola Scriptura* and Natural Revelation" later in this chapter.

10. One book that attacks Van Til's presuppositionalism and advocates the traditional approach is R. C. Sproul, John H. Gerstner, and Arthur W. Lindsley, *Classical Apologetics* (Grand Rapids: Zondervan, 1984). On the other side would be my *DKG* and any book of Van Til's, such as *Defense of the Faith*. See my review of the Sproul-Gerstner-Lindsley volume in *Westminster Theological Journal* 47, 2 (Fall 1985): 279–99. I've included it as Appendix A at the end of this book.

In saying that traditional apologists espouse "neutrality," I am not arguing that they seek to put their Christian commitment aside in doing apologetics.[11] Indeed, many of them believe that their type of apologetic is warranted by Scripture and is thus very much a "setting apart of Christ as Lord." They do, however, tell the unbeliever to think neutrally during the apologetic encounter, and they do seek to develop a neutral argument, one that has no distinctively biblical presuppositions. But does this kind of "neutrality" exist? No. Paul asks, "What partnership has righteousness with lawlessness? Or what fellowship has light with darkness? What accord has Christ with Belial? Or what portion does a believer share with an unbeliever?" (2 Cor. 6:14ff.). We are either for Christ or against him; no one is unbiased (Matt. 12:30).

Through the history of apologetics, it has been common for Christians to claim some kind of neutral ground, some criteria or standards that both believer and unbeliever can accept without compromising their systems.[12]

11. My friend R. C. Sproul, in correspondence, insists that the classical tradition, notably Aquinas and Sproul (!), does not claim "neutrality," but rather appeals to God's general revelation—his revelation in nature, history, and conscience. (See the discussion of Romans 1 later in this chapter and the discussion of natural revelation.) In this connection, however, Aquinas distinguished not between natural and special revelation, but rather between reason and faith—that is, between reasoning unaided by revelation and reasoning aided by it (*Summa Contra Gentiles*, 1. Q3. A2). Further, he (unlike Sproul, interestingly) had very little practical awareness of the effects of sin on human reasoning, so that he was able to use the views and arguments of the pagan philosopher Aristotle uncritically, with a few notable exceptions. Unlike Calvin, Aquinas did not believe that one needs the "spectacles of Scripture" to rightly interpret God's revelation in nature. In my view, Aquinas saw Aristotle's reasoning as neither pro- nor anti-Christian, but neutral. As for Sproul himself, I have nothing critical to say about his exposition of the effects of sin on unbelieving reasoning in Romans 1. He clearly denies the neutrality of unbelieving thought (see *Classical Apologetics*, 39–63). Thus, he recognizes that the apologetic encounter between believer and unbeliever is not between two parties who are seeking to think neutrally, but between an unbeliever who is biased against the truth and a believer who is seeking to correct that bias and is therefore, inevitably, biased in the opposite direction. But I don't find this discussion consistent with the treatment of autonomy on pages 231–40. To encourage the unbeliever to think autonomously is to encourage him to think without the correction of revelation—that is, to think "neutrally" (which is actually to think disobediently, replacing God's standards with the unbeliever's own). (For more detail on this point, see my review of *Classical Apologetics*, noted earlier.) My guess is that the three authors of this book were not entirely agreed among themselves. Making comparisons with books and articles that these gentlemen have written independently, I would guess that the treatment of Romans 1 is the work of Sproul and the discussion on pages 231–40 is the work of Gerstner. I am happy to welcome R. C. Sproul as an honorary presuppositionalist, but I do hope he will keep talking to his colleagues about this matter.

12. Here are two frequently cited examples: "Bring on your revelations, let them make peace with the law of contradiction and the facts of history and they will deserve a rational man's assent," and "Let reason be kept to: and, if any part of the Scripture account of the redemption of the world by Christ can be shown to be really contrary to it, let the scripture, in the name

There are, of course, usually some propositions that both believer and unbeliever can agree to. And those kinds of agreements are apologetically useful. Indeed, as we indicated earlier, some unbelievers, like the devils, might even confess that Jesus is the Son of the Most High God. But we mislead the unbeliever if we tell him that we are using the same standards of truth, rationality, and knowledge as he. To tell him this is misleading even if he is willing to do lip service to scriptural standards. For his grand passion, his basic commitment, is to attack and undermine the truth as the Christian understands it.

I am far from wishing to declare this tradition worthless. But on the precise point at issue, the question of neutrality, I do believe that its position is unbiblical. Peter's reasoning in our theme verse is very different. For Peter, apologetics is certainly not an exception to our overall commitment to Jesus' lordship. On the contrary, the apologetic situation is one in which we are especially to "honor Christ the Lord as holy," to speak and live in a way that exalts his lordship and encourages others to do so as well. In the larger context, Peter is telling his readers to do what is right, despite the opposition of unbelievers (1 Peter 3:13–14). He tells us not to fear them. Surely it was not his view that in apologetics we should set forth something less than the truth, out of fear that the truth itself might be rejected.

Peter tells us, on the contrary, that the lordship of Jesus (and hence the truth of his Word, for how can we call him "Lord" and not do what he says [Luke 6:46]?) is our ultimate presupposition. An ultimate presupposition is a basic heart-commitment, an ultimate trust. We trust Jesus Christ as a matter of eternal life or death. We trust his wisdom beyond all other wisdom. We trust his promises above all others. He calls us to give him all our loyalty and not allow any other loyalty to compete with him (Deut. 6:4ff.; Matt. 6:24; 12:30; John 14:6; Acts 4:12). We obey his law, even when it conflicts with lesser laws (Acts 5:29). Since we believe him more certainly than we believe anything else, he (and hence his Word) is the very *criterion*, the ultimate *standard* of truth. What higher standard could there possibly be? What standard is more authoritative? What standard is more clearly known to us (see Rom. 1:19–21)? What authority ultimately validates all other authorities?

The lordship of Christ is not only ultimate and unquestionable, not only above and beyond all other authorities, but also over all areas of

---

of God be given up." The first quote is from Edward J. Carnell, *An Introduction to Christian Apologetics* (Grand Rapids: Eerdmans, 1948), 178. The second is taken from Bishop Joseph Butler, *Analogy of Religion* (New York: Harper and Brothers, 1898), 5.

human life. In 1 Corinthians 10:31 we read, "Whether you eat or drink, or whatever you do, do all to the glory of God" (cf. Rom. 14:23; 2 Cor. 10:5; Col. 3:17, 23; 2 Tim. 3:16–17). Our Lord's demand on us is comprehensive. In all that we do, we must seek to please him. No area of human life is neutral.[13]

Surely this principle includes the area of thinking and knowing. The fear of the Lord is the very beginning of knowledge, says the author of Proverbs (1:7; cf. Ps. 111:10; Prov. 9:10). Those who are not brought to fear God by the new birth cannot even see the kingdom of God (John 3:3).

The point is not that unbelievers are simply ignorant of the truth. Rather, God has revealed himself to each person with unmistakable clarity, both in creation (Ps. 19; Rom. 1:18–21) and in man's own nature (Gen. 1:26ff.). In one sense, the unbeliever knows God (Rom. 1:21). At some level of his consciousness or unconsciousness, that knowledge remains.[14] But in spite of that knowledge, the unbeliever intentionally distorts the truth, exchanging it for a lie (Rom. 1:18–32; 1 Cor. 1:18–2:16 [note esp. 2:14]; 2 Cor. 4:4). Thus, the non-Christian is deceived and "led astray" (Titus 3:3). He knows God (Rom. 1:21) and does not know him at the same time (1 Cor. 1:21;

13. This was the insight of the great Dutch thinker Abraham Kuyper. He saw that the lordship of Christ requires radically different Christian forms of culture. Christians should be producing distinctively Christian art, science, philosophy, psychology, historical and biblical scholarship, and political and economic systems. And Christians should educate their children in distinctively Christian ways (note the God-saturated education urged in Deuteronomy 6:6ff. after the challenge to love God exclusively). For many of us, such considerations mandate home-schooling or Christian schools for our children, for how can we otherwise compete with up to seven hours a day of public-school secularism mandated by law? In any case, Christians may not take the easy road, uncritically following the thinking of the unbelieving world. Consider Kuyper's famous remark: "No single piece of our mental world is to be hermetically sealed off from the rest, and there is not a square inch in the whole domain of our human existence over which Christ, who is Sovereign over all, does not cry: 'Mine!'" James D. Bratt, ed., *Abraham Kuyper: A Centennial Reader* (Grand Rapids: Eerdmans, 1998), 488.

14. Some have tried to stress the past (aorist) form of "know" in Romans 1:21 to prove that the knowledge in view is past, not continuing into the present. Paul's purpose in this passage, however, is part of his larger purpose in 1:1–3:21, which is to show that all have sinned and therefore that none can be justified through the works of the law (3:19–21). In chapter 1 he shows us that even without access to the written law, Gentiles are guilty of sin before God (chapter 2 deals with the Jews). How can they be held responsible without access to the written law? Because of the knowledge of God that they have gained from creation. If that knowledge were relegated to the past, we would have to conclude that the Gentiles in the present are not responsible for their actions, contrary to 3:9. The past form is used (participially) because the past tense is dominant in the context. That is appropriate because Paul intends to embark on a "history of suppressing the truth" in 1:21–32. But he clearly does not regard the events of verses 21–32 merely as past history. He is clearly using this history to describe the present condition of Gentiles before God. Therefore, the aorist *gnontes* should not be pressed to indicate past time exclusively. As the suppression continues, so does the knowledge that renders the suppression culpable.

2:14).[15] Plainly, these facts underscore the point that God's revelation must govern our apologetic approach. The unbeliever cannot (because he will not) come to faith apart from the biblical gospel of salvation. We would not know about the unbeliever's condition apart from Scripture. And we cannot address it apologetically unless we are ready to listen to Scripture's own principles of apologetics.

But this means not only that the *apologist* must "honor Christ the Lord as holy," but also that his *argument* must presuppose that lordship. Our argument must be an exhibition of that knowledge, that wisdom, which is based on the "fear of the Lord," not an exhibition of unbelieving foolishness. Therefore, apologetic argument is no more neutral than any other human activity. In apologetic argument, as in everything else we do, we must presuppose the truth of God's Word. We either accept God's authority or we do not, and not to do so is sin. It doesn't matter that we sometimes find ourselves conversing with non-Christians. Then, too—perhaps especially then (for then we are bearing witness)—we must be faithful to our Lord's revelation.[16]

To tell the unbeliever that we can reason with him on a neutral basis, however that claim might help to attract his attention, is a lie. Indeed, it is a lie of the most serious kind, for it falsifies the very heart of the gospel—that Jesus Christ is *Lord*. There is no neutrality. Our witness is either God's wisdom or the world's foolishness. There is nothing in between. Even if neutrality were possible, that route would be forbidden to us.

When I oppose neutrality, what I oppose is appealing to something other than God's revelation as the *ultimate* standard of truth. It's certainly permissible to appeal to the dictionary as a standard of linguistic usage, or to the U.S. Constitution as a standard for American law. To do this is not to appeal to an ultimate standard. So, similarly, we can agree with unbelievers on certain things: the sky is blue, $2 + 2 = 4$, the Red Sox won the World Series. In one sense, this is common ground, but it is not neutrality in the above

---

15. Obviously, there is some complexity here that requires further explanation. Different kinds of knowledge are in view, for the Christian's knowledge of God (which the unbeliever lacks) is very different from the unbeliever's own knowledge of God (Rom. 1:21, 32). Further, there is psychological complexity: the unbeliever knows things at one level of his consciousness that he seeks to banish from other levels. To put it as simply as I can, he knows God, he knows what God requires, but he does not want that knowledge to influence his decisions, except negatively: knowledge of God's will tells him how to disobey God. See *DKG*, 1–61.

16. This is absolutely fundamental to a Reformed apologetic. The same God-breathed Scripture that informs us of sin, Satan, and the Savior equally speaks with unique authority in regard to the ethics of knowledge and our approach to apologetics.

sense. I think it's perfectly acceptable to start with present areas of agreement and work on from there. In one sense, there are all kinds of agreements, beginning with "the sky is blue." Neutrality is not agreeing on matters like that, but agreement on such things as worldview and epistemology. Agreeing that the sky is blue can push you either to deeper disagreements or to deeper agreements brought about by the work of the Spirit.

These propositions held in common can have apologetic value: If we can agree that the sky is blue, for example, how is it that such agreement is possible? If the world is a world of chance, how could anybody agree on anything? Agreement presupposes a world made by God, designed to be orderly and designed to be known by rational minds. You can see that this kind of argument is presuppositional. It's appealing to the true knowledge of God that the unbeliever has but suppresses (Rom. 1)—a knowledge that he has in common with the believer. To argue this way is very different from saying, "Let's assume that the Bible can be false, and let's judge its truth on the higher authority of our senses and logic."

Now for a further bit of nuance. Cornelius Van Til uses the term *presupposition* to indicate the role that divine revelation ought to play in human thought. I don't believe that he ever defines the term. I define it for him as a "basic heart-commitment." For the Christian, that commitment is to God as revealed in his Word. While we maintain our ultimate commitment, we cannot accept as true or right anything that conflicts with that commitment. And yet in a few instances in Van Til's writings, he uses the term differently. For example, he urges the apologist to show "the non-Christian that even in his virtual negation of God, he is still really presupposing God."[17] Clearly, when the unbeliever presupposes God in this sense, he is not acknowledging God as his ultimate commitment. Van Til's point here is that in assuming the intelligibility of the world, the unbeliever implicitly concedes the existence of the God that he explicitly denies. This lesser sense of *presuppose* is related to Van Til's more common use of the term, but it is somewhat different. For the unbeliever to presuppose God in this context is for him to think, say, or do something, contrary to his own inclination, that indicates at some level of his consciousness a recognition of God's reality and significance.

There are also passages in Van Til and other works by presuppositionalists in which the word *presuppose* is predicated not of persons, but

---

17. Cornelius Van Til, *A Christian Theory of Knowledge* (Nutley, NJ: Presbyterian and Reformed, 1969), 13.

of things: arguments, methods, knowledge, academic disciplines, states of affairs (such as the intelligibility of the universe). In such contexts, the word can be taken to mean "necessary condition," or "that which legitimizes." Perhaps we may relate these uses to our basic definition by saying that if some thing X presupposes Y, then Y is that to which a person must be committed if the person is to give an intelligible account of X. Finally, there is the phrase *reasoning by presupposition*, which for Van Til designates the "transcendental argument" for Christian theism. We will discuss this form of argumentation further in chapter 4. We need to keep these distinctions in mind if we're going to get our footing in understanding how presuppositionalists speak.

Circular Argument?

Does this mean that we are called to embrace circular argument? Only in one sense. We are not called to use arguments such as this: "The Bible is true; therefore, the Bible is true." One can certainly say that there is a kind of circularity in presuppositional apologetics, but the circularity is neither vicious nor fallacious. It sounds circular to say that our faith governs our reasoning and also that it is in turn based on rationality. But it is important to remember that the rationality of which we speak, the rationality that serves as the rational basis for faith, is God's own rationality. The sequence is as follows: God's rationality → human faith → human reasoning. The arrows may be read "is the rational basis for." So in this sense, the sequence is linear, not circular.

But if faith is in accord with God's own thought, then it goes without saying that it will also be in accord with the best human reasoning, which images God's. God gave us our rational equipment not to deceive us, but so that we might gain knowledge. Apart from sin, we may trust it to lead us into the truth; and even to sinners, the facts of God's creation bear clear witness of him to the human mind (Rom. 1:20).

In biblical argument, therefore, there is both reasoning and evidence: the clear revelation that God has given of himself in the created world. So it is both right and proper to use evidences and human logic to confirm faith. Scripture does this very thing, frequently calling on people to look at the evidences of the truth (Ps. 19:1; Luke 1:1–4; John 20:30–31; Acts 1:1–3; 26:26; Rom. 1:19–20). Biblical religion is unique in its appeal to history as the locus of divine revelation. God has plainly revealed himself both in nature and in historical events. So it is quite legitimate, as we will see, to argue on the basis of evidence, such as the testimony of five hundred witnesses to the resurrection (1 Cor. 15:6). Eyewitness accounts may be used argumentatively as follows:

- Premise 1: If Jesus' postresurrection appearances are well attested, then the resurrection is a fact.
- Premise 2: His postresurrection appearances are well attested.
- Conclusion: Therefore, the resurrection is a fact.

This is not a circular argument on any reasonable definition of circularity. And yet a certain circularity becomes evident when someone asks, "What are your ultimate criteria for good attestation?" or "What broad view of human knowledge permits you to reason from eyewitness testimony to a miraculous fact?" The empiricist philosophy of David Hume, to use only one example, does not allow for that kind of argument. The fact is that the Christian here is presupposing a Christian epistemology—a view of knowledge, testimony, witness, appearance, and fact that is subject to Scripture. In other words, he is using scriptural standards to prove scriptural conclusions.[18]

Does that procedure deserve to be condemned as circular? Everyone else reasons the same way. Every philosophy must use its own standards in proving its conclusions; otherwise, it is simply inconsistent. Those who believe that human reason is the ultimate authority (rationalists) must presuppose the authority of reason in their arguments for rationalism. Those who believe in the ultimacy of sense-experience must presuppose it in arguing for their philosophy (empiricism). And skeptics must be skeptical of their own skepticism (a fact that is, of course, the Achilles' heel of skepticism). The point is that when one is arguing for an ultimate criterion, whether Scripture, the Qur'an, human reason, sensation, or whatever, one must use criteria compatible with that conclusion. If that is circularity, then everybody is guilty of circularity.[19]

18. This epistemology is uniquely biblical in the sense that an unbeliever cannot consistently accept it. Indeed, the revelation of God in creation and in Scripture is central to it. Any theory of knowledge must specify the ultimate standard or criterion for determining truth and falsity. The Christian's ultimate standard is God's Word in Scripture; the unbeliever's ultimate standard must be located elsewhere. See *DKG*, in which this epistemology is worked out in some detail.

19. Granted these clarifications, I don't care very much whether the Christian apologist accepts or rejects the term *circular* to describe his argument. There are obvious dangers of misunderstanding in using it, dangers that I sought to brave in *DKG*. But I am more inclined now to say to my critics, "Granted your definition of circularity, I don't believe in it."

Does this fact eliminate the possibility of communication between believer and unbeliever? It might seem so. The Christian argues on biblical criteria that the resurrection is a fact. The non-Christian replies that he cannot accept those criteria and that he will not accept the resurrection unless we prove it by, say, the standards of Hume's empiricism. We reply that we cannot accept Hume's presuppositions. The unbeliever says that he cannot accept ours. Does that end the conversation?

Certainly not, for several reasons.

1. *At one level, the unbeliever already knows the truth.* In the first place, as I have said, Scripture tells us that God has revealed himself clearly to the unbeliever, even to such an extent that the unbeliever knows God (Rom. 1:21). Although he represses that knowledge (vv. 21ff.), there is at some level of his consciousness a memory of that revelation. It is against this memory that he sins, and it is because of that memory that he is held responsible for those sins. At that level, he knows that empiricism is wrong and that Scripture's standards are right. We direct our apologetic witness not to his empiricist epistemology or whatever, but to his memory of God's revelation and to the epistemology implicit in that revelation. To do that, to accomplish such meaningful communication, we not only may but must use Christian criteria, rather than those of unbelieving epistemology. So when the unbeliever says, "I can't accept your presuppositions," we reply: "Well, let's talk some more, and maybe they will become more attractive to you (just as you hope yours will become more attractive to me) as we expound our ideas in greater depth. In the meantime, let's just keep using our respective presuppositions and move along to some matters that we haven't discussed."

2. *Our witness to the unbeliever never comes alone.* In the second place, if God chooses to use our witness for his purposes, then he always adds a supernatural element to that witness—the Holy Spirit, working in and with the Word (Rom. 15:18–19; 1 Cor. 2:4–5, 12ff.; 2 Cor. 3:15–18; 1 Thess. 1:5 [cf. 2:13]; 2 Thess. 2:13–14). If we have doubts about our own ability to communicate, for whatever reason, we need not doubt the ability of the Holy Spirit. And if our witness is fundamentally his tool, then our strategy must be dictated by his Word, not by our supposedly commonsense suppositions.

3. *We all already do this.* In the third place, this is in fact what we do in similar cases that are not normally considered religious. Imagine someone living in a dreamworld—perhaps a paranoid, who believes that everyone is out to kill him. We'll call him Oscar. Let's say that Oscar presupposes this horror, so that every bit of evidence to the contrary is twisted and made

to fit the conclusion. Every kind deed, for example, becomes in Oscar's view evidence of a nefarious plot to catch him off guard and plunge a knife into his ribs. Oscar is doing what unbelievers do, according to Romans 1:21ff.—exchanging the truth for a lie. How can we help him? What shall we say to him? What presuppositions, what criteria, what standards would we employ? Certainly not his, for to do that would lead us to embrace his paranoia. Certainly not "neutral" criteria, for there are none. One must either accept his presupposition or reject it. Of course, the answer is that we reason with him according to the truth as we perceive it, even though that truth conflicts with his deepest presuppositions. On some occasions, he might answer, "Well, we seem to be reasoning on different assumptions, so we really cannot get anywhere." But on other occasions, our true reasoning might penetrate his defenses. For Oscar is, after all, a human being. At some level, we assume, he knows that not everyone is out to kill him. At some level, he is capable of hearing and being changed. Paranoids do sometimes, after all, revert to sanity. We speak the truth to him in the hope that that will happen, and in the knowledge that if words are to help at all in this situation, they must convey the truth, not further error, to bring healing.[20]

I take it, then, that a presuppositional approach to apologetics is warranted not only in Scripture, but also in common sense.

4. *We never run out of topics for discussion.* In the fourth place, Christian apologetics can take many forms. If the unbeliever objects to the "circularity" of the Christian's evidential arguments, the Christian can simply change to another kind of argument, such as an "offensive" apologetic against the unbeliever's own worldview or epistemology. That apologetic will also be circular in the precise sense noted above, but less obviously so. It could be presented Socratically, as a series of questions: How do *you* account for the universality of logical laws? How do *you* arrive at the judgment that human life is worth living? And so on. Or perhaps, as the prophet Nathan did with King David, when David would not otherwise repent of his sin (2 Sam. 11–12), we can tell the unbeliever a parable. Maybe we can tell the one about the rich fool (Luke 12:16–21). Van Til advocated a frank and explicit comparison of the competing worldviews. How might this interaction with a non-Christian look when we are bound to speak from Christian presuppositions? In very general terms, it goes like this:

---

20. This foreshadows some of the discussion of point of contact in chapter 4. The unbeliever lives in God's world and has this knowledge divinely implanted into the fabric of his humanity.

BELIEVER: The gospel is true because X, Y, Z.

UNBELIEVER: But your argument presupposes the truth of Scripture.

BELIEVER: Yes, but everyone presupposes something. You presuppose the autonomy of human reason.

UNBELIEVER: But how can you argue the truth of Scripture by appealing to Scripture? That's circular.

BELIEVER: No more circular than appealing to reason to prove reason.

UNBELIEVER: Well, then, you have your presupposition and I have mine. Does that mean that we cannot reason together at all?

BELIEVER: No, there is still a lot that we can talk about. Let's put your presupposition on the table, with your arguments, and I'll do the same with mine. We can compare the two. I think I can show that your argument "deconstructs"—that is, that it cannot even work within your own presuppositional framework.

UNBELIEVER: Good! Show me how you do that.

Those who believe that presuppositionalism eliminates communication between believer and unbeliever underestimate God's power to reach the unbelieving heart. They also underestimate the variety and richness of a biblical apologetic, the creativity that God has given to us as his spokespersons, and the many forms that a biblical apologetic can take.

5. *Not all circularity is created equal.* In the fifth place, I have, in *DKG* and elsewhere, distinguished between "narrowly circular" and "broadly circular" arguments. An example of the former would be: "The Bible is the Word of God because it is the Word of God." That might itself be a way of saying, "The Bible is the Word of God because it says it is." I agree with any nonpresuppositionalist that this narrowly circular argument is not an apologetic claim in a serious sense. In fact, it acts as a contrast to those arguments that I believe have real apologetic value. But is there *no* truth at all in the narrowly circular argument? Let us formulate the argument a bit more formally:

- Premise 1: Whatever the Bible says is true.
- Premise 2: The Bible says that it is the Word of God.
- Conclusion: Therefore, the Bible is the Word of God.

Both premises are true from an evangelical viewpoint, and they do validly imply the conclusion. So the conclusion is true *because* the two premises are true. We believe that the Bible is the Word of God because it says that it is the Word of God. A profound truth is vividly displayed in this narrow argument, namely, that there is no authority higher than Scripture by which Scripture may be judged, and that in the final analysis we must believe Scripture on its own say-so. Nevertheless, the narrow argument has some obvious disadvantages. In particular, an unbeliever will likely dismiss it out of hand, unless a great deal of explanation is given. We may overcome those disadvantages to some extent by moving to a broader circular argument. That broader argument says, "The Bible is the Word of God because of various evidences," and then it specifies those evidences. Now, the argument is still circular in a sense, because the apologist chooses, evaluates, and formulates these evidences in ways controlled by Scripture. But this argument tends to hold the unbeliever's attention longer and to be more persuasive. *Circularity*, in the sense that I have conceded it, can be as broad as the whole universe, for every fact witnesses to the truth of God.[21]

God's Responsibility and Ours

The relation of divine sovereignty to human responsibility is one of the great mysteries of the Christian faith. It is plain from Scripture in any case that both are real and that both are important. Calvinistic theology is known for its emphasis on divine sovereignty—for its view that God "works all things according to the counsel of his will" (Eph. 1:11). But in Calvinism there is at least an equal emphasis on human responsibility.

An equal emphasis? Many would not be willing to say that about Calvinism. But consider the Calvinistic emphasis on the authority of God's law—a more positive view of the law than in any other tradition of evangelical theology. To the Calvinist, human beings have duties before God. Adam failed to fulfill his duty and plunged the human race into sin and misery. But Jesus fulfilled his duty and brought eternal salvation to his people. Although God is sovereign, human obedience is of the utmost importance. God will fill and subdue the earth, but only through human effort (Gen. 1:28–30). He will gather his elect from all nations into his church, but only through faithful human preaching (Matt. 28:18–20; Acts 1:8; Rom. 10:13–15). Salvation comes to people solely by God's sovereign grace, without any human effort; yet we are to receive that salvation by grace and "work [it] out" with "fear and trembling" (Phil. 2:12)—not in spite of, but because of the fact that "it is God who works in you, both to will and to work for his good pleasure"

---

21. God controls and directs all of creation; therefore, all facts are on the side of the apologist. For more observations on this circularity, see *CVT*, 299–309.

(v. 13). You see that typically God's sovereignty does not exclude, but engages human responsibility.[22] Indeed, it is God's sovereignty that grants human responsibility, that gives freedom and significance to human choices and actions, that ordains an important human role within God's plan for history.

It is important for us to maintain this balance between divine sovereignty and human obedience in apologetics. We have already seen that apologetics cannot be successful apart from a supernatural element, namely, the testimony of the Holy Spirit. In that sense, apologetics is a sovereign work of God. It is he who persuades the unbelieving mind and heart. But there is also a place for the human apologist. He has the same place as the preacher mentioned in Romans 10:14. Indeed, he is the preacher.

Apologetics and preaching are not two different things. Both are attempts to reach unbelievers for Christ. Preaching is apologetic because it aims at persuasion. Apologetics is preaching because it presents the gospel, aiming at conversion and sanctification. Yet the two activities do have different perspectives or emphases. Apologetics emphasizes the aspect of rational persuasion, while preaching emphasizes the seeking of godly change in people's lives. But if rational persuasion is a persuasion of the heart, then it is the same thing as godly change. God is the persuader-converter, but he works through our testimony. Other terms are also roughly synonymous (or perspectivally related): *witnessing, teaching, evangelizing, arguing,* and the like.

Another way of putting it is this: the Spirit is the One who converts, but he normally works through the Word. Faith wrought by the Spirit is trust in a message, a promise of God.[23] As the earth was made by Spirit and word together (Gen. 1:2–3; Ps. 33:6 ["breath" = Spirit]), so God re-creates

---

22. These points have many important applications apart from apologetics, such as the following: (1) Christians often object that some kinds of scientific or technological progress amount to "playing God." Thus, they develop generalized objections to birth control, genetic research, ecology, space exploration, or whatever—even to medical care in general. For further discussion, see *DCL*, chaps. 37, 40. At some points, to be sure, God has set limits (e.g., to fetal-tissue experimentation), but the lordship of God in these areas does not preclude a responsible human role—quite the contrary. (2) Some Christians insist that since God sovereignly builds his church, we ought not to make human plans and study human techniques of church growth. Granted that some growth schemes are not pleasing to God, the fact remains that there is room for human responsibility here, too. Denying this is like saying, "God converts and sanctifies people, so preaching is unnecessary, or at least we can ignore the techniques of effective preaching."

23. We are, of course, speaking of faith as exercised by adult human beings of normal intelligence. The Spirit also works in the hearts of infants (2 Sam. 12:23; Luke 1:41–44; 18:16; Acts 2:39)—and presumably also in the hearts of people who are without the gifts of speech or even thought. That is very mysterious. Some theologians would describe the Spirit's work in such cases as regeneration without faith; others would describe it as a regeneration producing faith

sinful human beings by his Word and Spirit (John 3:3ff.; Rom. 1:16ff.; James 1:18; 1 Peter 1:23). As we have seen, the Spirit's work is necessary, but he works by illumining and persuading us to believe God's words (1 Cor. 2:4; 1 Thess. 1:5).[24] Thus, as I indicated above, the Spirit is necessary, but the preacher-apologist is also necessary. The work of the preacher-apologist is to present the Word. And his job is not just to read the Word, but to preach it—that is, to expound it, to apply it to his hearers, to display its beauty, its truth, its rationality. The preacher-apologist seeks to combat the unbeliever's false impressions and present to him the Word as it really is. It is to this testimony that the Spirit also bears witness.

This discussion will suffice to answer those who oppose the work of apologetics out of fear that it is an attempt to play God. There need not be any such competition between God's work and ours, as long as we recognize both God's ultimate sovereignty and his determination to use human agents to accomplish his purpose. Apologetics, rightly understood, is not playing God; it is merely practicing a divinely ordained human vocation.

Our discussion of divine sovereignty and human responsibility will also help us to answer those who insist that the Bible needs no defense. Charles Spurgeon is sometimes quoted (from somewhere!) as saying, "Defend the Bible? I would as soon defend a lion." Well, it is certainly true that Scripture, attended by the Spirit, is powerful (Rom. 1:16; Heb. 4:12–13). And it does defend itself, giving reasons for what it says. Think of all the "therefores" in Scripture, such as in Romans 8:1 and 12:1. Scripture does not merely tell us to believe and do certain things; it tells us to do them for certain reasons. This is Scripture defending itself, indicating its own rationale. But of course, when we as human preachers expound Scripture, we, too, must expound that rationale. Thus, we defend Scripture by using Scripture's own defenses. Indeed, Scripture not only defends itself but goes on the attack against sin and unbelief! Still, remarkably enough, Scripture itself calls us to be its defenders (Phil. 1:7, 16, 27; 2 Tim. 4:2; 1 Peter 3:15). To defend the Bible is ultimately simply to present it as it is—to present its truth, beauty, and goodness, its application to present-day hearers, and, of course, its rationale. When that message is preached so that people understand, the Bible defends itself. But the Bible will not defend itself to those who have never heard its message. Spreading that message is a human task, the task of human defenders. Listen to the apostle Paul: "Preach the word; be ready

---

in "seed form," that is, a disposition to hear and obey a word of God that as yet the person is unable to understand.

24. See also Appendix Q, "The Spirit and the Scriptures," in *DWG*, 615–39.

in season and out of season; reprove, rebuke, and exhort, with complete patience and teaching" (2 Tim. 4:2).

Sola Scriptura

"The Bible needs no defense" can also be used somewhat differently: as a way of invoking the Protestant principle *sola Scriptura*, the sufficiency of Scripture. Some fear that apologetics (which over the years has been notorious for injecting nonbiblical philosophical notions into Christian theology) may be seeking to subject Scripture to the judgment of something beyond Scripture. That is, of course, a great danger for the traditional apologetic, and it can happen unintentionally even when an apologist seeks to be presuppositional. But when apologetics is consistently presuppositional—that is, when it frankly recognizes that its own methods are subject to biblical norms—then it will avoid this danger.

Sola Scriptura, after all, does not require the exclusion of all extrabiblical data, even from theology. It simply requires that in theology and in all other disciplines, the highest authority, the supreme standard, must be Scripture and Scripture alone. As Westminster Confession of Faith 1.6 puts it, it is as "the whole counsel of God" that Scripture may not be added to. There can be no objection to mentioning extrabiblical data in apologetics, as long as those data are not presented as "counsel of God" on the same level as Scripture. Human thought, even theology, requires the use of extrabiblical data, for we are always dealing with the contemporary world in which God has placed us. Obviously, physics, sociology, geology, psychology, medicine, and so forth must respond to data beyond the Scriptures. Theology must do the same, because it is not a mere *reading* of Scripture, but an *application* of Scripture to human need.[25] Theology, therefore, always faces the danger of elevating the theologian's own conception of human need to a position of equal authority to, or even greater authority than, the Scriptures. But through prayer and meditation on God's Word, that danger can be avoided.

Therefore, to defend the Bible according to its own standards, even when we use extrabiblical data in the process, is not to add anything to Scripture as our supreme standard. It is simply to expose, as we saw above, the rationality of Scripture itself.

---

25. See *DKG*, 76–88, 93–98. Despite its focus on human need, this definition does full justice to the authority and sufficiency of Scripture. *Sola scriptura* does not require that human needs be ignored in theology, only that Scripture have the final say about the answers to those needs (and about the propriety of the questions presented).

It is sometimes hard to rid ourselves of the notion that when we argue the truth of Scripture based on facts outside of Scripture, we are elevating those facts (ultimately our own fact-gathering) to a position of greater authority than Scripture. It seems that we are measuring Scripture by those facts—that we are judging Scripture on the basis of their (presumably higher) authority. Van Til himself seemed to fear this, though not consistently.[26] But this is not necessarily the case. When I say, "There is design in the world; therefore, God exists," I might in fact be getting the premise from Scripture itself! (Surely Scripture teaches that there is design in the world!) In addressing the unbeliever, I might be addressing the knowledge that, according to Romans 1:18ff., he has obtained from creation. Indeed, when I say that, I could very well be expressing the certainty of my heart that design is unintelligible apart from the biblical God, and therefore that the very existence of design implies his reality. It is not that my concept of design is something by which I judge the Bible; rather, the Bible tells me what must be true if design is to exist.

What about using extrabiblical historical or scientific data to confirm biblical teachings? Surely, some might say, to do that implies that we have more confidence in this data than we do in the Bible, that we consider this data to have more credibility. And again, my reply is negative. I have far more confidence in the truth of the biblical history than I have in the reliability of, for example, Josephus.[27] But he does occasionally confirm biblical statements, and I think it is perfectly legitimate to mention that fact in apologetic discussions. The point is not that Josephus is more authoritative

---

26. For example, in *Defense of the Faith*, 336, Van Til criticizes arguments that "started from human experience with causation and purpose and by analogy argued to the idea of a cause of and a purpose with the world as a whole." He objects that "if you start with the ideas of cause and purpose as intelligible to man without God when these concepts apply to relations within the universe, then you cannot consistently say that you need God for the idea of cause or purpose when these concepts apply to the universe as a whole." True enough. But arguments about cause and purpose do not necessarily assume that "cause and purpose are intelligible to man without God," even as they "apply to relations within the universe." In fact, an apologist might very well advance such an argument because of his conviction that cause and purpose are not at all intelligible without God. Indeed, if Thomas Aquinas's causal argument is sound, it makes, in effect, that precise claim. His causal argument implies that if God doesn't exist, there is no *complete* causal explanation for anything, and therefore nothing can rightly be called *cause*. (Thomas himself may or may not have thought along those lines; I am deducing what is implicit in his argument. But whether he did or not is a question of his personal piety, not a question about the value of his argument.) Thomas is usually considered (by Van Til and others) to represent the antithesis of Van Til's presuppositional method, but in this case the antithesis is not obvious. I explore more examples of this sort in *CVT*.

27. Josephus is a well-known Jewish historian who lived from approximately A.D. 37 to A.D. 100 and thus was a younger contemporary of the apostles.

than, say, Luke. It is rather that even the non-Christian Josephus at points recognized the facts that Scripture records.[28] And modern skeptics, who are often willing to believe even the least reliable non-Christian historians in preference to God's Word, must take note that even first-century non-Christian historians wrote as one would expect them to, granted the truth of Scripture.

Again, this sort of argument does not add anything to Scripture in a way that would compromise the *sola Scriptura* principle. It adds nothing to our stock of supremely authoritative truth. That is in the Bible and nowhere else. Further, in one sense, arguments such as the causal argument or the Josephus argument, even though they involve extrabiblical data, aim simply at communicating the Scripture "as it really is." After all, to see Scripture rightly, it helps to see it in its various *contexts*: the context of its contemporary culture (with writers such as Josephus) and the context of the overall universe (including cause and purpose). To see Scripture rightly is to see how it fits and illumines those contexts. In that sense, a proper causal or historical argument does not go beyond Scripture. It simply shows the applicability of scriptural truth to some area of the world, and thus it displays the Bible in its full meaning.[29]

I conclude that we may use extrabiblical data in apologetics, but not as independent criteria to which Scripture must measure up. How ridiculous it would be to imagine that God's Word must be considered false if it fails to agree with Josephus or Eusebius or Papias—or with some anthropologist's theories about "early man"! Precisely the opposite is the case. We should simply present Scripture as it is, that is, as sometimes agreeing with other writings and sometimes not. That is what we would expect if God's Word were to enter a world of finitude and sin. And that very fact can, by God's grace, be persuasive. Our job is to present the Bible as it is, and to do so we must often refer to it in various contexts.

28. John Calvin taught that reason confirms (or corroborates) the truth of Scripture. Christian faith, according to Calvin, demands no rational argumentation for its final support (grounding this conviction in the internal witness of the Holy Spirit); nevertheless, he claimed that Christian faith provides a "knowledge with which the best reason agrees." See his *Institutes of the Christian Religion*, ed. John T. McNeill, trans. Ford Lewis Battles, 2 vols. (Philadelphia: Westminster Press, 1960), 1.6.5.

29. Note that *DKG*, 76–100, equates *meaning* with *application*. Scripture is written for people who live in the world. It is written for people with eyes and ears, people who will read it in the context of the rest of their lives. It expects us to apply its teaching to what is happening around us. Indeed, it says, to properly understand Scripture *is* to apply it to these situations (Matt. 16:3; 22:29; Luke 24:25; John 5:39–40; 20:31; Rom. 15:4; 2 Tim. 3:16–17; 2 Peter 1:19–21).

Sola Scriptura and Natural Revelation

To relate Scripture to its contexts is to relate it to natural revelation. Natural revelation is the revelation of God in everything that he has made (Pss. 19:1ff.; 104:1ff.; Rom. 1:18ff.), including human beings, who are his image (Gen. 1:27; 9:6; James 3:9). Every human being is surrounded by God's revelation, even within himself. This includes, of course, the unbeliever. As I stated earlier, the unbeliever knows God clearly (Rom. 1:21) but seeks to repress that knowledge in various ways.

Natural revelation reveals the eternal power and nature of God (Rom. 1:20). It also reveals his moral standards (1:32) and his wrath against sin (same verse; cf. v. 18). But it does not reveal God's plan of salvation, which comes specifically through the preaching of Christ (Rom. 10:17; cf. vv. 13–15). We have that preaching of Christ in definitive form in the Scriptures, and on the authority of Scripture we continue to preach the gospel to the world.

Why do we need two forms of revelation? For one thing, direct divine speech shortens the "learning curve." Even unfallen Adam needed to hear God's direct speech that supplemented and interpreted God's revelation in nature. He didn't need to figure everything out for himself; in many cases, that might have taken a long time or indeed been impossible for the finite mind. So as God's faithful covenant servant, Adam accepted this help gratefully. He accepted God's interpretation of the world until he made the tragic decision to accept Satan's interpretation instead.

But after the fall, at least two other reasons for special divine speech entered the picture. One was man's need of a saving promise, a promise that could never be deduced from natural revelation alone. The other reason was to correct our sinful misinterpretations of natural revelation. Romans 1:21–32 shows what people do with natural revelation when left with no other word of God. They repress it, disobey it, exchange it for a lie, disvalue it, and honor those who rebel against it.[30]

---

30. This passage is instructive for understanding an essential point of tension between presuppositionalism and apologetic methods that advocate natural theology. Paul's discussion in Romans 1 is familiar territory for apologists whose approach closely aligns with natural theology. Yet Paul's teaching in this passage undermines any notion that arguments can be derived exclusively from general revelation that would act as a stepping-stone to biblical faith. This is primarily because Romans 1 explicitly teaches that—apart from the regenerating work of the Holy Spirit—even the evidence presented by God himself ("For what can be known about God is plain to them, because *God has shown it to them*," v. 19) is twisted, perverted, and suppressed in the service of idolatry. This is not to say that the content of natural-theology arguments is false (i.e., that God is the final origin of causation, design, and ethics), only that in order for them to operate in a biblical manner, and to their fullest potential, they must be interpreted by Scripture.

Thus, God has given us Scripture, or *special revelation*,[31] both to supplement natural revelation (by adding to it the message of salvation) and to correct our misuses of natural revelation. As Calvin said, the Christian should look at nature with the "spectacles of Scripture." If even unfallen Adam needed to interpret the world according to God's verbal utterance, how much more do we!

The point is not that Scripture is more divine or more authoritative than natural revelation. Natural revelation is every bit the word of God and absolutely authoritative. The difference is that Scripture is a verbal divine utterance that God gives us to supplement and correct our view of his world. We must humbly accept that assistance. In doing so, we do not make Scripture more authoritative than natural revelation; rather, we allow the Word (with its ever-present Spirit) to correct our *interpretations* of natural revelation.[32]

To allow Scripture this corrective work, we must accept the principle that our settled belief[33] as to Scripture's teaching must take precedence over what we would believe from natural revelation alone.[34] God gave Scripture as the covenant constitution of the people of God, and if it is to serve us in that way, it must take precedence over all other sources of knowledge. It is wrong, for example, to suggest (as many do) that the "two books of nature and Scripture" should be read side by side, carrying equal weight in every respect. That sort of argument has been used to justify relatively uncritical Christian acceptance of evolution, secular psychology, and so on. In such arguments, Scripture is not permitted to

31. *Special revelation* in Reformed theology includes special utterances of God's voice (as in Exodus 19–20); the words of Jesus, prophets, and apostles; and the written Word that records and preserves the oral forms of God's speech. My own view is that the distinction between general and special revelation is not adequate to characterize all the forms of revelation described in Scripture and that additional categories are needed. See, e.g., *DWG*, 330–31. But the traditional twofold distinction will have to do for now.

32. Granted, our interpretations of Scripture also need to be corrected at times. But this is the proper order: Scripture itself corrects our interpretations both of Scripture and of nature. Can natural revelation (e.g., knowledge of ancient languages) sometimes correct our understanding of Scripture? Yes, but only insofar as such correction appears upon reflection to be justified by the scriptural text itself. So Scripture has a primacy over all else. See *DKG*, pt. 2, "The Justification of Knowledge."

33. The adjective *settled* is important; I am, of course, not advocating dogmatic adherence to ideas based on half-baked exegesis and rejection of, say, scientific theories on the basis of such sloppy theologizing. Cf. *DKG*, 152–53, on cognitive rest.

34. This is not, of course, to say that our settled beliefs concerning the teaching of Scripture are infallible. See *DKG*, 134–36, on the subject of certainty. But I repeat: those settled beliefs must take precedence over our beliefs, settled or not, from other sources. Otherwise, we do not allow Scripture to be a true corrective to our understanding of natural revelation.

do its corrective work, to protect God's people from the wisdom of the world (see 1 Cor. 2:6–16). Hence *sola Scriptura*.

Nevertheless, natural revelation, rightly understood through the "spectacles of Scripture," is of tremendous value to the Christian, and specifically to the apologist. As we look at nature with God's help, we see that the heavens really do "declare the glory of God" (Ps. 19:1). We see some of the very interesting ways in which human beings image God.[35] We see how it is that God furnishes the rational structure of the world and of the human mind, so that the two structures are adapted to each other. We see through science the astonishing wisdom of God's plan (see Ps. 104). We see through history and the arts what evils result when people abandon God and what blessings (and persecutions, Mark 10:30!) follow those who are faithful to him.

Traditional apologists have not always understood nature to be revelation of God. Aquinas did not distinguish between natural and special revelation, but between reasoning with and reasoning without the assistance of revelation. It is easy to understand how such views can be characterized as "autonomous" or "neutralist." Other traditionalists, however, have made much of the concept of natural revelation, even describing their method as one that presents natural revelation (somehow apart from special) to the unbeliever.

Certainly there can be no objection to presenting natural revelation to the unbeliever. We must, however, be careful that our statements about natural revelation are in line with scriptural teaching—that we are looking at nature through the "spectacles of Scripture." Showing natural revelation to the unbeliever is not an invitation to him to reason neutrally or autonomously or to ignore the Scriptures. Therefore, in a sense, natural and special revelation must never be separated in an apologetic encounter.[36]

35. Meredith G. Kline, *Images of the Spirit* (Grand Rapids: Baker, 1980), and James B. Jordan, *Through New Eyes* (Brentwood, TN: Wolgemuth and Hyatt, 1988), have some remarkable insights in this area.

36. Some have asked, "If nature and Scripture may never be understood apart from each other, then how can you say that the unbeliever, who sharply separates (even opposes) nature and Scripture, knows God?" But my claim is not that nature by itself gives no true knowledge. That claim would be contradicted by Romans 1:19–20. Rather, my claim is that only an obedient response to the biblical message can provide the needed supplement and corrective to the unbeliever's use of natural revelation, so that his knowledge of God (Rom. 1:21) becomes a knowledge in love (1 Cor. 8:1–3; 1 John 2:5; 4:8), a saving knowledge. Obviously, what the apologist seeks to communicate is not a knowledge (however correct) buried in the mind beneath layers of rationalization, darkness, foolishness, and lies (Rom. 1:18, 21–23), but a knowledge affirmed with confidence and delight, a knowledge that transforms the life, turning hatred into love.

Such a presentation of the Word, then, may include many sorts of arguments and evidences. Presuppositionalists are often accused of rejecting the use of evidence. This simply is not so.[37] The use of extrascriptural evidence, therefore, may be seen as part of a godly use of Scripture itself. It is an obedient response to Scripture's own view of the world. In principle, presuppositionalists have a higher view of evidence than some evidentialists do. In presuppositionalism, evidence is not a merely probable witness to the truth of Christianity; rather, it is sure and certain. God's normative interpretation of it is the *only* rational interpretation of it.[38] Therefore, presuppositionalism does not involve any general prejudice against the use of extrabiblical data; such prejudice is impossible in any apologetic that seeks to address current issues. We do not reject the use of evidences, even the use of theistic proofs. We only insist that these be *scriptural* arguments—that is, arguments that appeal to scriptural criteria.[39] In Scripture's teaching, nature points to God; so the obedient Christian apologist will show the unbeliever the various ways in which nature reveals God, without claiming neutrality

37. Even in otherwise astute and learned books, Van Til is all too frequently misrepresented in this regard. As a recent example, on page 288 of *Can You Believe It's True? Christian Apologetics in a Modern and Postmodern Era* (Wheaton, IL: Crossway, 2013), John S. Feinberg claims that Van Til (and many of his disciples) commends the faith "without offering any evidential support for it." Contrary to these claims, we have the words of Van Til himself: "I *would* therefore engage in historical apologetics. (I do not personally do a great deal of this because my colleagues in the other departments of the Seminary in which I teach are doing it better than I could do it.) *Every bit of historical investigation, whether it be in the directly Biblical field, archaeology, or in general history, is bound to confirm the truth of the claims of the Christian position.* But I would not talk endlessly about facts and more facts without ever challenging the non-believer's philosophy of fact. A really fruitful historical apologetic argues that every fact is and must be such as proves the truth of the Christian theistic position." Van Til, *Defense of the Faith*, 257 (emphasis added).

38. Presuppositionalists should have a uniquely high view of the use of evidences in Christian apologetics. A robust doctrine of both creation and providence demand it. Despite the inversion of man's sinful heart and futility to which creation has been subjected (Rom. 8), neither can ultimately perjure itself in its ongoing witness to God. *Everything* testifies to the truth of Christianity: the beauty and brokenness of creation, the blessedness and wretchedness of humanity, the flow and flux of history—all point to the truth of Scripture's portrait of God, mankind, and the world around us.

39. See my *DKG*, 140–49, 352–54; Cornelius Van Til, *Christian-Theistic Evidences* (Philadelphia: Presbyterian and Reformed, 1961). Van Til approves of theistic arguments in many places: see his *Defense of the Faith*, 197–98, 255; *An Introduction to Systematic Theology* (Phillipsburg, NJ: Presbyterian and Reformed, 1961), 179–80, 197, 314; *A Christian Theory of Knowledge* (Nutley, NJ: Presbyterian and Reformed, 1969), 292; *Common Grace and the Gospel* (Nutley, NJ: Presbyterian and Reformed, 1972), 179ff., 190ff. For a contemporary defense of presuppositionalism against the twin charges of fideism and fallacious circular reasoning, see Appendix D, "Between Scylla and Charybdis: Presuppositionalism, Circular Reasoning, and the Charge of Fideism Revisited."

and without allowing the use of non-Christian criteria of truth.[40] Thus, while he appeals to natural revelation, he inevitably appeals to Scripture at the same time. Indeed, the very purpose of Scripture (as I emphasized in *DKG*) is application, the use of Scripture to illumine situations and persons outside itself. "Viewing creation in the light of Scripture" and "applying Scripture to creation" are the same activity, seen from different perspectives.[41]

Granted this approach, there need be no competition between presuppositions and evidences. Our scriptural presupposition authorizes the use of evidence, and the evidence is nothing more than the application of Scripture to our situation. The use of evidence is not contrary to *sola Scriptura*, but a fulfillment of that principle.

Values

What is the use, the purpose, the value of apologetics? Since apologetics and preaching are perspectivally related, the benefits of the two are the same. As preaching leads to the conversion of the lost and the edification of the saints, so does apologetics.

40. The greatest difference between the traditional approach to apologetics and presuppositionalism is over epistemic neutrality. Van Til's critics often fault his method with question-begging and assuming the truth of Christianity before it has been proved. Harold Netland, "Apologetics, Worldviews, and the Problem of Neutral Criteria," *Trinity Journal* 12 (1991): 39–58, and more recently John Feinberg in *Can You Believe It's True?* both make the claim that some "neutral" criteria are needed to adjudicate between competing worldviews. In *Dissonant Voices* (Grand Rapids: Eerdmans, 1991), 183–89, Netland lists these neutral criteria as basic logical principles, self-defeating statements, worldview coherence, adequacy of explanation, consistency with knowledge in other fields, and moral assessment.

When John's Feinberg's brother, Paul, suggested seven nearly identical criteria of truth, my chief objection was Feinberg's omission of the criterion of scripturality. Of the proposed list, I said, "They, too, play important roles in apologetic argument and in all human knowledge. Scripturality is the major test, but consistency, correspondence, and the others can be helpful when governed by biblical presuppositions. Without those presuppositions, however, they need direction." *Five Views on Apologetics*, 197. Contrary to the sometimes oversimplified claims to neutral criteria, it must be remembered that "Christians and non-Christians simply do not agree on what constitutes empirical correspondence, comprehensiveness, simplicity, and the rest. Logic is not neutral. It can be used to glorify God or to resist him." Ibid., 197–98. At bottom, these criteria are *not* neutral. They are grounded in the nature and comprehensive plan of the God revealed in Scripture. While the law of noncontradiction can be known, recognized, and employed apart from submission to God's Word (because of the non-Christian's creation as *imago Dei* and the Spirit's preserving work of common grace), the apologist should not ultimately be satisfied with such a relatively superficial concession. The Christian should—given the opportunity—lovingly ask the non-Christian how these criteria line up with his worldview. While unbelievers make use of these criteria (that is to say, there is formal agreement), they properly belong within a biblical worldview and therefore are anything but neutral.

41. In *DKG*, the former was called the situational perspective; the latter, the normative perspective.

The specific work of giving an intellectual rationale has its useful-ness within these broader contexts. For the believer, apologetics gives reassurance to faith as it displays the rationality of Scripture itself. That rationality also gives to the believer an intellectual foundation—a basis for faith and a basis for making wise decisions in life. Apologetics is not itself that foundation, but it displays and describes the foundation presented in Scripture, as well as the way in which we should, according to Scripture, build on that foundation.

For the unbeliever, God might use apologetic reasoning to sweep aside rationalizations, arguments by which the subject resists conversion. Apolo-getics might also provide evidence conducive to a change in conviction. We are not saying that the unbeliever lacks evidence. He is surrounded by evidence in creation (Ps. 19:1ff.; Rom. 1:18ff.) and in himself (Gen. 1:26ff.) for the existence of God, and there is plenty of evidence in Scripture for the truth of other Christian doctrines. But an apologist can formulate that evidence, and do so in provocative ways, drawing the unbeliever's attention to it. And he can apply it to the unbeliever's particular objections.

For those who never come to faith, apologetics still might be doing God's work. Like preaching, again, it adds to their condemnation. Failure to repent and believe, despite faithful presentations of the truth, leads to more severe condemnation (Luke 12:47ff.).

Dangers

James warns us, "Not many of you should become teachers, my broth-ers, for you know that we who teach will be judged with greater strictness" (James 3:1). If we do not teach, our errors affect only ourselves; but if we do, our errors can affect others also. Thus, errors in those who teach are more serious and will be judged more severely. The apologist is, as we have indicated, a teacher; therefore, the scriptural warnings about teachers apply to apologists.

Can we be more specific? In our theme verses, 1 Peter 3:15–16, Peter urges apologists to keep "a good conscience," so that those who slander them will be "put to shame." It is interesting that Peter does not urge apologists to be intelligent and knowledgeable (although such qualities are certainly helpful), but to lead consistently godly lives. He gives us a practical standard for a discipline that we are inclined to regard as theoretical.[42]

---

42. Compare the mostly practical criteria for the teaching office in 1 Timothy 3:1–7; Titus 1:5–9. Cf. *DKG*, 324.

The fact is that every apologetic presentation has important practical contexts. Our communication with unbelievers consists not only of what we say, but also of how we live before them. If our life contradicts our doctrine, then our apologetics is hypocritical and loses credibility. But if our life and doctrine are consistent, then those who try to make us look bad will themselves lose credibility. They will, in the end at least, be put to shame.

To be still more specific: apologists are subject to the same sins that everyone else is, but over the years, they have been especially prone to sins in two areas. In terms of Ephesians 4:15, which urges us to speak the truth in love, we may say that apologists have sometimes been guilty of speaking falsehoods and sometimes of speaking without love. The first is often condemned in the New Testament polemic against false teaching (2 Tim. 3; 2 Peter 2; etc.). It is remarkable how many heresies are traceable to apologetic motives. Someone will think, "If I am going to present Christianity more persuasively, I will have to show that it is compatible with the intellectual movements of my time. I must present Christianity as 'intellectually respectable.'" Thus, various Christian doctrines are compromised, replaced by the doctrines of popular philosophy. The second-century apologists (Justin, Aristides, Athenagoras) were for the most part deeply committed Christians, but they compromised the Christian doctrine of creation, accommodating it to the Gnostic philosophical notion of a continuum of being between God and the world. This led to an almost impersonal concept of God (the unknowable being at the top of the scale) and a subordinationist view of the Trinity (Son and Spirit subordinate to God the Father, so that they could interact with the world, as the Father could not). Similar motivations are evident in Clement of Alexandria and Origen, in Thomas Aquinas, and more recently in Schleiermacher's *Speeches to the Learned Despisers of Christianity* and the many modern theologians from Bultmann to Tillich to Pannenberg who want to show "modern man" the intellectual value of Christianity. Very often the apologetic motive has led to doctrinal compromise. That doesn't mean that the apologetic motive is wrong; as we have seen, that motive in itself is scriptural. But the historic pattern and Scripture's explicit admonitions should lead us to be highly cautious. And don't be an apologist unless your first loyalty is to God—not to intellectual respectability, not to truth in the abstract, not to the unbeliever as such, not to some philosophic tradition.

Contributing to such failures are other sins: misdirected love, underestimation of human sin (as if what the unbeliever needs is merely a better argument), ignorance of God's revelation (especially of biblical presuppositionalism), and intellectual pride.

The opposite violation of Ephesians 4:15 is speaking without love.[43] Unfortunately, many contentious or quarrelsome people are attracted to the discipline of apologetics. In their hearts, they are unhappy unless they are in the midst of controversy; and if no controversy is going on, they will create one, picking fights over matters that could easily be overlooked or resolved peacefully. Scripture speaks often of this spirit and always negatively (Prov. 13:10; 18:6; 19:13; 26:21; Hab. 1:3; Rom. 2:8; 1 Cor. 1:11; 11:16; Phil. 1:16; Titus 3:9). One would do well to meditate on these passages before beginning a career in apologetics!

This sort of contentiousness comes from pride, according to Proverbs 13:10. When one is too proud to "take advice" from others, he insists on his own way until he is forced to desist. Far from being wise, such people are foolish (Prov. 18:6) and under the direction of the devil himself (James 3:13–16). James goes on to say, "But the wisdom from above is first pure, then peaceable, gentle, open to reason, full of mercy and good fruits, impartial and sincere. And a harvest of righteousness is sown in peace by those who make peace" (vv. 17–18). Paul even tells us that "knowledge" without love is not true knowledge: "We know that 'all of us possess knowledge.' This 'knowledge' puffs up, but love builds up. If anyone imagines that he knows something, he does not yet know as he ought to know. But if anyone loves God, he is known by God" (1 Cor. 8:1–3).

To defend the Christian faith with a quarrelsome spirit is to defend Christianity plus quarrelsomeness—a self-destructive hybrid. True Christianity—the Christianity that we are called to defend with word and life— says, "Blessed are the peacemakers, for they shall be called sons of God" (Matt. 5:9),[44] and "If possible, so far as it depends on you, live peaceably with all" (Rom. 12:18).[45]

---

43. I am aware, of course, that one can commit both violations at once: speaking falsehoods without love!

44. See my *Evangelical Reunion* (Grand Rapids: Baker, 1991) and Dennis Johnson's sermon on "Peacemakers," added as an appendix.

45. I grant that many passages of the Bible from the prophets, Jesus, and the apostles do not sound very "peaceful." These men were willing to use very strong, angry language when necessary. On many occasions, however, they showed much patience and gentleness. In my view, strong language is appropriate against people who (1) claim to have some religious teaching authority, and (2) are proclaiming false doctrine on serious matters, leading believers astray, or are dishonoring orthodox doctrine by ungodly lives, and (3) have ignored clear and graciously expressed warnings that their conduct displeases God. The Protestant Reformers used similarly strong language (which can usually be justified on these principles). Most of those today who

Hear also Peter, again in our theme text, urging the virtues of "gentleness" and "respect." Gentleness is the way of love and peacemaking, a trait quite opposed to the contentious spirit. In circles such as my own that emphasize (rightly, in my view) a militant orthodoxy, gentleness is the most neglected of the biblical virtues. Is it possible to be militant and gentle at the same time? Of course. Let the Lord Jesus himself and his apostles show us the way.[46]

"Respect" is the ESV translation of the Greek word *phobos*, "fear." The translations that use the term *fear* perhaps intend it to be taken as the fear of God (the NASB says "reverence"), or at least the apologist's perception of the spiritual dangers of the situation. *Respect* would mean treating the unbeliever as what he is—a person created in the image of God. It would mean not talking down to him, but listening to him—not belittling him, but taking seriously his questions and ideas. Either idea would be in accord with other scriptural teachings. The bottom line is that we should relate the apologetic encounter to God and his purposes, rather than allow our own emotional evaluation of the unbeliever to dictate our approach to him.

---

are seeking to emulate the biblical and Reformation writers in this respect are overdoing it, in my opinion. They should learn to give at least equal attention to peacemaking. See again my *Evangelical Reunion*, especially the appendix containing Dennis Johnson's sermon.

46. Note the preceding footnote in this respect.

2

THE MESSAGE OF THE APOLOGIST

The apologist's message, ultimately, is nothing less than the whole of Scripture, applied to the needs of his hearers. But in an apologetics text such as this one, it is important to provide a brief summary of the content of Scripture to give direction to the apologetic witness. That is not difficult. The teachings of Scripture can be summarized; indeed, there are such summaries in Scripture itself (John 3:16; Rom. 6:23; 1 Cor. 15:1–11; 2 Cor. 5:17–6:2; Eph. 2:8–10; Phil. 2:5–11; 1 Tim. 2:5–6; Titus 3:3–8; 1 Peter 3:18).

These texts show us that there are different ways of summarizing the biblical message, each of which carries at least a slightly different emphasis. We may call these emphases *perspectives*. For the purposes of the present book, it will be useful to summarize the message of Scripture from two perspectives: first, Christianity as a philosophy, and second, Christianity as good news.

Philosophy

By "Christianity as a philosophy," I mean that Christianity provides a comprehensive view of the world (a worldview).[1] It gives us an account

1. Such language has its dangers, of course. *Philosophy* sometimes connotes an approach to the truth by way of autonomous speculation, and I certainly want the reader to erase any such nuances from his mind when he reads here of Christianity as a philosophy. Further, there has been a historical tendency, unfortunately connected with apologetics, to force Christianity into a structure dictated by an autonomously produced philosophy. That tendency I renounce altogether. As I've said elsewhere, I do not make a sharp distinction between a Christian theology and a Christian philosophy. Philosophy generally is understood as an attempt to understand the world in its most broad, general features. It includes metaphysics or ontology (the study of being, of what "is"), epistemology (the study of knowing), and theory of value (ethics, aesthet-

not only of God, but also of the world that God made, the relation of the world to God, and the place of human beings in the world in relation to nature and God. It discusses metaphysics (the theory of the fundamental nature of reality), epistemology (the theory of knowledge), and values (ethics, aesthetics, economics, etc.). Thus, it is a viewpoint on *everything*. There are, I believe, distinctive Christian views on history, science, psychology, business, economics, labor, sociology, education, the arts, the problems of philosophy, and so on. As we saw earlier, our Lord's authority is comprehensive; whatever we do must be related to Christ (1 Cor. 10:31; etc.).

Christianity therefore competes with Platonism, Aristotelianism, empiricism, rationalism, skepticism, materialism, monism, pluralism, process thought, secular humanism, New Age thought, Marxism, and whatever other philosophies there may be—as well as other religions, such as Judaism, Islam, Hinduism, and Buddhism. One of the more unfortunate repercussions of America's distorted view of "the separation of church and state" is that public-school children are able to hear advocacy of every system of thought except those that are arbitrarily labeled "religious."[2] Who is to say that the truth might not be found in, or even limited to, one of these religious positions? Is it even remotely fair, in terms of freedom of thought and speech, to restrict public education to allegedly secular viewpoints? Is this not brainwashing of the worst kind?[3]

Further, the extreme separationists often seem to be more opposed to the public expression of Christianity in particular than to religion in

---

ics, etc.). The only philosophy I recommend here is the truth of Christianity itself, derived from the Scriptures, by which certain philosophical implications (i.e., implications as to the general features of God and the world) can be derived. If one seeks to develop a Christian philosophy, then he will certainly be doing so under the authority of Scripture, and thus will be applying Scripture to philosophical questions. See *DKG*, 85–86.

2. Of course, every system of philosophy is religious, not in the sense that it advocates certain rites of worship, but in the more important sense that (1) it is committed at some point to faith-presuppositions, just as religions are, and (2) it offers a comprehensive worldview and comprehensive solutions for the troubles of human beings.

3. To those who are offended by the advocacy of religion in the classroom, it should be replied that Christians have just as much right to be offended by the teaching of various secular philosophies, which disavow our need for God. Christians ought to express this offense (including their offense at having to pay for this brainwashing with their taxes) more consistently and severely. Why should "offensive" teaching be limited to "religious" expression in some arbitrarily narrow sense? Of course, if a more evenhanded view of these matters were to prevail, we would all have to equally accept the burden of possibly being offended, or we should eliminate public education entirely. Education in which people of all convictions are enrolled, but in which no one is offended, is not worthy of the name.

general. Too often, they have no objection to presentations in schools favoring Eastern mysticism or modern witchcraft—only to Christianity. Inconsistent as it might appear, however, this specifically anti-Christian behavior makes some sense. For as we will see, it is Christianity, not Eastern mysticism or witchcraft or Native American chanting, that really stands against the natural drift of the unregenerate mind. Christianity is excluded from the schools even though (or perhaps because) it is the only genuine alternative to the conventional wisdom of the modern establishment.

But that "conventional wisdom" has given us enormous increases in divorce, abortion, single-parent families, latchkey children, drugs, gangs, crime rates, AIDS (and related health concerns such as the resurgence of tuberculosis), homelessness, hunger, government deficits, taxation, political corruption, degeneracy of the arts, mediocrity in education, noncompetitive industry, interest groups demanding "rights" of all sorts (rights without corresponding responsibilities and at the expense of everyone else), and pollution of the environment. It has given us the messianic state, which claims all authority and seeks to solve all problems (secular "salvation"), but which generally makes things worse. It has brought about the appalling movement toward "political correctness" on university campuses, which once plausibly claimed to be bastions of intellectual freedom. It has allowed the language of polite society to degenerate into the language of blasphemy and mutual contempt. It has created an atmosphere in which popular music ("rap") urges people to kill police.

Under these circumstances, shouldn't we consider some alternatives that are opposed to the conventional wisdom? Or is there indeed, perhaps, only one such alternative? If so, and I will argue that there is, surely we ought to take that alternative very seriously.

To show that Christianity is *the* alternative, allow me to expound here the content of Christianity as a philosophy—as metaphysics, epistemology, and value theory (focusing on ethics). Christianity as gospel (i.e., as good news) is also important in this connection, perhaps more so. But that will come later. In our time (as opposed to, say, six hundred years ago), people are ignorant of the basic Christian worldview. It will be helpful if they understand that, so that the gospel will make sense to them. So I will present Christianity first as philosophy, then as gospel.[4]

---

4. For readers interested in seeing a broad sketch of Christianity as a philosophy, see *DG*, part 2, "A Philosophy of Lordship," 185–237, and also chapter 1 of my *A History of Western Philosophy and Theology* (Phillipsburg, NJ: P&R Publishing, 2015).

Metaphysics

The four most important things to remember about the Christian worldview are: first, the absolute personality of God; second, the distinction between Creator and creature; third, the sovereignty of God; and fourth, the Trinity.

God, the Absolute Personality

God is "absolute" in the sense that he is the Creator of all things and thus the ground of all other reality. As such, he has no need of any other being (Acts 17:25) for his own existence. He is self-existent and self-sufficient ("*a se*"). Nothing brought him into being; he always was (Pss. 90:2; 93:2; John 1:1). Nor can anything destroy him; he will always be (Deut. 32:40; Ps. 102:26–27; 1 Tim. 6:16; Heb. 1:10–12; Rev. 10:6). His existence is timeless, for he is the Lord of time itself (Ps. 90, esp. v. 4; Gal. 4:4; Eph. 1:11; 2 Peter 3:8).[5] He knows all times and spaces with equal perfection (Isa. 41:4; 44:7–8). In the words of answer 4 of the Westminster Shorter Catechism, "God is a Spirit, infinite, eternal, and unchangeable, in his being, wisdom, power, holiness, justice, goodness, and truth."

This definition emphasizes not only God's absoluteness but also his personality. "Spirit" in Scripture is personal, and God is Spirit (John 4:24). As Spirit, God speaks (Acts 10:19), leads (Rom. 8:14), bears witness (vv. 16–17), helps (v. 26), prays (same verse), loves (15:30), reveals (1 Cor. 2:10), and searches (same verse). Although the Greek word for *Spirit* (*pneuma*) is grammatically neuter, the New Testament sometimes emphasizes the personality of God's Spirit by referring to him with a masculine pronoun (e.g., John 16:13–14). Also clearly personalistic are the catechism's references to the attributes of wisdom, power, holiness, justice, goodness, and truth. These qualities are often ascribed to God in Scripture.

The great question confronting modern humanity is this: Granted that the universe contains both persons (such as you and me) and impersonal structures (such as matter, motion, chance, time, space, and physical laws), which is fundamental? Is the impersonal aspect of the universe grounded in the personal, or is it the other way around? Secular thought generally assumes the latter—that persons are the products of matter, motion, chance, and so on. It holds that to explain a phenomenon in terms of personal intentions (e.g., "This house is here because someone built it

5. See *DG*, 543–75; *NOG*, 143–59.

to live in") is less than an ultimate explanation, less than fully explana-tory. On this view, an ultimate explanation, a fully satisfying explanation, requires the ultimacy of the impersonal (e.g., "The person built the house because the atoms in his brain moved about in certain ways"). But is that a necessary assumption?

Returning to Scripture, the biblical writers do not hesitate to ascribe the events of the natural world directly to God. *He* waters the land (Ps. 65:9–11). *He* sends the lightning and the wind (135:5–7). *He* spreads the snow, frost, and hail and then sends his word to melt them (147:15–18). So the biblical view of the natural world is intensely personalistic.[6] Natural events come from God. This is not to deny that there are forces in nature itself, perhaps even "natural laws" in some sense, though it would be hard to prove the existence of such laws from Scripture. But behind all the forces of nature itself is the force of the personal Lord.

Let us think through the consequences of both views. If the impersonal is primary, then there is no consciousness, no wisdom, and no will in the ultimate origin of things. What we call reason and value are the unintended, accidental consequences of chance events. (So why should we trust reason, if it is only the accidental result of irrational happenings?) Moral virtue will, in the end, be unrewarded. Friendship, love, and beauty are all of no ultimate consequence, for they are reducible to blind, uncaring process. No one was more clear-eyed and eloquent as to the consequences of this view than Bertrand Russell, who nevertheless upheld it as "the world which science presents for our belief":

> That man is the product of causes which had no prevision of the end they were achieving; that his origin, his growth, his hopes and fears, his loves and his beliefs, are but the outcome of accidental collocations of atoms; that no fire, no heroism, no intensity of thought and feeling, can preserve an individual life beyond the grave; that all the labors of the ages, all the devotion, all the inspiration, all the noonday brightness of human genius, are destined to extinction in the vast death of the solar system, and that the whole temple of man's achievement must inevitably be buried beneath the debris of a universe in ruins—. . . only within the scaffolding of these truths, only on the firm foundation of unyielding despair, can the soul's habitation henceforth be safely built.[7]

6. Cf. Gen. 8:22; Job 38–41; Pss. 104:10–30; 107:23–32; 145:15–16; 147:8–9; Acts 14:17; many other passages.

7. Bertrand Russell, "A Free Man's Worship," in *Why I Am Not a Christian*, ed. Paul Edwards (New York: Simon and Schuster, 1957), 107.

But if the personal is primary, then the world was made according to a rational plan that can be understood by rational minds. Friendship and love are not only profound human experiences, but fundamental ingredients of the whole world order. There is Someone who *wants* there to be friendship, who *wants* there to be love. All the wonderful things that we find in personality—intelligence, compassion, creativity, love, justice—are not ephemeral data, doomed to be snuffed out in cosmic calamity; rather, they are aspects of what is most permanent, most ultimate. They are what the universe is really all about. Moral goodness is part of the great design of the universe. If personality is absolute, there is One who cares about what we do, who approves or disapproves our conduct. And that person has some purpose for evil, too, mysterious as that might seem to us (see chapters 6 and 7 on this subject). Beauty, too, does not just happen for a while; it is the art of a great craftsman. And if indeed the solar system comes to a "vast death," there is One who can deliver us from that death, if it pleases him to do so. So it may be that some of our thoughts, plans, trust, love, and achievements have eternal consequences after all, consequences that impart to all these things a great seriousness, but also humor: humor at the ironic comparison of our trivial efforts with "eternal consequences."

What a difference! Instead of a gray world of matter and motion and chance, in which anything could happen, but nothing much (nothing of human interest) ever does, the world would be the artistic creation of the greatest mind imaginable, with a dazzling beauty and fascinating logic. It would be a history with a drama, a human interest, a profound subtlety and allusiveness more illuminating than the greatest novelist could produce. That divine history would have a moral grandeur that would turn all the world's evil to good. Most amazingly: the world would be under the control of a being somehow, wonderfully, akin to ourselves! Could we pray to him? Could we know him as a friend? Or would we have to flee from him as our enemy? What would he expect of us? What incredible experiences might he have in store for us? What new knowledge? What blessings? What curses?[8]

I suspect that many who profess unbelief nevertheless *wish* that something like that were true. It is the work of the apologist not only to argue for the truth, but to portray it as it is, in all its beauty, and not neglecting its dark tones. As we thus describe its attractiveness, but also its challenge, we perform an apologetic service. For very often, before someone confesses the

8. The thrust of this paragraph originates in my memory of a remarkable sermon preached by Francis Schaeffer many years ago.

truth, that person comes to the point of *wishing* it were true. That is all to the good. Wishing does not make anything true or false, and it is slander to claim that Christianity is mere wish-fulfillment. But a person with a wish to be fulfilled is often on the road to belief. A consistent unbeliever does not find the biblical worldview appealing; he turns from it.

Absolute personality! A personal absolute! I have not studied every non-Christian religion, and I would not wish to say that only Christianity holds to a personal absolute. Variants of Hinduism and Buddhism are sometimes described as "theistic." According to some African animistic religions, there is behind the world of spirits a singular personal being who holds all accountable.[9] But it is certainly the case that the major contender for "absolute-personality theism" in our day is biblical religion.[10]

The major religions of the world, in their most typical (one tends to say "authentic") forms, are either pantheistic (Hinduism, Taoism) or polytheistic (animism, some forms of Hinduism, Shinto, and the traditional religions of Greece, Rome, Egypt, etc.). Pantheism has an absolute, but not a personal absolute. Polytheism has personal gods, but none of these is absolute. Indeed, although most religions tend to emphasize either pantheistic absolutism or personal nonabsolutism, we can usually find both elements beneath the surface. In Greek polytheism, for example, the gods are personal but nonabsolute. Yet this polytheism is supplemented by a doctrine of fate, which is a kind of impersonal absolute. Similarly, behind the gods of animism is Mana, the impersonal reality.[11] People seem to have a need or a desire for both personality and absoluteness, but in most religions these two elements are separated and therefore compromise each other, rather than reinforcing each other. Thus, of the major religious movements, only biblical religion calls us with clarity to worship a personal absolute.

9. These sects, of course, do not challenge the claim of Christianity to be unique, because the differences between them and Christianity outweigh the similarities. If these sects are similar in worshiping an absolute personality, that is not surprising, in view of the teaching of Romans 1:18–20 that God is clearly revealed in creation. That there are so few instances of this confirms the teaching of Romans 1:21ff. about unbelievers' suppression of the truth.

10. By "biblical religion" I refer to Christianity itself, together with the Christian heresies. Christian heresies are religions that are influenced by the Bible, but that deny the central biblical gospel. Among the Christian heresies are not only those designated as such in history (Arianism, Gnosticism, Sabellianism, Docetism, Eutychianism, etc.), but also the historical rivals of Christianity, namely, Judaism and Islam. Also among the Christian heresies are the modern cults and denials of the gospel: Jehovah's Witnesses, Mormonism, liberalism, and so on.

11. Buddhism is hard to classify. In its original form, it might have been atheistic; there are problems in interpreting the Buddhist concept of *nothingness*. Clearly, though, there is no personal absolute in the mainstream forms of Buddhism.

Meditate on that fact: the fundamental Christian worldview is virtually unique to biblical religion. Why should that be? One would think that
fair-minded people (bereft of evidence,[12] forced to speculate), faced with the
question of which was more ultimate, the personal or the impersonal, would
be equally divided. But no—they almost always gravitate toward the view
that if there is any absolute at all, that absolute must be impersonal. (And
if there is no absolute, that is the same as *chance* or *fate* being absolute—an
equally impersonalist view.) Modern science is no more an exception today
than it was in Russell's time. When scientists seek the causes of things, they
almost always assume that the personal elements in the universe can be
explained by the impersonal (matter, laws, motion), rather than the other
way around. And when scientists seek for absolutes—for example, the "origin of the universe"—they seek for an "elementary particle," a universal law
("theory of everything"), an initial motion (the "big bang"), or a combination of these. Why is this so? Is it not initially at least equally plausible that
impersonal matter, motion, and force can be explained by the decisions of
a person? We have all observed how persons create and harness impersonal
objects and forces to do their bidding. In a factory, human workers produce
a tractor (designed and planned by people); a farmer uses that tractor to
plow his field. But we have never seen a plowed field produce a farmer, or a
tractor produce a workforce.[13] The very idea seems ludicrous. Yet to many
well-educated scientists, the primacy of the impersonal goes without saying. It is, as it were, their presupposition. They adopt it not on the basis of
evidence (for what evidence could prove the negative proposition that there
is no God?), but by an irrational faith[14] that is opposed to Christianity.[15]

The only even remotely plausible explanation of this situation is the
one given in the Bible: that though God's existence is clearly revealed to all
(Rom. 1:18–20), rebellious mankind seeks to suppress that revelation and
thus to operate on the assumption that the God of Scripture does not exist.

12. I do not believe, of course, that we are actually bereft of evidence, but that is the way the
situation appears to many people.

13. The great irony in all this is that all our known experience points in the direction of
personalism over impersonalism. Perhaps someone might cite the evolution of life as the result
of an unguided and blind process as counterevidence, but this would beg the very question
under discussion.

14. I do not believe that all faith is irrational, though some would define it that way. In my
view, Christian faith is based on divinely revealed evidence. Non-Christian faiths are irrational.

15. Does it follow, then, that a Christian who is a scientist should avoid discussions of
elementary particles and such? No, but he should not regard such discussions as leading to the
most ultimate answers. The most ultimate answers are in the Bible.

Is this not the most likely reason for the almost universal, but irrational, preference for impersonalism over personalism?

The Christian apologist should lay more emphasis than did Cornelius Van Til on the issue of impersonalism versus personalism. It is this issue, as we have seen, that distinguishes the Christian worldview from all others. To emphasize it gives the apologist several advantages: (1) Inquirers sometimes tell us that there is no point in investigating Christianity, for if they did that, they would also have to investigate all the other religions, philosophies, ideologies of the history of thought—an impossible task, to be sure. We can reply that they should give special attention to Christianity, for on the crucial question whether the universe is governed by a person or by impersonal principles, Christianity is unique. It is consistently personalistic, and all its rivals are in the opposite camp.[16] (2) The emphasis on personalism also addresses the loneliness of modern secular people. It offers them an ultimate friendship, ultimate love, something that they will never find in a non-Christian view of the world. And (3) it assures them of an ultimate rationality—and (4) an ultimate justice—governing the world order: assurances possible on no other basis.

In this section I have not, of course, proved that biblical personalism is true. I have merely set it forth, over against its antithesis, to show the reader one fundamental aspect of the apologetic task. We are called to stand firmly against the almost universal presupposition that the universe is fundamentally impersonal. We must not allow the unbeliever to suppose what he usually supposes—that *of course* the impersonal is more ultimate. We must challenge him to consider the alternative. And if he says that he is certain of his impersonalism, and if he despises anyone who thinks otherwise as superstitious or stupid, we must ask him to give for his view the kind of proof that he demands of us. And once we show him that his impersonalism is the product of irrational faith, we will be in a good position to present the one alternative to that impersonalism: the alternative presented in Scripture.

The Creator-Creature Relationship

According to Scripture, God is both transcendent and immanent. His transcendence is simply the fact that he is radically different from us.

---

16. Special attention should be given to the modifier: "[Christianity] is *consistently* personalistic." As my discussion of the one-and-many problem argues, my contention is not that Judaism and Islam are examples of impersonalism but rather that in important ways they lack or compromise the robust absolute-personality theism taught in Scripture. See footnote 21 below for more on how I would approach these "Christian heresies."

He is the Creator and we are his creatures. He is absolute, as we saw in the previous section. We are not. Even his personality is different from ours, for his is original and ours is derivative. God is wholly personal and in no way depends on the impersonal, while we are dependent on impersonal matter (the "dust," Gen. 2:7) and forces to keep us alive.

God's immanence is his involvement in all areas of creation. Because he is absolute, he controls all things, interprets all things, and evaluates all things.[17] Because of his omnipotence, his power is exerted everywhere. It is indeed inescapable, and therefore omnipresent. His personality also motivates his immanence. It motivates him to be involved with creation in still other ways. For we are, despite the great differences between ourselves and God, akin to him. We are his "image" (Gen. 1:26–27). According to Scripture, God continually seeks to converse with, to have fellowship with, and to dwell with his people. He spoke to Adam in the garden of Eden, and when our first parents sinned, he continued to visit mankind, to make covenants, and to adopt families (Noah, Abraham, Israel) to be his own. At various points in history, God has actually (in some mysterious sense, which detracts in no way from his general omnipresence) localized his presence in space and time, dwelling in a particular location (the burning bush, Mount Sinai, the tabernacle, the temple, the person of Jesus, the church as the temple of the Holy Spirit).[18]

God is the planner of, and the main actor in, human history. Ultimately, it is with him that we have to do. From Genesis to Revelation, the ultimate question facing humanity was this: How are we to respond to God and his word? The same is true today: behind all the challenges and difficulties of this life, our ultimate challenge is whether or not we will honor God and obey his Word.

It is important that we maintain biblical views of the transcendence and the immanence of God. Transcendence reminds us of the Creator-creature distinction. God is the Creator and we are creatures. We can never become God, losing our creaturehood, nor can God lose his deity.[19] Christian theologians have sometimes erred in this matter, speaking as though salvation turned men into God.[20]

---

17. See later sections of this chapter for more analysis of these categories.

18. For more, see ST, pt. 2, "The Biblical Story," 53–115.

19. In the incarnation of Jesus Christ, God did not lose or diminish his deity to become man; rather, he added a human nature to his divine nature.

20. I am willing to accept the pleas of my Eastern Orthodox friends that they do not mean this literally. But their "deification" language is confusing. Others, after all, such as the ancient Gnostics and modern pantheists, have used such language literally.

And non-Christians of all persuasions radically deny the biblical Creator-creature distinction. Atheists deny it, of course, but so do pantheists, who hold that the world itself is divine in character. It is denied in secular humanism, in which the human mind is adored as the ultimate standard for truth and rightness. It is denied in Kantian philosophy, in which the human mind is the author of the forms of its experience. It is denied in existentialism, in which man creates his own meaning. It is denied in those forms of naturalistic science that claim in effect that the universe is its own creator. It is denied in Eastern religions and Western New Age thought, which urge people to look to "the God within" and to "create their own reality" by visualization.[21]

Liberal theologians,[22] who refuse to be subject to the Bible and who freely incorporate non-Christian ideas into their theologies, also regularly deny the biblical Creator-creature distinction. They insist on thinking autonomously (i.e., recognizing no absolute standard outside themselves), denying the Creator's authority over them. They regularly picture God's transcendence not as his absoluteness (as defined above), but as his remoteness, his "beyondness." In liberalism (and in so-called neoorthodoxy), God is "wholly other"—so far beyond us that we cannot (even with the help of revelation) speak or think correctly about him. Thus, the liberal theologian not only evades the authority of Scripture, but also gives to that evasion a theological rationale.

It is equally important to maintain a biblical view of God's immanence. Again, the point is not that God loses his deity or that man becomes God. Non-Christian thinkers, including liberal theologians, often use the rhetoric of immanence to suggest that the world is really divine in some sense, or that God is identical with the historical process (so Hegel, secular theology, and liberation theology). Process theologians use the rhetoric of immanence

21. I grant that this point is harder to make against what I have called the "Christian heresies," those faiths that share substantial elements of the biblical worldview. I do, however, find Creator-creature confusion, for example, in the remarkable freedom with which these religions allow themselves to manipulate, deny, reinterpret, and supplement the biblical message. Scripture is God's Word and is not open to such manipulation, addition, or subtraction (Deut. 4:2; 12:32; 2 Tim. 3:16–17; Rev. 22:18–19). And occasionally, as in Mormonism, which teaches that God was once a man and that people supposedly become gods, the confusion is quite explicit.

22. Note that by "liberalism" I do not mean only the classical liberalism of Schleiermacher, Ritschl, and their disciples of the nineteenth and early twentieth centuries. As indicated below, I include neoorthodoxy and also the fashionable theologies of our time: process theology, liberation theology, pluralist theology, theologies of hope, history, and story, and so on. Theology is "liberal" if it finds its ultimate authority somewhere other than in the Scriptures. For a survey of liberal approaches to Scripture, see DWG, chaps. 3–7.

(e.g., "God is really related") to deny divine sovereignty, eternity, and omniscience in their biblical senses. And Karl Barth, the father of neoorthodoxy, adds to the notion of God as "wholly other" the contradictory notion that God is "wholly revealed" in Christ.

The "wholly revealed" version of immanence contradicts the biblical doctrine of transcendence; the "wholly other" view of transcendence contradicts the biblical doctrine of immanence. Both of these counterfeits stem from unbelief, from the suppression of truth described in Romans 1:21ff., for both indicate a desire to escape responsibility to God's Word. If God is "wholly other," then of course he cannot speak to us. If he is "wholly revealed," then he is on our level and not entitled to speak with authority.

As Van Til put it, the Christian worldview involves a "two-level" concept of reality. Van Til used to walk into class and draw two circles on the board, one under the other, connected by vertical lines of "communication." The larger, upper circle represented God; the smaller, lower circle represented the creation. All non-Christian thought, he argued, is "one-circle" thought. It either raises man to God's level or lowers God to man's. In any case, it regards God, if it acknowledges him at all, as man's equal, as another part of the "stuff" of the universe. Christian apologetics must make no compromise with such notions.

The biblical Creator-creature relation, like the biblical doctrine of God's absolute personality, is something beautiful. No longer do we have the intolerable burden of playing God—of trying to be ourselves the ultimate standard of truth and right, with all the attendant anxieties of that position. Rather, we can rest in the bosom of our Creator and learn from him wondrous things of how the world was made and his purposes for us. Then we can integrate our own small and brief experience with his revelation, seeking to apply that revelation to ourselves. And what we cannot understand will never threaten us, for we can accept that as the secret of our loving Father.

The Sovereignty of God

In *DKG* I wrote at some length about God's lordship, which I understand to mean his control, authority, and presence. I understand the traditional term *sovereignty* to be a synonym of *lordship*, in all three respects.[23]

---

23. Granted, it is a bit awkward to describe *presence* as an aspect of *sovereignty*, but presence does follow from control and authority if those attributes connote (as they must) universal power and universal interpretation. God's presence is not physical (he does not have a body), but it is precisely a presence of power and authority.

In the present volume I discuss God's presence in the previous section, and I allude to his authority in chapter 1, in the earlier sections of this chapter, and in the subsequent section on epistemology. That leaves the subject of control.

It is important to the Christian worldview that God directs all things, or, as Ephesians 1:11 has it, that "[God] works all things according to the counsel of his will." The relationship between Jacob and Esau was foreordained before they were born (Rom. 9:10–26). Paul uses this relationship as a figure for the broader relation of Jews to Christians. God works all things together for the good of those who love him (Rom. 8:28).

The doctrine that God foreordains and directs all events is generally regarded as Calvinistic, and I am not embarrassed to be called a Calvinist. But other Christian traditions also accept this doctrine, sometimes in spite of themselves. Take Arminianism, for example. The Arminian makes much of human "free will," insisting that our free decisions, especially those of religious significance, are not foreordained or otherwise determined by God. He seeks thereby to reinforce the doctrine of human responsibility (a doctrine with which, in itself, the Calvinist has no quarrel). But the Arminian also recognizes (1) that God foreknows the future exhaustively, and (2) that he has created the world knowing what the future will bring. For example, before the foundation of the world, God knew that Joe would make the free decision to become a Christian. Somehow, then, before Joe was born, God knew of his free decision. So even at that time, Joe's free decision must have been inevitable. Why was it inevitable? Not because of Joe's free will, for Joe was not yet born. Not because of God's predestination, because the Arminian denies that possibility from the outset. It would seem that the inevitability in question had some source other than either Joe or God.[24] But ultimately, God's predestination remains the key element. For God is the One who (1) foreknows Joe's decision and (2) creates the world in such a way that Joe's decision will be made. The decisive factor is God's foreknowing creation. Creation is what sets the whole universe in motion. Is it too much to say that God's foreknowing creation *causes* Joe to make the decision he makes?

Thus, even Arminianism implicitly concedes the Calvinist point without admitting it. Therefore, some Arminians today have abandoned the

---

24. That is a scary possibility! In rejecting "divine determinism," the Arminian in effect embraces a determinism coming from some mysterious other source—another god? the devil? world history? impersonal laws? In any case, this idea certainly does not leave much room for free will.

premise that God foreknows everything and have moved to a view more akin to that of process theology.[25] But this move is exceedingly dubious scripturally.

The main point is that Christians who honor Scripture as God's Word regularly recognize—theological formulations to the contrary notwithstanding—that God rules over all of nature and history. The doctrine of divine sovereignty is the possession of the whole church.

This divine rulership is important to apologetics because it destroys the unbeliever's pretense of autonomy. If God creates and governs all things, then he interprets all things. His plan is the ultimate source of the events of nature and history, and his plan never fails. Therefore, his plan determines what things are, what is true or false, and what is right or wrong. For us to make judgments in these areas, we must consult his revelation (in nature and Scripture), seeking humbly to think God's thoughts after him. We may not claim that our mind, or anything else in creation, is the ultimate standard for being, truth, or right.

The Trinity

Finally, the Christian God is three in one. He is Father, Son, and Holy Spirit. There is only one God (Deut. 6:4ff.; Isa. 44:6). But the Father is God (John 20:17), the Son is God (John 1:1; Rom. 9:5; Col. 2:9; Heb. 1:10ff.), and the Spirit is God (Gen. 1:2; Acts 2; Rom. 8; 1 Thess. 1:5).[26] Somehow they are three, and somehow they are one. The Nicene Creed says that they are one "being" but three "substances," or, differently translated, one "substance" and three "persons." I prefer simply to say "one God, three persons." The technical terms should not be understood in any precise, descriptive sense. The fact is that we do not know precisely how the three are one and the one is three. We do know that since the three are God, they are equal, for there is no superiority or inferiority within God. To be God is to be superior to everything. All three have all the divine attributes. All three are "Lord." All three have the relations to creation that we have earlier ascribed to God. All three are members of the upper circle in Van Til's drawing.

---

25. My full-length treatment on "openness" theology can be found in *NOG, passim.*

26. There are many hints of the Trinity in the Old Testament: the "Spirit," the "Word," the "angel of the Lord" as a divine being; the prophecies of a divine Messiah, whose coming is the coming of the Lord (Ps. 110:1ff.). One may even find the three persons together in Isaiah 63:9–10. The Old Testament God is no "blank unity." But of course, this doctrine is not fully revealed until the New Testament, when there are distinct "comings" of the Son and the Spirit. See *DG,* 633–37.

Even if some question exists about the doctrines we discussed earlier, there is little debate that the doctrine of the Trinity is unique to Christianity. There are interesting triads (threefold distinctions) in other religions, such as the Hindu gods Brahma, Vishnu, and Siva. Many people intuitively grasp that there is something remarkable about the number three. But the Hindu gods are three gods, not one God in three persons, and other alleged parallels between non-Christian religions and the Trinity collapse upon examination. Essentially, rivals of Christianity ignore or deny the Trinity. Despite Hegel's triads, there is nothing like it in secular philosophy. There is nothing like it in the other major religions of the world. And even in the Christian heresies there is little of the Trinity. Indeed, in these heresies the doctrine of the Trinity is often the first to be denied.

Why is the Trinity important to apologetics? Well, what happens when unitarianism (the view that God is merely one) is substituted for Trinitarianism? One result is that the God so defined tends to lose definition and the marks of personality. In the early centuries of the Christian era, the Gnostics, the Arians, and the Neoplatonists worshiped a non-Trinitarian God. That God was a pure oneness, with no plurality of any kind. But one what? A unity of what? In answer to those questions, nothing could be said. Anything we say about God would suggest a division, a plurality, at least between subject and predicate. "God is X" creates, they said, a plurality between God and X. So we cannot speak of God at all. To such thinkers, God's nature was, in modern terms, "wholly other." It could not be described in human language, for (among other reasons) the human mind cannot conceive of a blank oneness. The logical conclusion, then, would seem to be not to speak of God at all. But the ancient unitarians would not accept that conclusion. Therefore, in answer to the question "One what?" they pointed to the creation: God is a perfect unity of those things that are separated in the creation. But if God is defined merely in terms of creation, then he is relative to creation. And indeed, these early unitarians saw reality as a "chain of being" between the unknowable God and the knowable world (a world that was actually a divine emanation: God in his plurality). God was relative to the world, and the world was relative to God.

Anti-Trinitarianism always has that effect. It leads to a "wholly other" God, rather than a God who is transcendent in the biblical sense. Paradoxically, at the same time, it leads to a God who is relative to the world, rather than the sovereign Lord of Scripture. It leads to a blank "One" rather than the absolute personality of the Bible. It makes the Creator-creature distinction a difference of degree rather than a difference of being. Thus, for example, Islam's doctrine of predestination often has the ring of an impersonal determinism rather than of the wise and good planning of the biblical Lord. And Islam's Allah can make arbitrary changes in his very nature, in contrast with the abiding, dependably personal character of the God of Scripture. The doctrine of the Trinity reinforces the earlier points we have made about God and the world.

The New Testament has a remarkable answer to the question "One what?" It answers, "One unity of Father, Son, and Holy Spirit"! It is interesting that when the New Testament most strongly emphasizes the unity of God, it cannot seem to resist naming more than one of the Trinitarian persons. First Corinthians 8:4ff. and Ephesians 4:4–6 are examples of this. Note also the teaching in 1 Corinthians 12:4–6 on the unity of the church as stemming from the one God. John 17:3 and Matthew 28:19ff. are also relevant. Our instinct resists this phenomenon. If I had been writing these texts, I would have wanted to avoid confusing matters by alluding to the Trinity in contexts where I was emphasizing God's oneness. But the biblical writers thought otherwise, because to them the Trinity confirmed, rather than compromised, the oneness of God. God's oneness is, precisely, a oneness of three persons.

Since God is both three and one, he can be described in personalistic terms without being made relative to the world. For example, God is love (1 John 4:8). Love of what? If we immediately answer "love of the world," then we have a problem. For on that account the divine attribute of love depends on the existence of the world. And to say that God's attributes depend on the world is to say that God himself depends on the world.[27] This is the route to the "wholly revealed." Should we say, then, that *love* is merely a metaphor for something mysterious? That is the route to the "wholly other." We can see the logic of Gnosticism, Arianism, and Neoplatonism: If God is a mere one, he is either "wholly other" or relative to the world—or somehow both. But he is not a mere one. He is one in three. His love is initially the love of the Father, Son, and Spirit for one another (John 17). His love, therefore, like his being, is self-existent and self-sufficient. It does not depend on the world (though it surely fills the world), and it need not be swallowed up in religious agnosticism.

The Trinity also means that God's creation can be both one and many. Secular philosophy veers between the extremes of monism (the

---

27. This, of course, is contrary to the doctrine of aseity. For a discussion of how aseity informs apologetic practice, see "Divine Aseity and Apologetics," reprinted as Appendix E in the present volume.

world is really one; plurality is an illusion)[28] and pluralism (the world is radically disunited; unity is an illusion).[29] Secular philosophy moves from one extreme to the other, because it does not have the resources to define a position between the two extremes, and because it seeks an absolute at one extreme or another—as though there must be an absolute oneness (with no plurality)[30] or else a universe of absolutely unique, unconnected elements, creating an absolute pluralism and destroying any universal oneness.[31] To find such an absolute in either direction is important if the philosopher is to find an adequate standard apart from the God of Scripture. Thus is revealed philosophy's religious quest—to find an absolute, a god, in the world. But the Christian knows that there is no absolute unity (devoid of plurality) or absolute plurality (devoid of unity). These exist neither in the world nor in the world's Creator. If either of these existed in the world, it would be a sort of unitarian god, but there is no God but the Trinitarian Lord. Such a unitarian god would be unknowable, for we cannot know a blank oneness or an utter uniqueness. And if that perfect oneness or perfect uniqueness is the metaphysical essence of reality, then nothing can be known at all. But the Christian knows that God is the only absolute, and that that absolute is both one and many. Thus, we are freed from the task of trying to find utter unity or utter disunity within the world. When we search for ultimate criteria or standards, we look not to some "maximum unity" or "utter uniqueness" within the world, but to the living God, who alone furnishes the ultimate criteria for human thought. Thus, the Trinity also has implications for epistemology.[32]

Epistemology

I have extensively discussed epistemology in *DKG* and have outlined my major epistemological concerns in chapter 1 of this volume.[33] Consider also the points made above under "The Sovereignty of God"—that God

---

28. Examples: Neoplatonism, Spinoza, Hegel.

29. Examples: Democritus, Epicurus, Leibniz, the early Wittgenstein.

30. Such as the "Being" of Parmenides, "the One" of Plotinus, and the "God or Nature" of Spinoza.

31. Examples: Aristotle's *infima species*, the "particulars" of medieval nominalism, and Leibniz's monads.

32. This is the best I can do to explain Van Til's claim that "the Trinity solves the 'one and many problem.'" Instinctively, I feel that Van Til is right about this, but the point is terribly difficult to formulate coherently. No doubt my formulation can be improved on. Cf. *CVT*, 71–76.

33. Philosophically sophisticated readers might also be interested in my article "Christianity and Contemporary Epistemology," *Westminster Theological Journal* 52, 1 (Spring 1990): 131–41.

as Lord interprets everything definitively, so that when we want to know something, we must seek to think his thoughts after him. And note my Trinitarian epistemology in the previous section. Since I have already said the most important things on this subject, the present section will be short.

God is not only omnipotent, but also omniscient. As we have seen, he controls all things by his wise plan. Hence, he knows all things (Heb. 4:12–13; 1 John 3:20). All our knowledge, therefore, originates in him. Thus, "the fear of the LORD is the beginning of knowledge" (Prov. 1:7).

God is not only the origin of truth, but also the supreme authority for knowledge. Authority is part of his lordship. God has the right to command and be obeyed. He has, therefore, the right to tell us what we must believe.[34]

Fallen man wants to think autonomously, subject only to his own criteria of truth, free to ignore those of God. But God's grace takes away our bondage to autonomous ways of thinking and enables us instead to think according to God's Word (Jer. 31:31ff.; Matt. 11:25–28; John 17:3; 1 Cor. 2:6–16; Eph. 4:13; Phil. 1:9; Col. 1:9ff.; 3:10; 2 Tim. 2:25; 2 Peter 1:2ff.; 3:18; 1 John 4:7).[35] The Holy Spirit illumines our minds to know the truth (1 Cor. 2:12ff.; 2 Cor. 4:6; Eph. 1:17ff.; 1 Thess. 1:5; Heb. 6:4; 10:32). The fear of the Lord leads to knowledge and wisdom (Prov. 1:7; parallels). But when sinners try to gain knowledge without the fear of the Lord, that knowledge is suppressed, distorted (Rom. 1:21–25; 1 Cor. 1:18–2:5). This is not to say that every sentence they utter is false. It is to say that their basic worldview is twisted and unreliable. Their most serious epistemological mistake is, typically, to assert their own autonomy: to make themselves, or something other than the biblical God, the final standard of truth and right.

---

34. This is the great offense to modern man, indeed to all non-Christian thinkers of all ages—the thought that someone else has the right to tell us what to believe. Philosophy itself may well have developed out of rebellion against the traditional religions, as it sought to find answers to problems determined not by religious traditions but by independent—autonomous—human thought. To tell these intellectuals that their whole movement toward "free thought" (so often praised rhapsodically) was a mistake is to offend them at a very deep level. I will grant to them that it is wrong to allow one's mind to be enslaved to merely human traditions. (In fact, such enslavement continues to be a problem even in the most purportedly "freethinking" circles. How often we hear from our intellectual mentors that we must question all the certitudes of our forefathers—but must never be "politically incorrect"!) But where God speaks, his words must take precedence over all our cherished conceptions. Accepting such a humble stance is not easy for an intellectual. Once again we see that salvation must be by divine grace!

35. I apologize for deluging the reader with "proof texts." See my DKG, especially 1–49, for some analysis of their teaching. I do think, however, that for the most part these texts speak for themselves without commentary, at least to most high school graduates. On "proof texts," see ibid., 197.

So rationalistic philosophy declares human reason to be the final standard. Empiricism, recognizing the flights of speculation to which unbridled "reason" is prone, demands that all ideas be ultimately account-able to human sense-experience. And skepticism, recognizing that both human reason and sense-experience are prone to error, declares (on its own authority!) that truth is unattainable.[36] Kantian and existentialist thought in effect make man the very source of significance in his experi-ence. Liberal theologians are all too eager to go along with these traditions, and the Christian heresies continue to manipulate the biblical message as they see fit.

As we saw under "Metaphysics," again it is evident that true Chris-tianity is *the* alternative to the conventional wisdom, to the consensus of philosophers, religionists, liberal theologians, and popular thinkers. Our time is one in which everyone seems to claim autonomy, the right to "do your own thing." God calls that foolishness (1 Cor. 1:18–2:5); he says that it comes from the devil (2 Cor. 4:4).

The apologist must not only refuse to compromise with these dis-torted epistemologies, but also summon unbelievers to abandon them. For such epistemologies are part of the unbeliever's sinful suppression of the truth. Like the distortions in metaphysics, they represent his desire to escape from responsibility, to avoid hearing the voice of God telling him what to do.[37]

We cannot consistently issue such a challenge if, as has often been done traditionally, we build our own apologetics on one of those non-Christian epistemological options.

Ethics

Ethics investigates such matters as good and evil, right and wrong. Like Christian metaphysics and epistemology, Christian ethics is distinctive.

God is perfectly good and just (Gen. 18:25; Ps. 145:17). As Lord, he is, as we have seen, the supreme authority over his creatures. Under "Episte-mology" we saw that God is the supreme criterion of truth and falsehood. Under "Ethics" we must observe that God is also the supreme standard of what is good and evil, right and wrong. And he has expressed his standards in his words to us (Deut. 4:1ff.; 6:4ff.).

---

36. But is that declaration true?

37. This is another example of how apologetics and evangelism dovetail into each other. The apologist calls the unbeliever to nothing less than moral and intellectual repentance.

Unbelievers, we are told, know not only of God's existence, but also of his standards, his requirements (Rom. 1:32). Yet they disobey those laws, and, further, seek to evade that responsibility (Rom. 1:26–32).

Again, the history of philosophy illustrates how human thinkers seek to avoid responsibility to God by claiming autonomy. They don't want to obey God's laws, and so they set themselves up as the ultimate judges of what is right. Teleological ethics seeks to base values on sense-experience, but it cannot bridge the gap between the *is* of experience and the *ought* of value. Deontological ethics claims a source of duty beyond experience, but that source is ultimately mysterious—to the point where it lacks all usefulness. Subjectivist ethics bases its judgments on mere feeling, but why should one person's feelings command anyone else's attention or behavior?[38]

After the philosophers, the liberal theologians come running in, waving the banner of autonomy. Joseph Fletcher's "situation ethics" comes from their group, leading the flock of more recent ethicists—the Callahans, Childresses, Gustafsons, Kervorkians, Spongs. And the newspaper columnists, the talk-show hosts, and the politicians follow suit. Abortions become legitimate for no other reason than that people want to have them. It is a "choice." Thus develops the conventional wisdom—and thus develop the ills of a society governed by that wisdom. If ethical autonomy is really true, then of course we can justify gangs, drugs, sadistic rap music, and all the rest. But if we are responsible to God, we ought to retreat from these social fashions with enormous haste.

Christianity is *the* alternative. Only Christianity flies right in the face of human claims to autonomy. Only Christianity, therefore, has the answer to lawlessness.

Good News

But Christianity is not just an alternative to the secular philosophies or a set of moral standards better than those of current society. It is *gospel*, good news. In this respect, too, it is unique—a genuine alternative to the conventional ways of thinking. Scripture teaches that human beings, made in God's image, sinned against him (Gen. 3:1ff.). We today bear the guilt of Adam's first sin (Rom. 5:12–19) and the weight of our own sins against God (Rom. 3:10ff.). Our problem, therefore, is not finitude (as we are told by some pantheists, New Age thinkers, and the like), and the solution to the

---

38. For a fuller examination of these three ethical approaches, see *DCL*, chaps. 6–8. The apologetically minded reader will note the transcendental thrust of that discussion.

problem is not for us to become God. Nor is our chief problem to be found in our heredity, environment, emotional makeup, poverty, or sicknesses.[39] Rather, the problem is sin: willful transgression of God's law (1 John 3:4). According to Scripture, existing evils of heredity, environment, sickness, and so on are due to the fall (Gen. 3:17–19; Rom. 8:18–22).

And what is the solution? "For God so loved the world, that he gave his only Son, that whoever believes in him should not perish but have eternal life" (John 3:16). Jesus died for our sins and was raised for our justification (Rom. 3:20–8:11; 1 Cor. 15:1–11). The scriptural directive is not for us to work harder to achieve God's favor (Rom. 3:20), but to accept God's mercy through Christ as a free gift (Eph. 2:8–10).

No philosophy, no liberal theology, not even any Christian heresy offers any solution to human sin, beyond encouragements to try harder. However persuasive they may be in other respects, these ideologies agree that there is no free gift of divine forgiveness through the sacrifice of Jesus. Empiricism, rationalism, idealism, Judaism, Islam, Mormonism, the Jehovah's Witnesses—all are religions of works-righteousness, which is self-righteousness. They offer us only the hollow advice to try harder, or the false and morally destructive claim that God will forgive without demanding anything.

Allow me to draw the application that evangelism is part of apologetics (as the reverse is also true—perspectivally!). The apologist must always be ready to present the gospel. He must not get so tangled up in arguments, proofs, defenses, and critiques that he neglects to give the unbeliever what he needs most.

We see that Christianity, both as philosophy and as good news, is *the* alternative to the conventional wisdom. This uniqueness of Christianity is itself of apologetic significance. Uniqueness does not itself entail truth, but when all the other alternatives march along like Tweedledum and Tweedledee, all claiming implausibly to be able to explain the personal by means of the impersonal, all claiming autonomy (and thus denying God's sovereignty), all claiming to find ultimates not in God but in creation, all offering as a solution to our predicament nothing more profound than works-righteousness—indeed, without a dime's worth of difference among these conventional ideologies—it certainly makes sense to give a high priority to investigating Christianity and its claims. Indifference to such uniqueness is not wise.

---

39. Jay Adams and others have pointed out the tendency in modern culture to explain moral problems by medical models: mental illness, homosexuality as genetic, and so on.

3

APOLOGETICS AS PROOF: SOME METHODOLOGICAL CONSIDERATIONS

In the remaining chapters, I intend to discuss more fully the three forms of apologetics defined in the first chapter: proof, defense, and offense. In this chapter and the next three, the subject will be *proof*, or finding a rational basis for faith.

Faith, Scripture, and Evidence

Faith is not mere rational thought, but it is not irrational either. It is not "belief in the absence of evidence"; rather, it is a trust that rests on sufficient evidence. This fact is evident in Scripture. Abraham's willingness to sacrifice his son Isaac (Gen. 22) is often presented as an example of a faith that contravenes moral and rational norms. But this analysis often fails to take account of the fact that Abraham had a very firm basis for doing what he did—namely, the command of God. What God says can be neither irrational nor immoral, for his Word defines rationality and morality for us. When God tells us to do something, we need no greater rational basis for doing it. So faith does not believe despite the absence of evidence; rather, faith honors God's Word as sufficient evidence. Romans 4:20–21 describes Abraham's faith—always in the New Testament a model of Christian faith—as follows: "No distrust made him waver concerning the promise of God, but he grew strong in his faith as he gave glory to God, fully convinced that God was able to do what he had promised."

Another example: I have often asked students to paraphrase Paul's argument for the resurrection in 1 Corinthians 15:1–11. They often mention the postresurrection appearances, especially to the five hundred eyewitnesses, most of whom were still alive when Paul wrote (v. 6). But they almost always miss the main thrust of the apostle's argument.[1] The main thrust is perfectly clear from the structure and content of the passage: you should believe in the resurrection because it is part of the apostolic preaching! Note verses 1–2: "Now I would remind you, brothers, of the gospel I preached to you, which you received, in which you stand, and by which you are being saved; if you hold fast to the word I preached to you—unless you believed in vain." And verse 11: "Whether then it was I or they, so we preach and so you believed."

Paul is telling the Corinthians that they came to faith through his preaching, which included the preaching of the resurrection. He warns them not to cast doubt on the resurrection, for if Christ has not been raised, their faith will be in vain. If the resurrection is subject to doubt, all the rest of the message will also be subject to doubt, and then "we are of all people most to be pitied" (1 Cor. 15:19; see also vv. 14–18).

The ultimate proof, the ultimate evidence, is the Word of God.[2] Eyewitnesses are important, but they die, and memories of them fade. Only if their testimony is preserved in God's written Word will that testimony have continuing value down through the history of the world.

To trust God's Word as ultimate evidence is not to deny the importance of reasons. God does not always reveal the reasons for what he says and does, but as a wise, true, and faithful God, and as the very standard of rationality, he always has a reason—of that we may be confident. Often he does reveal his reasons to us. Abraham knew that God had a reason for commanding him to sacrifice his son, even though that reason was hidden at first. Later, he came to know in some measure what that reason was: to test his faith (Gen. 22:16–18). In the light of the completed canon, we can see more of the reason: God was teaching us to experience something of his own agony in giving up his own Son to death on our behalf.

Scripture often contains its own reasons for the things it says. When Paul tells us in Romans 8:1 that "there is now no condemnation for those

---

1. Perhaps they miss it because they have been influenced by the evidentialist apologetic literature, which focuses almost exclusively on the data just mentioned.

2. This is also the case when Scripture encourages "testing" its claims. It is true that both prophets and apostles stressed the need for evidence. But more often than is usually acknowledged, the evidence demanded is God's Word itself.

who are in Christ Jesus," he adds the word *therefore*.[3] *Therefore* indicates a reason. Specifically, Paul is saying that *because of* the saving work of Christ already described, there is no condemnation. We should believe that we are not condemned, and we should believe it on the grounds or reasons offered in chapters 1–7. Here Scripture does not merely proclaim the truth; it also proclaims reasons for believing the truth. And just as its truths are authoritative, so also are its reasons. We have an obligation not only to believe scriptural truth, but also to believe it *for scriptural reasons.*

Therefores abound in Scripture, together with many other indications of authoritative reasoning. When we proclaim Scripture, therefore, we may (and must, if we want to be complete in our exegesis) also proclaim that authoritative reasoning process, the biblical rationale.

Showing biblical reasons for biblical truth is a very important part of apologetics. An unbeliever asks, "Why did Jesus curse the fig tree in Matthew 21:19ff.? That seems like such a cruel and petty thing to do!" The believer should answer by showing from Scripture itself the symbolism of approaching judgment and therefore the point of Jesus' object lesson.

This does not mean, however, that direct scriptural proof is the only apologetic evidence that God permits us to use. As we have seen, Scripture itself directs us to consider evidence outside itself.[4] For the first-century believers, at least, the five hundred eyewitnesses of 1 Corinthians 15:6 were a valuable resource, even a supplement to the apostle's word. Certainly Paul's argument in chapter 15 implies that if people have doubts, they can look up the witnesses. Of course, the witnesses' testimony is to be evaluated by way of a biblical view of evidence—not by theories such as those of David Hume and Rudolf Bultmann, which reject all supernatural claims from the outset.

Paul argues, as we have seen, that God is clearly revealed in the creation (Rom. 1:18–21). We may infer that there is evidence in creation, God's "general revelation," which, in a way similar to the evidence provided by the witnesses mentioned in 1 Corinthians 15, supplements the evidence of Scripture itself. But that evidence must also be assessed on biblical criteria.

---

3. You know the old saying: when you see a *therefore* in Scripture, you should always look to see what it's "there for."

4. Review at this point chapter 1's discussion of *sola Scriptura*. We should also remind ourselves (see the discussions in *DKG*) that it is impossible to make a sharp distinction between arguments based on "Scripture alone" and arguments based on combinations of Scripture and natural revelation. Usually when we cite Scripture, we are citing a version of Scripture, the product of textual criticism and translation principles based in part on natural revelation. Indeed, the very citing of one text rather than another represents a human choice based on factors (audience, need) that cannot be deduced from Scripture alone. *DWG*, 239–57.

As I argued in chapter 1, we may freely use extrabiblical evidence as long as we use it in ways acceptable to Scripture.[5]

The Concept of Proof

Cornelius Van Til says that "there is absolutely certain proof for the existence of God and the truth of Christian theism."[6] He continues:

> The Reformed apologist maintains that there is an absolutely valid argument for the existence of God and for the truth of Christian theism. He cannot do less without virtually admitting that God's revelation to man is not clear. It is fatal for the Reformed apologist to admit that man has done justice to the objective evidence if he comes to any other conclusion than that of the truth of Christian theism.[7]

What do we mean by *proof* in this sort of discussion? The most uncontroversial examples of proof are those in mathematics, where propositions are derived by strictly logical inference from axioms. Axioms are propositions that are considered self-evident or, at least, are assumed for the purposes of the discussion. On this understanding, a proof for God's existence might go somewhat like this:

- Premise 1: What Scripture says is always true.
- Premise 2: Scripture says that God exists.
- Conclusion: Therefore, God exists.

Here, the truthfulness of Scripture would be one axiom, and the teaching of Scripture that God exists would be another. The conclusion then follows by strict logic.

On our previous analysis, this argument is a sound one. The first premise is true because Scripture is God's Word and therefore inerrant. The second premise is obvious and uncontroversial. The logical path from premises to conclusion is likewise unimpeachable. In one sense, then, this argument is one form of "absolutely certain proof for the existence of God."

5. For a discussion of the type of circularity involved in this procedure, see the discussion of circularity in chapter 1.

6. Cornelius Van Til, *The Defense of the Faith*, ed. K. Scott Oliphint, 4th ed. (Phillipsburg, NJ: P&R Publishing, 2008), 126.

7. Ibid., 126–27.

But there is something lacking here. Practically speaking, we would not be likely to use this proof in our witness to non-Christians. Most intelligent unbelievers today would dismiss it simply by denying the biblical authority on which it is based. The circle is too narrow.[8] In one sense, the problem is not with the proof, but with the unbeliever: he ought to accept biblical authority, and therefore he ought to accept our proof. But of course he doesn't.

One way to approach this problem is to revise our concept of proof somewhat by incorporating the unbeliever's response. That is to say, it is not sufficient for a proof to be based on true premises and sound logic; it must also be persuasive. We might say that an argument, in order to be a proof, must be persuasive to every rational person.

I do think that persuasion is an important concept,[9] but I do not agree that it should be incorporated in the concept of proof. That would limit our proofs to those that actually persuade people. But in fact, Scripture teaches that good proofs do not always persuade, for unbelievers repress the truth. This repression is not always successful; sometimes unbelievers recognize truths, even truths about God.[10] But it is nearly impossible to predict what a given unbeliever will suppress and what he will admit in spite of himself. Ultimately, the only cure for repression is the regenerating work of the Holy Spirit. Therefore, as we construct arguments, we have little idea of what sort of argument will be persuasive to any particular individual or audience. *No argument is guaranteed to be persuasive to all people.* Not even arguments from Scripture alone are guaranteed in that way, though we know from the discussion above that they are pleasing to God. To have such a guarantee, we would have to be able to predict both the devious process of suppression and the mysterious workings of the Holy Spirit.

One might note that this process of suppression is not rational. Therefore, unbelievers do not fall into the category of *rational person* in the proposed definition of proof. Then that definition is of no apologetic significance. For the whole point of apologetics is to present the truth to unbelievers. The question then becomes: How should we present the truth to nonrational persons? What constitutes a proof in the apologetic situation?

8. Review the distinction in chapter 1 (and in *DKG*, 131, 303–4) between broad and narrow circularity. The argument in question is narrowly circular because the first premise is so clearly dependent on the conclusion. Of course, all valid deductive syllogisms are circular in the sense that the conclusion is already implicit in the premises. But in this case the circularity is so obvious that it almost begs the unbeliever to challenge the premises.

9. See *DKG*, 119, 131, 355–58.

10. The Pharisees described in the New Testament are obvious examples.

Perhaps we can remedy the situation by defining proof as that which *ought* to persuade, rather than as something that actually persuades. But this definition brings us back to the narrowly circular proof that we originally considered. The unbeliever ought to accept that proof together with the scriptural authority it presupposes. As a matter of fact, he ought to believe in God without any such argument at all, simply on the basis of God's revelation in creation (Rom. 1:18–21, again). If our task is simply to put the unbeliever into a position in which he ought to believe, then we are best advised to do nothing, for he is in that position already.

I think it is right to define proof as that which ought to persuade. But that does not help us to show what is missing in the narrowly circular type of argument, for such arguments fit that definition of proof. At this point we must invoke a godly pragmatism within the overall teaching of Scripture. Broader arguments just seem to work best. Many unbelievers demand that we consider the facts of their experience, which seem to them to refute Christianity. The apologist is not obligated to refuse such requests, for God is revealed in all creation. Even those facts that unbelievers use to oppose Christianity can be seen to have God's mark on them. Even evil is quite unexplainable apart from a Christian theistic worldview (see chapters 7 and 8). It is therefore useful for the apologist to deal with such demands on their own terms, making a case based on data from both general and special revelation.

The only restrictions on apologetic argument that emerge from our discussion so far are these: (1) The premises and logic of the argument must be consistent with biblical teaching (including biblical epistemology). (2) The premises must be true and the logic valid. (3) The specific subject matter of the argument must take into account the specific situation of the inquirer: his education, his interests, his questions, and so on. This third point means that apologetic argument is "person-variable."[11] No single argument is guaranteed to persuade every unbeliever or to assuage every doubt in a believer's heart. But since every fact testifies to the reality of God, the apologist has no shortage of resources, but rather a great abundance.

The Need for Proof

In one sense, not everybody needs a theistic proof. Some people, such as W. K. Clifford, have said that it is wrong to believe anything without

11. See the discussion of this in *DKG*.

evidence. But that initially plausible view has been effectively countered in our time by philosophers Alvin Plantinga and Nicholas Wolterstorff.[12] They point out that we believe many things that we cannot necessarily prove. That other persons have minds like mine, for example, is a very difficult proposition to prove to someone disposed to challenge it. Or take my belief that Violet Frame is truly my mother, or my belief that my wife really loves me, or my belief that $2 + 2 = 4$. Such "basic" beliefs (as Plantinga calls them) are easy to accept as being obviously true, especially when alleged proofs for them are complicated and hard to follow.

I would agree with Clifford that we should not believe anything without having evidence in the objective sense. That is, one should not believe anything unless there is objective evidence to support it. Clifford, however, intends to say more, namely, that we should not believe anything without proof—that is, without being able to formulate an argument based on evidence. (This is having evidence in a subjective sense.) I believe that there is more than adequate evidence for the truth of Christianity, but I do not believe that someone must be able to formulate a proof using that evidence in order to justify his belief in Christ.

Evidence has its own persuasive value, quite apart from our verbal formulations of it. When I see someone drive to my home in a Postal Service truck, wearing a uniform, I infer that that person is going to bring me mail. I know that; it is a kind of logical process. I could formulate a syllogism: When people in Postal Service trucks and uniforms drive to my house, it is for the purpose of delivering mail; Mr. P. has driven to my house in a Postal Service truck and wears a uniform; therefore, I can expect him to bring me mail. But why bother with the syllogism? The objective evidence is sufficient; formulating a subjective argument will only waste time.

When we consider the heavens (Ps. 8:3) and observe the incredible vastness of the universe and the magnificence of its order, that experience has a persuasive value equal to, and perhaps beyond, that of any verbal teleological or cosmological argument.

Indeed, Scripture teaches that God's existence is obvious, and many of us would testify that his existence is obvious to us as well. Scripture never argues the existence of God; rather, it states that he is clearly revealed (Rom. 1:18ff.), and it ridicules those who deny him (Ps. 14:1). The "fool" in the psalm who says "There is no God" says it not out of intellectual error,

---

12. See Alvin Plantinga and Nicholas Wolterstorff, eds., *Faith and Rationality* (Notre Dame, IN: University of Notre Dame Press, 1983). Compare my review of it in *DKG*, 382–400.

but out of moral blindness (see the following verses). He has repressed the truth, as have the unbelievers described in Romans 1:21ff. Or, to put the same point differently, he is blinded by Satan (2 Cor. 4:4).

In contrast to such fools, many people grow up with God and receive him gladly. They hear about God in church, in Sunday school, around the family dinner table, and in Christian school. They see their parents making decisions based on the Word of God. They learn Scripture verses and catechism from memory. God is literally the head of their home. They could no easier doubt God's existence than they could doubt the existence of their own father or mother.[13]

Indeed, for people of this sort, trying to prove God's existence would be at best a theoretical exercise, at worst a form of impudence. What should we think of a child who demands proof that his father really is his father before he agrees to obey? Clearly—in most cases!—he is avoiding responsibility. He ought simply to believe and obey, without "proof."

Scripture never rebukes childlike faith; indeed, Jesus makes such faith a model to be followed by adults (Luke 18:16f.). One who requires proof might be doing it out of ungodly arrogance, or he might be thereby admitting that he has not lived in a godly environment and has taken counsel from fools. God's norm for us is that we live and raise our children in such a way that proof will be unnecessary.

Still, as we saw in the previous section, there are some who claim that proof is necessary *for them.* As we have seen, Scripture does more than simply rebuke them. It provides much persuasive testimony of God's reality and also points us to sources outside itself where more testimony can be found. Often the most effective thing is for the inquirer simply to read the Bible. God's Word is powerful as the Spirit drives it into the heart. Another valuable piece of advice to an inquirer is simply to be as open as he can be to the creation itself. That, too, clearly reveals God, as we have seen, even when that data is not formulated into an argument. Think of how many, many people have looked at the stars or the wonders of the earth and sea and concluded that someone must have planned and made it all. That conclusion, however vague, is a confession of our God of absolute personality. And in one way, it goes beyond any teleological or cosmological argument. It is as though a teleological argument based on star-formation were repeated billions of times—once for each star.

13. Compare Van Til's pamphlet *Why I Believe in God* (Philadelphia: Committee on Christian Education, Orthodox Presbyterian Church, n.d.).

But as we have seen, it is possible to go beyond these general recommendations and produce specific arguments for God's existence. A wise man does not really need these; they are for fools. But God is very patient and gracious with such fools as we all once were.

Once we get beyond simply pointing the unbeliever to the creation and the statements of Scripture, proof becomes a fairly complicated matter. Since everything is created and directed by God, nothing may be properly understood apart from him. That means that any fact may become the focal point for an apologetic; the apologist may show how that fact derives its intelligibility from God. We may use a wide variety of approaches and methods, consistent with our overall presuppositional commitment. Since proof is person-variable, we are particularly interested in choosing an argumentative approach that makes contact with the individual or group we are talking to. That decision is not an easy one.

It is interesting in this connection to ask how people actually come to faith in Christ. I have not made a scientific survey of the conversion testimonies of Christians, but I have heard a great many of them in my life, and I can make some rough generalizations. For one thing, few Christians, when asked to list the factors that led them to trust in Christ, list any argument or proof at all. For most, the issue is not intellectual; for them, Christianity was, in an intellectual sense, believable enough. The issue was, rather, that the person was not yet motivated to repent of sin, seek forgiveness, and obey the Christian revelation. That motivation, supernatural in origin, came through various experiences—often merely a very vivid retelling of the gospel of Jesus, especially such a retelling connected by loving, winsome behavior. (As I indicated earlier, behavior is part of communication; our lives are part of our apologetic.)

Then comes a theistic proof, possibly unstated, but representing the following sort of thought process:

- Premise 1: If Jesus is Lord and Savior, then he is reliable.
- Premise 2: If he is reliable, then God exists.
- Premise 3: He is Lord and Savior.
- Conclusion: Therefore, God exists.

This is a somewhat narrowly circular argument, but it is very persuasive to many people;[14] it represents the actual thought process that brings

14. In practice, of course, it is likely to be much broader, especially since much evidence will be demanded to establish premise 3.

many to faith in God. Apologists often routinely assume that an inquirer must consider theistic proofs before he or she considers the specific case for Christianity, but in real life the reverse order is often the case: it is Jesus who assures us that God is real.[15]

Many different orders of argumentation are possible, for three reasons. First, Christianity is a package; its doctrines are interrelated; each, rightly understood, will lead to the others. Second, at some level everyone knows that the Christian God exists, although each person requires supernatural help to embrace that truth in love. The Spirit works in mysterious ways, and his use of us apologists is not limited to the strategies described in apologetics textbooks. Third, proof is person-variable, and different people respond to different approaches.

For some inquirers, it does seem to be necessary to discuss the existence of God before we discuss Jesus. They simply insist on it, and we have no reason to refuse. When they ask a question, we should be ready to answer it, even if that question is "How can I believe that God exists?" (Recall 1 Peter 3:15–16.) And indeed there are some Christians—not a great many, but some—who will testify that a proof of God's existence helped them to believe in Christ, or at least that a proof took away one of their excuses for unbelief. The great writer and scholar C. S. Lewis described his quest for God as very much an intellectual journey, and in his case I have no doubt that it was. His writings, in turn, bore much spiritual fruit. Perhaps there are some that we can help today by arguing for the existence of God.

As we do the difficult job of selecting the appropriate strategy for our situation, we want to find an approach that (1) will be intellectually understandable to our inquirers, (2) will arouse and maintain their interest, (3) will perhaps interact with some area in which they admit weakness or uncertainty, pressing it harder, (4) will contain some element of surprise, so that their prepared responses will be nullified and they will be forced to think, (5) will set forth the truth without compromise, and (6) will by its manner communicate the love of Christ.

15. One of my correspondents asks, "Who believes that Jesus is the Son of God without first believing that there is a God who can have a Son?" But we must keep reminding ourselves that unbelievers are not ignorant of God. They know God, but suppress that knowledge (as that particular correspondent is certainly aware!). The theistic proof is only a prod, a stimulus, to bring what is suppressed to the surface, if God will so use it. We all have, indeed, many beliefs of which we are only dimly aware, which in some circumstances we might even deny, but which can be brought out through challenges of various sorts. And surely many people are, shall we say, reassured of God's reality by considering Jesus.

Point of Contact

The phrase *point of contact* is rather ambiguous. Some readers might assume that it simply refers to some common interest that the apologist might share with an inquirer for the sake of friendship and conversation, an interest that could eventually lead to an opportunity to present the gospel. But in theology (chiefly with Barth and Van Til), the phrase has a somewhat more technical meaning.

The issue provoking the use of this phrase is this: Granted that the unbeliever is totally depraved, what is there in him, if anything, that is capable of receiving God's grace? The Arminian answers, "Man's reason and free will." Karl Barth answers, "Nothing at all." In Barth's view, God's grace creates its own point of contact. This position coheres with Barth's view that the reception of grace has no intellectual element. Grace brings us no "propositional revelation" that the unbeliever by grace comes to understand and trust. It is rather a "bolt out of the blue," which makes no contact at all with the thinking or will of the unbeliever.

Orthodox Calvinists,[16] however, recall that God made man in his image—an image that is marred by sin, but not destroyed. Van Til argues that part of that image is knowledge of God, which, though repressed (Rom. 1), still exists at some level of man's thinking. That is the point of contact to which the apologist appeals. He does not appeal merely to the unbeliever's reason and will, for his will is bound by sin and his reason seeks to distort, not affirm, the truth. We do not ask the unbeliever to evaluate Christianity through his reason, for he seeks to operate his reason autonomously and thus is deep in error from the outset. Rather, says Van Til, we appeal to the knowledge of God that he has (Rom. 1:21) but suppresses.

But how do people suppress the truth of God's revelation? We might be tempted to think of *suppression* in psychological terms, as when someone relegates an unwelcome truth to his subconscious or unconscious. But that is not the biblical picture. The enemies of God in the Bible, from the Egyptians (Ex. 14:4), to the Pharisees, to Satan himself, often consciously acknowledge the existence of God. In Romans 1, the suppression is seen in idolatrous worship and illicit sexual behavior. The unregenerate deny their knowledge of God by their ethical rebellion.

In contrast, when the Bible describes the believer's knowledge, that knowledge is always accompanied by obedience and holiness. John

---

16. Barth opposes historic orthodoxy on this and many other matters.

says, "And by this we know that we have come to know him, if we keep his commandments" (1 John 2:3). Scripture closely relates epistemology to ethics.

So the difference between unregenerate and regenerate knowledge of God may be described as ethical. The unregenerate represses his knowledge of God by disobeying God. This disobedience might lead in some cases to psychological repression, or explicit atheism, but it does not always. The apologist should recognize, therefore, that the unbeliever's problem is primarily ethical, not intellectual. He rejects the truth because he disobeys God's ethical standards, not the other way around.

This ethical rebellion does, however, always inject an element of irrationality into the thinking of the unregenerate. To know God and his commandments, even his "eternal power" (Rom. 1:20), and yet to rebel against him, is supremely futile. In this sense, unbelief is foolishness (Ps. 14:1). Consider Satan, who knows God in some respects better than we do, yet who seeks to replace God on the throne. In some ways, Satan is highly intelligent and knowledgeable. But in the most important sense, he is supremely irrational. It is important for the apologist to understand that in the final analysis, the position of the non-Christian is like this: often intellectually impressive, but at a deeper level ludicrous.

Further, as we have seen, God's common grace restrains the non-Christian's distortions of the truth. So even Satan uses the truth for his own purpose, and there are some unregenerate human beings, such as the Pharisees, who are relatively orthodox. So that suppression is never complete. The unbeliever would like to snuff out his knowledge of the true God, but he cannot. Indeed, it is this knowledge, however he may distort it, that enables him to go on living in God's world.[17] Thus, the unbeliever, contrary to his own assumptions, often says things that agree with the truth as the Christian sees it. The effect of sin on reasoning does not mean that the Christian and the non-Christian disagree over everything, although if both were consistent with their presuppositions, that would be the case. Defining the possible extent of that agreement is difficult. The Pharisees acknowledged so much of God's truth that Jesus actually commended their teaching (Matt. 23:3), while deploring their works (vv. 3–39). Thus, as we appeal to the unbeliever's native knowledge of God, we might find him agreeing with us, at least part of the time.[18]

17. I recall Van Til's illustration of the little girl slapping her daddy's cheeks while being held on his lap. Without his support, she could not continue her assault.

18. See *DKG*, 49–61.

So how can we tell whether an apologist is using a correct or an incorrect point of contact? When someone argues "Causality, therefore God," is he appealing to the unbeliever's pretense of autonomous knowledge, or is he speaking to the unbeliever's repressed knowledge of the truth? It is not easy to tell, without knowing much more of that apologist's work. If he tells us, of course, then we know, assuming that he is trustworthy. If we know something of his views of epistemology, we can at least make a good guess. Can we tell by what he says to the unbeliever? Well, yes, if he tells the unbeliever what his point of contact is. But he might never do that.

Incidentally, is it necessary in an apologetic encounter to tell the unbeliever what our point of contact is? Certainly the point may be made if it comes up naturally, and I would not recommend intentional concealment; but I cannot think of any reason why it must be part of any apologetic encounter. We can surely appeal to the unbeliever's repressed knowledge even when we do not say that this is what we are doing.

In the absence of such explicit statement, it is hard to tell what an apologist is appealing to. Was C. S. Lewis appealing to and therefore compromising with unbelieving autonomy in the argument of his *Mere Christianity*? Or was he appealing to the unbeliever's repressed knowledge of God? Probably he was not doing either self-consciously, for he was not aware, so far as I know, of that particular issue.

Perhaps the major issue in evaluating an apologetic is simply whether it is true. If it is true, then whatever the apologist might think about the point-of-contact problem, his argument will nevertheless address the unbeliever in the right place. If what the apologist says is true, it will address the unbeliever's repressed knowledge of God, whether or not the apologist specifically intends to do that. And if the unbeliever seeks, as sometimes he will, to integrate that truth with his unbelieving worldview, he will find that it is not so easily domesticated. A truth, any truth, will introduce awkwardness, if not contradiction, into an unbelieving system. That will happen no matter what the apologist's views and intentions concerning the point of contact might be.

The apologist's intentions concerning the point of contact are therefore not particularly relevant to the external description or evaluation of his apologetics. Yet these intentions are relevant to its internal description and evaluation. For the question of the point of contact boils down to this: are we accepting and thus addressing the unbeliever's distorted worldview, or are we accepting and thus addressing the undistorted revelation that he holds within himself despite his distorted worldview?

Here again, Van Til has identified a spiritual issue that is not easily defined by methods or other externals. Van Til may have thought that using a positive or a "merely probable" argument was a sure sign that the apologist was not aiming at the right point of contact. But we cannot so easily assess others in this connection. What we can assess is ourselves—our motives, our loyalties. Are we so impressed by unbelieving "wisdom" that we seek to gain the approval of unbelieving intellectuals based on their own criteria? That danger, as we saw in chapter 1, has been very real in the history of apologetics. We can guard against it by reminding ourselves that our job is to rebuke unbelieving criteria, not affirm them. Our appeal is not to those criteria, but to that knowledge of God that the unbeliever has "deep down," as Van Til liked to say. The point-of-contact issue, therefore, is a spiritual one, one by which we examine our motives, not one by which we can quickly assess the intentions of our fellow apologists.

4

APOLOGETICS AS PROOF: TRANSCENDENTAL ARGUMENT

In this chapter, we will spend some time discussing the transcendental argument for the existence of God (hereafter TAG), a form of argumentation that has become something of the bread and butter of presuppositionalists. Cornelius Van Til understood the need to set forth the truth without compromise to require a specific kind of argumentation, which he called *presuppositional* and sometimes *transcendental*. Many of his followers have focused on the latter name.[1] We saw in chapter 1 the importance of reasoning on the basis of Christian presuppositions. But Van Til took his presuppositionalism one step further, arguing that such reasoning requires the use of a particular type of *argument* and the rejection of all others. We will discuss TAG in terms of its background, presenting the contours of the argument in broad outline, and by raising some questions.

Background[2]

The term *transcendental* became a major philosophical concept first in the writings of the highly influential thinker Immanuel Kant (1724–1804). Kant believed in a sort of God, but he was not an orthodox Christian; indeed, he advocated the autonomy of human thought—its independence from any allegedly authoritative revelation—in the strongest possible terms. Kant was dismayed by the skeptical implications of

1. In the preface, I indicated some dissatisfaction with the term *presuppositionalism*, and it would certainly be tempting to replace it with *transcendentalism* if the latter term were at all well understood. I don't believe it is, however, and we will see some confusing ambiguities in it later on.

2. Some material in the "Background" and "TAG in Outline" sections of this chapter appears in a similar form in my article "Transcendental Arguments," in W. C. Campbell-Jack and Gavin J. McGrath, eds., *New Dictionary of Christian Apologetics*, consulting ed. C. Stephen Evans (Downers Grove, IL: InterVarsity Press, 2006), 716–17. Used by permission of the publisher.

the philosophy of David Hume (an equally strong advocate of intellectual autonomy). In Hume's empiricism, all proof (except in mathematics and logic) is reducible to sense-experience. But Hume discovered that on that basis one could not prove any propositions concerning physical causes, moral values, God, human freedom, or the human self.[3] Kant was unwilling to accept Hume's pure empiricism (although he granted that we could not know anything beyond our experience), for he saw that it would destroy all human knowledge. But since he was also unable to accept the methods of his rationalist teacher Christian Wolff, Kant came to advocate transcendental argument as a new means of grounding the certainty of mathematics, science, and philosophy. That method does not try to prove that genuine knowledge is possible; rather, it presupposes that it is. If not, there is no point to any discussion or inquiry. Now, given that knowledge is possible, said Kant, we should ask what the conditions are that make knowledge possible. What must the world, the mind, and human thought be like if human knowledge is to be possible? The transcendental method then goes ahead to ask what the necessary conditions of human knowledge are.

Hegel and others in the idealist tradition followed Kant in this transcendental method, although they came to very different conclusions. Van Til studied under idealists at Princeton University in the 1920s and emerged advocating a kind of transcendental method that was distinctively Christian. Like Kant, Van Til was unhappy with empiricism and rationalism, and with traditional ways of combining reason and sense-experience such as that of Aquinas. Kant found these approaches to knowledge logically invalid. But for Van Til, they were also wrong in a distinctively theological way. Traditional methodologies applied to apologetics, said Van Til, assume that human sense-experience, human reason, or both can adequately function

---

3. David Hume stood in the philosophical school of British Empiricism, a tradition that taught that all knowledge is derived from sense-experience. If a claim to knowledge cannot—at least in principle—be tasted, touched, seen, heard, or smelled, it contributed nothing to the understanding. This radical view logically led to his notorious skepticism, the conclusions of which surprise people to this very day. For example, we do not perceive causation. We see one event followed by another. We do not, and cannot, perceive the *necessity* of the connection of those events. In philosophical terms, we "see" a *succession* of events—the green billiard ball moves after the red billiard ball strikes it—not *causation*. Likewise, there are no empirical grounds to believe that the future will be like the past. We have had no experience of "the future" as such. Finally, we do not perceive a continuing "self." Looking into a mirror cannot remedy the situation, since all we perceive is a body, not an enduring "self." This line of reasoning led to Hume's claim that beliefs in the existence of God, a continuing self through time, the principle of causation, and the uniformity of nature were based on "habits of the mind."

without God, that is, "autonomously" or "neutrally." So at the very outset of an apologetic argument, they concede the whole game. They adopt a presupposition contrary to the conclusion they wish to argue. They seek to gain knowledge of God by adopting a nontheistic epistemology. The only alternative, Van Til argued, is to adopt a theistic epistemology when arguing for the existence of God. Kant answered the question "What are the conditions required for an intelligible universe?" with his phenomena-noumena distinction and his transcendental aesthetic and analytic. Van Til answered that same question, but answered differently: the condition of universal intelligibility is the biblical God. But that approach seems to be viciously circular: presupposing God in our epistemology and then using that epistemology to prove his existence. Van Til answered the charge of circularity by claiming that the Christian circle is the only kind that renders reality intelligible on its own terms.

TAG in Outline

This principle was not only a fact, but an argument for the existence of God. Without God, there is no meaning (truth, rationality, etc.); therefore, God exists. To Van Til, this was the only legitimate proof of God's existence. He said that all legitimate theistic proof reduces to the "proof from the possibility of predication." God exists, in other words, because without him it would not be possible to reason, to think, or even to attach a predicate to a subject (*predication*). A proof with any lesser conclusion, Van Til argued, makes God something less than he is. We should not use arguments, he said, that prove that God is, for example, merely a first cause or an intelligent designer or a moral legislator.

Van Til noted that in Scripture God is the source of all reality, and hence all truth, all knowledge, all rationality, all meaning, all actuality, and all possibility. The Bible does make this kind of radical claim, that creation not only implies but presupposes God. For God is the Creator of all, and therefore the source of all meaning, order, and intelligibility. It is in Christ that all things hold together (Col. 1:17). So without him, everything falls apart; nothing makes sense. When we ascribe existence to anything in the world, we must ascribe existence to God. So we must regard God's existence as more sure, more certain, than the existence of anything else. Thus Scripture teaches that unbelief is foolish (Ps. 14:1; 1 Cor. 1:20). So if one asks with Kant what the conditions are that make knowledge possible, the answer must first of all be the existence of the God of Scripture.

Even when someone argues against Christian theism, Van Til said, he presupposes it, for he presupposes that rational argument is possible and that truth can be conveyed through language. The non-Christian, then, in Van Til's famous illustration, is like a child sitting on her father's lap, slapping his face. She would not be able to slap him unless he supported her. Similarly, the non-Christian cannot carry out his rebellion against God unless God makes that rebellion possible. Contradicting God assumes an intelligible universe and therefore a theistic one.

My own "nutshell" exposition of TAG would be something like this: God *must* exist if there is to be any meaning to the world. In a biblical worldview, God is the basis for all reality, and therefore for all rationality, truth, goodness, and beauty. Unless God exists, there is no reason to assume the possibility of meaningful communication. This claim can be further conjugated into specific arguments about (1) logic, (2) the uniformity of nature, and (3) moral standards. So unless God exists, there is no reason to assume the validity of logic, the uniformity of nature, the obligatoriness of moral standards. Of course, besides these, specific arguments can be developed from any data of experience: language, aesthetic experience, human psychology, and the like. Van Til maintained that Christian theism is the presupposition of all meaning, all rational significance, all intelligible discourse.

Here are some of TAG's more specific claims.

Logic Demands the Existence of God

God is logically necessary in the sense that without him, the use of logic would be impossible. He is the source of all order in the world and in the human mind, including logical order. So God acts and thinks in accordance with the laws of logic. This does not mean that he is "bound by" these laws, as though they were something "above" him that had authority over him. The laws of logic and rationality are simply the attributes of his own nature, and the logical structure of the world and the human mind is based on the fact that God's rationality, his wisdom, is reflected in the creation. As he is righteous, so he is logical. To be logical is his natural desire and pleasure. Nor does he create the laws of logic, as if they were something that he could change at will. Rather, they are necessary attributes, inalienable qualities, of all his thinking and acting.

So if logic itself is based on God's nature and existence, he is, in that sense, logically necessary. Without him, therefore, we could not even speak rationally. Human logical systems don't always reflect God's logic perfectly.

But insofar as they do, they are necessarily true. If logic cannot exist without God, then to deny that God exists while affirming the law of noncontradiction is like denying the existence of the sun while affirming the existence of its rays. Of course, an unbeliever might deny this view that logic cannot exist without God, but since that is the very point in dispute, it would beg that question.

My point here is not merely that if God doesn't exist, for example, the law of noncontradiction will fail. Rather: *it does not even make any sense to talk about a world in which God doesn't exist.* If God does not exist, we cannot argue either the presence or absence of logic in the world. I grant, of course, that on such a supposition it is more natural to believe that logic is absent. But transcendental theism is even more radical than that. For if God is our transcendental presupposition, then without him arguments both for and against the existence of logic are meaningless. This is not to say that God's existence can be proved by logical axioms alone, or that "God doesn't exist" can be shown to be contradictory (though I think it is contradictory in a sense). The point, rather, is that God's existence is necessary to the very existence of logic, for God is the very source of logical truth. So there is no logically possible world in which God does not exist.[4]

Ethics Demands the Existence of God

As Ivan puts it in Dostoyevsky's *Brothers Karamazov,* if God does not exist, "everything is permitted." This is one way of saying that notions of good and evil lose their force when people cease to acknowledge God. Our current cultural climate has especially confirmed the rightness of Dostoyevsky's claim: we've grown noticeably more secular over the past thirty years, banning God from public education and the marketplace of ideas, and our culture's moral tone has declined. Is this merely historical coincidence, or is there a profound relationship between ethics and belief in God? TAG argues that this relationship is far stronger than a passing correlation between ethical behavior and theistic belief. Ethical behavior and standards do not merely demand the belief in God, but presuppose his existence.

All non-Christian ethical systems of thought are fraught with problems that disqualify them from consideration as *the* code of ethical conduct.

---

4. Notice here how epistemological considerations can lead to metaphysical conclusions. For human knowledge to be possible, certain metaphysical conditions (including the existence of God) must be satisfied. We have the option, of course, of denying that human knowledge is possible. But such radical skepticism cannot be advanced as a rational view. On any rational view of the matter, therefore, God exists, and exists necessarily. For further elaboration on this point, see James N. Anderson and Greg Welty, "The Lord of Non-Contradiction: An Argument for God from Logic," *Philosophia Christi* 13, 2 (2011).

For example, secular theories cannot show why moral standards *obligate*. Philosophers have attempted to show this by basing moral obligation on abstract ideas (Plato), logical deduction (Kant), the idea of utility (Bentham, Mill), intuition (Moore), feeling (Hume). All these philosophers have adequately refuted one another. Moral standards can be obligatory only if their source is a *person* who *deserves* absolute obedience and reveals his will to human beings. But that leaves us with the responsibility of presenting a positive case for Christianity. As the claim is made according to the traditional moral argument, a supreme moral law demands a supreme moral legislator. This claim is certainly true. But more can be said than just that. See my discussion in chapter 5 for more details. What we can say now is this: The question of morality is like that of logic. Morality is first based in God's nature, not on his arbitrary fiat, nor on some principle independent of him. God could not will that cruelty is good, for cruelty is not good; it is incompatible with God's own nature.

When I say that ethics demands, and indeed *requires*, God, I do not mean that atheists and agnostics never recognize moral standards. Even the Bible recognizes that they do (Rom. 1:32). Indeed, some say that they believe in absolute principles, though that, of course, is rare. I contend, rather, that an atheist or agnostic is not able to give an adequate *reason* for believing in absolute moral principles.[5] And when people accept moral principles without good reason, they hold to them somewhat more loosely than others who accept them on a rational basis. Nor do I wish to suggest that people who believe in God are morally perfect. Scripture tells us that this isn't so (1 John 1:8–10). The demons are monotheists (James 2:19), but belief in the one God doesn't improve their morals. Something more is needed to become good, and that, according to the Bible, is a new heart, given by God's grace in Jesus Christ (2 Cor. 5:17; Eph. 2:8–10).

Science Demands the Existence of God

God has ordained a basic uniformity to nature. These regularities in the natural world are what scientists seek to describe with formulas and theories. The so-called scientific method assumes the general regularity and repeatability of an experimental procedure to validate a given hypothesis. Unless we assume predictability and regularity in nature, it is impossible for

5. The point at issue in a transcendental presentation of the moral argument is not one of individual ethical principles (do not lie, steal, murder, etc.), but one of metaethical justification. (Why, and on what basis, should we agree that lying, theft, and murder are morally condemnable?)

experimental science to conduct its work. Theologically, these regularities in the natural world are expressions of God's covenant with Noah to keep the seasons regular "while the earth remains" (Gen. 8:22). Without God, there is no basis for assuming any uniformity. And without this uniformity, we could have no assurance that antitoxins used today will not poison us tomorrow.

Many believe that "natural laws" in this sense are absolute, operating without exception. Yet Scripture gives us no assurance that these laws *always* hold. But science does not presuppose any absolute uniformity of nature; indeed, modern science allows for areas of randomness in the universe. There are exceptions to this uniformity, because God is after all a person and, like human persons, works according to his personal intentions, not according to rigid patterns. God is free to work either through or outside of these natural laws. These unusual occurrences we normally call *miracles*. Miracles are not necessarily violations of or exceptions to natural law; sometimes they even have natural explanations. (See, e.g., Exodus 14:21, where God dried up a portion of the Red Sea by sending "a strong east wind.")[6] There is no scientific consensus that scientific explanations must never presuppose God. Of course, divine providence is not in itself a scientific explanation.[7] But there is no scientific rule to the effect that proper scientific explanations may not in turn presuppose divine providence.

Does this admission undermine science? Such irregularities mean that scientists must be humble enough to claim something less than absolute universality for their formulations of natural laws. But I think that should not be too high a price for them to pay, since the alternative is no basis for science at all.[8]

Questions

I agree with Van Til that theistic argument should have a transcendental goal. To summarize Van Til's TAG:

1. Presuppose a biblical epistemology in all your reasoning.[9]

6. For a thorough discussion of natural law and miracle, see *DG*, chap. 13. For more on miracles in the present volume, see chapter 6.

7. This is an important point: Providence is not a scientific explanation; it is the necessary precondition for scientific explanation itself.

8. See the fine discussion in Vern S. Poythress, *Redeeming Science* (Wheaton, IL: Crossway, 2006), 13–31, 179–80.

9. Refer back to chapter 1.

2. Argue that God is the presupposition of all meaning and intelligibility, so that you must presuppose him in order to prove him. [Respond, then, to the charge of circularity, as I have.]

3. Show that any system that rejects the biblical God loses intelligibility because it is caught up in the dialectic of rationalism and irrationalism.[10]

Now, you notice that Van Til's formulation of TAG states a set of conclusions to be reached, but not an argumentative strategy for reaching those conclusions.[11] Although Van Til calls it an "argument," it really is a conclusion rather than an argument.[12] Certainly our purpose is to prove nothing less than the full biblical teaching about God—that he is absolute personality, transcendent and immanent, sovereign, Trinitarian. And indeed, part of that teaching is that God is the source of all meaning. Certainly we must not argue in a way that misleads the inquirer to think that God is anything less than this. But I have some questions.

1. First, I question whether TAG can function without the help of subsidiary arguments of a more traditional kind.[13] Although I agree with Van Til's premise that without God there is no meaning, I must grant that not everyone would immediately agree with that premise. How, then, is that premise to be proved? If I say, "The existence of physical laws presupposes a personal God," that statement cannot be the end of the argument. The unbeliever has the right to ask, "Why do you think that?" So Bahnsen himself, in the Stein debate, compares a theistic view of physical law (and logic, and morality) with as many non-Christian theories as he has time for, and argues that the Christian view is cogent and the others are not. But that is simply a traditional apologetic argument from causality, similar to Aquinas's first two "ways": physical law exists, therefore God exists. Is it that the meaning-laden character of creation requires a sort of designer? But that is the traditional teleological argument. Is it that the meaning-structure of reality requires an efficient cause? That is the traditional cosmological argument. Is it that meaning entails values, which in turn entail a valuer?

10. See chapter 9 for more on this.
11. Or, as I've said in *CVT*, 315, he has presented (1) a conclusion, (2) a logical model, and (3) a practical strategy.
12. I've tried to supplement it by adding actual premises and arguments for reaching that conclusion. That is what my "moral argument" in chapter 5 is all about. Some followers of Van Til think that any resort to such arguments in effect denies Van Til's transcendental method. I disagree.
13. Among presuppositionalists, this has been an important topic of discussion. This second edition greatly expands my view.

That is a traditional values argument. It seems to me that if Aquinas argued correctly in showing that God is the first cause of everything, then God is the transcendental condition of everything: of meaning, coherent thought, and predication, as well as motion, causality, and contingency. On that understanding, Aquinas's argument, like Van Til's, is transcendental and presuppositional. If that is true, then Van Til's argument might not be as original as he thought it was. I certainly reject Aquinas's view of autonomous natural knowledge. But his cosmological argument is legitimate as part of a legitimate TAG.[14]

Some presuppositionalists have defended the uniqueness of Van Til's argument by pointing out that for Van Til it is not enough to say with Aquinas that causality proves God. For Van Til, it is important that even the *denial* of causality proves God. For if God is the transcendental ground of intelligibility, causality cannot be meaningfully affirmed *or denied* unless God exists. So Van Til argued that even atheism presupposes theism; even the denial of God presupposes God.[15] This double argument, that either the affirmation or the denial of something presupposes God, fits in well with some definitions of presupposition in modern analytic philosophy. For P. F. Strawson, Bas van Fraassen, and others, to say that A *presupposes* B is to say not only that A implies B, but also that not-A implies B. Van Til would modify Aquinas's argument to say not only that causality implies God, but also that the *denial* of causality implies God. To construct an argument with that double premise is to argue by presupposition, to argue transcendentally.

In my ongoing discussion with Don Collett[16] on this issue, for example, I have been willing to use this definition of presupposition in describing Van Til's position, rather than describing his argument as a mere implication,

14. Practically, the difference is that the traditional apologetic has not always been aware of its own transcendental thrust. And it has sometimes argued as though God were simply another fact to be proved rather than the hinge on which all rationality hangs. And therefore, traditional apologetics has been insufficiently aware (I purposely use the language of degree) of the antithesis between Christian and non-Christian views of knowledge.

15. One problem here is that to say that atheism presupposes theism supposes that atheism can be stated coherently. But if atheism presupposes theism, then it bears in itself a contradiction that destroys its coherence. If it is incoherent, it is unclear how it can be said to presuppose anything. What Van Til would probably say is that atheism, stated as a philosophical position, does have some coherence—by borrowed capital from theism—or that its coherence can at least be assumed "for the sake of argument." So in what follows I will mostly assume that and ignore this particular problem. But at a later point of this discussion, I will need to look at a related issue.

16. "Reply to Don Collett on Transcendental Argument," *Westminster Theological Journal* 65, 2 (2003): 307–9, available at http://www.frame-poythress.org/frame_articles/2003ReplytoCollett.htm.

a *modus ponens*. But I still wonder if Collett isn't exaggerating the difference between presupposition (Strawson's sense) and implication. Isn't it more like this, that Strawson's presupposition embraces two implications?[17] A presupposes B = if A, then B, and if not-A, then B. "If A, then B" is one traditional implication. "If not-A, then B" is another. So why shouldn't we look at "A presupposes B" as a shorthand for talking about two traditional implications at the same time?

Collett would say that I have missed the point here. What is unique about presuppositional arguments in the Strawson/van Fraassen mode is that you can do this:

- If A, then B. (Meaning that B is the presupposition of A.)
- Not-A.
- Therefore B.[18]

Although this is "analogous" to traditional *modus ponens* and *modus tollens* arguments, it is not one of those traditional forms. In fact, most observers who are not in on the discussion of presuppositions would dismiss this argument as a formal fallacy.

I'm willing to grant that the argument above is valid, given the Strawson/Van Til understanding of presupposition. But we need to get back to basics here. A good deductive argument, in apologetics, needs to have three qualities. It needs to be *valid* (i.e., it follows the laws of logic), *sound* (its premises are true and therefore its conclusion is true), and *persuasive* (it is effective in bringing people to believe the conclusion).[19] Many arguments are valid and sound, but not persuasive, such as this one:

- God's Word never errs.
- The Bible is God's Word.
- Therefore, the Bible never errs.

17. This is a difficulty with Collett's thesis. It appears that for Collett, "A presupposes B" is equivalent to "A → B" as well as "not-A → B". But if this is the case, TAG can be expressed as two "ordinary" *modus ponens* arguments: one from the first half of the conjunct and one from the second half. Thanks to James Anderson for this insight.

18. Of course, you can also do this: "If A, then B. A. Therefore B." This looks like a traditional *modus ponens*, and is not controversial. What is unique about presuppositional arguments conceived in this way is that "If A, then B" and "not-A" will together imply B, and that both this and the former argument are valid.

19. Alert readers will note my three perspectives here: validity is normative (following laws); soundness is situational (stating true facts about the world); and persuasiveness is existential (appealing to the hearts and minds of its audience).

This argument is certainly valid, and most evangelical Christians will regard it as sound, as I do. But skeptics will typically not find it persuasive. They will have many questions about and objections to the premises, and until those are dealt with, they will not consider adopting the conclusion. The same may be said about the Collett version of TAG. Take this argument about causality:

- If causality exists, God exists (in the sense that God is the presupposition or transcendental ground of causality).
- There is no causality.
- Therefore, God exists.

Given Collett's analysis, this is a valid argument. The truth of the premises we may assume here for the sake of argument, and on that assumption the argument is sound. But it would not be persuasive to anyone inclined to skepticism. Most would reply, I think, that the first premise needs to be argued.[20] *Why* should anyone grant that the God of the Bible is the presupposition of causality?

So the Collett argument needs many subarguments if it is to be persuasive. And I think those subarguments will use traditional argument forms, mainly *modus ponens* and *modus tollens*. How can we prove that God is the transcendental ground of causality? Not by repeating the Collett TAG again and again, for that is what is problematic. We need to establish the first premise. How do we do that? By showing that it is meaningless to speak of causality unless God exists. How do we do that? Perhaps by showing (with traditional apologists) that an infinite series of causes is unintelligible, and that to deny that infinite series is to affirm God. Or maybe there are other ways. But in any case, we are trying to prove TAG's first premise by using traditional arguments—which was my point all along.

The next step, after we have proved that God is the transcendental ground of causality (or anything else), will be an argument like this:

- If God is the transcendental ground of X, he exists.
- God is the transcendental ground of X.
- Therefore, God exists.

That, like the supporting arguments for the second premise, is a traditional argument, in this case a *modus ponens*. So in these two ways—(1) the

---

20. The second one, too, of course. But we assumed that only for the sake of argument.

supporting arguments for God's being the transcendental ground, and (2) the argument from God's being the transcendental ground to God's existing—traditional arguments are legitimate and indeed necessary.

To look at this from another perspective: Van Til's TAG seems to me to say this:

- If anything is intelligible (coherent, meaningful), God exists.
- Something (causality, motion, banana peels, Augustine) is intelligible (coherent, meaningful).
- Therefore, God exists.

But this is a traditional *modus ponens*. To put it into Collett's mode, you would have to be able to say:

- If anything is intelligible, God exists.
- Nothing is intelligible.
- Therefore, God exists.

But then God is not merely the transcendental ground of intelligibility; he is the transcendental ground of intelligibility and nonintelligibility, meaningfulness and meaninglessness. This dissolves, for me, the original meaning and attractiveness of TAG. Again, I want to retreat into common sense. Do we really want to say that even a meaningless, unintelligible world would presuppose God? What would *presuppose* even *mean* in a meaningless world? Indeed, if "nothing is intelligible" (the second premise above), then not even God is intelligible, not even to himself. And then what kind of God would he be? I must reluctantly conclude that at this point the transcendentalizing of apologetics implodes into nonsense.[21]

2. Second, I do not agree that the traditional arguments necessarily conclude with something less than the biblical God. Take the teleological argument, that the purposefulness of the natural world implies a designer. Well, certainly the God of Scripture is more than a mere designer. But the argument doesn't say that he is merely a designer, only that he is a designer, which he certainly is. Similar things can be said about the other traditional theistic proofs. It would be wrong to think of God merely as a first cause, but the cosmological argument does not entail such a conclusion.

---

21. Have I just formulated a *reductio*?

3. It should also be remembered that the traditional arguments often persuade. They work because (whether the apologist recognizes this or not) they presuppose a Christian worldview. For example, the causal argument assumes that everything in creation has a cause. That premise is true according to a Christian worldview, but it is not true (at least in the traditional sense) in a worldview such as that of Hume or Kant. So understood, the proof is part of an overall Christian understanding of things, and there can be no legitimate objection to it. Once one defines *cause* as Hume or Kant does, however, the argument goes nowhere. Now, many people can be led to accept the existence of God through the traditional argument because they agree to a Christian concept of cause. This is part of God's revelation that they have not repressed—what Van Til calls "borrowed capital." But once they become more sophisticated and philosophical (i.e., more self-conscious about suppressing the truth), they are likely to raise objections to such proofs on the basis of a more consistently non-Christian frame of reference. At that point, the apologist must be more explicit about differences of presupposition, differences of worldview, differences in concepts such as causality. Then the argument becomes more explicitly transcendental. But not every inquirer requires this, and for many it actually hinders communication. So one must recognize the "person-variability" of apologetics and deal with each inquirer according to his or her lights. For some (usually unsophisticated) inquirers, one or more of the traditional arguments might be sufficient.

4. Van Til's slogan "Christian theism is a unit" should be understood with such qualifications. I agree that the slogan is true in the sense that one cannot compromise one doctrine without compromising others, and in the sense that accepting one doctrine provides a logical motivation for accepting others. But I do not think that the whole of Christian theism can be established by a single argument, unless that argument is highly complex! I do not think an argument should be criticized because it fails to prove every element of Christian theism. Such an argument might be part of a system of apologetics that as a whole establishes the entire organism of Christian truth.

5. If we grant Van Til's point that a complete theistic argument should prove the whole biblical doctrine of God, then we must prove more than that God is the author of meaning and rationality. Ironically, at this point, Van Til is not sufficiently holistic! For besides proving that God is the author of meaning, we must (or may in some cases) prove that God is personal, sovereign, transcendent, immanent, and Trinitarian, not to mention infinite,

eternal, wise, just, loving, omnipotent, omnipresent, and so forth.[22] Thus, for another reason (in addition to the fact, already discussed, that it cannot function without the help of subsidiary arguments of a more traditional kind), TAG requires supplementation by other arguments.

6. All this suggests a further reason why no single argument will prove the entire biblical doctrine of God. To generalize: any argument can be questioned by someone who is not disposed to accept the conclusion. Such questions might require further arguments to defend the original arguments, and so forth. Since no single argument is guaranteed to persuade every rational person, no argument is immune to such additional questioning.

Therefore, Van Til's TAG (like every other argument) is not sufficient, by itself, to prove the existence of the biblical God to everyone's satisfaction. Nor do transcendental considerations exclude arguments that are intended to prove only part of the biblical doctrine of God.

Nevertheless, much that Van Til says about these matters is biblically true and important. There is probably not a distinctively "transcendental argument" that rules out all other kinds of arguments. But certainly the overall goal of apologetics is transcendental. That is, the God we seek to prove is indeed the source of all meaning, the source of possibility, of actuality, and of predication. The biblical God is more than this, but certainly not less. And we should certainly not say anything to an inquirer to suggest that we can reason, predicate, assess probabilities, and so on, apart from God.

TAG and the Trinity

Some have claimed that the presuppositional approach is merely theistic, as opposed to distinctly Christian.[23] So, as the argument goes, a Muslim could just as easily employ Van Til's TAG as could a Christian. Steve Hays

---

22. One may, of course, maintain that *author of meaning* includes all these other attributes. But this fact is not immediately obvious. An inquirer might well ask for additional argument to show this relationship, just as he (despite his innate knowledge of God) asked for initial proof of God's existence.

23. This original objection to Van Til's apologetic was made by John Warwick Montgomery in his article "Once upon an A Priori," in *Jerusalem and Athens: Critical Discussions on the Philosophy and Apologetics of Cornelius Van Til*, ed. E. R. Geehan (Nutley, NJ: Presbyterian and Reformed, 1971), 380–92. A more recent presentation was put forth by John Johnson, "Is Cornelius Van Til's Apologetic Method Christian or Merely Theistic?," *Evangelical Quarterly* 75, 3 (2003): 257–68.

and I have responded to this claim in detail elsewhere,[24] but some clarifying points need to be made here.

In the next chapter, I will introduce readers to the epistemological argument for God's existence. There I will argue that the epistemological argument reduces to the ethical, and the ethical argument shows that there must be an absolute person. *Person* here includes *interpersonal* attributes, such as love. So the God presupposed by ethics, epistemology, and logic must be multipersonal. (And of course, there is the argument we laid out in chapter 2 that God must be one and many if he is to account for the one-and-many nature of the world.) So my argument shows that God is multipersonal. If one asks why this God must be precisely three persons, I have no apologetic argument to that effect. But Reformed theology (like other traditional theologies) has always said that the doctrine of the Trinity comes from special revelation, not natural. So the doctrine of the Trinity as such might not be the subject of apologetics. Perhaps the most that apologetics can do is to establish the existence of a God who is one and many.

Can we get more specific? How would a Christian defend his faith against a rival theism such as Islam? To briefly summarize my approach to Islam: (1) Muslims and Christians agree that the Bible is divinely inspired, but Muslims argue that the Bible has been mistranslated and distorted, and that God has corrected those distortions in the Qur'an. (2) But there is no historical basis for the claim that the Bible has been distorted in this way. (3) Therefore, differences between the Bible and the Qur'an must be resolved in the Bible's favor. (4) Insofar as Islam compromises the biblical doctrine of God, it loses the only possible transcendental ground of science, logic, and ethics. So TAG does not appeal to bare theism. It presupposes the distinctives of the Christian doctrine of God. The logical structure of Christianity is not formally parallel to unbelief in the way that Shadokism is formally parallel to Gibiism in Montgomery's parable.[25] Islam, or any other non-Christian system, does not believe in a Trinitarian, sovereign, Creator God who redeemed his people from sin through the work of his Son and revealed his will in a holy book. Judaism and Islam do have some formal parallels, since these movements have been influenced, as I've argued earlier, by the Bible. And of course, there is the formal parallel that both Christians and non-Christians do have presuppositions. But no non-Christian system contains all the content of the Christian message. And if one of them did,

24. See John M. Frame and Steve Hays, "Johnson on Van Til: A Rejoinder" (2005), available at http://www.vantil.info/articles/johnson_on_vt.html.

25. Montgomery, "Once upon an A Priori," 384–85.

what would we say about it? Only that it was Christianity, expressed in a different language.

Must we bring up TAG explicitly in every apologetic encounter? I would say no.[26] To be sure, part of the lordship of Christ is his lordship over our intellectual life. Surely evangelistic apologetics is never complete without a presentation of Christ as Lord and as Lord of all. From here, we may well go on to stress his lordship over certain specific areas of life. Jesus told the rich young ruler to sell all his goods and follow Jesus (Matt. 19:16–30), in effect declaring his lordship over our wealth and economic life. He displayed his omniscience by telling the Samaritan woman of her multiple marriages and immorality (John 4:7–18), and then described a coming change in the very worship of God (vv. 19–26), thus declaring himself Lord over our marital and sexual lives and even over our relationship with God. To the Pharisees, he declared himself Lord of the Sabbath (Mark 2:28). But he didn't specifically describe all the areas of his lordship to every inquirer; he restricted himself to mentioning those areas that were of particular temptation to each individual.[27] Now, we should not hesitate to declare the intellectual lordship of Christ (in the manner, e.g., of 1 Corinthians 1:18–2:16) to would-be intellectuals, or others who are particularly afflicted with the desire, the prideful ambition, to think autonomously. But the majority of inquirers would probably not need to hear this point specifically. "Christ is Lord" covers this field—and many more—implicitly. If someone has a particular problem recognizing Christ's intellectual lordship, then we should make an issue of it; otherwise, not.

Still, modern "apostles to intellectuals" will find many occasions to stress the transcendental direction of apologetics. Autonomy has been routinely assumed in secular thought since the days of Greek philosophy (and its Eastern counterparts).[28] Intellectuals are often proud of their autonomy (sometimes called *neutrality, unbiased objectivity*, etc.), and that pride must

26. See point 3 above.

27. TAGs can be developed from the concepts of causality, design and purpose, morality, beauty, and human dignity, depending on the concerns and interests of the person with whom we are speaking. Recall the concept of person-variability in *DKG*, 151–52.

28. Greek philosophy was itself in part a reaction against the traditional religions, an attempt to gain knowledge entirely apart from religious revelation. Descartes' "fresh start" inaugurating modern philosophy was another housecleaning, seeking to rid philosophy of any dependence on religious tradition and building up the body of human knowledge afresh from man's own "clear and distinct ideas." The empiricists and Kant pushed the principle of autonomy to even further extremes, and so has the development of secular thinking in all fields since their day. Existentialism and poststructural thought insist in the strongest terms that meaning is a human creation.

be abased. An intellectual will often agree to submit to Christ as Lord in every area except that of the mind. *Sacrificium intellectus*, "sacrifice of the intellect," is a dreaded concept among modern thinkers. "Oh, yes, Jesus is Lord; but we must believe in evolution, because all the best scholars do." "Jesus is Lord, but all the best Bible scholars deny biblical authority and inerrancy." In reply, it is important for us to tell inquirers that Jesus demands all, not some, of our loyalty (Deut. 6:4ff.; Mark 8:34–38). And that includes loving him with the mind—which may well entail holding some unpopular views on scholarly matters (1 Tim. 6:20).

Negative and Positive Arguments

Van Til does not just stress the use of transcendental or presuppositional arguments. He also insists that if arguments are to be authentically presuppositional, they must be "negative" rather than "positive." A negative or "indirect" argument is sometimes called a *reductio ad absurdum*. An indirect proof or *reductio* in mathematics is a proof in which one assumes a proposition ("for the sake of argument," as Van Til puts it) in order to refute it. One tentatively adopts, say, proposition A and then deduces from it a logical contradiction or some proposition that is obviously false. That shows that A is false. (One must be careful here: the contradiction or falsity in the conclusion might be due not to the falsity of A, but to some logical fallacy or additional premise used in the course of the argument.)

In theistic argument, the indirect argument would run like this: "God doesn't exist; therefore, causality (or whatever—ultimately everything) is meaningless." Since we are unwilling to accept the conclusion, we must negate the premise and say that God does exist. Certainly arguments of this form are often useful.[29] But I have a question about them:

Are indirect arguments really distinct from direct arguments? In the final analysis, it doesn't make much difference whether you say "Causality, therefore God" or "Without God, no causality, therefore God." Any indirect argument of this sort can be turned into a direct argument by some creative rephrasing. The indirect form, of course, has some rhetorical advantages, at

---

29. Greg Bahnsen utterly bewildered atheist spokesman Gordon Stein in a debate some years ago with TAG, developed along these lines. Stein was ready to answer the traditional proofs, but not this one! This debate has taken on something of a legendary status in Van Tillian circles. A complete transcript of the debate can be found at http://www.bellevuechristian.org/faculty /dribera/htdocs/PDFs/Apol_Bahnsen_Stein_Debate_Transcript.pdf. For more of Bahnsen's debates, visit www.cmfnow.com.

least.[30] But if the indirect form is sound, the direct form will be, too—and vice versa. Indeed, if I say, "Without God, no causality," the argument is incomplete unless I add the positive formulation "But there is causality, therefore God exists," a formulation identical to the direct argument. Thus, the indirect argument becomes nothing more than a prolegomenon to the direct.[31]

In *Defense of the Faith*, Van Til says:

> The method of reasoning by presupposition may be said to be indirect rather than direct. The issue between believers and nonbelievers in Christian theism cannot be settled by a direct appeal to "facts" or "laws" whose nature and significance is already agreed upon by both parties to the debate. The question is rather as to what is the final reference point required to make the "facts" and "laws" intelligible. The question is as to what the "facts" and "laws" really are. Are they what the non-Christian methodology assumes that they are? Are they what the Christian-theistic methodology presupposes they are?[32]

We should not overlook Van Til's modifying statements. Van Til does not appear here to be against appeal to fact per se, only to facts or laws "whose nature and significance is already agreed upon by both parties to the debate." When a Christian makes an appeal to facts or laws, he must present them as they "really are." Could this imply that Van Til thought it was possible to present a direct proof that does not assume autonomy, neutrality, or brute fact? I am not completely sure that Van Til was always consistent on this point.

Therefore, I think Van Til's restriction of the apologist to the exclusive use of negative arguments is unreasonable. I am plagued by an analogy (albeit a weak analogy) of a child who sticks her hand into a bag of marbles, pulls one out, and then demonstrates the supremacy of her marble by criticizing the other marbles in the bag. Surely she must offer positive argumentation for the marble in her hand.[33] Even if one grants that the various manifes-

---

30. See the previous footnote. The indirect form tends to take overconfident unbelievers by surprise.

31. As for Van Til's objection that a direct argument assumes that we understand something (e.g., causality) apart from God, see my reply in the section "*Sola Scriptura*" in chapter 1. But even if we grant this objection, it would bear equally against the negative argument.

32. Van Til, *Defense of the Faith*, 122.

33. Yet one point needs to be conceded to this "negative" approach: An *exhaustive* negative argument (i.e., a negative argument against every alternative to Christian theism) is equivalent to a positive argument for Christian theism. Once all rivals are removed from the table, Christian-

tations of non-Christian thought known to man cannot account for the intelligibility of experience, one may still ask whether Christian thought can and, if so, how it can. For all we know, there is a third alternative.

Of course, opponents try to show that there is no third alternative. Either the God of the Bible exists or he doesn't. Either the Bible is true or it isn't. Presuppose the unbelieving alternative, and you *must* embrace rationalism and irrationalism. Since both destroy meaning, biblical theism must be correct. I am moved by this line of argument. But I still think it is more complicated than they imagine to show this in every case. And when you get down to specifics, the alternatives become more diverse.[34]

In other words, it's not simply a matter of claiming that the Christian worldview can account for laws of logic, science, morality, and so forth. If that were the case, the atheist would have every right to make the claim that the atheistic worldview can account for laws of logic and so on. That is to say, the Christian would be merely begging the question. I'm under the impression that positive argumentation is inescapable. I also reject the tendency among some Van Tillians to equate negative arguments with transcendental arguments. Positive arguments can be just as transcendental in their thrust as negative ones, and negative arguments are just as likely as positive ones to express a spirit of autonomy.[35]

Van Til had a wonderful eye for spiritual problems in apologetic encounters. He saw the need to rebuke intellectual pride, to reject the spirit of autonomy, to hold fast to the universal lordship of Christ over all structures of meaning. But Van Til tended to think that these problems were best handled by restricting apologetics to certain formulated methods. Unfortunately, the suggested methods, even apart from their other difficulties, do not necessarily eliminate the spiritual problem: the sinful attitude of the would-be intellectual. Sinful attitudes can be present no matter what kind of argument we employ. We must indeed be diligent to rebuke these sins. Jesus' lordship must be clearly set forth in word and in deed. But that

---

ity is the last one standing. But this concession does not invalidate my overall point. In fact, it proves my larger point that we do not need to choose between negative and positive arguments.

34. This is not to say that apologists cannot group worldviews into larger classes (monist, pantheist, atheist, deist, theist, etc.) and refute those groups as classes. I do this very thing in *DCL*, where I group world religions into (surprise!) three categories: (1) religions based on fate, (2) religions of self-realization or self-transcendence, and (3) religions of law without gospel. See *DCL*, chap. 5. For a helpful survey of world religions, see Derek Cooper, *Christianity and World Religions: An Introduction to the World's Major Faiths* (Phillipsburg, NJ: P&R Publishing, 2013).

35. Remember that someone can be relatively orthodox intellectually and still be rebellious against God.

spiritual result is not guaranteed by a transcendental (actually epistemologi-cal) emphasis or a negative argument. To trust such frail reeds is to court disaster. Nothing less than the whole armor of God (Eph. 6:10–18) will allow us to gain victory over Satan's intellectual devices.

Absolute Certainty and Probability

What now becomes of Van Til's claim that there is an "absolutely cer-tain argument" for Christian theism? He seems to think that transcendental arguments, which are negative arguments, are absolutely certain. But I have, I think, cast some doubt on the clarity of these concepts and the legitimacy of Van Til's attempt to limit apologetics to these types of arguments.

Certainty is a somewhat problematic concept. I have discussed it in *DKG* in terms of believing psychology and the assurance of salvation.[36] We should begin with the biblical conviction that God wants us to be certain of the truth of Christ (Luke 1:4) and of our own salvation (1 John 5:13). Regenerate knowledge of God is a knowledge that, as we have seen, presup-poses God's Word. A presupposition is held with certainty by definition, since it is the very criterion of certainty. Besides this logical fact, the believer is assured by the supernatural factor of God's Spirit concerning both the truth of the gospel (1 Cor. 2:4–5; 1 Thess. 1:5) and his own relationship to Christ (Rom. 8:16). It is true that believers do sometimes doubt both the truth of God and their own salvation, but they have the resources and the right, both logical and supernatural, to come to full assurance on at least the major points of the gospel message.[37]

This is the certainty that we seek to communicate in apologetics, as in preaching and witnessing.[38] It is the certainty of a person concerning the revelation of God.

But the word *certain* has been attached not only to persons, but also to evidence. "Certain" evidence is evidence warranting certainty of belief. "Probable" evidence warrants a level or degree of belief less than certainty, but possibly of great importance. Scripture speaks of the certainty of the evidence that God has given us for his truth. General revelation is so

---

36. *DKG*, 134–36.

37. See the cited section in *DKG* for complications. For example: few Christians have full assurance as to the meaning of "baptized on behalf of the dead" in 1 Corinthians 15:29. Since we are unsure of its meaning, we cannot "presuppose" it in the fullest sense (although we can presuppose that Scripture's statement is true), and for some reason God's Spirit has determined not to give the church assurance concerning any interpretation of this passage.

38. Recall my earlier point that these differ only in emphasis or perspective.

plain and clear that it obligates belief and obedience—leaving us without excuse (Rom. 1:19–20). John speaks of Jesus' miracles ("signs") as warranting belief (John 20:30f.), and Luke speaks of the "convincing proofs" (Acts 1:3 NIV) that Jesus presented to the disciples after the resurrection. The evidence for Christian theism, therefore, is "absolutely certain." Or, to put it in moral terms, there is no excuse for disbelief. The evidence obligates belief.

We have seen that certainty can apply both to human beings and to evidence. But Van Til also applies it to argument. What might be meant by "absolutely certain argument"? We are inclined, perhaps, to assimilate the phrase to one of the other two uses: a certain argument is one that either conveys certain evidence (objective certainty) or necessarily creates certainty in the persons who hear it (subjective certainty). As to the second sense: we saw earlier that no single argument is guaranteed to create certainty in all its hearers. And if we modify our concept to say that the argument "ought" to bring certainty, we must remember that people have an obligation to believe in God—indeed, at some level they do believe in him—from the evidence alone, apart from any argumentative formulation of the evidence. So no argument *creates* an obligation to believe.[39] In the subjective sense, then, there are no certain arguments.

What of the objective sense? We may think of arguments conveying evidence in the way we think of preaching conveying God's Word. As we saw in chapter 1, apologetics is a form of preaching, and of course we may also equate "evidence" with "God's Word," since the evidence is nothing less than God's ("certain") self-revelation. Now, the Second Helvetic Confession says that "the preaching of the Word of God is the Word of God." This is a dangerous equation if it leads preachers to presume their own infallibility. But of course, the sentence was not so intended. Rather, the point is that when a preacher sets forth the Word of God truly, that Word does not lose its authority from being placed on a preacher's lips. The content of Scripture is always authoritative, whether written on pages, chiseled in stone, recorded on magnetic tape or computer disk, exemplified in a life (2 Cor. 3:2–3), or spoken through a preacher's mouth. The same can be said of the apologist as he presents evidence through his arguments. Insofar as his argument communicates truly the evidence that God has revealed in nature and Scripture, it

---

39. Of course, an argument could *intensify* that obligation somehow. Granted, there is more to be said on this point.

may be said to convey the certainty of that evidence. But insofar as the argument obscures, misconstrues, or distorts the evidence, insofar as it fails (whether because of sin or because of some mere inadequacy) to present that evidence as it is, it lacks authority and therefore may not boast absolute certainty.

An argument, therefore, is absolutely certain in the objective sense insofar as it is a clear communication of God's revelation. Now, Van Til tended to describe as "absolutely certain" those arguments (and only those) that were presuppositional or transcendental in thrust and negative in form. In view of our earlier discussion of TAG and negative form, I would resist that restriction of the concept. Absolute certainty pertains to all those arguments that convey the truth, whether positive or negative, whether focused on predication or on some other datum.

At one time I was inclined to argue differently for Van Til's "absolute certainty," namely, by appealing to the very circularity (even broad circularity) of the arguments in question. For example, if in using a causal argument we presuppose the existence of God, does not the argument reduce to "God exists, therefore God exists"—a narrowly circular argument that, since its premise is scriptural and its logic uncontroversial, is, on our criteria above, "absolutely certain"? I once said yes, but now I would reject this approach. As I indicated in chapter 1, the presuppositions of an argument are not among the premises of the argument. Therefore, the circularity in view is not what is normally called circularity in logic textbooks. Also, the precise claim made by this sort of argument is not "You should believe that God exists because God exists." Rather, it is "You should believe that God exists because (to be sure, on a theism-compatible epistemology) causality implies God's existence, and I can show that by reasons A, B, C, D . . ." We are, in other words, offering a more or less complicated argument for God's existence. But when we do this, even assuming a biblical epistemology, there is room for error to enter in and for a possible loss of "absolute certainty."

Now, is there any room for arguments that claim only a probability of being true? Van Til thought that if we claim anything less than absolute certainty, we are "virtually admitting that God's revelation to man is not clear."[40] Again, however, it is important for us to distinguish between evidence, argument, and subjective certainty. Van Til's point is strong in the area of evidence. As we noted earlier, the evidence for Christian theism is

---

40. Van Til, *Defense of the Faith*, 126.

absolutely compelling; it may not be described as merely probable. As for subjective certainty, again we should note that God has provided the means for it in the large, clearer areas of scriptural truth, but it sometimes escapes us in those or other areas. Our lack of certainty, then, does sometimes lead us, in all honesty, to say "probably."

As for argument, one might describe as "probable" those arguments that, because of their inadequate or incomplete presentation of the evidence, fail to be absolutely certain. The inadequacy might be due to sin or to a lack of understanding. For example, I might consider formulating an argument for God's existence based on the second law of thermodynamics. But since my understanding of that law is quite imperfect, I would not trust myself in that situation to adequately convey the absolute truth of God's evidence. So I would be inclined in that case to use the word *probably* a great deal. My account of Christian fallibility is as follows: (1) We are not God, so we cannot know anything exhaustively, even God's revelation. (2) As sinners, we repress the truth. (3) In regeneration, that repression is overcome only gradually. (4) Even though we have a right to psychological certainty about the basic truths of the faith (above), it is always objectively possible that we can be wrong. (5) Therefore, we ought to be humble even about the knowledge we hold as certain.

TAG articulates Christian certainty argumentatively. I am certain about the basic truths of Christianity, and indeed I regard these as the very standard of certainty. So nothing can be certain if these are not true. TAG seeks to show that there is no knowledge, meaning, predication, and so on unless these are true. TAGs are humanly formulated arguments, however, and therefore fallible. To speak of "probability" is to acknowledge that fallibility. Practically, this means: (1) We should be willing to confess that much of what we believe and many of the arguments we offer are not even psychologically certain, for they deal with matters other than the "basic truths." (2) Even our arguments about basic truths could be wrong, for those arguments are usually not themselves basic truths. (3) Even our beliefs about basic truths could be objectively wrong, though we have a right to be psychologically certain about them.

I don't believe that Scripture forbids us to explore areas that we don't entirely understand; quite the contrary (Gen. 1:28ff.). Nor do I think that Scripture forbids us to formulate tentative ideas concerning how relatively unknown phenomena relate to God. To do so, and to use the word *probably* in this connection, is not to say that the revealed evidence for God is merely probable; it is rather to say that one portion of the evidence, not well understood by a particular apologist, yields for him an argument that is at best possible or probable.[41] Van Til himself recognizes something like this distinction: "We should not tone down the validity of this argument to the probability level. The argument may be poorly stated, and may never be adequately stated. But in itself the argument is absolutely sound."[42]

What is this "argument" that is "absolutely sound," even though the statements of it might all be inadequate? Evidently, Van Til has in mind a kind of "ideal argument" that might never be adequately stated by an actual apologist. What he seems to be saying is that if there could be an argument that would perfectly reproduce the inherent clarity of God's revelation, that argument would be absolutely sound, valid, certain.[43] But it is possible (!) that no *actual* argument, including Van Til's, has ever measured up to that standard.

But then it is illegitimate for him to demand that all *actual* (as opposed to *ideal*) apologetic arguments claim certainty for their conclusions. Rather, an apologist, recognizing that he is *not* presenting the full evidential force of divine revelation, ought to be honest and admit that his argument conveys something less than absolute certainty. Another way of making that admission is to state that the argument is "probable." I would prefer to say that the evidence is absolutely sound, and that the argument conveys that evidence with more or less adequacy. Insofar as the argument conveys the evidence truly, it also conveys the absolute certainty inherent in the evidence.

A Strategic Sketch

To wrap things up at this stage in our discussion, although I disagree with Van Til's insistence that only negative arguments (*reduc-*

---

41. In modern philosophy, at least three kinds of probability are under discussion: *frequency*, the occurrences of a phenomenon relative to a statistical sample; *logical*, the likelihood of a hypothesis relative to a body of evidence; and *subjective*, the degree of belief warranted by the rational odds. Frequency probability can be disregarded in our present context. The logical probability of the truth of Christianity relative to its evidence is "1" or absolute certainty. But in the subjective sense, both the apologist and his hearers are often left with uncertainties because of inadequacies in the formulation of the argument and in its reception. And when there is suspicion of at least some legitimacy to uncertain reasoning, we may speak of some degree of probability. (Thanks to K. Scott Oliphint for reminding me of these distinctions.)

42. Van Til, *Defense of the Faith*, 255.

43. Van Til uses *sound*, *valid*, and *certain* more or less interchangeably, passing over the distinctions among these terms commonly made by philosophers.

tios) are legitimate, the *reductio* is an excellent kind of argument in its openness and adaptability. With an empiricist, you reduce empiricism to absurdity. With a postmodernist, you reduce postmodernism to absurdity, etc., etc. And with a *reductio*, it is easier to raise presuppositional issues.

But if I had to suggest a step-by-step approach, with somewhat typical university people in mind, it would be something like this:

1. The universe is either ultimately personal or ultimately impersonal.
2. If it is ultimately impersonal, it cannot justify rational discourse, including whatever you may be saying to me.
3. Therefore, if you want to carry on rational discourse, you must presuppose that the universe is ultimately personal.
4. Only the Bible, and views derived from the Bible, contains a consistently personalistic account of the world.
5. Therefore, we should give careful consideration to the Bible and assess its truth on the assumption that a personal God may have inspired it.
6. Pray that God's Spirit would open blind eyes to that truth.

Points 1–2 have been laid out in our discussion of absolute personalism in chapter 2. Points 3–4 are the thrust of the transcendental argument(s) that I have developed in this chapter and will continue to develop in the next.

Some Conclusions: A Presuppositionalism of the Heart

On this account of transcendental direction, negative argumentation, certainty, and point of contact, there is less distance between Van Til's apologetics and the traditional apologetics than most partisans on either side (including Van Til himself) have been willing to grant. I am not at all saddened by this implication. This way of thinking opens to the presuppositional apologist many, and perhaps all, of those arguments generally associated with the traditional apologetics in the past. We should no longer be embarrassed, for example, to argue for the existence of God on the basis of cause, purpose, and values. These can be elements in an overall argument that has a transcendental purpose (indeed, that has more than a merely transcendental purpose).

I would also conclude that the word *probability* deserves to be rehabilitated in Reformed apologetics. We dare not concede that the evidence for God's existence or the justification for believing in God's existence is merely probable. To do that would be, as Van Til says, to deny the objective clarity of revelation. But to be honest, we ought to admit that many of our arguments are only probable,[44] if only because there is so much room for error in their formulation.

Certainly, however, I have not removed all the differences between Van Til and his critics. The issue of neutrality (discussed in chapter 1) is still a high barrier between the two schools of thought, and on that matter Van Til is definitely right. Legitimate apologetic argument presupposes the truth of Scripture, and it renounces the idea of human intellectual independence or autonomy. Its aim, as Van Til says, is not to teach some kind of bare theism, but to confirm the full riches of biblical doctrine, including the teaching that God is the source of all meaningful predication.

There is also a residual Van Tillian point that needs to be made concerning proof. Van Til says, "If, therefore, he [the Christian] appeals to the unbeliever on the ground that nature itself reveals God, he should do this in such a manner as to make it appear in the end that he is interpreting nature in the light of Scripture."[45]

We have seen that Van Til is wrong to disavow direct arguments on the ground that they presuppose an autonomous understanding of the premises. A direct argument can, as easily as an indirect one, spring from the conviction that nothing is intelligible except through God. In the quotation above, Van Til seems almost to recognize that possibility.[46] Yet he adds a warning—and an important one. There is always the danger of communicating to the unbeliever—through body language, a cocksure tone of voice, or omissions of significant points—that one has adopted an autonomous stance. In the above quote, Van Til urges us to find some way—whether in the argument itself or in the behavior/language accompanying the argument—to communicate that our stance is not a neutral one. Van Til would most like for us to communicate that idea by

---

44. We must remember, of course, the distinctions made earlier in our discussion of how fallible arguments can convey infallible truth infallibly.

45. Cornelius Van Til, *An Introduction to Systematic Theology: Prolegomena and the Doctrine of Revelation, Scripture, and God*, ed. William Edgar, 2nd ed. (Phillipsburg, NJ: P&R Publishing, 2007), 315.

46. The words "nature itself reveals God" suggest a direct argument more naturally than they suggest an indirect one.

using indirect rather than direct arguments.[47] We have seen that this is an illegitimate requirement. But there are other ways to communicate our Christian "bias." Our whole attitude as apologists, our personal piety, our way of speaking—all of these can show the unbeliever that we are committed to the God of Scripture and not to the advancement of our own intellectual status or to the "search for truth" in the abstract or to victory in a battle of wits. All of this is part of the process of communication, and it affects the content of what we actually do communicate. It was not easy for Van Til to talk about such subtleties, but these things, not some rigid restrictions on apologetic form, represent God's way of dealing with what is essentially a spiritual problem. We can compare my approach to Van Til's using the chart on the following page.[48]

It may no longer be possible to distinguish presuppositional apologetics from traditional apologetics merely by externals—by the form of argument, the explicit claim of certainty or probability, and so forth. Perhaps presuppositionalism is more an attitude of the heart, a spiritual condition, than an easily describable, empirical phenomenon. To call it *spiritual* is certainly not to say that it is unimportant—quite the contrary. Our biggest need in apologetics (as in all other areas of life) has always been spiritual at the core. And our "presuppositionalism of the heart" is not something vague and indefinable. The presuppositionalism that we are talking about is (1) a clearheaded understanding of where our loyalties lie and how those loyalties affect our epistemology, (2) a determination above all to present the full teaching of Scripture in our apologetic without compromise, in its full winsomeness and its full offensiveness, (3) especially a determination to present God as fully sovereign, as the source of all meaning, intelligibility, and rationality, as the ultimate authority for all human thought, and (4) an understanding of the unbeliever's knowledge of God and rebellion against God, particularly (though not exclusively) as it affects his thinking. And if some apologists maintain these understandings and attitudes without wanting to be called Van Tillians or presuppositionalists, I am happy to join hands with them.

---

47. Again I would say that Van Til has a tendency to confuse issues of piety (What is my deepest loyalty, my presupposition?) with issues of method (What comes first in my argument? Should I prove the conclusion directly or disprove its opposite?). Certainly our piety must govern our method, but we must be careful before we, in effect, impute evil motives to apologists who simply prefer to do things in a different order.

48. This chart is taken from my discussion in *CVT*, 300–301.

	Van Til	Frame
Proof	There is an "absolutely certain proof" for Christian theism.	We need to distinguish between the certainty of evidence for Christian theism (which is absolute) and our human arguments (which are fallible and often uncertain).
Neutrality	All reasoning must presuppose divine revelation. Reasoning is never religiously neutral.	I agree with enthusiasm.
Presuppositions	All reasoning must presuppose the absolute-personal Trinitarian Lord who exercises total and absolute rule over his creation.	Again, I agree with enthusiasm.
Antithesis and Common Grace	Our reasoning must take into account both the noetic effects of sin and the restraining influence of common grace.	I agree, but nuance is needed.
Suppression	The unbeliever suppresses the truth by a dialectic of rationalism and irrationalism.	Agreed.
Evidence	We may freely use logical arguments and present evidences for the truth of Scripture. But we shouldn't do this "endlessly" without challenging the unbeliever's philosophy of fact.	Agreed, with the proviso that we be permitted to vary our approach based on the nature and questions of our audience. We don't always need to explicitly speak of epistemology.
Proving Christian Theism	We should always seek to prove Christian theism "as a unit."	Yes . . . but. To some extent it is legitimate to prove one fact about God at a time, being careful not to distort the whole in expounding the parts.
Certainty or Probability?	Our arguments should claim absolute certainty, never mere probability.	See the first point above. It is legitimate in some cases, and even unavoidable, to use arguments that claim only probability.
Should We "Supplement" the Unbeliever's Knowledge?	We should not produce arguments that merely "supplement" the unbeliever's knowledge. We should seek to overturn the very foundations of his thought.	If we reject an extreme view of antithesis, we must recognize that there will be elements of truth in unbelieving thought. This is not to deny the importance of overturning the foundations of unbelieving thought, for elements of truth in unbelieving thought are at variance with its foundational commitment.
Direct or Indirect Arguments?	A truly transcendental approach is indirect rather than direct.	Any indirect argument of this sort can be turned into a direct argument by some creative rephrasing. If the indirect form is sound, the direct form will be, too—and vice versa.

5

APOLOGETICS AS PROOF: THEISTIC ARGUMENTS

I will now present an example of a way to prove God's existence, taking into account the preceding introductory points. It will be rather different from the ways to God described in the preceding section. In a way, it will resemble the more traditional sorts of apologetic. Yet the ultimate conclusion is quite Van Tillian: nothing is intelligible unless God exists, and God must be nothing less than the Trinitarian, sovereign, transcendent, and immanent absolute personality of the Scriptures.[1]

This argument will not be appropriate for every witnessing situation—no argument is. As we have seen, apologetics is person-variable. Nonetheless, many educated adults from traditional Western culture should be able to follow its main thrust and appreciate its logical force. These are the people I am most used to dealing with. I leave to other apologists the important work of developing approaches more suited to those of other cultural and socioeconomic groups.

My argument is not absolutely certain.[2] Many readers will find problems in it. Certainly it is far from being a complete argument; at many points it could be improved by providing additional logical steps and clarifying

---

1. As indicated in the previous chapter, I do not believe that any single argument can prove all this. My argument is really a group of arguments, and no one of them by itself proves the entire conclusion. It would be unreasonable to expect every argument to prove the whole system at once. Yet every argument should contribute to the establishing of this conclusion and to nothing contrary to it. For there is no other God that we are interested in proving.

2. Except, of course, in the sense of chapter 3: that it conveys some of the evidence that God has revealed in Scripture and the world.

some concepts.[3] Yet it should have some persuasive value—granting that persuasiveness is very difficult to measure in apologetics.[4] I think it is logically sound and in keeping with scriptural norms. I believe that it draws the reader's attention to some data that God has created to testify of him. And the testimony of that revelation *is* absolutely certain. It will convince anyone who looks at it rightly.[5]

This proof should help the reader to see in what sense the evidence for God is "obvious." Romans 1:20 tells us that God's existence is "clearly perceived" in creation; but, alas, we so often look and fail to see. My moral argument begins with moral values—which, to be sure, cannot be literally seen, but which, nevertheless, all of us do and must acknowledge if we are to make rational judgments. Moral values, then, are pervasive; they enter into all our reasoning and all our decisions. They are inescapable and unavoidable—and they point to God. In that sense, the argument presents a God who is "obvious."

This argument should also help us to see how all intelligibility and meaning, and indeed all predication, depend on God. I intend to show that all such predication depends on moral values and that those in turn depend on God. This proof has, therefore, the force of TAG, though it is formulated in positive rather than negative form for the most part.

I will be arguing, in effect, "Moral values, therefore God." Let me immediately insist that we cannot understand moral values apart from God and then deduce his existence from them, as if the true God depended on values that have meaning apart from him. Quite the contrary. The syllogism will not work unless the moral values themselves are construed theistically. And if someone calls that "circular," I simply invoke my previous discussion on that matter.

This approach cannot, therefore, be characterized as "blockhouse methodology."[6] Indeed, Scripture itself tells us that God is the author of

3. This book is written in more of a theological than a philosophical vein. My intended readers are Christian workers and laymen with some higher education. Philosophers rightly demand more precision and detailed argument than are found here, and I am capable of meeting that demand up to a point. But I feel that to go through an elaborate philosophical demonstration would inhibit communication with my main intended audience.

4. The point, of course, is that we never know for sure what will lead an unbeliever, humanly speaking, to abandon his suppression of the truth and therefore be persuaded; or, in other words, we never know precisely what kind of argument the Holy Spirit will choose to use in a particular case.

5. And looking at it rightly, of course, for us fallen creatures, requires divine grace.

6. This is Cornelius Van Til's phrase describing those who begin with a foundation of autonomous reasoning and then attempt to establish Christianity as a second story, built on that foundation.

authentic moral standards—that they reflect his nature (Lev. 19:2; Matt. 5:48; 1 Peter 1:16).

I will seek to gain agreement on each premise before passing on to the next one. In my mind, I am not here appealing to the unbeliever's would-be autonomous knowledge, but to his true knowledge of God and creation, which he has by revelation, yet represses. Granted, it is hard to tell from the external course of the argument which of these procedures is which; we noted at the end of chapter 4 that it is difficult to distinguish presuppositional from traditional methods by externals alone.

The conclusion of the argument will not be some bare theism acceptable to many religions and philosophies, but the distinctive God of Scripture. And the argument proceeds by way of the standards and methods of a biblical epistemology.

This argument is not the means by which I came to faith, and it is not the ground of my present trust in Christ. Yet it should put some truths of Scripture into focus for some people.

Atheism and Agnosticism

My moral argument integrates beliefs and moral values in a way that will be more fully explained in later sections.[7] Our values determine our beliefs in the same way that they determine our other behavior.

People sometimes have in their minds conflicting beliefs, however offensive that may be to logic. In such cases, we are often inclined to ask, for example, "What does Susan *really* believe?" One test is to observe behavior. One's dominant belief will most often or most profoundly govern one's behavior. As Scripture says, "Thus you will recognize them by their fruits" (Matt. 7:20).

There are many who claim to be neither theists nor atheists, but agnostic. They claim that they do not know whether or not God exists. Of course, Scripture denies that anyone can be agnostic: God is clearly revealed to all (Rom. 1:18–20), so that all know him (v. 21), although they repress the truth (vv. 21ff.). In one sense, everyone is a theist, for everyone knows God. But in another sense, unbelievers are atheists, for they seek to erase, to deny, this knowledge and to live on atheistic presuppositions. In this model, no one is an agnostic.

There is no agnosticism by the scriptural "behavior test." If someone were genuinely agnostic, he would be frantically trying to find ways of

7. It is also explained in *DKG*, 62–64, 73–75, and elsewhere.

hedging bets: at least giving lip service to God, who after all might one day judge him. But as a matter of fact, most professing agnostics do not hedge their bets in that way. Rather, they totally ignore God's Word in their decision-making. They never go to church, never seek God's will, never pray. In other words, they behave exactly like atheists, not as if they were in some halfway position between atheism and theism.

There are some exceptions. I do want to leave the door open for cases in which the Holy Spirit is leading toward Christ someone who has not yet finalized the intellectual issues. People in that position might be described as genuine agnostics. But their openness to the Word of God does not allow them to remain agnostic forever (John 7:17). There might also be some agnostics who do in fact hedge their bets. One of my correspondents claims to have been that kind of agnostic before he became an explicit Christian. Whether such hedging is the hypocritical pose of an unbeliever or the first baby steps of a believer is not usually clear to human observers (and perhaps not even clear to the person taking those steps), although it is clear to God. This phenomenon does not disprove the ultimate antithesis, that everyone is either for God or against him. But if an argument (such as that below) is successful in dealing with atheism, it will be successful with agnosticism as well—even sincere agnosticism.

We should always remember, however, that there is no halfway house between being God's friend and being his enemy. "Choose this day whom you will serve," said Joshua (Josh. 24:15). "No one can serve two masters," said Jesus (Matt. 6:24). And "Whoever is not with me is against me" (12:30).

Therefore, the argument that follows is directed to atheists. Others, however, are welcome to read on.

The Moral Argument

Traditional theistic arguments have sometimes focused on causality, sometimes on purpose and/or design, and sometimes on ontology (the nature of being in general). More recently, various arguments that focus on moral values have emerged. My argument is of the latter sort; at least that is how it begins. As it develops, it incorporates the more traditional categories.

Moral values, after all, are rather strange. We cannot see them, hear them, or feel them, but we cannot doubt that they exist. A witness to a bank robbery can see the thief walk into the bank, pull out his gun, speak to the teller, take the money, and walk out. But the witness does not see what is perhaps the most important fact—the moral evil of the robber's action. Yet that evil is unquestionably there, just as moral good is unquestionably present when a motorist stops to help someone whose car has broken down on a dangerous stretch of highway.

What are moral values, and how can we come to know them? Some have argued that although right and wrong cannot be directly seen or heard, they do arise from experience. "Right" behavior tends to be rewarded, but "wrong" behavior tends to lead to bad consequences. Thus, we form the concepts of right and wrong on the basis of consequences. These consequences, however, are not at all uniform in our experience. As the psalmists often complained, the wicked sometimes prosper and the righteous sometimes die penniless. And even if the consequences were uniform, that uniformity would be of dubious moral relevance. As David Hume pointed out, "X brings good consequences" does not logically imply that "X is morally good." Statements about facts (without presupposed principles of moral evaluation) cannot entail any conclusions about morality. Valueless facts do not imply values. *Is* does not imply *ought*.[8]

Some would say that these values are merely individual subjective feelings. On this view, I call the thief's action "evil" or "wrong" because I am emotionally repulsed by robbery. Well, it's easy enough to describe other people's ethical standards as subjective or emotional. But few of us, if any, would be willing to describe our own standards that way. When we call an action "evil" or "wrong" (rather than, say, merely "repellent"), we normally intend to say something objective. Robbery is not wrong because we dislike it; rather, we dislike it because it is wrong. Our evaluation of robbery, in other words, is not just our own subjective taste; it is a judgment that we are obliged to make and that, moreover, we believe everyone else is also obliged to make. Those who make the wrong judgment are not merely creatures with odd emotions; they have violated a basic principle that binds human beings. Those who approve of robbery and murder are not merely mistaken, not merely odd in their emotional makeup; they are wicked. They are violating a norm[9] that is just as real as the law of gravity.[10]

8. Otherwise, if we could show that wickedness on the whole brought prosperity, then we could draw the conclusion that we ought to be wicked; then wickedness wouldn't be wicked, but good.

9. A norm is a divine law or standard, in this case one that tells us what values are indeed objective and should therefore be honored. One of my correspondents insists that all values are subjective, but that norms are objective. I take that to be a matter of definition. My friend can define these terms as he likes; I don't think my definitions violate any linguistic invariables. But in substance we are agreed: our subjective concepts of what is right and wrong must be brought into line with the objective revelation of God, however we describe it.

10. Of course, the difference between moral norms and physical laws such as the law of gravity is that one can violate moral laws, but not physical ones. On the other hand, maybe the difference is not so great, for one cannot violate moral laws with impunity. It is just as true that

Is it possible that moral values are, if not individual subjective feelings, merely the subjective feelings shared in a given culture and passed down from generation to generation? Well, again, as a matter of fact we do not generally regard moral values as mere cultural tastes (like the Polish taste for pierogies). When we hear of cannibalism in a far-off tribe, our response is not "Well, that's their particular taste (!)" but rather, "That is wicked." So if these values are culturally subjective, we must try very hard to change our reactions to things.[11]

So as a matter of fact, we act and think as if these values were objective, rather than merely subjective. Theoretically, of course, it is possible that we are wrong in thinking this way. But if we deny objective values, we should be aware of the price we must pay. For denying objective values is something far more drastic than merely denying conventional, parochial standards of behavior. It is to deny rationality itself.

For what is truth, after all? It is many things, but among them, it is certainly an ethical value. The truth is what we ought to believe and what we ought to speak with one another. And those *ought*s are *ought*s of ethical value. If they were merely subjective, we would be free to believe and maintain whatever we liked, unconstrained by evidence, logic, or revelation. If ethical values were merely subjective, we could make no ethical case against someone who refused to consider facts and who consequently lived in a dreamworld of his own making.

The assertion that ethical values are merely subjective is self-contradictory, like all other statements of subjectivism or skepticism. For the subjectivist is telling us that we have an objective moral obligation to agree with subjectivism, while telling us that no one has an objective moral obligation to do anything. Subjectivists regularly make this error. Jean-Paul Sartre, for example, argued vehemently against objective values, but he also demanded that we admire those who "live authentically" by affirming their own freedom and creating their own meaning. If "authentic existence" is not an objective value, why should we admire it or, indeed, care about it at all? And if it is, then Sartre has refuted himself.

Before we consider the origin of moral values, let us note one more point: ethical values are hierarchically structured. "We should seek to make

---

"the wages of sin is death" (Rom. 6:23) as that "what goes up must come down." With moral laws, of course, we often have to wait awhile for the consequences to take effect, but some physical laws are that way, too: for example, we are still experiencing effects of the sun's formation.

11. For further discussion of non-Christian ideas concerning the source of morality, see my *Perspectives on the Word of God* (Phillipsburg, NJ: Presbyterian and Reformed, 1990), 39–50.

our children feel good" is one ethical value, but for most of us it is second-ary to the value "We should seek to teach our children self-discipline." In many cases, there is a conflict between these two values; a good parent will in such cases follow the second maxim, granting it more authority than the first. Conceivably, however, there are maxims even more important and authoritative than the one about self-discipline. For example: "We should teach our children to be kind to others." Eventually, as you climb this lad-der, you reach a maxim that is higher than any others in the context. For Christians, in the context of child-rearing, that maxim would be: "We should teach our children to love God with all their heart and love their neighbor as themselves" (see Matt. 22:37–40). And in the broadest context, the highest maxim is that we should all love God and neighbor perfectly.

Hierarchies do change with time, for our ethical values change. Even our highest commitments change from time to time.[12] But at any single moment, there is one principle that takes precedence over all the others, one that prevails over all the others in governing our behavior. That highest value is not only objective but also absolute, for it takes precedence over all others and serves as a criterion for the truth of others.

To Christians, that absolute would be God's will as expressed in Scrip-ture. To Muslims, it would be the will of Allah, expressed in the Bible and especially in the Qur'an. To some, it would be the Golden Rule. To some, it would be the principle to be kind. To others, it would be the maxim "Live and let live." To others, "Do no harm." People can argue with one another as to which of these should be regarded as the highest ethical principle, the absolute norm. But all of us do acknowledge one; otherwise, we would make no moral judgments at all.

Now, where does the authority of the absolute moral principle come from? Notice that I am not asking where the conviction itself comes from, as if this were a causal argument. That is not the point—at least not yet. The question concerns the authority of that principle: why should we give to it the enormous respect that indeed we do give to it?

Ultimately, only two kinds of answers are possible: the source of abso-lute moral authority is either personal or impersonal. Consider first the lat-ter possibility.[13] That would mean that there is some impersonal structure

---

12. Of course, once a person is born anew by the Spirit of God, God's grace preserves his fundamental commitment. This is the doctrine of perseverance (see John 10:28ff.; Rom. 8:29ff.). But even in the Christian life there are ups and downs—times in which we are more, and other times in which we are less, governed by what is on the whole our ultimate presupposition.

13. Note here elements of a Van Tillian *reductio*.

or law in the universe that sets forth ethical precepts and rightly demands allegiance to them. But what kind of impersonal being could possibly do that? Certainly if the laws of the universe reduced to chance, nothing of ethical significance could emerge from it. What of ethical significance can we learn from the random collisions of subatomic particles?[14] What loyalty do we owe to pure chance?

Of course, most antisupernaturalists find ethical value not in pure chance, but in some sort of impersonal structure in the universe. Perhaps it is conceived on the model of physical law: just as what goes up "must" come down, so in the moral sphere one "must" love one's neighbor. But as I indicated earlier in a note, there are significant differences between physical and moral laws. And the main question here is: How can an impersonal structure create *obligation*? (Again, we have a major *is-ought* problem.) Or: On what basis does an impersonal structure demand loyalty or obedience?

One thinks of the fatalism of ancient Greek religion, in which, essentially, fate calls the tune for history. When the tragic hero learns of his fate, he might fight it, but in time he will be crushed by that all-controlling destiny. Here, impersonal fate is stronger than anything else. It cannot be resisted. But does that fact imply that we ought to submit to it? Is one nobler if he submits or if he fights? Some Greek thinkers, at least, seemed to think that one who fights fate is noble, even if fate eventually crushes him. Is that not also our own instinct? The fact is that an impersonal principle such as fate is insufficient to create an *ought*, to rightly demand loyalty and obedience.

Where, then, does the *ought* come from? What is there that is capable of imposing an absolute obligation on human beings? For the answer, we must leave the realm of impersonal principles and turn to the realm of persons. Obligations and loyalties arise in the context of interpersonal relationships. In terms of Reformed theology, we may put it this way: obligations, loyalties, and therefore morality are covenantal in character.

When I receive a bill from a man who has repaired my roof, I feel an obligation to pay it. It is not just that that person (plus the police!) is, like the Greek fate, strong enough to crush me. In the personal arena, there is always another factor: I recognize in the roof repairman a person like myself. And I have the sense about him that he deserves to be paid. Or, to put it differently: when we agreed that he would fix my roof, I promised to pay him. That promise created an obligation, and I would have little respect for myself if I did not keep that promise.

---

14. Remember what we said earlier about the *is-ought* relation.

We learn morality, typically, in the family—another deeply personal, covenantal environment. Parents rightly demand the obedience of their children, not only because parents are bigger and can spank, but also because they presumably have greater wisdom and experience, greater compassion and goodness, and deep responsibility and love for their children. Beyond all that, they bear authority simply because they are parents, even when, so far as we can tell, they do not deserve that authority. Other adults might be wiser and more compassionate than one's parents, but the word of the parent still counts for more—unless it contravenes a still higher moral authority.

Our obligations to repairmen and even to parents are not absolute. If the repairman's bill is ten times his estimate, a higher moral arbiter, the court, might have to be involved. If parents tell a son to murder somebody, it is best that he resort to higher moral authorities, perhaps to his absolute or ultimate moral authority. But where does *that* authority come from?

If my reasoning so far has been correct, then that authority can come only from what we called in chapter 2 a *personal absolute* or an *absolute personality*.[15] If obligations arise from personal relationships, then absolute obligations must arise from our relationship with an absolute person. If we obey our parents because they are wiser and more experienced than we are, because they are responsible for us, and because they care for and love us, then we obey the absolute person because he is *supremely* wise, experienced, responsible, good, and loving. And if our parents deserve honor even above and beyond what their good qualities deserve, simply because they are parents, then the absolute person *supremely* deserves our honor, simply because he is the ultimate personal authority.

Moral standards, therefore, presuppose absolute moral standards, which in turn presuppose the existence of an absolute personality. In other words, they presuppose the existence of God. But what God? Well, consider again the argument of chapter 2. Of all the major religious traditions, only biblical religion affirms a God who is both personal and absolute. We have also seen that the idea of absolute personality is closely linked to the ideas of a Creator-creature distinction, divine sovereignty, and the Trinity. Compromise these and you compromise the personality of God. This

---

15. While Van Til emphasized in a number of places that the *personality* of God has important apologetic implications, I don't know if he ever explicitly used this kind of formulation. In that sense it is mine. He believed that a large part of the error of Arminianism is to make God subordinate to impersonal factors (chance, brute fact, abstract logic). He emphasized that only a person can be a concrete universal, that is, an adequate explanation of finite reality. So I think my moral argument fits well into the Van Tillian scheme of things. See *CVT*, 58–61.

precise pattern of thought is found only in the Bible and in traditions that are heavily influenced by the Bible. Is it, then, too much to say that morality presupposes the God of the Bible? I think not.

Other divine attributes, too, are evident from the logic of the moral argument. The fact that God himself thinks, knows, plans, and speaks is evident from the very meaning of personhood. God's justice is implicit in the fact that he is the very source, the very definition, of moral standards. He himself can never be charged with injustice (see chapter 7). And he is truth, for he is the very criterion of truth and can therefore never be charged with falsehood. (Recall from earlier in this chapter how truth is itself a moral concept.) We may never doubt his word.

If God is truly absolute, then he is without beginning or end. The reason is that just as we cannot rationally understand the present without taking his absolute standards into account, so we cannot conceive of any past or any future without him. A past without God would be chaos, from which order could never emerge; the same would be true for a future without God. Indeed, God is *a se* (self-sufficient and self-existent); no circumstances are conceivable without him, and so it is impossible for him not to exist.[16]

And since he is absolute, he must be one (though with the Trinitarian complexity we have noted). For there can be only one final, ultimate standard for morals and knowledge.[17]

And there are no limitations on his knowledge, power, or presence; that is, he is omniscient, omnipotent, and omnipresent. Why? Because if something existed, but God did not know it, that something would exist apart from God's intelligent planning, creation, and providence. That something, therefore, would be intelligible apart from God. In that case, God would not be the origin of the world, but only of part of it. But we have seen that that is impossible. The world has only one origin, and that is personal. Therefore, God is omniscient. Similarly, if something could be done,[18] but God could not do it, then its "doability" would be measured by something other than God. Therefore, he is omnipotent. And if he is omniscient and

16. Put positively, he exists necessarily.

17. If there are two, and they sometimes disagree, then either only one of them is God (if one of them is right all the time) or there is no ultimate standard at all (if neither is right all the time). If there are two, and they always agree, then the fact of that agreement, together with its grounds or reasons, is our actual standard: a singularity, not a duality. If the reason is a unity underlying a Trinitarian type of complexity, which is the most likely reason, then that especially confirms the Christian position.

18. By limiting my discussion to what "can be done," I am ruling out logical impossibilities such as the making of round squares. Omnipotence does not mean the ability to do illogical things.

omnipotent, he must be omnipresent. Since God does not have a body, his power can be at work (by his knowledge, of course) in all particular locations only if he is in some sense present everywhere.

The argument is transcendental. Rather than offering straightforward empirical evidence for God, it asks the deeper question: what must be the case if evidential argument and knowledge (and hence objective moral standards) are to be possible?

The argument, of course, does not prevent anyone from choosing unbelief. One can do that in the face of any argument, no matter how strong the argument may be. Human beings, tragically, are able to act irrationally. Further, the argument itself leaves open the theoretical possibility that we are wrong in claiming an objective knowledge of morality. One could therefore reason that we are wrong about this and therefore about God. Of course, that reasoning would also lead to a denial of objective truth and thus to an end of reasoning itself. So the choice is this: either accept the God of the Bible or deny objective morality, objective truth, the rationality of man, and the rational knowability of the universe. Some might maintain that they don't care much about this. They might say that they can go on living happily enough without having a rational basis for thinking and acting. For these people, other forms of gospel communication might be needed. But let no one say that Christianity lacks a rational basis or that non-Christian "conventional wisdom" is more rational than Christianity.

Here, however, we come to a problem that emerges when we say that God is the ultimate standard of ethical value and obligation. When we ascribe goodness to God and also make him the standard for identifying and evaluating goodness, the two statements generate a kind of circularity.

If I say that Bach's music is the greatest ever written, I make a meaningful, if disputable, claim. But if someone asks my criteria for greatness in music, and I reply, "Likeness to Bach's," then the significance of my claim seems to be reduced. Bach's superiority then becomes tautological and trivial, for of course, of all composers, Bach's music is most like Bach's. An admirer of Mozart, or even of Lawrence Welk, could use the same circular argument, and it would be equally unconvincing. Or imagine my claiming to be the world's greatest basketball player, and then defining basketball greatness as whatever I do on the court. On that definition, my apparently audacious claim becomes true, but utterly uninteresting.

Similarly, some have argued that if we say, "God is good," but then make God the standard or criterion of goodness, we make the initial claim meaningless. If we say both "God is good" and "Good is whatever God is," then God's "goodness" could be anything at all. When we make God our standard of goodness, he could hate the righteous, reward wickedness, and betray his friends, but those actions would be good, simply because God did them.

So Plato, in Euthyphro, poses the question whether piety is what the gods say it is, or whether the gods command piety because of its intrinsic nature, apart from their own wishes. In Plato's mind, the former makes the nature of piety arbitrary, one that could be changed on the whim of a god. But the second alternative, which Plato certainly prefers, means that piety is independent of the will of the gods, something to which the gods' opinions are subject. So either piety is arbitrary or the gods are subject to something higher than themselves.

Some philosophers have identified a similar problem in biblical theism: if good is what God says, then goodness is subject to the arbitrary whims of a personal deity.[19] But if goodness is independent of God, then he is subordinate to the abstract concept of goodness. The same problem would arise with righteousness, truth, wisdom, beauty, or any other attribute that served as a model or criterion for the same attributes imaged in creation.[20]

In my view, this problem arises from the inability of Plato and other philosophers to see goodness as something personal. Many of them never seem to question the view that such things as goodness and truth are impersonal.[21] They reason that since goodness is an abstract entity, it cannot be identical with a person.

I question this assumption. It is plausible to argue this way on the human level, for human goodness is shared by many and thus should not be identified absolutely with any one of us. And of course, the behavior of

19. See C. Stephen Evans, *Philosophy of Religion* (Downers Grove, IL: InterVarsity Press, 1985), 68–96; R. W. Hepburn, *Christianity and Paradox* (New York: Pegasus, 1958), 128–54; C. B. Martin, "The Perfect Good," in *New Essays in Philosophical Theology*, ed. Antony Flew and Alasdair C. MacIntyre (London: SCM, 1955), 212–26. See also the literature on the "divine command theory" of ethics, such as Robert Adams, *The Virtue of Faith* (Oxford: Oxford University Press, 1987); Paul Helm, ed., *Divine Commands and Morality* (Oxford: Oxford University Press, 1981).

20. The very objection was again voiced by Bertrand Russell in his now-classic *Why I Am Not a Christian* (New York: Touchstone Books, 1967), 12.

21. Similarly, many scientists and philosophers of science assume that the impersonal aspects of the universe are more fundamental than the personal aspects. So they tend to believe that explanations of phenomena in terms of impersonal realities (matter, motion, time, space) are more basic than explanations in terms of personal choice. On this assumption, scientists prefer theories that reduce the personal to the impersonal. This explains the objectively implausible preference for naturalistic evolution over creation as an explanation for the forms of living beings.

APOLOGETICS AS PROOF: THEISTIC ARGUMENTS 107

one human being cannot define goodness.[22] Since goodness is not a human person, some conclude, it must be something impersonal, an abstract object.

But when we think of goodness as an attribute of God, we must surely think differently. Remember that not one of God's attributes is strictly communicable.[23] In that sense, God's goodness is strictly his own. It is not shared by anybody else, but God has imaged it in the creation. Before creation, only God existed, and his goodness was not shared with anyone but the persons of the Trinity. Indeed, it was nothing less than God's own nature.[24] So God's goodness is God, and therefore personal.

So goodness is the behavior and self-revelation of a person, not a general or abstract concept. Certainly it would be wrong to regard the behavior of any mere human being as the criterion of goodness. But of course, God is unique.

So the good is not, as in Plato's view, an abstract form superior to God. Is the good, then, what God says it is? Yes, but God's word is not arbitrary. God commends goodness to us because he is himself supremely good. His commands to us are based on what he himself is.[25] So it is true to say that goodness is what God says it is, and it is also true to say that God commends the good because it is good.

A mere human being cannot be the standard of goodness because his nature is not perfect. His commands would indeed be subject to the suspicion of arbitrariness. As a finite and fallen creature, he might indeed declare what is good today to be bad tomorrow. People such as Adolf Hitler, Josef Stalin, and Jim Jones, who have demanded absolute allegiance from their followers, have typically led them into sin, error, and death. But God's word cannot be arbitrary in this way, for God is supremely and unchangeably good.

A form of circularity here is unavoidable. When we say that God is good, we evaluate God's conduct on the basis of his own revelation. God is both supremely good and the ultimate standard of goodness. Does this

22. I am not here denying the sinlessness of Jesus. But we can appreciate his sinlessness more fully if we understand how audacious it is to claim that any man is sinless.

23. See *DG*, chap. 19.

24. See ibid., chap. 12.

25. Obviously, there are differences between what is good for God and what is good for man. For example, God has the right to take human life for his own purposes; we do not. We have an obligation to worship a being other than ourselves; God does not. God's prerogatives, his "rights," are different from ours. But the differences as well as the similarities between God's ethics and ours are based on his nature. Both the uniqueness of God's nature and the resemblances between God and his creaturely images are important to ethics.

circularity fall prey to the criticisms that apply to the examples I mentioned above (regarding Bach, Mozart, Welk, and myself)?

I think not, for these reasons:

1. Whatever may be said of their music, Bach, Mozart, and Welk are human beings. None is fit to be the absolute criterion of musical excellence. To make Bach the ultimate standard of musicality is to ignore the fact that musical excellence occurs in types of music very different from Bach's. So there are objections to using human beings as ultimate criteria, entirely apart from questions of circularity—objections that do not apply to God.

2. This circularity is very similar to the circularity I have discussed earlier. There is always a kind of circularity when we are dealing with an ultimate standard. If one's standard of truth is human reason, one can argue for that standard only by a rational argument, an argument that presupposes the truth of its conclusion. Similarly, if God is the supreme standard of truth and rationality, one may argue for that standard only by presupposing it. For if the conclusion is true, this is the only kind of argument permissible. Likewise, when we argue that God is good, we must appeal to the only true standard of goodness that there is, namely, God. We have no other choice.

The same circularity is present in any attempt, Christian or non-Christian, to establish a criterion of goodness. Let's say that someone tries to prove that goodness is an abstract form, without any personal exemplification. He must then somehow derive specific ethical content from that form. But then it becomes his task to show that these ethical principles are in fact good. If his abstract form is indeed the supreme standard, then he must show the content of the abstract form to be good by reference to the abstract form. That argument is circular, too. So if theistic reasoning is circular at this point, its circularity is shared by all other forms of reasoning.

3. Some might argue that circularity still presents a problem, despite the observations above. For even though this circularity is shared by all religions and philosophies, they might say, it is still circularity and therefore objectionable. But if it is, the whole enterprise of reason is invalidated, and we are forced into radical skepticism. Yet that sort of objection is self-refuting. If the circularity of reason invalidates reason itself, then it invalidates the objection as well. Besides, skepticism itself is a self-refuting position. Any argument for skepticism presupposes *some* knowledge.

4. Our subjective uneasiness with this circularity stems in part from our tendency to reduce the differences between God and man (see point 1 above) and in part from our failure to understand concretely how we actually learn about God's goodness. The biblical writers never say that God

is good because he says he is good, and that he says he is good because he is good. That would be narrow circularity. Rather, they describe and praise God's mighty acts of deliverance, his kindness in providence, and his grace in salvation. These are big, bold, obvious evidences of goodness. They overwhelm believing readers and call from us almost involuntarily the confession that God is good. At this stage of our thinking, there might seem to be no circularity at all.

But as we think more deeply, we realize that of course we learn of these evidences from God himself. We learn them from God's Word, and the biblical writers themselves learn them from God's inspiration. There is also general revelation: God reveals his goodness through his actions in the course of nature and history, both in the experience of the biblical writers and in our own. So everything we know about God's goodness comes from him. God's revelation is both our ultimate criterion of truth and our sole source of knowledge about God's goodness. We believe that God is good, then, because God tells us that he is good. So the circularity is present. But it is a broad circularity, not a narrow one. It is a circularity loaded with content, full of evidence, and richly persuasive. We are literally surrounded by evidence of God's goodness.

So when someone says that for God to be his own standard allows him to be an arbitrary despot, declaring what is good today to be evil tomorrow, the critic is not dealing with the reality of God's revelation. The God who reveals himself in all creation is simply not that kind of person. We do not know him as an arbitrary despot. We have heard of arbitrary despots, but our God is not like them.

God has made us to hear his voice, as obedient children listen to a loving father. We know him because he knows us and addresses us. He declares his goodness, and he demonstrates it richly. We don't merely know the bare fact that God is good; we know him. We learn to trust someone by observing his or her behavior. With God, there is far more evidence than that, for all creation presents to us his actions and his love.

God's goodness is not always obvious on the surface, especially when we experience injustice or suffering. But in the end we will see that even that injustice and suffering manifests the goodness of God. Then believers will see his wrath as justice and our sufferings as his fatherly discipline (Heb. 12:4–12).

The choice is between God and chaos, God and nothing, God and insanity. To most of us, those are not choices at all. Believing in an irrational universe is not believing at all. It is, as we have seen, self-contradictory. But if someone has resolved to live without logic, without reason, and without standards, we cannot prevent him. He will, of course, accept logic and rationality when he makes his real-life decisions, and so he will not live according to his theoretical irrationalism. In many apologetic situations, it is useful to point this out.[26] But for a tough-minded irrationalist, logical inconsistency is not a problem. Still, at some level he knows he is wrong. God still speaks, around and in the unbeliever.

The Epistemological Argument

Epistemological arguments traditionally start with the phenomenon of human rationality and ask how that can be. How is it possible that the human mind correlates so well with the structure of the world that people can make sense of the world? There must be a rational structure in the world that mirrors (or is mirrored by) the rational structure of the human mind.

If the world developed by pure chance, it would be highly unlikely that human experience would mirror the reality of the world in the way that we usually assume it does. Why should we assume that chance has equipped me with eyes and a brain so that I can actually see what I'm doing? Isn't it equally possible that when I think I'm a seminary professor typing at my desk in Florida, I am really a cockroach running around the New York City subway?

The theory of evolution, of course, tries to show (usually on a nontheistic basis) the likelihood of human rationality's developing into a reliable interpreter of the world. But even if evolution were true (and there are some pretty impressive scientific and philosophical witnesses against it these days), why would pure chance have given rise to evolution itself—a system so meticulously and rationally (!) calculated to maximize the preservation of species?

Certainly, again, the hypothesis of absolute personality explains the data far better than the hypothesis of ultimate impersonality. An absolute personality can make a rational universe because he himself is rational and his plan for creation and providence is therefore rational. And the absolute personality is able to make man in his image and to equip him to understand the universe as much as he needs to. Why should one prefer the hypothesis of ultimate impersonality, when that creates such an enormous

---

26. Perhaps the most persuasive element of Francis Schaeffer's apologetic was his emphasis that irrationalists (or relativists or subjectivists) cannot live consistently with their beliefs. Indeed, when one tries to live as if there were no rational order (arbitrarily stepping in front of moving cars, etc.), one is not likely to live very long! That message had a strong impact on many minds.

gap between the nature of the creator (nonrational) and the nature of the universe, including human beings (rational)?

The case becomes even stronger when we recall what was said in the previous section: truth is an ethical value. The rational quest, like the ethical quest, is covenantal. It essentially amounts to discovering the will of an absolute person. Ethics discovers his will for our actions; epistemology discovers his will for our beliefs.[27]

Even logic itself is value-based. If I confess that "all men are mortal" and that "Socrates is a man," what is it that requires me to confess that "Socrates is mortal"? The laws of physics certainly do not stop anyone from making errors in logic. Is it that being logical leads to success and happiness? But it doesn't, always. Is there some abstract, impersonal principle of rationality that imposes such a conclusion on me? But why should I be required to act in accord with such a principle? Why should I not rather rebel against it, as a logical Prometheus? Is logic an evolutionary development to ensure the preservation of the human species? But even assuming that evolution were true (and it is no more than an unproved theory), it is not clear that being logical always or even usually preserves life; after all, cockroaches have inhabited the world much longer than man. Furthermore, if evolution seeks to ensure the preservation of species, then it would seem to have personal characteristics or to be the tool of a person. If it is entirely impersonal, with no personal causes, then it has no power to make logic normative. And if logic is not normative, we have no obligation to it. On that basis, even "preservation of the species" is only a concept; no one has an actual obligation to carry it out.

No, the power of logic is normative and ethical. It tells us what we ought to confess as a conclusion, granting our confession of premises.[28] And if it is ethical, it is covenantal; like moral values, it rests on the dependable word of a trustworthy person, a Lord, our absolute divine personality. Thus, when unbelievers use logic to raise objections against Christianity, they are using something that, manipulate it how they may, points in the opposite direction.

Metaphysical Arguments

Most of the arguments traditionally used in apologetics begin with some fundamental reality in the universe and try to show that that reality

---

27. For more on the correlation between epistemology and ethics, see *DKG*, 62–64, 73–75, 108, 149, 248.

28. It is, of course, a bit more complicated than this. See *DKG*, 247–51.

presupposes, implies, or somehow requires God.[29] These are called *meta-physical* arguments, and the most common ones start from purpose, cause, and being itself. Let us consider them in turn.

Purpose: The Teleological Argument

The teleological argument is perhaps the strongest argument of all when it is considered informally, but it has always been one of the weakest when theologians and philosophers have tried to state it formally. Even Immanuel Kant, the most influential modern critic of the proofs for God's existence, found "the starry heavens above" (together with "the moral law within") to be a remarkable testimony to the reality of God. Yes, indeed:

> When I look at your heavens, the work of your fingers,
> the moon and the stars, which you have set in place,
> what is man that you are mindful of him,
> and the son of man that you care for him? (Ps. 8:3–4)

The psalmist probably had only a small bit of our modern understanding of the size and complexity of the universe. We today have so much more reason to admire God's work in the cosmos and to wonder why he should give attention to such tiny beings as ourselves.

We also cannot help but be impressed by the intricacy of the microcreation. The amazing programming of the DNA code, the intricacy and precise balance of the many tiny parts needed to produce sight through the eye—this, too, boggles the mind. The wisdom of it goes far beyond the most sophisticated human technology, and when we see that this kind of wisdom is spread through all the molecules and atoms in the billions of stars throughout this immense universe, we begin to get a sense (albeit a very inadequate sense) of the Creator-creature distinction. Evolution? Well, as I noted earlier, many are critical of evolution today, and the Word

---

29. In my view, there is no logical difference between presuppositions and conclusions. In a logical argument, belief in the premises commits (obligates!) you to belief in the conclusion; it also obligates you to believe in what the premises presuppose. Logically, then, presuppositions are one kind of conclusion. Psychologically, however, there is a greater difference. We believe the presuppositions of a premise more firmly than we believe the premises themselves, and the presuppositions serve as criteria for evaluating the premises. These facts are not true of nonpresuppositional conclusions. To tell the difference between someone's presuppositions and his nonpresuppositional conclusions, we must either hear that person's own testimony or else have a divine insight into his heart. So for the most part, we don't have this information. But we can still exhort one another to presuppose what we ought to presuppose. Once again, we see that a legitimate presuppositionalism is essentially "presuppositionalism of the heart."

of God denies in decisive terms the evolution at least of man (Gen. 2:7).[30] The fact that the ability to see requires the independent development of all sorts of organs and powers and their eventual cooperation toward the production of sight makes it difficult indeed to suppose that the process happened "naturally," either by natural selection or by random mutation. Indeed, many evolutionists, recognizing the great complexity and remarkable achievement of evolution itself (assuming it to be true), have posited a divine origin for it.

All of this is teleological reasoning. As Thomas Aquinas put it, when we see unintelligent things (atoms, matter, energy) working together for a purpose, we generally attribute that to an intelligent designer. *Teleological* means "pertaining to purpose or goal."

Intuitively, we feel the power of such thinking. But how do we formulate it into an argument?[31] Historically, most such attempts have been unsuccessful. There is, for one thing, counterevidence for design, sometimes called *dysteleology.* The existence of evil is the strongest piece of counterevidence (we will discuss that in a later chapter). For another thing, David Hume proposed alternative explanations for the order of the world: polytheism and organism (i.e., the world is like a giant vegetable rather than a designed piece of machinery). And Hume also objected that to posit a designer of the world is to go beyond our experience: we have seen watches designed and manufactured, but we have never seen a world designed and made.[32]

Even on Christian presuppositions (Hume's, of course, were not Christian), one may object to the teleological argument. For to say that the world looks like something "designed" is to state an analogy between the world

30. I also take Genesis 1 to indicate that there are certain divisions among living things, called "kinds" in the text (which are not necessarily equivalent to the "species" identified in modern biology), which can never be transgressed by the process of natural selection: each creature reproduces only "after its kind." And even Darwin recognized that the evidence from geology and biology is consistent with this picture. Far from there being a continuum of creatures between one general type and another, as one would expect on the evolutionary hypothesis, there are distinct types that reproduce within clear genetic limits.

31. Notice again (as I emphasized in the previous chapter) the important difference between evidence and argument. The evidence is powerful, the arguments not necessarily so. In this case, the distinction is especially plausible. For the intuition lying behind the teleological argument incorporates a vast amount of data. The macrocreation, the microcreation, and the world in which we normally function are all huge. Intuitively, the mind is impressed with the sheer vastness of the design, the myriads of details we observe. We could never begin to formulate all these details in a formal argument or group of formal arguments. This is one reason, at least, why the intuitive teleological argument has been far more admired than the formal, logical version of it. As Pascal said, "The heart has its reasons that reason cannot know."

32. See David Hume, *Dialogues concerning Natural Religion* (various eds.).

and objects designed by human beings. But we are not interested in show-ing that the world was made by human beings! We want to show that it was made by One who radically transcends human beings. A perfect analogy between the world and objects of human design would actually be counter-productive to Christian apologetics; if anything, it would prove that man, rather than God, created the world.

A naive teleological argument may in this way be counterproductive to the Christian's case, but some of Hume's objections are actually produc-tive. If the world is designed and made by God, then we would expect both analogy and disanalogy between the world and the products of human design. On a Christian view, the world is something like an object of human design, because it is designed; but it is also unlike such objects, because it is a product of divine design. Thus, dysteleology[33] actually favors the Christian conclusion; even the existence of evil can be listed among the evidences for Christianity! The evidence—both apparent teleology and apparent dyste-leology—is what we would expect if the world was planned and made by a transcendent God. The same thing is true for the disproportion between the making of watches and the making of the world. Of course, we did not see the world made; if we had, we would have been God. That disproportion is precisely what we would expect on the theistic hypothesis.

But once we grant all this, do we still have an argument? Granting that teleology and apparent dysteleology are both compatible with Chris-tian theism, can we then argue: "Both teleology and apparent dysteleology exist; therefore, God exists"? I do not find that argument persuasive! And then Hume reminds us of his alternative explanations of the world order, and it becomes hard to show that the evidence points exclusively to God. Is there, then, any way to capture the powerful intuitive force of teleological reasoning in the form of an argument that is not subject to such objections?

In my view, we can do this simply by making the teleological argument equivalent to the epistemological argument that we considered earlier. The two arguments share the teleological intuition. Like the teleological argu-ment, the epistemological argument begins with the observation that the universe is a rational order, accessible to the human mind. When presenting the epistemological argument, I stated this point in general terms, while in presenting the teleological, I followed the usual procedure of including some specific illustrations. But in both cases, the fundamental point is the

33. I prefer to call it *apparent dysteleology*, because ultimately everything does exist for God's purposes (Rom. 8:28).

same. Still, there is one advantage in the epistemological formulation: it is built on the premise that truth and rationality are moral values. Thus, the epistemological argument was reduced, in turn, to the moral argument, and the two arguments yielded the same theistic conclusion.[34]

In the teleological argument as well, it makes a difference when we are able to see truth and rationality as moral virtues. Our ability to distinguish between apparent teleology and apparent dysteleology, and our ability to speak intelligibly about the limits of our knowledge and about alternative explanations for data, implies that we have (or think we have) access to criteria by which to resolve questions of this sort. Ultimately, then, we have access to the values of rationality and truth. And if these are indeed moral values, where does their authority come from? Once again we must answer: from the absolute personality, the biblical God.

The essential antithesis discussed earlier between the two worldviews, absolute personality versus ultimate impersonality, eliminates consideration of Hume's alternative explanations. They all boil down to the impersonalist alternative. Even Hume's polytheistic suggestion boils down to

---

34. Greg Bahnsen once critiqued my approach to the traditional arguments on the ground that—wittingly or unwittingly—I "presuppositionalized" them. See Bahnsen's *An Answer to Frame's Critique of Van Til: Profound Differences between the Traditional and Presuppositional Methods* (Willow Grove, PA: Kirkland Printing, 1988). The arguments found in the first edition of this book, Bahnsen argued, are subtly reformulated in accordance with Reformed and Van Tillian convictions. There may be something to this claim. Whereas Van Til "reduced" all theistic argument to the transcendental argument (or, as he called it, the argument from the possibility of predication), I explicitly reduce them to the moral argument. In doing so, I make them more explicitly personalistic. The two payoffs to this "reduction" are that it naturally leads to (1) the distinctives of presuppositionalism (heart-commitments, antithesis, common grace, etc.), and, more importantly, (2) the gospel of the Lord Jesus Christ. The moral argument highlights the fact that not only is there an absolute personal basis and standard for ethical norms, but also we are naturally in contact with this personal absolute by way of our creational constitution. The argument also underscores that humans failed to live up to the moral standard that they themselves approve. In turn, this moral failure implies their alienation from God. But this alienation should not be understood as the result of something equivalent to an innocent error in moral calculus. Humanity is at odds with its Maker, and this hostility permeates all of life (including what we will accept as rational or irrational). This personal (and therefore covenantal) relationship can be mended only by the initiative of God.

My motivation is the Reformed conviction that all of life is lived *coram Deo*. God himself is man's most fundamental context. *Christian* apologists should never leave the personal relationship that the non-Christian already has with God too far behind in their discussions. All of this brings apologetics and evangelism close together. This is different from much of the apologetic tradition, in which God is posited as the metaphysical ground for causality, design, or ethics. That is certainly true, but the tradition has had difficulty integrating these apparent philosophical abstractions with the ethical call to repentance in response to the Christian gospel. Our relationship to our Creator is both metaphysical and ethical. Evangelism and apologetics are both perspectives on the one endeavor of faithful Christian witness.

impersonalism, unless the plural deities are themselves products of the absolutely personal God. For only one being can be the ultimate warrant for moral and epistemological values.

Cause: The Cosmological Argument

The cosmological argument is somewhat broader than the teleological. For while the teleological focuses on one phenomenon within the world (that of purpose or design), the cosmological asserts that *every* finite reality, whether it appears to be designed or not, must be dependent on an infinite God, simply because of its finitude. There are many kinds of cosmological arguments. Thomas Aquinas's *Summa Theologica* lists five proofs, three of which are generally regarded as cosmological.[35] The first is an argument from motion: every motion is caused by a previous motion, a process that ultimately requires an "unmoved mover." The second is an argument from cause: every effect is caused by something else; the whole process requires a "first cause" or "uncaused cause." The third is an argument based on necessity and contingency: not everything can be contingent; somewhere there must be something that exists necessarily.[36] A summary of these arguments looks like this:

Argument From . . .	Requires . . .
Motion	Unmoved Mover
Causation	Uncaused Cause
Contingency	Necessary Being

I will consider here only the argument from cause, which is the clearest and the most intuitively cogent. The *Kalam* argument of Al-Ghazali, recently expounded by William Lane Craig, denies that there can be an actually infinite series of events succeeding one another in time. Therefore, the

35. The fifth is teleological, the fourth hard to classify. I think it is based on the notion that the criterion for X must be maximally X. My epistemological and moral arguments also make the case that values require criteria and that the only adequate criterion is the absolute personal God.

36. Something "exists necessarily" if it cannot fail to exist. Something "exists contingently" if it can fail to exist. Whether or not something contingent exists depends on factors outside itself. Therefore, "contingent existence" (such as ours) is "dependent existence." Necessary existence is aseity or self-existence.

universe had a beginning, which must be explained by a divine cause. The Thomistic-Aristotelian form seeks to prove that there is a present (or perhaps supratemporal) reality whose existence is necessary to explain the present phenomenon of causality.[37] My remarks will pertain equally to both forms.

Belief in causes is an aspect of a commitment to reason. Roughly speaking, causes are reasons and reasons are causes.[38] To say that event A has a cause is to say that there is some reason why event A took place.

Those who believe that reason is essentially reliable, and therefore that the universe is susceptible of rational analysis, are attracted to the proposition that all events in the world have causes.[39] To deny that is to claim that some events are irrational happenings. But the rational quest can never remain content with such a claim. If some event took place without a reason, how could reason know it? For example, how could reason prove such a negative as "This event has no cause at all"? To prove that, one would have to assure oneself that all possible causes had been ruled out, and to reach that conclusion would require omniscience.

Further, the nature of reason is to inquire after causes. And if reason does not find a cause, it does not conclude that there is no cause; rather, it looks further—or else it sets the problem aside for future investigation.[40] Of course, there must be one exception to this rule. Once reason finds what it regards as the complete cause, the final and ultimate explanation for the phenomenon under consideration, then it must cease its inquiry. I will later claim that such completeness can be found in God. But rational people do not find such completeness in the creation as such.

Those who claim that some events in the world are uncaused are to that extent irrationalists. Like all irrationalists, they run into problems when they try to argue their case rationally! For there is no way to prove rationally

37. Thomas's proof, therefore, is compatible with the assertion that the world has no begin-ning in time. Yet he also maintains a temporal origin of the world on the basis of faith, apart from "reason."

38. I say "roughly," because there are many different kinds of reasons and many different kinds of causes, and they do not all correlate neatly. For example, I am comfortable with say-ing that God's actions have reasons (reasons lying within his own wisdom), but not that God's actions have causes, because a cause would normally be understood as something outside of God (although *cause* does not necessarily mean that).

39. I have stated this proposition, which is in effect the first premise of the argument, with some care. I would, of course, deny that God's existence has a cause, and I exclude that claim by adding the phrase "in the world" to my opening formulation.

40. Occasionally, scientists will claim that some event is causeless: for example, movements of some subatomic particles, the "big bang." But in my view, this claim can be only temporary. Eventually, either these theories will be abandoned or else some tireless scientist will renew the search for causes in these areas.

(apart, of course, from divine revelation) that any particular event in the world is causeless. And if some event was causeless, how could it have happened? From nothing, nothing comes, as the saying goes. Furthermore, if one event in the world lacks a cause, then the world as a whole lacks a cause. And if the world as a whole is without reason, then irrationalism triumphs.

The irrationalism that denies causation at some point in the world process is not so much a reasoned position as a failure of nerve. The irrationalist fails to find a cause here, there, or somewhere else, so he despairs and says there is none. But what gives him the right to make such a dogmatic assumption? Paradoxically, an element of rationalism enters here, for the irrationalist at this stage is so impressed with the authority of his own autonomous thought that he thinks that if he and others haven't found a cause of the event in question, there can be no cause.

Of course, as we saw earlier, an irrationalist can always justify himself by saying that to him rationality, logic, and moral value do not matter. To such a view, our reply is the same as before.

Nevertheless, granted the extent to which irrationalism has penetrated the thinking of our time, it is not surprising that the cosmological argument has often been disparaged. Indeed, the concept of cause itself has been revamped (e.g., by Hume and Kant),[41] so that while it may be said that everything has a cause, those causes cannot imply any conclusions about what was, is, or will be the case. Such concepts, however, fail to do justice to our basic intuition about cause, namely, that cause gives a reason why things happen.

Once that intuition is honored and irrationalism is excluded, the cosmological argument can make some progress. That every event in the world has a cause means that everything in the world happens for some reason. But suppose that there is no first cause, no uncaused cause, at the beginning of the process. In that case, there is no complete explanation, no complete reason, why any event takes place. If there is no first cause, the process of explanation keeps going on and on—an infinite regression for which there is no ending point. But if there is no end, then there is no "cognitive rest" (as I described it in *DKG*[42]). You just keep going on and on, from one partial reason to another, and your quest never ends. You never reach the complete reason that you set out to find. Thus, in the end irrationalism wins out. There is no final explanation for anything.

41. For Hume, causality is the frequent (but coincidental) accompaniment of one event by another. For Kant, it is a structure that the mind imposes on events.
42. *DKG*, 152–62.

The non-Christian rationalist is here in a quandary, for his motivations press him in two directions simultaneously. On the one hand, he wants to affirm that there *are* complete explanations of events; therefore, he wants to honor a first cause. On the other hand, if the rationalist honors the first cause, he will have to cease his rational quest and submit his mind to the conclusion implicit in the first cause. But he does not want to cease his rational quest. He wants always to have the privilege of asking why. But if he denies the possibility of a first cause, he becomes indistinguishable from the irrationalists.[43]

So in the end we are forced to choose between belief in a first cause and irrationalism. Irrationalism, as I pointed out earlier, is self-contradictory ("It is objectively true that there are no objective truths"). That leaves the cosmological argument in a strong position indeed.

Nevertheless, one might well ask: if it is possible for God to be self-existent and self-explanatory, causeless, and an ultimate reason, why can't the world be, too? If we may end our causal inquiry with God, why not stop with the world and be done with it? Well, the answer is that the world is not self-existent and self-explanatory; it is not causeless; it is not an ultimate reason.[44] We know this by the reasoning of our moral and epistemological arguments. The ultimate source of moral norms, of the norms of thought and logic, is personal, not impersonal. But if God is the ultimate source of these norms, then he is also the ultimate source of the world. The material world is not something separate from the rational and moral order. That order is the order of the material world. The ultimate source of rationality is the ultimate reason for everything, as we saw earlier. And "everything" includes the material aspect, as much as the moral and rational aspects, of the universe.

Notice, however, that in the final analysis the cosmological argument is epistemological in character. The question about rational causes is really the same as the question about rational order. It shows how, if we assume that the world is rational, we must assume that God is the author of reason. The point, as in our earlier epistemological argument, is that reason is covenantal. The search for causes and reasons will be self-defeating unless it is willing to rest ultimately in God.

---

43. Recall that we earlier found rationalism in the irrationalists; here we find rationalism reverting to irrationalism. From this we can observe that the two positions are not substantially opposed; they are only two emphases, two "perspectives," within the "conventional wisdom."

44. This is both taught in Scripture and corroborated by scientific evidence such as the second law of thermodynamics (the law of entropy) and big-bang cosmology.

Being: The Ontological Argument

The ontological argument is in some ways the most fascinating—and exasperating—of all the classical arguments. It can be presented as a sort of "find the fallacy" parlor game,[45] or it can be presented, as Anselm of Canterbury did, in a prayer of profound Christian devotion. To some it is a joke, to others the very foundation of reason and faith.

Of the greatest philosophical and theological minds down to the present, some have despised it, others have honored it. Parmenides, Plato, and Augustine used reasoning that prefigures the ontological argument in some ways. Anselm of Canterbury provided the most influential formulation of the argument itself. Aquinas rejected it, but Descartes, Spinoza, and Leibniz all accepted various versions of it. Jonathan Edwards (followed by *Classical Apologetics*) used a Parmenidean form of it that verges on a pantheistic conclusion. Kant developed an influential refutation, but that did not stop Hegel and his disciples from, some would say, building their whole philosophies around it. Most twentieth-century philosophers, such as G. E. Moore, Bertrand Russell, Jean-Paul Sartre, Antony Flew, Kai Nielsen, and J. L. Mackie, reject the proof, but many highly competent and distinguished philosophers have accepted versions of it, such as Norman Malcolm, Alvin Plantinga, and Nicholas Rescher. Process philosophers such as Charles Hartshorne place great weight on the ontological proof, but their version of it concludes with a process god, one very different from the orthodox God of Anselm.

Simplifying a few matters, we can formulate the ontological argument as follows:

- Premise 1: God has all perfections.[46]
- Premise 2: Existence is a perfection.[47]
- Conclusion: Therefore, God exists.[48]

The earliest critic of this proof was the monk Gaunilo, whose remarks Anselm graciously included in his own book, with a response by Anselm himself. Gaunilo said that this argument could prove not only a perfect being

---

45. I recall a party in my high school days where someone brought in a mathematical proof that 1 = 2 and dared us all to find the error in it. The error turned out to be a concealed division by zero. But the fallacy in the ontological argument, if such there be, is not at all easy to locate.

46. Anselm: God is "that than which no greater can be conceived."

47. Or, as in some formulations, "Necessary existence is a perfection."

48. Or "God exists necessarily."

such as God, but a perfect anything. For example, one could argue that a perfect island would have all perfections, and since existence is a perfection, the perfect island must exist. Anselm, however, replied in effect that a perfect island does not have all perfections. It is, after all, only an island, and therefore has only those perfections proper to islands. The ontological argument will therefore work in only one case, the case of a perfect being who has all perfections in limitless measure.

Others have objected that this proof makes a (quasi-Platonic) jump from "concept" to "reality." It says that since our concept of God includes his existence, he must exist in reality; but that does not follow. Plato, to be sure, thought that our concepts are recollections of the ultimate forms of things and therefore that all our concepts, especially those of ultimates, have correlates in the "world of forms." We know that Augustine and Anselm were both heavily influenced by Plato, and perhaps Plato is the ultimate source of their argument. But modern thinkers do not find Plato's speculations about forms to be cogent, and therefore we should not suppose that our ideas have correlates in reality.

But on the other hand, is it possible that none of our concepts correlates with objective reality? Such a view would be skepticism. To avoid that (and we have given reasons why skepticism, or irrationalism, is not an acceptable option), we must accept the fact that at least some of our mental concepts correspond to realities in the world. But which ones? Surely at least those that conceptualize ultimate criteria. For as we have seen, all thinking presupposes such criteria. And surely we must also presuppose the objective reality corresponding to our concept of the ultimate source of such criteria. Christians believe that that source is God. Others may believe that that source is something else.

Despite Plato's rather mythological presentation of his view, I think the paragraph above represents his actual rationale for the world of forms. Human thought presupposes criteria, he thought, which cannot be simply derived from sense-experience. Our idea of a perfect triangle is not derived from any specific object of the senses, but it must correspond to *something* real, or else it would not be useful as a criterion. The same is true for the forms of blue, red, courage, wisdom, humanity, and that "highest form," goodness. Plato's reasoning here is a kind of moral argument, like the one I proposed earlier. He concludes not to God, but to a plurality of impersonal forms, but we have seen that the source of moral values must be both one and personal.

So Anselm says that our concept of the source of all perfection, the being who has all perfections, must be objective, not merely a figment of our own thinking. Even if Anselm is under the influence of Plato here, I cannot deny the cogency of his basic reasoning. But this argument, like the others, is reducible to my earlier argument from moral values.

Of course, there are other objections to the argument. Immanuel Kant thought Anselm misunderstood the nature of existence, by treating it as a perfection of God. In Kant's view, existence is not a perfection, not even a property. It is not, indeed, a "real" predicate, though it can occupy the predicate position in a sentence such as "God exists." For existence, Kant said, doesn't add anything to our concept of something. True, when one defines a cocker spaniel, the fact that cocker spaniels exist is not usually part of the definition. And when I describe the Taj Mahal, I would probably not go out of my way to state that it exists. As Kant puts it, "a hundred real dollars do not contain a penny more than a hundred possible dollars."[49] So Kant thinks Anselm has erred by making existence one of God's attributes or properties.

But Kant admits that his financial position is better with real dollars than with possible ones. And we know that a real car is different from an imaginary one, and that a real unicorn, if it existed, would be different from an imaginary one. Clearly, one would not adequately define *phoenix* (to people who know nothing of it) without a predicate such as *fictional* or *mythical*, predicates that imply nonexistence. Existence is therefore different from other properties and predicates in some ways, but not in the sense that it makes no difference to the objects that have it. I know the difference, for example, between Secretariat and Black Beauty. Thus it seems that Kant's objection to the ontological argument fails, though it has generated and continues to generate much discussion.

Now let us turn to the last difficulty with this argument. The term *perfection*, as used in the argument, is fairly slippery. It presupposes an already known system of values. What is perfect to a Christian might not be perfect, for example, to a philosophical naturalist. Is existence a perfection, as the argument implies? Well, it is not a perfection in Buddhism, where Nirvana is explained as a form of "nothingness" and life is disparaged as "suffering." It is a perfection in Christianity, where God saw all that he had made and declared everything to be "good" (Gen. 1:31; cf. 1 Tim. 4:4).

In other words, the ontological argument proves the biblical God only if it presupposes distinctively Christian values and a Christian view

---

49. Immanuel Kant, *Critique of Pure Reason*, abr., ed., trans., and with an introduction by Norman Kemp Smith (New York: Random House, 1958), 282.

of existence. Substitute other values and you change the conclusion. This is why the ontological argument has been used to defend so many different kinds of God: polytheistic (Plato), pantheistic (Parmenides, Spinoza, Hegel), process (Hartshorne), monadic (Leibniz), and Christian (Anselm, Plantinga).

Remarkably, the prayer in which Anselm formulates his argument identifies him as a sort of Christian presuppositionalist. He indicates that he is not really in doubt as to God's existence, but that he is seeking a simple way to prove the God whom his heart "believes and loves." He seeks "not to understand, that I may believe, but to believe, that I might understand" (*credo ut intelligam*). Faith here is the basis for understanding, rather than the product of it. Indeed, even Anselm's reply to Gaunilo is an attempt to address not the unbeliever whom Gaunilo represents, but the Catholic whom Gaunilo is. And it is essentially an appeal to Gaunilo's "faith and conscience." Have we not found here another "presuppositionalist of the heart"?

My conclusion is that either the ontological argument is a Christian presuppositional argument (and thus is reducible to our earlier moral argument) or it is worth nothing.

6

APOLOGETICS AS PROOF: PROVING THE GOSPEL

Proving the truth of a historical narrative (such as the gospel, as presented in 1 Corinthians 15:1–11) is rather different from proving the truth of a general worldview. In the latter case, we can deal with common features of our experience, such as values, truth, cause, and purpose. But in the former, we are pretty much restricted to evidence relating to a historical period in the distant past. The primary sources are the Scriptures themselves. Extra-biblical sources confirm what the early Christians believed, but they do not add much to the biblical testimony concerning the events themselves.

While the existence and many attributes of God are "clearly perceived" in the creation (Rom. 1:18–20), the gospel message is not visible in the world as such. A preacher is needed to communicate the gospel (10:14–15).

This does not mean, of course, that we must simply accept the biblical account on blind faith. Scripture itself argues for its contentions; it presents what we have earlier called a *rationale*. It presents evidence for the truth of its message.

So our main task is to isolate the Bible's own argument for the truth of the gospel message. That argument is both explicit (as when Paul says that the risen Christ was witnessed by some five hundred people at once, 1 Cor. 15:6) and implicit (as when scholars trace the textual history of 1 Corinthians 15:1ff. back to an account written or presented orally only a few years after the resurrection). That is to say, sometimes Scripture provides an actual verbal argument for elements of the gospel; sometimes it simply states these elements, but in such a way and under such conditions that the reader finds the statement persuasive.

Our starting point must be the Christian worldview itself, as we have discussed it in previous chapters. We have seen that God exists as an absolute person and, to quote answer 4 of the Westminster Shorter Catechism, as "a Spirit, infinite, eternal, and unchangeable, in his being, wisdom, power, holiness, justice, goodness, and truth." I argued in chapter 2 that this conception presupposes a distinction, not a continuum, between God and the world, with God as absolute sovereign. Although I have perhaps not argued the doctrine of the Trinity,[1] I have tried to show that that doctrine reinforces the other elements of the Christian doctrine of God, while denial of the Trinity leads to the distortion and compromise of those elements.

I have also argued that absolute-personality theism is found mainly in the biblical tradition. Certainly, of all the major religious movements, only those influenced by Scripture conceive of God as absolute personality. Now, if our previous arguments are correct, and the world is created and governed by an absolute personality, this fact creates an immense presumption in favor of the biblical tradition. If the absolute personality cares about human behavior (and our moral argument implies that he does), we would expect him to present his case to man somewhere. Further, since God speaks clearly and expects us to hear and obey, we would not expect the location of that case to be obscure or to be debatable among God's people. But the Bible is the only major religious book that claims to fulfill that expectation, that claims to be the place where God presents his case to man. If God's speech has an obvious location, that location must be the Holy Scriptures. There simply is no other candidate.[2]

Inquirers, then, may be glad to know that the real issue is between biblical religion and "conventional wisdom." One does not need to study every world religion and philosophy thoroughly. Only two are of any impor-

---

1. It is common for theologians to say that the doctrine of the Trinity is known only through special, not natural, revelation. I don't know, however, of any scriptural reason to exclude the Trinity from natural revelation, and I have presented some reasons to suppose that a study of nature itself favors a Trinitarian conception of God. I would not, of course, claim to have presented absolutely certain proof! But if a proof for the existence of God allows for the possibility of a unitarian God, the question arises as to the sense in which it proves distinctively *Christian* theism. Interestingly, even Thomas Aquinas, who insists that the Trinity is known only from special revelation, nevertheless produces proofs from the nature of knowledge and love that, if sound, would have to be described as natural-theology proofs of the Trinity.

2. Recall that in past chapters we have judged the claims of Islam, those of modern Judaism, and in effect those of the Roman Catholic hierarchy, as well as the latter-day prophecies of the Mormons, Seventh-day Adventists, Christian Science, and others, as being dependent on the Bible and yet distortions of the biblical message. It would, of course, take a much longer book to debate those issues in detail.

tance. As Scripture puts it, we are faced with a choice between the wisdom of God and the wisdom of the world (1 Cor. 1:18–2:16).

In that sense, then, our theistic arguments have already settled the truth of the gospel, the total message of Scripture. Since there is no other logical candidate for a source of God's words, we must hear and obey that message.

I realize, of course, that this argument will not carry much weight with some people. It doesn't rule out every possibility that God's message to man might not exist, or that it might be found somewhere else. Therefore, I intend to continue bearing the burden of proof as we consider the claims of Scripture. To people who understand the full implications of my case for theism, the following argumentation is "gravy"—not strictly necessary, but useful. To others, it will be of some importance.

The reader here may profitably review the exposition in chapter 2 of the biblical "good news." To summarize: Scripture tells us of our creation in God's image, our fall (through Adam) into sin, and God's free gift of his only Son to die an atoning death for our sin and to raise us up with him in newness of life.

Scripture's Doctrine of Scripture

Why should we believe this? Essentially, because God has told us so in the Bible! The old song is right:

> Jesus loves me, this I know,
>> For the Bible tells me so.

The Bible presents us with a doctrine of the Bible. The Bible itself is not merely an incidental human record of Jewish history and early Christianity; rather, the Bible is God's self-witness. It is God speaking to us. Therefore, the doctrine of Scripture is part of the good news; Scripture itself is one element in the saving message. And the doctrine of Scripture is not found only in a few texts of the Bible. Rather, it pervades the Scriptures. God is very much concerned not only that we believe in Christ, but also that we believe the Word that tells us about Christ, the very Word of God. God has given us not only salvation in Christ, but also a wonderfully simple way to know about that salvation.

As Scripture describes its own status and presents its self-witness, we come to see an important part of the scriptural rationale for the gospel message. If we find Scripture's self-description to be credible, then at the same time, we will find the message of Scripture to be credible.

Crass as it might sound to modern religious speculators, it is evident from biblical history that God intends to rule his church through a book. God's church is to have a written constitution.

When God brings the Israelites out of Egypt and meets them as they are gathered around Mount Sinai, he adopts them as his people (Ex. 19). There he declares to them the "Mosaic covenant," which promises God's gracious blessings to them and requires their obedience. *Covenant* is a literary form of the ancient Near East, sometimes called the *suzerainty treaty*, instances of which have been found outside the Bible. In the suzerainty treaty, a great king imposes on a lesser king the status of a servant-ally. In the literary form of the treaty, the great king speaks as the author. He begins by giving his name. Then, in a historical prologue, he explains how he has helped the servant-king in the past. He then sets forth his law, the obligations of which the servant must perform. Then come the sanctions: blessings on the servant if he obeys, and curses if he disobeys. The treaty concludes with procedural details: dynastic-succession arrangements, keeping of the treaty documents, provisions for their public reading, and so on.[3] We can see this literary form in the Ten Commandments of Exodus 20,[4] and Meredith Kline has identified other passages (including the entire book of Deuteronomy) that reflect this form.

The written document is not at all peripheral to the covenant. Indeed, being the very provisions of the covenant, it *is* the covenant. To violate the document is to violate the covenant, and vice versa. The covenant is written by the great king and is kept in two copies, one in the sanctuary of the great king, the other in the sanctuary of the servant-king. The document is suited to the holiest places. As the kings revere their gods, they honor the covenant.

Similarly, in the covenant between God and Israel, the covenant document plays a major role. At first, that document includes only the two tables of the Ten Commandments.[5] In that document, God speaks as author, giving his own name in the usual location for the name of the great king. The passage strongly emphasizes God's authorship, for the tables are writ-

---

3. For more details, see Meredith G. Kline, *The Structure of Biblical Authority* (Grand Rapids: Eerdmans, 1972). Kline's work is the most important contribution to the evangelical doctrine of Scripture since Warfield.

4. "I am the LORD your God" (name of suzerain-author), "who brought you out of the land of Egypt, out of the house of slavery" (historical prologue); "You shall have no other gods before me," and so on (laws), "for I the LORD your God am a jealous God," and so on (sanctions).

5. Kline sees the two tables as two copies of the entire Decalogue rather than as one tablet with some commandments and another tablet with the rest. See *Structure of Biblical Authority*, 113–30.

ten by God's own finger[6] (Ex. 24:12; 31:18; 32:15–16; 34:1; see also Ex. 34:32; Deut. 4:13; 9:10–11; 10:2–4).

Later, more such words are added. In Deuteronomy 32, God teaches his people a song, by which they are to remember his mercies and remember to obey him. It is God's song, and Moses writes it down (31:22). It is a song of "witness" (31:19). But it is not (as modern theologians often have it) Israel's witness to God; it is God's witness against Israel (31:19). When the Israelites sin and break the covenant, the song will accuse and convict them.

The entire law is placed in the most sacred place of God, the ark of the covenant, as a witness against the people (Deut. 31:26). It is holy because it is God's own Word. For that reason, no one may add to or subtract from these words (Deut. 4:2; 12:32; cf. Josh. 1:7; Prov. 30:6; Rev. 22:19–20).

From time to time, until Malachi, God adds new words to the canon of Scripture. Prophets have God's word in their mouths (Deut. 18), and many of their prophecies are written down (see, e.g., Isa. 8:1; 30:8ff.; 34:16–17; Jer. 25:13).

Now, if you open the book of Deuteronomy almost at random, you will find passages where God calls the people to heed his "words, commandments, testimonies, ordinances, statutes, laws," and so on (note the eloquent redundancy). What words are these? Evidently, they are the written words of God that Moses has recorded. Psalm 119 and other Old Testament passages speak in reverent terms about God's words. (In Psalm 56:4, 10, the words of God are objects of religious praise.) What words are these? Again, they are God's written words.

Jesus speaks about the written law of the Old Testament in these words:

> Do not think that I have come to abolish the Law or the Prophets; I have not come to abolish them but to fulfill them. For truly, I say to you, until heaven and earth pass away, not an iota, not a dot, will pass from the Law until all is accomplished. Therefore whoever relaxes one of the least of these commandments and teaches others to do the same will be called least in the kingdom of heaven, but whoever does them and teaches them will be called great in the kingdom of heaven. (Matt. 5:17–19)

When Jesus makes belief in Moses the prerequisite to belief in his own word (John 5:45), and when he denies that Scripture should ever be broken (10:33–36), he is adding his witness to the teaching of the written

---

6. The second pair of tables, however, was written by God (Ex. 34:1) through Moses (34:27). Here Moses is the "secretary," but God is no less the author.

old covenant. When Paul speaks of Scripture as being "breathed out by God" (2 Tim. 3:16),[7] and when Peter says that the prophets spoke not by their own will or interpretive faculties, but rather by the Holy Spirit, they are talking about the written Word. To Jesus and the apostles, the whole Old Testament is the covenant document of the people of God.

What of the New Testament? In the nature of the case, it could not talk about itself as a completed collection of writings. Yet it leaves no doubt that God's purpose is to give such a collection to the church.

People sometimes suggest that while the Old Testament presents a religion of authoritative words, the New Testament is more "spiritual" and less focused on verbal revelation. But that is clearly untrue. In the New Testament, Jesus comes teaching God's will. His words are tremendously important, the supreme criterion for discipleship. Meditate on Matthew 7:21–27, 28–29; Mark 8:38; Luke 8:21; 9:26ff.; John 6:63, 68–69; 8:47; 12:27ff.; 14:15, 21, 23–24; 15:7, 10, 14; 17:6, 17; 1 Timothy 6:3; 1 John 2:3–5; 3:22; 5:2–3; 2 John 6; Revelation 12:17; 14:12. Without the words of Jesus, we are lost; without his words, we have no gospel.

The words of the apostles are also enormously important (see Rom. 1:16–17; 2:16; 1 Thess. 4:2; Jude 17ff.), including their written words (see 1 Cor. 14:37; Col. 4:16; 1 Thess. 5:27; 2 Thess. 3:14 [cf. 2:15]; 2 Peter 3:16).

Like the Old, the New Testament records a covenant, the "new covenant in my blood" (1 Cor. 11:25). Covenants in Scripture, as we have seen, are verbal in character.

Thus, it is clear that there are new covenant words for God's people. Without them, Christianity would be meaningless. We may expect, then, that God would place those words where all could find them without too much trouble. And indeed he did.

There was, of course, some controversy in the early church about which books belonged in the New Testament canon. But differences over the canon—unlike other disputes—never divided the church. And when all the books had been thoroughly read throughout the churches of the Roman Empire, and Athanasius of Alexandria had issued in 373 a list of the books accepted in his church as God's Word, there was no dissent. God had made himself known; his sheep had heard his voice; his Spirit had witnessed with the Word to the hearts of his people.

There is a certain prejudice in our time against written words. From some theological writers we get the idea that a written word is less authorita-

---

7. That is, "spoken by God."

tive than the "living voice" of a prophet, and that even the prophet's "living voice" is of lesser authority than the direct voice of God (e.g., as heard at Mount Sinai). Certainly the direct voice of God is more terrifying than the written words of God. But the Scriptures do not know of any distinction in authority whatsoever. The written Word has the same authority as the living prophet, the same as the divine voice. Obeying the written Word is the same as obeying God himself, and despising the written Word is despising God himself. God rules his church by a written constitution, by a book.

Thus it is that God's people gain their assurance of the gospel from the Word of God. How do I know that Jesus died for me? From Scripture. There is no higher authority, no greater ground of certainty—though of course the Holy Spirit enables us to believe, understand, and use the Scriptures rightly. The truth of Scripture is a presupposition for God's people.

Are we back to blind faith or narrow circularity? Not really. Those who have followed my argument so far understand that we have sought to justify an enormous presumption in favor of the biblical religious tradition, the only such tradition to honor a God of absolute personality. I have been emphasizing Scripture in this chapter in order to show the reader two things about that tradition. First, written revelation is not merely a peripheral element in that tradition, but the central constitutional authority. Second, Scripture, as that written constitution, is not merely a product of human thinking, not merely a historical source—rather, it is the Word of God. Therefore, if anyone wishes to follow the tradition of biblical religion, it will not be enough to have a general allegiance to the ideas of that tradition while maintaining the freedom to pick and choose the doctrines that one prefers. Rather, faithfulness to that tradition renounces autonomy and listens faithfully to the wisdom that one finds on the pages of God's book. The true disciple hungers and thirsts for more and more of God's Word; he lives by *every* word of God (Matt. 4:4).

In the traditional apologetic, inquirers are told *not* to presuppose the full authority of Scripture as God's Word until after that authority has been proved by the apologist. They are told, rather, to assume only that the Bible is a generally reliable historical text. In the first place, however, even the general reliability of Scripture is contested by many scholars (see the following section). In the second place, we should never tell inquirers to presuppose less than the truth. In the third place, the Bible's own argument for Christianity (which I am seeking to reproduce) presupposes its own authority in the fullest sense. In the fourth place, I recognize that people have to begin where they are. If one does not believe in biblical authority, he cannot simultaneously presuppose it. There are ways to communicate with someone in this position (cf. the story of Oscar in chapter 1), but it is a defective point of view,[8] and the apologist should never encourage it.

But What about Biblical Criticism?

For those who are not yet willing to confess Christ on the basis of the arguments above, I do have more to add—more about Scripture's own rationale for its teachings. But before we get to that, I must answer one substantial objection to the argument of the previous section.

It is a continual embarrassment to Bible-believing Christians that many professional Bible scholars and theologians, who are (in one respect) in the best position to defend the gospel, are themselves sharply critical of historic Christianity. This was not always the case. Until around 1650, most—including the most famous—theological scholars were staunch defenders of biblical supernaturalism. But then came the Age of Reason, when traditions were jettisoned, human autonomy lauded, and theories honored as much for their newness as for their truth. Rationalists presupposed (without proof) that supernatural events never occur and that the human mind functions best independently of any purported divine revelation. In other words, they adopted the concept of human autonomy. Although some of these people continued to believe in some sort of God, these presuppositions clearly amounted to flat denials of biblical theism. These denials were made not on the basis of Bible study, but before that study even began. These presuppositions were intended to govern the very method of Bible study itself; they were in no way influenced by the actual teaching of Scripture.

This meant that from this point on, in the view of the scholarly establishment, the Bible would have to be studied under nonbiblical assumptions, assumptions that flatly contradicted the teachings of historic Christianity.

Under that presupposition, it was obvious that the Bible had to be treated as any other book—that is, as a book with a merely human origin and merely human authority. Thus developed all sorts of theories about the origins of Bible books and passages, all bereft of any supernatural reference. Jesus was seen not as the Son of God and atoning Savior, but either as a mere teacher of morality or (later) as a misguided apocalyptic visionary. The miracle stories were routinely disbelieved and ascribed to the pious imaginations of the biblical writers.

---

8. Would it be more "politically correct" to say that such a person is "epistemologically challenged"?

Similarly, the Old Testament was carved up into various "sources" and "traditions." The first five books were ascribed to various unknown authors designated J, E, D, P, and sometimes J1, J2, and so on. This was called the "documentary hypothesis." The history of Israel was reconstructed. Genesis 1–11 was relegated to the category of myth, legend, or saga; the stories of Abraham, Isaac, and Jacob were also regarded as unhistorical. Some scholars even denied that there had been an exodus of God's people from the land of Egypt.

Again, these scholars routinely denied the supernatural. The evolutionary hypothesis was not only accepted as opposed to the biblical account of creation, but also used as a framework to determine the course of biblical history. The critics assumed that Israel's original religion was coarse and primitive, the religion of a local god whose chief concern was judgment and vengeance, and that it had developed by an evolutionary pattern into belief in an infinite God of covenant love.

The biblical concept of prophecy, which involves the placing of divine words in the mouth of a human being, and which includes the foretelling of future events, was simply denied as a matter of principle. Passages that appeared to give detailed predictions of future events were dismissed as fraudulent—as actually having been written after the "predicted" events.

This sort of liberal[9] thinking rapidly came to dominate the teaching of the European universities, which had always been overenthusiastic about newness and which had always manifested an intellectual pride that in turn fostered the spirit of autonomy. Later, it affected the churches as well. Some denominations capitulated entirely to liberalism, others resisted to some degree, and still others were created by orthodox people who could not remain in the older denominations that were dominated by liberal thought.

Liberal dominance continues today in most mainline universities, theological seminaries, and denominations. Today teaching is often based on Marxism ("liberation theology") and "process thought" rather than the Spinozistic rationalism and Kantian criticism of past centuries. But it is still antisupernaturalistic and especially opposed to the inerrant authority of Scripture. It continues to claim intellectual autonomy. The most famous scholars (e.g., Rudolf Bultmann, John Hick, the "Jesus Seminar") seem to be those who deny the most biblical teaching.

---

9. I use the word *liberal* to include all theology (including so-called neoorthodoxy) that does not accept the final authority of Scripture. I grant that there are many differences among liberal thinkers, just as there are differences among orthodox thinkers. But we do need some general terms to denote general movements, even though such terms are often disdained as "labels."

As before, these scholars offer no proof that their methodology is superior to that of historic Christian methods of Bible study. Instead, we are dogmatically told that man cannot believe in miraculous occurrences in the age of radios and airplanes. How the radio and the airplane refute, for example, Jesus' feeding of the five thousand is rather unclear. The critics' own belief in their methods is not based on proof in any normal sense. It is a presupposition, as Rudolf Bultmann admitted quite candidly in his famous essay "Is Exegesis without Presuppositions Possible?"[10] And it is a presupposition quite contrary to those of historic Christianity.

There does seem to be a tendency in biblical studies (not always mirrored in systematic theology) for liberal scholars to come to more and more conservative conclusions about the dating, authenticity, and historicity of biblical books. Although liberal scholars in the early nineteenth century routinely denied the accuracy of all biblical narratives relating to events before the time of Moses and insisted that many of the New Testament books came from the mid-second century, archaeological and documentary evidence has forced many scholars to accept the historicity of at least the settings of the patriarchal accounts. And all the New Testament books are now generally admitted to come from the first century. Interestingly, some of the scholars most radical in their theology (Adolf Harnack, John A. T. Robinson) have been most conservative in their historical judgments. Robinson, who propounded a flagrantly unbiblical theology in his infamous book *Honest to God*,[11] returned in a later book to claim that all the New Testament documents might have been written before A.D. 70.[12]

Nevertheless, the basic assumptions of liberalism continue to dominate the theological world. A few brave souls have attempted to cry out, "The emperor has no clothes!" Orthodox scholars such as C. F. Keil, Theodor Zahn, and Ernst Hengstenberg battled liberalism in nineteenth-century Europe, along with such American scholars as William Henry Green, B. B. Warfield, and Robert Dick Wilson. In the next generation, famous critiques of liberal methodology were put forward by J. Gresham Machen,[13] Oswald T. Allis,[14]

10. Rudolf Bultmann, *Existence and Faith*, ed. Schubert M. Ogden (New York: Meridian Books, 1960), 289–96.

11. Philadelphia: Westminster Press, 1963.

12. A. T. Robinson, *Redating the New Testament* (London: SCM Press, 1976).

13. J. Gresham Machen, *Christianity and Liberalism* (Grand Rapids: Eerdmans, 1923); *The Virgin Birth of Christ* (New York: Harper, 1930; Grand Rapids: Baker, 1967); *The Origin of Paul's Religion* (New York: Macmillan, 1921; Grand Rapids: Eerdmans, 1965). These are still very powerful works!

14. Oswald T. Allis, *The Five Books of Moses*, 2nd ed. (Philadelphia: Presbyterian and Reformed, 1949); *The Unity of Isaiah* (Philadelphia: Presbyterian and Reformed, 1950); *The*

and Cyrus Gordon (a Jewish scholar who questioned the documentary hypothesis). Still later, Eta Linnemann, once a disciple of Bultmann, dramatically renounced her great prestige as a German Bible scholar for the greater honor of being a servant of Christ.[15]

I am confident that as the reader studies books such as these with an open mind (and that might require in some a new work of the Spirit!), he will be persuaded that the liberal case has not been made and, indeed, that it is deeply flawed—intellectually, methodologically, and theologically. I have also been influenced in my own thinking by a couple of other writers who present the issues in a more popular, less technical way, though their professional credentials in these fields cannot be questioned. One is *Critique of Religion and Philosophy*,[16] by the philosopher Walter Kaufmann. Unlike the people noted above, Kaufmann is not susceptible of the derogatory epithet *fundamentalist*. In fact, Kaufmann was a strongly anti-Christian writer, and this book is, on the whole, an impassioned and reasoned attack on everything I hold dear. But one of Kaufmann's targets is also one of mine: the so-called higher biblical criticism.[17] His arguments against the documentary hypothesis (J1, J2, etc.) are powerful and bring out brilliantly the absurdity of the whole effort.

The other popular writer is C. S. Lewis, in his essay "Modern Theology and Biblical Criticism."[18] Lewis, too, was not a fundamentalist— unfortunately, he renounced biblical inerrancy. But he was a Christian supernaturalist and wrote some very impressive works of apologetics. Being a professor of early English literature at Oxford University, he was in the business of interpreting and evaluating ancient texts and was therefore able to look at the work of biblical scholars from a fresh, though sympathetic, viewpoint. Lewis says this of the prominent Bible critics: "They seem to me to lack literary judgment, to be imperceptive about the very quality of the texts they are reading."[19] To Bultmann's claim that the personality of Jesus

---

Old Testament: Its Claims and Its Critics (Nutley, NJ: Presbyterian and Reformed, 1972; Grand Rapids: Baker, 1972).

15. See Eta Linnemann, *Historical Criticism of the Bible: Methodology or Ideology?*, trans. Robert W. Yarbrough (Grand Rapids: Baker, 1990).

16. New York: Harper and Brothers, 1958.

17. *Lower criticism* is the determination of the proper biblical text by a study of the ancient manuscripts of Scripture. *Higher criticism* seeks to determine, apart from Scripture's own testimony, the truth of what Scripture claims, especially concerning the authorship, date, and origin of the books. Historic Christianity commends lower criticism and denies higher criticism so defined. The two phrases can, of course, be defined in other ways.

18. C. S. Lewis, *Christian Reflections*, ed. Walter Hooper (Grand Rapids: Eerdmans, 1967), 152–66.

19. Ibid., 154.

was unimportant to Paul and John, Lewis replies, "Through what strange process has this learned German gone in order to make himself blind to what all men except him see?"[20] And then he declares:

> These men ask me to believe they can read between the lines of the old texts; the evidence is their obvious inability to read (in any sense worth discussing) the lines themselves. They claim to see fern-seed and can't see an elephant ten yards away in broad daylight.[21]

Here are some of Lewis's other "bleats," as he called them:

> All theology of the liberal type involves at some point . . . the claim that the real behavior and purpose and teaching of Christ came very rapidly to be misunderstood and misrepresented by his followers, and has been recovered or exhumed only by modern scholars.[22]

> Thirdly, I find in these theologians a constant use of the principle that the miraculous does not occur.[23]

> What forearms me against all these [reconstructions of the "original" settings of biblical texts] is that I have seen it from the other end of the stick. I have watched reviewers reconstructing the genesis of my own books in just this way. . . . My impression is that in the whole of my experience not one of these guesses has on any one point been right; that the method shows a record of 100 per cent failure.[24]

But most biblical and theological scholars still more or less toe the party line established by the seventeenth-century rationalists. If one decides whom to follow by counting the number of recognized experts holding the various views, then one must be a liberal. On the other hand, if one can maintain a healthy skepticism toward conventional wisdom (isn't this what they always told us to do in college?) and a sense of humor about the really absurd nonsense that passes for scholarship in these circles,[25] one might find himself or herself opening up to radically unfashionable approaches.

---

20. Ibid., 156.
21. Ibid., 157.
22. Ibid.
23. Ibid., 158.
24. Ibid., 159–60.
25. My favorite example is the assumption that no saying of Jesus can be accepted as authentic unless it disagrees with the thinking of the early church; otherwise, the church, not Jesus, is

And if one is a Christian—if his or her ultimate loyalty is to Jesus—cannot one muster from that loyalty the courage to stand against even the frail reed of modern biblical scholarship? Many ancient Christians (and some modern ones) have had to do much more—to be burned alive, crucified, or thrown to lions—rather than renounce Christ. If Christ calls us to love God with all our heart, soul, mind, and strength, and to follow Jesus in all our activities, how can we deny to him the small favor of adopting unpopular, but Christian, positions on biblical scholarship? He offers us his own wonderful wisdom in his Word (1 Cor. 2:6ff.). How can we renounce that wisdom for the dry husk of modern fashion, that very unbelieving, yet popular, pseudowisdom that the Lord condemns in 1 Corinthians 1:18–2:5?

And if the reader is still an "inquirer": do not think for a moment that the prevalence of unbelief in the field of biblical scholarship will excuse you from confessing Jesus and the truth of his Word. Unbelief is prevalent in all areas of culture—science, politics, sociology, psychology, and on and on. It should come as no surprise that unbelief sometimes also inundates religion. Jesus indicted the religionists of his own time in the strongest terms. The arguments for true Christianity militate against unbelief in all areas, even when it bears a Christian label, and you should give heed to those arguments, not to the proud speculations of so-called scholarship.

We have seen the Bible's teaching about itself. I have given reasons to reject the approach of the standard biblical criticism. But is Scripture's teaching about itself credible? Consider: (1) No other doctrine is compatible with absolute-personality theism. If God is a person who speaks with absolute authority, then he reveals himself with nothing less than supremely authoritative speech or writing. If God revealed himself in such a way that we could freely criticize his words and believe something else instead, then he would not be the God revealed in Scripture. One does not talk back to the biblical God. His Word has supreme authority. And just as it cannot be disproved by something else of greater authority, so it cannot be proved in such a way. God's Word, like himself, must be supremely authoritative and therefore self-attesting. On the conventional wisdom, the biblical doctrine of Scripture is implausible; but if you presuppose a Christian worldview, no other doctrine of revelation is conceivable. (2) Like all other biblical teachings, the doctrine of Scripture will be credible to you if the Holy Spirit opens your mind to it. Otherwise, it will not be. As we might expect, faith in an

---

assumed to be the author of the saying. How preposterous! Would anyone take such a position concerning any other thinker, such as Luther (and his Lutherans) or Descartes (and his Cartesians)?

absolute personality is a supernatural gift. (3) This doctrine was taught by many different biblical authors, from many different times and settings, with many different strengths and weaknesses. None of them found fault with the Bible; all accepted it as their covenant constitution. (4) Above all, this doctrine was taught by Jesus, by the apostles whom he appointed to communicate his teaching, and by the prophets of the Old Testament, who anticipated his coming. Thus, Scripture is a necessary element in the great drama of redemption. The credibility of that redemption validates the Scriptures, and vice versa.

Scripture's Rationale for the Gospel Message

The Argument from Prophecy[26]

Scripture does not merely claim to be the Word of God. It also presents us with reasons for believing its claims. It presents its claims in a credible way.

In one sense, such credibility is not necessary. God could have put the words "Scripture is the Word of God" in the Bible and then, through the

---

26. The use of arguments for the truth of Scripture based on the fulfillment of Old Testament prophecy has a long and respected history in the apologetic tradition. For example, Justin Martyr, in his *First Apology* (chaps. 32–34), argued that the Old Testament predicted both the manner and place of Christ's birth. Contemporary presentations of this argument make the claim that the sheer number of Old Testament prophetic passages that converge on, and find their fulfillment in, the events of the birth, life, death, and resurrection of Jesus of Nazareth defy statistical probability, the likelihood of which is mathematically impossible apart from the superintending hand of divine providence. So Louis S. Lapides, referencing the work of Peter W. Stoner, claimed that the probability of a single person's fulfilling forty-eight messianic prophecies is "one chance in a trillion, trillion, trillion, trillion, trillion, trillion, trillion, trillion, trillion, trillion, trillion, trillion, trillion." Lee Strobel, *The Case for Christ: A Journalist's Personal Investigation of the Evidence for Jesus* (Grand Rapids: Zondervan, 1998), 183. In its most popular forms, the argument from prophecy fails to distinguish between different kinds of prophecy and different kinds of fulfillment. While it is certainly true that a number of prophecies are uniquely and singularly fulfilled in specific events in the life of Christ, the majority are not. Some Old Testament prophetic statements find their fulfillment in reoccurring cultural circumstances ("Rachel . . . weeping for her children," Jer. 31:15), typological identification ("Out of Egypt I called my son," Hos. 11:1), and even the self-conscious intent of Jesus to carry out prophetic statements (the triumphal entry). Most presentations give the impression that all messianic prophetic statements that find their fulfillment in the New Testament are of the predictive variety. But this is not the case. In fact, predictive prophecy is the *least* frequent category of messianic pronouncement. But the careful reader will observe that I approach the argument from a distinctly Reformed perspective. Here the prophecy argument is presented in terms of Old Testament themes, promises, offices, institutions, and events that find their hermeneutical center in the person and work of Jesus, Israel's Messiah and God incarnate. In the words of Westminster Confession of Faith 7.5, the Old Testament foreshadowed Christ "by promises, prophecies, sacrifices, circumcision, the paschal lamb, and other types and ordinances delivered to the people of the Jews."

persuasive power of the Holy Spirit, supernaturally convinced elect readers of the truth of that statement. But God's way is not to persuade people "magically" of the truth of his Word. The Spirit certainly does persuade, but he persuades us to believe inherently rational content. As in a sermon, it is not enough just to lay the facts before the congregation; one must present those facts winsomely, persuasively, with clarity and order. Otherwise, we have not presented the facts as they really are. So it is with Scripture's own presentation. In other words, the Spirit's work is not to persuade us of something for which there are no rational grounds, but rather to persuade us by illumining the rational grounds that obligate us to believe. Spirit-created faith is not "blind."

Thus, Scripture does not merely give us the bare statement "Jesus Christ is Lord." Rather, it presents Jesus in the context of a rich, complex historical drama. Jesus is the expectation of God's people over a period of several thousand years before his birth. After man's fall in the garden of Eden, God announces to the serpent (Satan):

> I will put enmity between you and the woman,
>   and between your offspring and her offspring;
> he shall bruise your head,
>   and you shall bruise his heel. (Gen. 3:15)

And so God's people began to look for a deliverer, one who would save them from the effects of the fall. He would be human, an "offspring" of the woman (Eve). Yet his victory would be in the supernatural realm: he would crush the head of Satan. And in the process, Satan would wound the deliverer ("bruise his heel").

The child of the promise is often threatened. Over and over again, circumstances arise that threaten to prevent his birth, but the woman's offspring is maintained by God's power. Wicked Cain kills righteous Abel (Gen. 4), the only one through whom the promise can be fulfilled. But God defeats Satan by giving to Eve a third son, Seth (v. 25), and in his time people first gather to worship the Lord (v. 26).

God himself endangers the "seed of promise" by demanding that Abraham sacrifice his son Isaac, the only son of Abraham through whom the promise can come. But as Abraham lifts the knife:

> The angel of the LORD called to him from heaven and said, "Abraham, Abraham!" And he said, "Here am I." He said, "Do not lay your hand on

the boy or do anything to him, for now I know that you fear God, seeing you have not withheld your son, your only son, from me." And Abraham lifted up his eyes and looked, and behold, behind him was a ram, caught in a thicket by his horns. And Abraham went and took the ram and offered it up as a burnt offering instead of his son. So Abraham called the name of that place, "The LORD will provide"; as it is said to this day, "On the mount of the LORD it shall be provided." (Gen. 22:11–14)

Here God teaches his people (1) that there is no higher test of covenant loyalty than to give up one's beloved son for another; (2) that God will preserve the seed of the promise so that it will certainly be fulfilled; (3) that a substitutionary offering is nevertheless necessary (cf. Gen. 22:8); and (4) that God thus provides for his people in all their needs, their greatest being the forgiveness of sins.

In Exodus 12–15, God delivers Israel, his people, from Egypt. In the process, he sends an "angel of death" to kill all the firstborn sons in the land. The families of Israel escape this curse by killing a lamb and placing some of its blood on the doorframes of their homes. When the angel of death sees the blood, he passes over that house and spares it. Here we see that: (1) God again demands a sacrifice. (2) The firstborn son represents his family, taking their fate on himself. Once again the seed of the promise is endangered. (3) Apart from that sacrifice, everyone—even the chosen people of God—deserves death. (4) Only substitutionary blood can avert the wrath of God. (5) That blood must be publicly displayed.

In Exodus 17, after God has delivered Israel from Egypt, the people complain that they have no water. They threaten to stone Moses, the leader, but the real object of their complaint is God himself. The Lord stands before the people (that is, he puts himself in the position of a defendant) by a rock, and at his command, Moses strikes the rock. The Lord symbolically receives the blow, and through the suffering of God, water comes from the rock to bless the people.[27]

It is not only the explicit prophecies of Christ, though there are a great many of them (e.g., Pss. 2; 110:1ff.; Isa. 7:14; 9:6–8; 11:1–16; 35:5ff.; 53; Jer. 31:33ff.; Dan. 9:20–27; Mic. 5:2; Zech. 9:9–12; 12:10; Mal. 3:1–5), that are important. The biblical narratives also lead people to expect a deliverer who can be no one other than Jesus Christ. Narratives fashion the values

27. For these and other remarkable readings from the Old Testament, see Edmund P. Clowney, *The Unfolding Mystery: Discovering Christ in the Old Testament*, 2nd ed. (Phillipsburg, NJ: P&R Publishing, 2013).

of a people. When they think of salvation, they think of a salvation that includes a perfect sacrifice. They expect (if they understand rightly) that God will somehow sacrifice himself in that perfect sacrifice and through it provide blessing. Otherwise, how can the ultimate salvation be greater than that of Exodus 17? And how can it be greater than that of Genesis 22, unless it exhibits a divine love, measured according to the giving of an only Son? How can it be greater than the salvation of Genesis 4, unless it brings together a people to call on God's name?

And though the deliverer is human, how can his mission be anything less than the coming of God himself (Pss. 2:12; 45:6; 110:1ff.; Isa. 42:6ff.; 43:1ff.; 59:15–20; Jonah 2:9)? How can he be tempted less than Adam was? How can his teaching ministry be any less authoritative and profound than that of Moses? How can his healing ministry be anything less than that described in Isaiah 35:5ff.? How can he provide for his people less abundantly than Moses and Elijah did? And if God is to suffer for his people, how can that suffering be less than that described in Psalm 22? There the King of Israel suffers mocking, scorn, and physical pains—a description that amazingly anticipates aspects of crucifixion.

So Israel learns from the Old Testament the nature of man's plight, the sort of sacrifice needed to deal with sin, the sort of suffering that must be involved, the remarkable combination of divinity and humanity required for the work of salvation, the divine self-giving. One would have expected that when Jesus came on the scene, at least after his crucifixion and resurrection, a lot of "pennies would have dropped." Suddenly all the pieces of the puzzle came together in Jesus. Hundreds of prophecies and narratives were involved, all pointing in various ways, from various perspectives, in only one direction—to Jesus. Alas, even the disciples of Jesus were blind to these extraordinary relationships until Jesus instructed them after his resurrection. What instruction that must have been! Suddenly the Scriptures took on a whole new shape, a form both strange and familiar, for there was always the sense of "surely, at some level, we knew this all along." They realized that that was the way the Scriptures *ought* to be interpreted.

The "argument from prophecy," then, is actually an argument from the whole Old Testament (see Luke 24:27; John 1:45; 5:39) and is in reality an appeal to the extraordinarily rational structure of Scripture itself. Here we have a wide variety of human authors, writing across many centuries, with very different interests, concerns, styles, and levels of intellectual sophistication, saying many different things, and yet, at the same time, saying one thing: Jesus is coming, and this is what he will be and do. Does this not indicate something of God's sovereignty over history? Does it not show that the Old Testament is more than an ordinary book? Does it not show some remarkable things about Jesus? Is this not a powerful witness to the Word of God? If you hesitate to agree, then read it and see. And claim the promise of John 7:17, accepting the responsibility that comes with it: "If anyone's will is to do God's will, he will know whether the teaching is from God or whether I am speaking on my own authority."

The New Testament Witness to Christ

Continue your reading into the New Testament, and see how the Old Testament expectation is fulfilled in Jesus. Open your heart to the remarkable person portrayed here: One whose ministry is endorsed by God the Father himself, speaking from heaven (Mark 1:11); One who is faithful to God, despite a more stringent temptation than Adam experienced (Matt. 4); a teacher who speaks with amazing authority (Mark 1:22); One whose power to heal is the power of God's word itself (Luke 7:1–10), and yet who declines to save himself from death (23:35), only to rise again from the dead (24:1ff.)!

Jesus speaks with amazing authority and wisdom, and he also claims to be God! In John 8:58 he takes upon himself the divine name "I am" (cf. Ex. 3:14), which the Jews consider too sacred to pronounce.[28] His relationship to the Father is unique—a sonship unlike that which all believers have with God. He speaks of God as "his own Father" (John 5:18), plainly distinct from the position of his disciples (20:17). He says that it is only through him that anyone else can become a "son" of God (14:6; 17:26). To see him is to see the Father (14:9). The Father has given him all things (Matt. 11:27), including a distinctive knowledge (John 5:26; 17:24). That he makes such claims, even claiming the power to forgive sins (Matt. 9:2–3; Mark 2:7; Luke 5:20–21), leads the Jews to accuse him of blasphemy. And when the high priest charges him with making such a claim, Jesus affirms it (Matt. 26:64). If Jesus' claims were false, he certainly was a blasphemer, and we can well understand why the strongly monotheistic Jews would be quick to accuse any man who claimed to be God. On this matter, they did understand him rightly.

What is perhaps even more amazing, however, is that many Jewish monotheists believed him. The apostle John begins his gospel by identifying Jesus as the powerful Word of God that created the world (Ps. 33:6;

---

28. See also John 18:5–6, where Jesus says "I am" (in the original Greek) and the soldiers coming to arrest him fall to the ground.

John 1:1–3) and then identifies that Word with God. Old Testament passages that speak of the Lord God are quoted by New Testament writers and applied to Jesus (compare Isa. 45:23ff. to Phil. 2:10–11; Isa. 2:10, 19, 21; 66:15 to 2 Thess. 1:7–9; Ps. 102:25–27 to Heb. 1:10–12). Jesus does everything that only God does in the Old Testament: he creates (John 1:3; Col. 1:16–17; Heb. 1:2), initiates a covenant (1 Cor. 11:25), controls the course of nature and history (Heb. 1:3), forgives sins (Isa. 43:25; 44:22; Mark 2:7; etc.), and saves his people (Isa. 40:3; 41:14; 43:25ff.; 45:21; 46:13; Titus 2:13). New Testament writers almost "casually" place Jesus on the side of God when they contrast God and man (see Gal. 1:1, 10, 12).

How could these Jews believe such a startling claim, one that apparently contradicted the monotheistic foundation of their early religious training?[29] Well, when Jesus taught the Scriptures to his disciples, they evidently saw that the day of salvation would be simultaneously a coming of the Lord and the coming of a human Messiah. Mysterious passages of Scripture that equated the Messiah with God (e.g., Pss. 2; 45:6; 110:1ff.) suddenly came to light. When they were compared with Jesus himself—his power, his authority, his saving love, his resurrection glory—the conclusion was inescapable. Jesus was God! In John 1:18 (the reading "only God"); 20:28; Acts 20:28; Romans 9:5; 2 Thessalonians 1:12; Titus 2:13; 2 Peter 1:1; 1 John 5:20, the Greek term *theos*, meaning "God," refers to Christ. Philippians 2:6ff. and Colossians 2:9 are perhaps even clearer in their testimony to Jesus' deity.

The personal impression made by Jesus on his disciples must have been entirely unprecedented. His words were quite different from those of any other teacher: "The crowds were astonished at his teaching, for he was teaching them as one who had authority, and not as their scribes" (Matt. 7:28–29). Peter knew he could find no one with words like those of Jesus: "Lord, to whom shall we go? You have the words of eternal life" (John 6:68). And perhaps even more amazingly, people who knew Jesus intimately were convinced that he had never done wrong. Peter referred to him as the One who "committed no sin, neither was deceit found in his mouth" (1 Peter 2:22). John, also a disciple, said, "You know that he appeared [in order] to take away sins, and in him there is no sin" (1 John 3:5).[30] To be a fit sacrifice,

29. Of course, the doctrine of the Trinity, as we have seen, does not compromise monotheism, but fulfills it. When the New Testament emphasizes monotheism, it also mentions more than one Trinitarian person (1 Cor. 8:5–6; Eph. 4:3–6). But a monotheist looking at this doctrine for the first time is more than likely in for a shock. And in the New Testament, many of those monotheists become avid opponents of Jesus. But amazingly enough, some of them believe.

30. Cf. Acts 3:14; 2 Cor. 5:21; Heb. 4:15; 7:26.

the Passover lamb of the Old Testament had to be perfect, without defect (Ex. 12:5). Jesus was the perfect Lamb of God, who takes away the sins of the world (John 1:29).

This concept of a perfectly sinless man is unique not only to our experience, but also to biblical history. Scripture does not idealize the great men among God's people. Though recognizing many as heroes of the faith (Heb. 11), Scripture presents their flaws: Abraham's cowardly deception, Moses' disobedience, David's adultery and murder, Solomon's harem, the wretched behavior of most of the kings of Israel and Judah. But of Jesus, the central figure, there is no critique. His sinlessness became proverbial in the early church. Coming from such witnesses, is that testimony not credible?

Miracle and Resurrection

Throughout Scripture, God does wonderful works so that people will know that he is the Lord (Ex. 6:7; 7:5, 17; 8:22; 9:14; 10:2; 11:7; 14:4, 18; 16:12; 29:46; etc.). This is a pervasive theme in the Old Testament. Miracles, therefore, constitute evidence of God's reality and of his nature and will as Lord. Thus, apologists have regularly appealed to biblical miracles to confirm the truth of Christianity. Yet there are some problems with relying too heavily on the miraculous for a persuasive apologetic. In the first place, few of us today would claim to have seen a miracle. What we find in Scripture are not miracles as such, but miracle stories and testimony concerning miracles. Second, Scripture warns us against putting too much confidence in miracles to convert unbelieving hearts. In Jesus' story of the rich man and Lazarus, the rich man in hell asks for someone of the dead to be sent back to tell the truth to his five brothers. Abraham replies, "If they do not hear Moses and the Prophets, neither will they be convinced if someone should rise from the dead" (Luke 16:31).

Indeed, that was the experience of Jesus himself. He wrought many miracles, but they rarely led people to faith. Often the enemies of Jesus admitted the miracle, but still refused to believe. And even the resurrection itself failed to convince many. Jesus had harsh words for those who demanded to see signs (Matt. 12:39; John 4:48).

Yet, as in the Old Testament, the signs were not without value. They were intended, as then, to show who was Lord. They confirmed the apostles as servants of God (2 Cor. 12:12) and their message as God's (Heb. 2:4). Miracles do have an epistemological function, even though they themselves will not convert an unbeliever. Unbelievers suppress the truth, as we have seen, and the truth of miracles is no exception. If he wants, an unbeliever can write off an apparent miracle by saying, "Well, yes, it happened, but a lot of strange things happen in the world. It doesn't mean anything." Yet a miracle may be the occasion, as in the case of doubting Thomas, for the Spirit to implant faith in the heart. Remember how Jesus tells Thomas to examine the evidence, but also to "stop doubting and believe" (John 20:27 NIV). Thomas replies in faith, "My Lord and my God!" (v. 28). All the signs recorded in the Gospel of John are there so that the readers may, like Thomas, believe and thereby have life in the name of Christ (v. 31).[31] Thus, not only the miracle, but even the report of the miracle, can be a divinely ordained means of knowing Christ as Lord.

In debates between Christians and non-Christians, miracles have often played an important role. These discussions tend to focus on three issues: (1) the possibility and probability of miracles, (2) the evidence for miracles, and (3) whether miracles serve as evidence for the truth of Christianity.

Are Miracles Possible or Probable?

In the context of a Christian worldview, the answer is obvious. Miracles are possible because the world is under God's sovereign control. It is God who, by his nature and decrees, determines what is possible. The regularities of nature are his covenantal gift to us, and they do not at all limit his ability to work in the world as he pleases.

We need not get into discussions of the supposedly random behavior of elementary particles to provide some small possibility of very unusual events taking place. According to present-day science, the smallest particles/waves of matter behave counterintuitively, but there is no known path by which these communicate their strangeness to processes involving much larger bodies. These observations have not moved many, if any, naturalistic scientists to believe in miracles. To rest the case for miracles on the whims of photons and quarks is to trust a frail reed. Rather, miracles are possible because God exists.[32]

But are miracles probable? Of course they are unlikely, because they are by definition extraordinary. But that fact does not reduce their probability

31. I have found it helpful, in trying to assess the efficacy of miracles, to think of them (as the Reformers thought of sacraments) as "visible words." Miracles have the same purpose and efficacy as the Word of God, except that they are more vivid, providing a spectacle to the eye, as well as the ears and brain. Like the Word, they communicate saving truth, but an observer can remain unmoved unless the Spirit creates a proper response.

32. Here I share Van Til's reservations of a "blockhouse" method of apologetics, which looks to affirm various elements of the Christian worldview independently. The case for miracles is inseparably tied to the case for God.

to zero. Probability, like possibility, is determined by God. In a Christian-theistic worldview, our question becomes: "How likely is it that God will bring about miracles?" To answer that question, we must know something about God, particularly about his intentions and goals.

God announced to Noah that the course of nature would proceed in a way that is generally regular (Gen. 8:22). But God's higher intention is to redeem a people for himself, and to do that, it is appropriate for him to perform unusual works, to accomplish salvation, apply it, and attest it. If the world were governed by impersonal forces, there would be no reason to expect departures from the basic functions of those forces.[33] But ours is a world ruled by a person, and he seeks fellowship with us. That is sufficient reason to expect that he will identify himself in the natural order, as the ruler of that order. And since he has ordained miracle as a mark of his lordship and an attestation of his revelation, we can say that miracle is significantly probable. This question of probability is closely related to the next point.

Is There Sufficient Evidence for Believing in Biblical Miracles?
David Hume says, in his famous essay "Of Miracles":[34]

> A miracle is a violation of the laws of nature; and as a firm and unalterable experience has established these laws, the proof against a miracle, from the very nature of the fact, is as entire as any argument from experience can possibly be imagined.[35]

I reject Hume's definition of miracle as a violation of the laws of nature and therefore consider the rest of this quotation to be irrelevant. Even granted his definition, however, he begs the question when he says that "a firm and unalterable experience has established these laws." If this argument is to stand as a proof against miracle, the experience establishing the laws must be universal and without exception. Hume argued that everything behaves naturally and regularly. But is there really such evidence? Certainly, in almost all our experience, things happen in regular patterns, to some extent describable by scientific law. But there is nothing in this experience to persuade us that irregularity is impossible, or that everything always behaves naturally and regularly. Experience tells us what is happening; it

33. On the other hand, there would in that case be no reason to expect regularity either.
34. David Hume, *An Inquiry concerning Human Understanding* (New York: Liberal Arts Press, 1955, 1957), 117–41.
35. Ibid., 122.

does not tell us what is or is not possible, or what "always" happens. We have not seen what everything always does, for we have neither seen everything nor seen things always. So when Hume begins his argument by saying that nobody has ever had experience of exceptions to these laws, experiences of miracle, he begs the question because that is precisely the question that needs to be resolved.[36]

But Hume does not quite want to argue that because natural laws are universal, miracles are metaphysically impossible. At least he does not want his argument to appear to assume that. An "argument from experience," as he explains earlier in the essay, is never absolutely certain, but is always more or less probable. We determine the level of probability by weighing one experience against another and, importantly, one *testimony* against another. So the rest of Hume's argument is about the credibility of testimony. His assumption (above) about the laws of nature leads him to say this about the level of testimony needed to establish a miracle:

> No testimony is sufficient to establish a miracle unless the testimony be of such a kind that its falsehood would be more miraculous than the fact that it endeavors to establish.[37]

He then argues that no report of a miracle has ever fulfilled this criterion. In no case, he thinks, has a miracle report come from witnesses who are absolutely trustworthy.[38] He believes that miracle reports tend to come from emotional excess and therefore exaggeration.[39] These reports tend to come from "ignorant and barbarous nations,"[40] are opposed by those of different religious persuasions,[41] and even at best should be rejected because of the "absolute impossibility or miraculous nature of the events which they relate."[42]

In this last quotation, he tips his hand. He wants us to believe that he is not begging the question by assuming at the outset the impossibility of miracle. But in the last quotation he clearly seems to be making that

---

36. Compare the bottom of page 122: "But it is a miracle that a dead man should come to life, because that has never been observed in any age or country." Never? Here he dismisses the apparent counterexamples of Scripture.

37. Ibid., 123.

38. Ibid., 124.

39. Ibid., 125–26.

40. Ibid., 126.

41. Ibid., 128.

42. Ibid., 133.

assumption. In his view, there simply cannot be any "violation of the laws of nature." His argument, essentially, is that no testimony can establish a report of something impossible.

Applied to the reports of miracles in Scripture, Hume's arguments are unpersuasive unless we assume a priori the impossibility of miraculous events. There is no reason to suppose that the biblical reports of miracles stem from emotional excess or exaggeration, and shouldn't the biblical writers be considered innocent at least until proven guilty? Nor is biblical Israel fairly described as an "ignorant and barbarous nation." The most that can be said is that the biblical writers lived before the advent of modern science. But clearly they understood that axe-heads normally do not float, that one cannot normally feed multitudes with a few loaves and fishes, and that men don't normally rise from the dead. They knew that Satan counterfeits God's miracles (Ex. 7:11–12, 22; 8:7, 17–18; Deut. 13:1–3; Matt. 24:24; 2 Thess. 2:9; Rev. 13:13), and so they had a proper skepticism about such things. And they also knew that unless miracles are unlikely, they cannot do what God intends for them to do.

And as for the opposition of contrary parties, we have no knowledge of such opposition in the Old Testament context. So far as we know, nobody questioned whether the plagues of Egypt took place, whether Elijah raised the son of the widow of Zarephath, or whether the axe-head really floated. In the New Testament period, the opponents of Christianity either resorted to transparent rationalizations (such as that the disciples must have stolen the body of Jesus) or else conceded the miracle and attributed it to Satan.

But the more fundamental criticisms of Hume's argument are epistemological:

1. He assumes a nontheistic view of the possibility and probability of miracles. For him, possibility and probability are determined entirely by autonomous human experience, without any consideration of who God is and what God's intentions are. His argument, indeed, *assumes* that the God of Scripture does not exist; for if God did exist, one would have to take him into account in judging the possibility and probability of miracle, as we did in the previous section.

2. Hume assumes at the outset that divine revelation plays no role in determining whether miracles have taken place. For the Christian, however, writers such as Moses, Luke, John, and Paul are perfectly credible witnesses, not because they are completely unprejudiced, sophisticated, scientific, and civilized, but because they are them-

selves prophets of God, inspired by God's Spirit. It is significant that although Paul in 1 Corinthians 15 appeals to numerous witnesses of the resurrection of Jesus (including five hundred most of whom are still living—a significant evidentiary point), his main argument for belief in the resurrection is that it is an integral part of the gospel he preached, a gospel that he received by revelation (Gal. 1:11–12). So if the dead do not rise, then

> our preaching is in vain and your faith is in vain. We are even found to be misrepresenting God, because we testified about God that he raised Christ, whom he did not raise if it is true that the dead are not raised. (1 Cor. 15:14–15)

The Corinthians should believe in resurrection because it is a central element in the gospel *revelation*.

Hume does not even consider the possibility of knowledge by divine revelation. Doubtless he would consider revelation, too, to be a miracle and therefore impossible and incredible. But in so dismissing the possibility of revelation, he cuts himself off from any communication from the God who is the only ground of rational discourse. If the testimony concerning miracles is the testimony of God himself, then it would fulfill his condition quoted earlier. For the falsehood of God's testimony would certainly be more miraculous (in Hume's sense) than the facts that God's testimony establishes.[43]

Do Miracles Serve as Evidence for the Truth of Christianity?

Are miracles an apologetic problem or an apologetic resource? In the theological and philosophical literature, they have been both. There have

---

43. The same must be said of many, including many scholars, who study the Bible with the presupposition that miracles, including revelation, never take place. The mainstream of modern biblical criticism began with writers such as Spinoza, Reimarus, and Strauss, who made precisely that assumption. They therefore routinely denied the historicity of anything in Scripture that appeared to them to be supernatural, and they sought to reconstruct the history of Israel and the story of Jesus in line with that assumption, an assumption precisely contrary to the assumptions of the biblical writers themselves and logically incompatible with all the distinctive teachings of Christianity. More recent Bible critics in the liberal tradition have sought to break away from such naturalistic assumptions, and they have been successful in various degrees. But they have not reconciled themselves to the fact that God as covenant Lord rules his people by a written Word, of which he is the author. So they, like Hume, have often operated on the assumption that the biblical writings reflect only the level of human knowledge typical of the culture of the human writers. These critics have not taken a firm stand on the Scriptures as the very *criterion* of historical truth. But that, nothing less, is the presupposition of Christian faith, the stance of the covenant servant of God.

been arguments about whether miracles have happened (their possibility, probability, and actuality), such as the arguments that we have considered above. But miracles have also been used as evidence for the truth of Christianity.

Certainly the miracles that occurred in the Bible were intended to convince. They do not merely "propose a decision,"[44] but they obligate their audience to make the right decision, to recognize and believe God. We saw earlier that miracles attest prophets. That miracles warrant belief in Christ is a frequent theme in John's Gospel. Jesus says:

> If I am not doing the works of my Father, then do not believe me; but if I do them, even though you do not believe me, believe the works, that you may know and understand that the Father is in me and I am in the Father. (John 10:37–38)

> If I had not done among them the works that no one else did, they would not be guilty of sin, but now they have seen and hated both me and my Father. (John 15:24)

Many see the miracles and don't believe (John 12:37–38); yet they *ought* to believe on the basis of the miracles. And many do (2:23; 4:53; 6:2, 14; 7:31; etc.). This is John's purpose in recording the signs: "that you may believe that Jesus is the Christ, the Son of God, and that by believing you may have life in his name" (20:31).

Peter addresses the Jews on the day of Pentecost, announcing:

> Jesus of Nazareth [is] a man attested to you by God with mighty works and wonders and signs that God did through him in your midst, as you yourselves know. (Acts 2:22)

The Letter to the Hebrews also cites "signs and wonders and various miracles" by which God testified to the salvation of Christ (Heb. 2:4). These statements clearly imply that those who experienced the miracles are thereby obligated to believe in Jesus as Lord. Thus, miracles are evidence, indeed decisive evidence, of the truth of Jesus.

The greatest miracle, the resurrection of Jesus, is particularly important as a warrant for belief. Jesus prophesied it in answer to the Jews' question, "What sign do you show us for doing these things?" (John 2:18). Peter on

---

44. G. C. Berkouwer, *The Providence of God* (Grand Rapids: Eerdmans, 1952), 225.

Pentecost, again, referred to the resurrection in calling the Jews to faith (Acts 2:24–36). If Christ is not raised, therefore, our faith is vain (1 Cor. 15:14).

Christianity is based on historical events, and God's mighty works in history warrant faith. Miracles are an embarrassment to many intelligent Buddhists, because Buddhism is not based on historical events. If Buddhism is true, it is true by virtue of its timeless wisdom, not by virtue of historical events. But Christianity in this respect differs from Buddhism, Hinduism, and many other world religions. In Scripture, God's miraculous deeds are important to our salvation and to our knowledge of salvation.

To say that miracles warrant faith is not to say that miracles automatically bring people to faith. People saw the miracles of Jesus and did not believe. Some were hardened by God so that they could not see the truth (John 12:37–40).

Nor is it always legitimate for people to demand miraculous evidence. Jesus regularly rebuked the Jews' demands for more and more signs (Matt. 12:38–45; 16:1–4; John 4:48; 6:30–40; cf. 1 Cor. 1:22). Abraham in Jesus' parable tells the rich man in hell that he should not ask someone to rise from the dead to bring his brothers to repentance: "If they do not hear Moses and the Prophets, neither will they be convinced if someone should rise from the dead" (Luke 16:31).

Miracles are revelation, but they are not the only form of revelation. All creation reveals God (Rom. 1:18–21), and Scripture ("Moses and the Prophets") is his written revelation. In these sources, there is enough revelation to make us all responsible to believe. Paul in Romans 1 exposes unbelief as willful and culpable. So no one can claim that because God has not shown him a miracle, he has an excuse for unbelief. Certainly the Jewish opponents of Jesus, who had already seen many signs,[45] had no right to demand more. No one may say that he will not believe without a miracle. In that sense, miracles are epistemologically superfluous. We don't absolutely need them, but in them God gives us more evidence than we strictly need. He piles on the evidence, to underscore the cogency of his Word and our own responsibility to believe.

That fact is especially important to us today, because for the most part we have not directly experienced the more spectacular kinds of miracles. The "argument from miracle" today is really an argument from miracle-*reports*, from testimony. In the earthly ministry of Jesus, his miracles and

45. Some said, "When the Christ appears, will he do more signs than this man has done?" (John 7:31).

words were somewhat independent sources of knowledge, each attesting the other (see John 10:38; 14:11), though of course these were also interdependent and mutually interpreting in many ways. But for us, Jesus' works and words are found in the same place: the pages of Scripture. For us, Jesus' words to "doubting Thomas" are especially appropriate:

> Have you believed because you have seen me? Blessed are those who have not seen and yet have believed. (John 20:29)

The miracle of the resurrection brought Thomas to faith. But no one may demand from God a similar individual miraculous attestation. Moses and the Prophets, with the New Testament, are sufficient.

My point is not that miracles themselves are irrelevant, since we are now left with only a written Word. Miracle is part of the persuasive power of the Word itself, illumined by the Spirit. The Bible is not just any old book; it is a book of miracles, miracles that accomplish and attest God's salvation. When Paul appeals to many witnesses in 1 Corinthians 15, those witnesses are part of Scripture's self-authentication. The miracles of Scripture play a significant role in persuading us that Scripture is true.

Some might find a circle here: we believe the miracles because of Scripture, and Scripture because of the miracles. It is true that Scripture is our ultimate standard—the covenant constitution of the people of God. And an ultimate standard cannot be proved by any standard other than itself. But the circularity does not render the argument unpersuasive. We are not merely saying that "the Bible is the Word of God because it is the Word of God," although that syllogism is strictly valid and sound.[46] But we recognize the specific ways in which Scripture attests itself, by presenting content that is wonderfully persuasive and cogent. And miracle is a large part of that.

Reading Scripture thoughtfully, under the Spirit's illumination, we encounter credible accounts of miracles that reinforce our confidence in the scriptural truths that those miracles attest. And we gain confidence that the miracles really happened, as we gain greater understanding of God's inspiration of the writers who report the miracles. And then, fortified with greater confidence that the miracles really happened, we gain a greater confidence in biblical inspiration. It is a spiral process, in which two realities reinforce each other, as we compare them again and again. That is the way of faith.

---

46. See the previous discussion on this.

I would mention again, however, contrary to the traditional approach, that the chief evidence for the resurrection is the Word of God itself. Paul's argument in 1 Corinthians 15:1ff. is made chiefly to remind the Corinthians that the resurrection of Jesus is part of the apostolic preaching, which they believe. But in the course of his argument, he does also refer to postresurrection appearances and witnesses to those appearances who are still living.

It appears that the apostles were able to proclaim the resurrection largely without fear of contradiction. There was simply no evidence on the other side. The Jews concocted the story that the disciples had removed Jesus' body, thereby conceding the reality of the empty tomb. But in the unlikely event that the disciples had done such a thing (risking their lives in the face of the Roman guards), would they have died to perpetuate the fraud?

The story of the resurrection was related too soon after the fact to be the product of legendary development. The ornamentation and elaboration characteristic of legends are not there. The story of the women discovering the empty tomb bears remarkable marks of authenticity. No one inventing such a story would have placed women in this role, because they were not acceptable as witnesses in Jewish courts of law.

Attempts to explain the resurrection as something other than a supernatural event have always fallen flat. Some have said that Jesus did not actually die on the cross, but only fell into a coma, from which he was roused in the tomb. But in such a weakened condition, Jesus could not have rolled away the heavy stone and appeared to the disciples as the triumphant Lord of heaven and earth. Some have said that the disciples engaged in a conspiracy, but that has been dealt with above. Some have explained the postresurrection appearances as hallucinations or "visions." But hallucinations do not work that way. They do not produce the same images in many persons, who then report that they have all seen the same thing.

The fact is, then, that the resurrection is as well established as any other fact in history—indeed better than most, for it is attested by the Word of God itself. One cannot deny it, save by a radical skepticism that calls all knowledge into question. Nor can it be written off merely as a "strange event," for the Word of God gives it tremendous significance: the resurrection vindicates Jesus' sacrifice for sin and allows us to claim in faith that we have been raised with him from sin to eternal life (Rom. 6).[47]

---

47. The New Testament has much to say about the theological and redemptive-historical significance of Christ's resurrection. Two particularly helpful works in this regard are Richard B. Gaffin Jr., *Resurrection and Redemption* (Phillipsburg: NJ: Presbyterian and Reformed, 1987), and N. T. Wright, *The Resurrection of the Son of God* (Minneapolis: Fortress, 2003).

God's Word makes this gospel "absolutely certain." Jesus—God in the flesh—has died as a sacrifice for the sins of his people and has been raised to glory. All who believe, who trust in this sacrifice for divine forgiveness (John 3:16) and who recognize Jesus as Lord (Rom. 10:9), will be saved from hell and raised to eternal friendship with God. Do you believe in him?

Conclusion

What Scripture teaches, it teaches credibly. It presents an extraordinary spectacle of many authors of different times, social strata, and literary skills, producing a story that is perfectly unified around the person of Jesus. The facts are presented with remarkable credibility (even the kings of Israel are shown "warts and all"), despite the radical uniqueness of Jesus and his message. Indeed, Scripture even presents a credible reason for its being so credible—its divine authorship as the covenant constitution of the people of God. So biblical religion alone, of all the religions and philosophies of the world, provides an authoritative answer to the question that we most need to ask of God: How can my sins be forgiven?

Is its credibility absolutely certain? Ultimately, yes, for it is the Word of God himself and therefore deserves to be presupposed as the highest standard of credibility. How can we be persuaded of that certainty? By the Holy Spirit's witness to us, reinforcing the credibility inherent in the text itself (1 Cor. 2:4; 1 Thess. 1:5).

7

APOLOGETICS AS DEFENSE: THE PROBLEM OF EVIL, PART 1— QUESTIONS, GENERAL PRINCIPLES, AND BLIND ALLEYS

Having considered apologetics as proof, we now turn to the second function of apologetics, that of defense. We have seen that the Bible defends itself in an important sense, but God also calls his people to defend his truth (Phil. 1:7, 16; 1 Peter 3:15). In defense, as in proof, Scripture supplies the fundamental standards and criteria that the apologist must employ. We are not, however, restricted to Scripture for the data of our arguments. All facts have apologetic significance because all facts are created and ordered by God. But Scripture supplies the presuppositions for every phase of Christian apologetics.

Is There a Problem of Evil? Is There an Answer?

In this chapter, we will consider what is perhaps the most serious and cogent objection that unbelievers have brought against Christian theism: the problem of evil. A typical formulation of it is as follows:

- Premise 1: If God were all-powerful, he would be able to prevent evil.
- Premise 2: If God were all-good, he would desire to prevent evil.
- Conclusion: So if God were both all-powerful and all-good, there would be no evil.

- Premise 3: But there is evil.
- Conclusion: Therefore, there is no all-powerful, all-good God.

Such is the philosopher's way of looking at the problem. But the essence of it is a concern to nonphilosophers as well. Who of us has not cried out, "Why, Lord?" when beset by tragedies in our experience? We simply feel a terrible discrepancy between our experience and what we believe God to be. That cry from the heart may be simultaneously a cry of pain, a cry for help, a cry for enlightenment, and a cry of doubt that questions our own deepest presuppositions. That "Why, Lord?" says everything that the philosophical argument says and more.

I said that this problem is perhaps the most serious and cogent objection to Christian theism. Professor Walter Kaufmann, mentioned in an earlier chapter, always referred to this as his strongest argument against Christianity—he had lost family members in the Holocaust. To him, the reality of evil was a "complete refutation of popular theism." Many people who have experienced the suffering and death of a child, or some other suffering that seems entirely undeserved, will hold a grudge against God, the intellectual content of which can be described in our premises and conclusions. Every Christian, perhaps, has at least wondered about this issue, and many of us have experienced periods of doubt on its account.

Alvin Plantinga, in *God, Freedom, and Evil*,[1] makes a useful distinction between a *defense* and a *theodicy*. The latter has the goal of justifying God's ways to men, of demonstrating the goodness of all his actions. The former merely seeks to show that the problem of evil does not disprove the God of the Bible. Is there an answer to the problem? That depends on what is meant by *answer*. If someone is seeking a theodicy that vindicates God's providence in every instance of evil, I certainly cannot supply that, and I doubt that anyone else can, either. Nor, I think, can we supply a totally satisfying theoretical reconciliation between divine sovereignty, goodness, and evil. The mystery of God's relation to evil is one that will, I am convinced, never be completely dissolved in this life, and I am not sure whether it will be in the next.

Another distinction that we should initially make is between natural and moral evil. The former includes anything that brings suffering, unpleasantness, or difficulty into the lives of creatures. Earthquakes, floods, diseases, injuries, and death are examples of natural evil. Moral evil is the

---

1. Grand Rapids: Eerdmans, 1977.

sin of rational creatures (angels and men). According to Scripture, moral evil came first. Satan's temptations and the disobedience of Adam and Eve led to God's curse on the earth:

> Cursed is the ground because of you;
>> in pain you shall eat of it all the days of your life;
> thorns and thistles it shall bring forth for you;
>> and you shall eat the plants of the field.
> By the sweat of your face
>> you shall eat bread,
> till you return to the ground,
>> for out of it you were taken;
> for you are dust,
>> and to dust you shall return. (Gen. 3:17–19)

God will remove this curse only on the final day, the consummation of Jesus' redemption, when he executes his final judgment and this world is replaced by new heavens and a new earth. In the meantime, the whole creation "has been groaning together in the pains of childbirth" (Rom. 8:22) "with eager longing for the revealing of the sons of God" (v. 19).

Scripture, therefore, gives us an explicit answer to the problem of natural evil. Natural evil is a curse brought on the world because of moral evil. It functions as punishment to the wicked and as a means of discipline for those who are righteous by God's grace. It also reminds us of the cosmic dimensions of sin and redemption. Sin brought death to the human race, but also to the universe over which man was to rule. God has ordained that the universe resist its human ruler until that ruler stops resisting God. So in redemption, God's purpose is no less than "to reconcile to himself all things, whether on earth or in heaven" (Col. 1:20). The unanswered question is the problem of moral evil: how can sin exist in a theistic universe? I will therefore focus on moral evil for the rest of this chapter and the next.

Jay Adams's book *The Grand Demonstration*[2] is in many ways a fine biblical study of the problem of moral evil. Dr. Adams is a colleague and friend of mine, a man who has been a great help to the church and to me personally, and I dearly love him in Christ. But there is something about this particular book that, to say the least, rubs me the wrong way. Adams is a problem-solver, and he doesn't like to see loose ends flying around—in counseling, in preaching, or in theology. He is very unhappy with wimpish

2. Santa Barbara, CA: East Gate Publishers, 1991.

talk that gives up on problems before the best solutions have been tried. And he doesn't seem to like the "maybe this, maybe that" approach that theologians employ when they cannot find something definitive to say. Adams wants to be able to say, "Thus says the Lord! Here is the answer, right here!" And so, his book says, he has found the answer to the "so-called" problem of evil.[3] In his view, all the wimpish theologians who have agonized over the problem down through the centuries (such as Augustine), who have mumbled "mystery" and tiptoed around the issue, have simply failed to see the answer that has been right there in black and white in front of their noses! That answer is Romans 9:17, "For the Scripture says to Pharaoh, 'For this very purpose I have raised you up, that I might show my power in you, and that my name might be proclaimed in all the earth.'"

God raises up evil people (and, by implication, all evil) so that by prevailing over them he can display his power and his name throughout the earth.

Adams's answer is a good one, certainly. But it does not remove all the mystery from evil. It does not completely answer the question we have posed. For the questions then arise: Why should the display of God's power and good name require the employment of that which is totally opposed to everything that God is? Cannot God display his power without contradicting his goodness? Cannot God display his name without making little babies suffer pain? How can a good God, through his wise foreordination, make someone to be evil, even when that God hates evil with all his being? How can he do that, even to display himself? Does the God so displayed, then, become something less than our God of love? To answer these sorts of questions, Adams must return to the traditional theodicies and, in the end—I think—return to mystery. *The Grand Demonstration* is a fine contribution to the discussion of the problem, but I do wish the tone of it were a bit less cocksure, a bit more open to the agonies of those who still have problems after they have heard Romans 9:17. The book is a help, but it is not "the" answer, and the "so-called" problem of evil will remain a problem to many sensitive readers of the book.[4]

My own verdict is that we are unlikely to find complete answers to all these questions—answers, that is, that are not subject to further questions.

But I do think we can provide answers in another sense. If what you want is encouragement to go on believing in the midst of suffering, Scrip-

---

3. The subtitle of Adams's book is *A Biblical Study of the So-Called Problem of Evil*.
4. See Adams's reply, reproduced as Appendix B in the back of this book.

ture provides that, and provides it abundantly. If you want help to go on trusting God despite unexplained evil, yes, we can help. And that is what I will seek to provide in what follows.

Focus on the Bible

In this chapter, I'm going to be focusing on what the Bible teaches concerning the problem of evil, following Jay Adams's good example. His book is itself rather unusual in this respect. Most books on the problem of evil deal with logical and experiential matters without much focus on the Bible, perhaps out of the conviction that the Bible cannot help very much. As I have indicated earlier, I do not object to using extrabiblical data in dealing with this issue, but I do believe that in this case the Bible itself brings us as close to an answer as we are likely to get. The problem of evil is so firmly connected in our minds with the holocausts of Hitler, Stalin, and Pol Pot, with the terrors of modern warfare and modern scenarios for eco-destruction, that we are often tempted to think of it as a modern problem—as though the prevalence of unbelief today were due to mankind's sudden realization that there is too much evil in the world to justify old-fashioned theism. But who in our modern experience has suffered more, with more apparent injustice, than the biblical Job, or meditated on that suffering more profoundly? Indeed, the Bible is preoccupied with the problem of evil. We will see it being raised over and over again on the pages of Paul's letter to the Romans. And we might even say that the whole Bible addresses the problem of evil, for the whole story turns on the entrance of sin and evil into the world and on God's plan for dealing with it.

There is another reason why people often object to dealing with the problem of evil from Scripture. And that is, simply, that they don't believe Scripture as God's Word. Liberal theologians of various kinds often claim to have Christian answers to the problem, but those answers consist in revising the theology of the Bible. They—and this is especially true today of the "process theology" school—think they can best solve the problem by revising the biblical doctrine of God. As long as we regard God as the majestic, sovereign absolute personality of the Scriptures, they say, there will always be a problem of evil, for supreme power will always conflict with supreme goodness. But, say the process thinkers, if we deny God's supreme power and total sovereignty, then we can solve the problem of evil: evil exists because God is not fully able to prevent it.

But such revisions of scriptural teaching always lose more than they gain. Perhaps we can solve the problem of evil simply by denying God's sovereignty! Well, let's go all the way back to worshiping birds—then there will be no chance at all that the problem of evil will arise! No, no. Somewhere along this line of reasoning, you end up with a god who is simply not worthy of worship. In my view, a god who is not sovereign—indeed, a god who differs at all from the biblical absolute personality—is an idol, and is to be despised rather than worshiped. A nonsovereign god is an idol of conventional wisdom, not the absolute personality of Christianity.

We need to sharpen our sense of proportion. It would be nice to have a solution to the problem of evil, but not at any price. If the price we must pay is the very sovereignty of God, the faithful Christian must say that that price is too high. After all, it is of little importance whether any of us discovers the answer to the problem of evil. It is possible to live a long and happy and faithful life without an answer. But it is all-important that we worship the true God, the God of Scripture. Without him, human life is worth nothing.

Who do these theologians and philosophers think they are, anyway? Why do they imagine that they are in a position to correct the Bible's teaching concerning God? For the most part, they are known for their scholarship, not, to put it mildly, for their piety. They are not prophets or priests; they are not known for the depth of their personal relationships with God. They are not candidates for sainthood on the Roman Catholic model, people who give their lifeblood for the poor and overwhelm us with their universal, unconditional love. Their only credentials are their academic degrees and academic positions. But such credentials have never qualified anyone as an expert on God. Some of us can at least get by, maintaining our credibility as teachers by sticking close to the Holy Scriptures. But the liberals proudly dismiss the teachings of Scripture as inferior to the brilliance and cogency of their own thoughts, thus exposing themselves as partisans of the wisdom of the world and enemies of the wisdom of God. Why, I ask, should anyone pay any attention to them?

Modern man must get it clear in his own mind once and for all that Christian doctrines are not subject to revision. A novelist may, of course, revise his novel if he doesn't like the way the narrative is turning out. But if one seeks to revise the law of gravity because of its sometimes troublesome consequences, he will not only fail, but look silly trying. Scripture in this respect is like the law of gravity, not like a novel. I might wish that Scripture taught something different from what it teaches, but what it says is so, and I have no control over that. To pick and choose among its teachings, to revise this and modify that, is just as foolish as trying to revise the law of gravity.

And if Scripture were wrong, how would we know what was right? Indeed, the actual truth, which itself will not be subject to revision, might be far harder for modern man to take than the supposed errors of the Bible.

So we will again look at Scripture. There are other methods, but in my mind, a direct inspection of biblical teaching is often the best way to defend the faith against objections. In that respect, our treatment of the problem of evil will furnish a model for the treatment of other difficulties.

What the Bible Does Not Say

The first thing we can learn from Scripture is what it does not say. Of course, as I have often said before, the apologist is not limited to repeating what is explicitly stated in Scripture. It is instructive, however, to see that many of the devices used by philosophers to solve the problem of evil are not present in Scripture. Very often there is a good reason why they are not present.

We will consider here most of the defenses and theodicies used in the historic discussion. We should note that some thinkers have combined two or more of the following strategies; some of them are compatible with others. Common defenses against the problem may be divided into three general types. The first focuses on the nature of evil, the second on the ways in which evil contributes to the overall good of the universe, and the third on God's agency with regard to evil.[5]

The Nature of Evil: The Unreality-of-Evil Defense

Some Eastern religions and Western cults (e.g., Buddhism and Christian Science) maintain that evil is really an illusion. Even some respected Christian thinkers, such as Augustine, have suggested that evil be classified under the category of nonbeing.[6] Augustine does not quite mean to say that evil is an illusion, but rather that it is a "privation," a lack of good being where good being ought to be. Still, he does use this idea to remove responsibility from God. God creates all being, but he is not responsible for nonbeing.

These explanations are quite inadequate. There is no reason for us to think that evil is an illusion. Further, saying that it is plays games with

5. For a parallel—though not identical—discussion of the problem of evil, see *ST*, chap. 14.
6. Of being, God says, "It is good" (Gen. 1:31; 1 Tim. 4:4). That would seem to indicate that only nonbeing can be evil.

words. For if evil is an illusion, it is a terribly troublesome illusion, an illusion that brings misery, pain, suffering, and death. If it is said that the pain is also illusory, I reply that there is no difference between illusory pain and real pain so far as the problem of evil is concerned. The problem just backs up a step and asks, "How could a good God give us all such a terrible illusion of pain?" One great advantage of Scripture's viewpoint is that it doesn't play games with suffering people. In Scripture, evil is treated quite simply as something that we must deal with, whatever its metaphysical status may be.

Nor is Augustine's version any more biblical.[7] Whatever we may say about the relative distribution of good (i.e., being) throughout the universe, Scripture is clear that that distribution is in God's hands. God is as responsible for the lacks and privations (if we wish to call them that) as he is for the good being of the universe. God works *all* things after the counsel of his own will (Eph. 1:11), as Augustine later in his life came to recognize. This includes sins and evils (Gen. 50:20; Isa. 10:5–10; Luke 22:22; Acts 2:23; 4:28; Rom. 9:1–29). It is true that all things are good, but the fallen human heart is evil, and because of that, human actions and attitudes are evil. And because of that, we describe many events in the world as evil because they express God's response to sin (Gen. 3:17–19). There is no point in creating a distinct metaphysical category (*nonbeing* or *privation*) for evil. The problem is simply that God is sovereign over all events, good and evil, and however one analyzes evil metaphysically, it is part of God's plan.

The Contribution of Evil

The Best-Possible-World Defense

The philosopher G. W. Leibniz and others have argued that this world, for all its evils, is nonetheless the best world that God could have produced. The reason is not the weakness of God, as in an upcoming defense, but rather the very logic of creation. Certain evils are logically necessary to achieve certain good ends. For example, there must be suffering if there is to be compassion for sufferers. So the best possible world will include some evil. God necessarily, on this view, makes the best world possible, including whatever evils may be required for the best overall result. Because of the very excellence of his standards, he can do nothing less.

---

7. We should, of course, give Augustine credit for recognizing that evil has no power of its own and is in some sense parasitic on goodness.

Scripture does teach that God observes the laws of logic,[8] not because there are laws "above" him to which he must conform, but because he is by nature a logical person. That God is logical is implied by the scriptural teachings that he is wise, just, faithful, and true—attributes that would be meaningless if God were free to contradict himself.

But does a perfect world logically require the existence of evil? God himself is perfect, but there is no evil in him. And according to Scripture, the original creation contained no evil (Gen. 1:31). Was it imperfect for that reason? The consummate new heavens and new earth—that is, the ultimate perfection of the created order—will also be without evil (Rev. 21:1–8). As for the earlier example, suffering may be necessary for the exhibition of compassion, but it is not necessary for the existence of compassion in a person. God has always been compassionate, even when there was no one for him to show compassion to.

And is God, because of his perfection, able to create only perfect beings? That might seem logical, but Scripture teaches otherwise. Indeed, in the Bible, God creates beings who lack perfection in many ways. Adam was created good, but not perfect. He was "alone," for one thing, and that was not good (Gen. 2:18). He was also untested; his righteousness had to be confirmed through trial (2:17; 3:1–21). Satan himself was most likely created good, but was from the beginning capable of rebellion against God. Thus, even in the good creation there were imperfections. And so it goes throughout the historical providence of God. There is much that is imperfect that will be perfected (or destroyed) only in the new heavens and new earth.

Of course, Leibniz's view is not that everything God makes is perfect, but that the world as a whole is perfect, granted the logical necessity of some evil. While rejecting the idea of the logical necessity of evil, I would grant the possibility that, taking the whole historical sequence into account, including God's glorious redemption of sinners, this is the best world that God could have made. But that is only a possibility. If God can make imperfect individual beings, if God can make a whole world that is imperfect and requires renovation, surely it is possible that he can determine a whole historical sequence that is imperfect in comparison with other worlds that he might have made. So the bottom line is this: I don't know whether this world (taken as a complete historical sequence) is the best possible world. So far as I know, God is free to make things that are either imperfect or

---

8. I am, of course, talking about God's own logic, which may not be identical to any humanly devised logical system. Logic as a human science strives, like all other human sciences, to think God's thoughts after him, but it does not always do so perfectly.

perfect. So we cannot solve the problem of evil by saying that we know a priori that this is the best possible world and that all evils are logically necessary for its perfection.

The Free-Will Defense

The most common defense among professional philosophers today is based on human free will.[9] The free-will defense says that evil came about by the free choice of rational creatures (Satan or Adam or "everyman"). Since that free choice was in no sense controlled or foreordained or caused by God, he cannot be held accountable for it.[10] Therefore, the existence of evil does not compromise God's goodness.[11]

Scripture does teach that man is, or can be, free in certain senses. (1) He does what he wants to do, acting in accord with his desires, whether those are holy or wicked.[12] (2) Adam had the freedom or ability to choose either good or evil. The fall removed this freedom from us, for fallen creatures can[13] do only what is evil (Gen. 6:5; 8:21; Isa. 64:6; Rom. 3:10ff.). But redemption restores this freedom to those who believe (2 Cor. 5:17). (3) Redemption brings to us an even higher freedom, a freedom from sin and its effects altogether (John 8:32). "Freedom from sin" is the usual meaning of *freedom* in the New Testament. (4) We are free in the sense that we are not the helpless

---

9. One of the most influential formulations is that of Plantinga, *God, Freedom, and Evil.*

10. Strictly speaking, Plantinga's argument is based not on the actuality of free will in this sense, but on the mere possibility of it. Yet if we have reason to believe, as I do, that free will in this sense is not actual, I cannot see that Plantinga's argument will be very cogent. In this sense, Plantinga's book is a brief for an Arminian concept of human freedom, though it was published while he taught at Calvin College, a supposedly Calvinistic institution.

11. Plantinga combines this traditional free-will defense with a form of the greater-good defense, which we will discuss in the next chapter. Essentially, he claims that the divine gift of free will, even with the attendant possibility of evil, makes for a better overall good than there would be in a universe without such freedom. In general, we will see that the greater-good defense contains some biblical truth, but I doubt that free will in Plantinga's sense actually is a greater good.

12. This is sometimes called *compatibilist* freedom, since it is compatible with the causal determination of human choices.

13. The *can* here is a moral-spiritual *can*, not a *can* of physical or mental ability. Sinners have the physical and mental capacity to obey God, but they lack the moral-spiritual motivation. Their problem is a heart problem, not a lack of some capacity or other. The problem is that despite their capacities, they *will* not obey; and that *"will* not" is so deeply ingrained, so intensely reiterated, so much a part of their very nature, that in an important (but unique) sense they "cannot." I do think there is some confusion between Calvinists and Arminians on this point. In certain obvious senses, fallen man *can* do right, and his responsibility depends on that "ability." As Cornelius Van Til emphasized, depravity is ethical, not metaphysical; it does not involve a decline in our physical capacities, skills, or IQs, but a misuse of these. Calvinists need to be clearer in admitting that, while making the proper distinctions.

victims of historical determinism. Scripture does not allow us to plead a deficiency in heredity, environment, psychological balance, or self-esteem, for example, as an excuse for violating God's commandments. We are, in all our actions (1 Cor. 10:31), responsible to obey the Lord.

Further, Scripture does agree with the defenders of free will in teaching that the blame for sin rests on man, rather than on God. Even when Scripture specifically mentions God's foreordination of an evil event, the blame for the evil rests exclusively with the human perpetrators (see Gen. 50:20; Acts 2:23; 4:27).

But Scripture does not teach—in fact, it denies—free will in the sense that it is used by the free-will defense. For on that view of freedom,[14] man's free choices are not in any way foreordained or caused by God. Yet Scripture frequently speaks of God's determining our free choices (see Gen. 50:20; Acts 2:23; 4:27; also 2 Sam. 24:1, referring specifically to evil choices; also Prov. 16:9; Luke 24:45; John 6:44, 65; Acts 2:47; 11:18; 13:48; 16:14; Rom. 8:28ff.; 9; Eph. 2:8–9; Phil. 1:29). And certainly the free choices of human beings are included among the general statements of Romans 11:36 and Ephesians 1:11.[15]

It is remarkable that in Romans 9, where the problem of evil is explicitly raised, Paul does not resort to the free-will defense; rather, he contradicts the assumptions of that defense. He raises the question why so few Jews have believed in Christ. This is a matter of some agony for him (vv. 2–5), for these are his people and, historically, the people of God, the heirs of the promise. We should note that this very question presupposes a strong view of the sovereignty of God. For why would the problem of evil arise here at all unless Paul were assuming that faith is a gift of God? The problem is that God has taken Israel to be his people, yet he has largely withheld from them the gift of faith.

Paul's answer is that since the time of Abraham, the "people of God" have been divided between those who actually belong to God by faith and those who are only physically descended from Abraham. What causes this division? Here, Paul could easily have said "human choice."[16] But he does not say this. Rather, he traces the division back to "God's purpose of election"

14. That view was taught by Pelagius, Molina, and Arminius, among others in church history. In secular philosophy, it is called the *incompatibilist* (cf. note 12) or *libertarian* view.

15. Even Arminians must reluctantly admit that God in some sense controls our free choices. They can escape this conclusion only by moving toward even more unbiblical positions, such as process theology and open theism. See the discussion of divine sovereignty in chapter 2 and in *NOG, passim*.

16. Had he said this, he would not have been wrong, even on a Calvinistic basis. For Calvinists also accept the importance of human choice. The question is whether that choice is

(Rom. 9:11), adding: "not because of works but because of him who calls" (v. 11). Indeed, God foretold the fate of Esau and Jacob before they were born, indicating that he had foreordained their destiny (vv. 12–13).

In Romans 9:14, the problem of evil comes to the fore: was God unjust to ordain evil for Esau before he was even born? No, says Paul. Why? The free-will defense would say that God foresaw Esau's autonomous free choices and therefore determined to punish him. But Paul traces the evil to God's own free choice:

> I will have mercy on whom I have mercy, and I will have compassion on whom I have compassion. (Rom. 9:15, quoting Ex. 33:19)

He then reiterates: "So then it depends not on human will or exertion, but on God, who has mercy" (Rom. 9:16). Then comes verse 17,[17] which tells us that God's purpose for raising up evil Pharaoh was to declare God's name throughout the earth. "So then he has mercy on whomever he wills, and he hardens whomever he wills" (v. 18).

In Romans 9:19, the problem of evil comes up again: Why does God still blame us? And again, the answer is not "Because God does not control our free choices." Rather, the answer is that he has full rights over us to do whatever he (sovereignly!) chooses to do.

Scripture never uses the free-will defense in any passage where the problem of evil is up for discussion. You will not find it in the book of Job, in Psalm 37, or in Psalm 73. Indeed, all these passages presuppose the usual strong view of divine sovereignty.

So the free-will defense is unbiblical. There are also problems with its internal coherence. If, as in classical Arminianism, our free choices are literally causeless, then they are not caused by our character or our desires any more than they are caused by God. And if this is the case, our "free choices" are totally accidental happenings unconnected with anything in the past. They are surprises, worse than hiccups occurring at awkward times. A person with an upright character and no previous inclination toward theft would, walking past a bank, suddenly, on some strange impulse, go inside and rob the bank without even wanting to.[18] Surely this is not what

---

itself a gift of God. Had Paul referred to human choice in this context, he would simply have sidestepped that issue.

17. Adams's key verse!

18. Of course, libertarians usually do admit that our character and desires "influence" our free choices, but without "determining" them. What that usually means, however, is that character and desires somewhat limit the alternatives available for free choice and perhaps incline us to choose in one direction or another. But of course, we may choose against inclination on this

we normally think of as free choice. And such chance happenings can hardly be the ground of moral responsibility, since, as we saw in previous chapters, they are essentially irrational. They are events of which there is no first cause, no origin in an absolute personality.

On the other hand, if the Arminian-libertarian sees free choice as caused by character and desire, then he is introducing factors that themselves have causes[19] in heredity and environment, causes that precede the conscious life of the individual. He is substituting an impersonal cosmic determinism for the personalistic "determinism" of biblical Christianity. I do not see this as any sort of gain for moral responsibility.

The Character-Building Defense

The third unbiblical defense based on contribution of evil in God's plan that we will consider is sometimes called *Irenaean*, after the church father Irenaeus, who employed it. In modern times it has been urged by John Hick,[20] who calls it the "soul-making" theodicy.[21]

The argument is that man was created in a state of moral immaturity. For man to come to full maturity, it was necessary for him to undergo various forms of pain and suffering.

It is true that suffering sometimes builds character. Hebrews 12 says that believers experience God's fatherly discipline and chastisement. Just as an earthly father's spankings bring discipline to a child's life, so our heavenly Father puts us through trials so that we will learn habits of godliness.

I think it is unbiblical, however, to turn this principle into a full-scale theodicy. For one thing, Scripture teaches that Adam was not created morally immature with a need to develop character through suffering. He was created good, and had he obeyed God, he would not have needed to experience suffering. Suffering is the result of the fall (Gen. 3:17).

Furthermore, Scripture teaches that not all suffering builds character. Unbelievers suffer and often learn no lessons from it. And not all character improvement comes through suffering. Believers are created anew in Christ

---

view, and that choice emerges, again, as a sheer accident. Thus, even with these qualifications, a person might make a "free choice" that is quite out of character, and simply by chance. For a more comprehensive discussion of the nature of libertarian freedom, along with its biblical and philosophical problems, see *DG*, 137–45.

19. If they do not, then they are evidently accidents, and the argument of the previous paragraph pertains to them.

20. See John Hick, *Evil and the God of Love* (New York: Harper & Row, 1966).

21. Recall that *theodicy* means literally "justification of God." It is used to describe proposed solutions to the problem of evil.

(2 Cor. 5:17). The basic change from sin to righteousness is a gift of God's grace. Moreover, our sanctification will be perfected in heaven—not through a purgatory of suffering, but through God's own action.

The Stable-Environment Defense

C. S. Lewis, in *The Problem of Pain*,[22] argues that a stable environment is necessary for human life. We know one another through regular and stable signs of one another's presence (facial appearance, voice, etc.). To live happily and productively requires a universe of regular law, so that we can make plans and fulfill them. If, when I reached for my comb in the morning, it randomly turned into a tortoise, I would not be able to develop a dependable plan and practice of combing my hair.

But, says Lewis, a stable environment opens up the possibility of evil. It means, for example, that the law of gravity will not be temporarily repealed to save me from falling down the stairs.

True enough. But does a stable environment necessarily produce evil? Is it a sufficient cause for evil? Certainly not. God created Adam (concerning whose literal existence, I gather, Lewis had some doubts) and placed him in a stable environment, but without evil and pain. I don't know how this worked—did God revoke physical laws now and then to protect Adam, leaving enough regularity for a fairly normal everyday life, or did God simply foreordain that Adam would not run afoul of these laws? However it was, there was no pain and suffering until the fall. Heaven will, certainly, be another stable environment, but one without evil.[23]

And how does a stable environment bring about evils of the human heart, the spirit of rebellion against God?

So although some evils may certainly be traced proximately (see below) to natural laws in a stable environment, these are not a sufficient explanation for evil. The Bible never refers evils to such a source. To do so would be to blame creation rather than our own hearts.

Evil and God's Agency

The Divine-Weakness Defense

Many have urged some sort of divine weakness or inability as the solution to the problem of evil: God does not overcome all evil because he

22. London: Geoffrey Bles, 1940.

23. The reader may notice that several of the proposed defenses fail to take into account either the goodness of the original creation or the perfection of heaven, or both. An adequate defense or theodicy must be consistent with these biblical teachings.

cannot do so—although he does do his best. This is the answer of process theology[24] and also of Harold S. Kushner's popular book, *When Bad Things Happen to Good People*.[25] This solution denies the historic Christian doctrines of divine omnipotence, omniscience, and sovereignty, while seeking to preserve God's attribute of goodness. Yet Scripture itself not only fails to teach this solution, but firmly contradicts it. God's omniscience (Ps. 139; Isa. 46:10; Heb. 4:11–13; 1 John 3:20), omnipotence (Ps. 115:3; Isa. 14:24, 27; 46:10; 55:11; Luke 18:27), and sovereignty (Rom. 11:33–36; 1 Tim. 6:15–16) are central to the biblical doctrine of God.

One may prefer to believe in a weaker god than the absolute personality of the Scriptures, but he should be aware of the cost of such a preference. He may thereby get a solution to the problem of evil, but he loses any sure hope for the overcoming of evil. He gains intellectual satisfaction at the cost of having to face the horrible possibility that evil might triumph after all. Surely there is something ironic about calling this a "solution" to the problem of evil.

The Indirect-Cause Defense

The indirect-cause defense differs from other defenses we have discussed in that it is rather commonly found in Reformed theology. Cornelius Van Til endorses it in a discussion of Calvin's use of it against Pighius.[26] Gordon Clark also makes use of it.[27] The argument seems to be that since God is the indirect rather than the direct cause of evil, he bears no blame for it.

Clark explains the distinction this way: God is the ultimate cause of my book, but he is not its author; I am. Therefore, I bear responsibility for its contents, not God. The author is the closest cause to the effect, the "proximate" cause. If I hit billiard ball A, and it hits B, and B hits C, then I am the ultimate cause of C's movement, but the movement of B is the proximate cause or author.

It is true that in Scripture God's relation to evil is indirect. It was not God who tempted Eve, but the serpent.[28] James 1:13 persuades us that such

---

24. As, for example, in David Ray Griffin, *God, Power, and Evil* (Philadelphia: Westminster, 1976). Cf. his *Evil Revisited* (Albany, NY: State University of New York Press, 1991).

25. New York: Schocken Books, 1981.

26. Cornelius Van Til, *The Defense of the Faith*, ed. K. Scott Oliphint, 4th ed. (Phillipsburg, NJ: P&R Publishing, 2008), 242–47.

27. Gordon Clark, *Religion, Reason, and Revelation* (Philadelphia: Presbyterian and Reformed, 1961), 238–41.

28. Even with this statement, however, there are problems. If God in providence "concurs" with second causes, maintaining them and directing them to their effects, then the distinction

is always the case with temptation. And it is also true that in Scripture moral blame attaches only to creatures. It is therefore tempting (!) to find a connection between these two facts.

But indirectness of causality does not in itself mitigate responsibility— at least on the human level. If I hire a hit man to kill someone, I am as responsible for the murder as the man who actually pulls the trigger. Scripture warns us that enticing someone else to sin is itself a sin (Deut. 13:6ff.; Rom. 14). Is God so different from creatures in this respect that the indirectness of his role in evil insulates him against moral censure? Scripture never says that he is different in that way.

And if that were the only solution we had to the problem of evil, it would certainly be a most inadequate one. For it would picture God as some kind of giant Mafia boss who keeps his hands legally clean by forcing his underlings to carry out his nasty designs. Is that picture a biblical one? Is it compatible with the goodness of God that Scripture teaches us?

The Ex Lex Defense

In the volume just cited, Gordon Clark also presents another theodicy, which, if sound, would render his indirect-cause defense wholly beside the point. That he includes both defenses may indicate some lack of confidence in one or the other, although you couldn't tell that from reading the text.

His argument is that God is *ex lex*, which means "outside the law." The idea is that God is outside or above the laws he prescribes for man. He tells us not to kill, yet he retains for himself the right to take human life. Thus, he is not himself bound to obey the Ten Commandments or any other law given to man in Scripture. Morally, he is on an entirely different level from us. Therefore, he has the right to do many things that seem evil to us, even things that contradict scriptural norms. For a man to cause evil indirectly might very well be wrong, but it would not be wrong for God.[29] Thus Clark neatly finesses any argument against God's justice or goodness.

There is some truth in this approach. As we will see, Scripture does forbid human criticism of God's actions, and the reason is, as Clark implies, divine transcendence. It is also true that God has some prerogatives that he forbids to us, such as the freedom to take human life.

Clark forgets, however, or perhaps denies, the Reformed and biblical maxim that the law reflects God's own character. To obey the law is

---

between indirect and direct causes is not easily made. See *DG*, 175–77, 287–88.

29. But on this basis, it would also not be wrong for God to cause evil directly. That is why I said that this argument makes the indirect-cause argument beside the point.

to imitate God, to be like him, to image him (Ex. 20:11; Lev. 11:44–45; Matt. 5:45; 1 Peter 1:15–16). There is in biblical ethics also an imitation of Christ, centered on the atonement (John 13:34–35; Eph. 4:32; 5:1; Phil. 2:3ff.; 1 John 3:16; 4:8–10). Obviously, there is much about God that we cannot imitate, including those prerogatives mentioned earlier. Satan tempted Eve into seeking to become "like God" in the sense of coveting God's prerogatives (Gen. 3:5).[30] But the overall holiness, justice, and goodness of God is something that we can and must imitate on the human level.

So God does honor, in general, the same law that he gives to us. He rules out murder because he hates to see one human being murder another, and he intends to reserve for himself the right to control human death. He prohibits adultery because he hates adultery (which is a mirror of idolatry— see Hosea). We can be assured that God will behave according to the same standards of holiness that he prescribes for us, except insofar as Scripture declares a difference between his responsibilities and ours.[31]

But on this basis, the problem of evil returns. If God prohibits us from tormenting others, how can he allow his creatures to be tormented? If he abides (essentially, with some exceptions) by the standards revealed in Scripture, how can he plan and foreordain evil and cause it to take place? Thus, we cannot agree with Clark's *ex lex* defense. It simply is not biblical. The problem remains to be solved.

An Ad Hominem Defense

Some Christian apologists have approached the problem of evil on the theory that the best defense is a good offense. Thus, when an unbeliever questions the consistency of God's sovereignty with his goodness in the face of evil, the apologist replies that the unbeliever has no right even to raise the question, for he cannot, on his basis, even distinguish good from evil.

30. John Murray said that the difference between the two ways of seeking God's likeness appears to be a razor's edge, while there is actually a deep chasm between them.

31. Oddly, Clark, who is usually accused of being a Platonic realist, at this point veers into the opposite of realism, namely, nominalism. The extreme nominalists held that the biblical laws were not reflections of God's nature, but merely arbitrary requirements. God could as easily have commanded adultery as forbidden it. I mentioned this once in a letter to Clark, and he appreciated the irony, but did not provide an answer. Why, I wonder, didn't he deal with moral law the same way he dealt with reason and logic in, for example, *The Johannine Logos* (Nutley, NJ: Presbyterian and Reformed, 1972)? There he argued that God's reason/logic was neither above God (Plato) nor below God (nominalism), but God's own rational nature. Why did he not take the same view of God's moral standards?

The point is correct, as far as it goes. As I argued earlier, moral values presuppose the absolute personality revealed in Scripture. If there is no such God, then the world is governed either by chance or by impersonal laws, neither of which commands the loyalty required by moral values. If, like the unbeliever, we seek to think and live without God, we have no basis for identifying or describing good and evil.

It is also useful to bring this point to the unbeliever's attention. He, in a way, has a more serious problem than the believer does. If the believer faces the problem of how there can be evil in a theistic world, the unbeliever faces the problem of how there can be either good or evil in a nontheistic world. In terms of the larger apologetic enterprise, this sort of truth needs to be driven home to the unbeliever.

Unbelievers must surely not be allowed to take their own autonomy for granted in defining moral concepts. They must not be allowed to assume that they are the ultimate judges of what is right and wrong. Indeed, they should be warned that that sort of assumption rules out the biblical God from the outset and thus shows its character as a faith-presupposition. The unbeliever must know that we reject his presupposition altogether and insist on subjecting our moral standards to God's. And if the unbeliever insists on his autonomy, we may get nasty and require him to show how an autonomous self can come to moral conclusions in a godless universe.

Valuable as this point is in itself, however, it is not really an answer to the problem of evil. It is an ad hominem argument; that is, it is addressed to the person rather than to the issue. The unbeliever asks how we account for evil, and we reply that he has a worse problem. He may indeed, but we have not thereby answered his question. And he might well reply, "Well, I grant that atheism has its share of problems, but for now let us talk about yours. I am pointing to what looks like a contradiction in your system. Whether or not my system is an adequate alternative is quite irrelevant to the question. Even if I were a Christian,[32] I would still have the same question, and I would like to have an answer to it."

Scripture does, as we will see, rebuke people who raise the problem of evil in certain ways. And Scripture is not entirely averse to some types of ad hominem response. But its typical responses are rather different from the one presently under discussion. We must hasten, then, to discover positively what Scripture does say.

---

32. In Van Tillian language, "When I consider Christianity on its own presuppositions, for the sake of argument."

8

APOLOGETICS AS DEFENSE: THE PROBLEM OF EVIL, PART 2— A BIBLICAL RESPONSE

In the previous chapter, we examined several solutions that various philoso-phers and theologians have put forward to solve the problem of evil, and we found them to be unbiblical or at least inadequate. In this chapter, we will see what the Bible itself says about the problem of evil. I propose that Scripture presents us with three ways of faithfully looking at evil:

Normative Defense:
God sets the standards

Situational Defense:
greater good

Existential Defense:
a new heart

Let us now look at this in greater detail.

God Is the Standard for His Actions[1]

Scripture never assumes that God owes us an explanation for what he does. In a number of biblical passages, the problem of evil arises for the

---

1. Students of the triadic system explained in *DKG* will identify the three sections of this chapter as normative, situational, and existential, respectively.

reader, but the text itself never comments on it. For example, we often wish that God had told us much more in Genesis 3, the story of the entrance of evil into the world. Where did the serpent (Satan) come from? If he was originally good along with the rest of the creation (Gen. 1:31), how did he become evil? Why was he allowed into the garden to tempt Eve? Why, indeed, did a good God foreordain this entire event to take place? If he foreordained the response of Adam and Eve, by what right does he punish them? All these questions naturally arise in the context, but the passage does not answer them. Indeed, when Adam in effect raises the problem of evil by blaming God for giving him the wife who tempted him (3:12), God offers no rationale for what he has done. Rather, he points out Adam's own wickedness, imposes a curse on him,[2] and then leaves the scene.

The same pattern is present in Genesis 22, where God tells Abraham to sacrifice his beloved son, the child of the promise. The reader naturally wants to know how such a command is compatible with God's goodness. Granting that God prevented it from being carried out, was this not a horrible trifling with a father's love? But God does not explain. Unlike Adam, Abraham never raises the issue, and God commends his quiet, unflinching obedience, his faith that God will provide the lamb (Gen. 22:15–18; cf. Rom. 4:17–25; Heb. 11:8–19).

By his failure to defend himself, God is claiming his sovereign right to be trusted and believed, whatever suspicions his actions might provoke in human minds. In the final analysis, he is sovereign in the granting and withholding of mercy. He makes that clear in Exodus 33:19, which is, in context, an exposition of his very name: "I will be gracious to whom I will be gracious, and will show mercy on whom I will show mercy." In his decisions, he will not submit to man's judgment. He reserves the right to behave in a way that might offend human values, that might even appear, from a human viewpoint, to contradict his own values. And when that happens, he is not under man's judgment. He is not obligated to explain.

This is one of the main themes of the book of Job. Job believes that he is suffering unjustly, and he demands an interview with God (23:1–7; 31:35ff.). He imagines that he will ask questions of God, and that God's answers will in turn vindicate his (Job's) righteousness. Well, God does grant the interview (see chaps. 38–42), but not on Job's terms. God, not Job, asks the questions. The Lord says to him, "Brace yourself like a man; I will question you, and

---

2. This is, to be sure, also a blessing, because it permits Adam to go on living and allows history to continue until the deliverer comes to defeat Satan.

you shall answer me" (38:3 NIV). The questions deal with mysteries of the universe, somewhat sarcastically pointing up Job's ignorance:

> Where were you when I laid the foundation of the earth?
>> Tell me, if you have understanding.
> Who determined its measurements—surely you know!
>> Or who stretched the line upon it? (Job 38:4–5)

The point is that if Job is so ignorant concerning God's works in the natural world, how can he expect to understand the workings of God's mind in distributing good and evil (cf. John 3:12)? In this stylized debate, Job confesses utter defeat. He puts his hand over his mouth—a sign of shame and also an admission that this would-be indicter of God has nothing to say (Job 40:4). But God initiates another round (40:6–41:34). There is the same result. No hint is given of any weakness in God! Job admits, "I know that you can do all things, and that no purpose of yours can be thwarted" (42:2). And he confesses his sin in claiming to know more than he really did:

> Therefore I have uttered what I did not understand,
>> things too wonderful for me, which I did not know. . . .
> I had heard of you by the hearing of the ear,
>> but now my eye sees you;
> therefore I despise myself
>> and repent in dust and ashes. (Job 42:3–6)

Notice how the charges are reversed. Job, like Adam, intended to bring charges against God. But the result, again as in Adam's case, is that the complainer is convicted of sin.

Notice also that Job never learns why he has had to endure suffering. The reader knows a bit more than Job, for he can read the prologue, in which Satan is permitted to tempt Job in order to prove his faithfulness. But that is not a complete explanation of why Job suffered. The reader then wants to know why God allowed Satan to do such a thing. Did God not know that Job was faithful? Who was it that needed additional proof? Why did God have any interest in convincing Satan of anything? (Why should he even assume that Satan's question was sincere?) Why was the bizarre wager made? Indeed, what was Satan doing in heaven anyway? And why was Satan created and permitted to make evil choices in the first place?

The book provides no answers to these questions. In the end, the reader is in the same position as Job himself. But in the end, the reader's questions must be handled in the same way that God handled Job's questions. For, like Job, we were not there when God laid the foundations of the earth. None of us knows who marked off its dimensions or stretched a measuring line across it. We need, too, to be cautious in probing the problem of evil. I don't believe it is sinful merely to pose questions. But when our questions take on the quality of accusations, when they express actual doubt of God's goodness, when we put ourselves in the proud position of demanding an answer, then we can expect a rebuke from God like the rebukes he gave to Job and to Adam.[3]

Let us note the same pattern in a few more passages. In Ezekiel 18:25, there is a brief exchange: "Yet you say, 'The way of the Lord is not just.' Hear now, O house of Israel: Is my way not just? Is it not your ways that are not just?" Again, a complaint against God's justice is reversed. For details, look at the context.

Another interesting passage in this connection is Matthew 20:1–16, Jesus' parable of the workers in the vineyard. Some work only one hour, others all day, but they all receive the same pay.[4] Some complain about unfairness (i.e., the problem of evil). But the master (God) replies, "Friend, I am doing you no wrong. Did you not agree with me for a denarius? Take what belongs to you and go. I choose to give to this last worker as I give to you. Am I not allowed to do what I choose with what belongs to me? Or do you begrudge my generosity?" (vv. 13–15).

Note here some of the same themes that we observed earlier: (1) The charges are reversed: the complainer is accused of envy. (2) The sovereignty of God is underscored ("Am I not allowed . . . ?") in contrast to any weakness-of-God theologies. (3) The reason for the uneven distribution is not given; the master senses no obligation to provide it. To these we may add (4) the reliability of the master's word ("Did you not agree . . . ?"). The master offered a denarius, and that is what he gave. His revelation is dependable; he is not a liar.[5] Thus, whatever problems might be connected with God's

3. And I expect that some of those rebukes will be visited on the theologians who are so insistent on a solution to the problem of evil that they are willing to turn their backs on the sovereign God revealed in Scripture.

4. This is not to be construed as a biblical model for labor-management relations! In the context of Matthew's Gospel, it seems to focus on the fact that Gentiles are soon to share the blessings of God with the Jews, and that the two groups will receive the same blessings, even though the Jews have been God's people for a much longer time. Note a similar point in the parable of the prodigal son (Luke 15:11–32), in which the returning profligate receives a blessing far greater than the older brother thinks is fair (vv. 28–32).

5. Reformed theology distinguishes between God's decretive will and his preceptive will. The former governs whatever comes to pass; the latter expresses what God wants us to believe and to

distribution of good and evil, we may not conclude that his Word, in which he promises blessings for his people, is unreliable.[6] And notice also that (5) a true interpretation of the facts actually vindicates the master's character. As the master sees it (and he, of course, is right!), the disparity in pay shows not unfairness to those who worked all day, but generosity to those who worked only an hour. A proper perspective—proper presuppositions—can make a great difference in how we evaluate things!

Finally, let us look at Paul's letter to the Romans, which also has a great concern for theodicy. Indeed, Romans is to the New Testament what Job is to the Old—the book most systematically focused on the problem of evil. Of course, we usually think of Romans as a description of how God justifies sinful people, together with the implications of that justification. That is true enough. But 3:26 indicates that Paul is concerned here not only with the justification of man, but also with the justification of God (theodicy). Specifically, how can God justify sinners without himself being subject to charges of injustice?

Thus, Romans often takes the form of dialogue between Paul and imaginary (or real?) objectors, who raise the problem of evil in various ways. For example, in 3:3 someone asks whether the unbelief of some Jews nullifies the faithfulness of God. Is God unjust to promise blessing to Israel and then to withhold from some the faith that is necessary to receive the blessing? Here is the problem of evil, applied to one aspect of God's plan. Interestingly, Paul, like the previous writers that we have considered, does not sense any obligation to answer that question. Rather, he rebukes it, as God rebuked Adam, Job, and the Israel of Ezekiel's time, and as the landowner in Jesus' parable rebuked his complaining workers: "By no means![7] Let God be true though every one were a liar, as it is written, 'That you may be justified in your words, and prevail when you are judged'" (v. 4, quoting Ps. 51:4). Note here again the familiar themes: the complainers

---

do. The former is secret until it is carried out in history; we cannot use it to predict the future. Nor can we use it alone to direct our lives; for such direction, God has given us his preceptive will in the Scriptures. (Of course, God's preceptive will must be applied to our circumstances, which in turn arise from his decretive will. To that extent, the decretive will is involved in God's guidance of our lives.) Jesus' parable tells us, then, in these theological terms, that although the structure and motivations of God's decretive will are highly mysterious, that mystery casts no doubt on the reliability of his preceptive will.

6. Again, this is contrary to the suppositions of many theologians.

7. This exclamation translates the Greek *me genoito*, literally "may it not be" (sometimes translated "certainly not"). It is a strong expression of abhorrence. The KJV translates it "God forbid." That is misleading, since the word *God* is not found in the Greek; but that added word does help to convey the strength of the expression.

have charges directed at them; God's word is vindicated; God rejects the supposed obligation to explain himself; God's sovereign rights are honored and his character is vindicated.

But in the very next verse the objector comes back: "But if our unrighteousness serves to show the righteousness of God, what shall we say? That God is unrighteous to inflict wrath on us?" (Rom. 3:5). Paul quickly reminds us (and God!) that this is not his objection, but one of an opponent: "I speak in a human way" (v. 5). And again, the questioner is strongly rebuked: "By no means! For then how could God judge the world?" (v. 6). Paul again upholds God's sovereign right as the supreme Judge, without showing how God can avoid a charge of injustice in this connection.

In the next instance, Paul's answer is even more of a rebuke and even less of an explanation:

> But if through my lie God's truth abounds to his glory, why am I still being condemned as a sinner? And why not do evil that good may come?—as some people slanderously charge us with saying. Their condemnation is just. (Rom. 3:7–8)

The last four words are the extent of Paul's answer.[8]

Note also Paul's shortness with questions in Romans 3:31; 6:1–2, 15ff.; 7:7. There are some actual answers here, as opposed to those we considered earlier. These questions don't deal with God's own character as directly. But they do indirectly, and to that extent Paul's responses contain at least a touch of rebuke.

The dialogue on the problem of evil resumes in earnest in Romans 9.[9] The question of verse 14, "Is there injustice on God's part?" (in hating Esau before his birth), receives Paul's usual answer: "By no means!" But why must we say that God is just in this connection? Because God has mercy on whom he will have mercy (v. 15, quoting Ex. 33:19). In other words, God has the sovereign right to do what he wishes, and no further explanation is necessary. Anyone who continues to accuse God (as in v. 19) is himself subject to the accusation that he is talking back to God, like a clay pot that questions the purposes of the potter who made it (vv. 20–21). The potter

---

8. One is reminded of the gag line, " 'Shut up,' he explained."

9. Notice, however, that the pattern of rhetorical questions in the book is transformed into a great hymn of divine victory and human redemption in Romans 8:31–39. The questions in the letter begin as unbelieving questions; later they have some measure of sincerity about them; in Romans 8, they become expressions of mature faith! But chapter 9 brings regression, as we will see.

is sovereign over the clay in both control and authority. So much for the weakness-of-God and free-will defenses!

Romans confirms, therefore, what we have seen elsewhere in Scripture. (1) We have no right to complain against God, and when we do, we expose ourselves as disobedient. (2) God is under no obligation to give us an intellectually satisfying answer to the problem of evil. He expects us to trust him in spite of that. (3) God's sovereignty is not to be questioned in connection with the problem of evil; it is rather to be underscored. (4) God's Word, his truth, is altogether reliable. (5) As a matter of fact, God is not unjust. He is holy, just, and good.

To summarize: God, as sovereign Lord, is the standard of his own actions. He is not subject to human judgment; on the contrary, our judgment is subject to his Word. Once we are thus clear on our epistemological situation, we can be assured, despite our questions, of God's good character, for on that matter the Word of God is clear.

This is not to say with Gordon Clark that God is *ex lex*, although it sounds similar and may indeed meet some of Clark's concerns. God honors essentially the same law that he gives us, for the fundamental law for man is, given the differences between Creator and creature, the law of God's own nature. God's righteousness is the standard for our righteousness. But as sovereign Lord, God may sometimes do things that appear to our finite minds to be contrary to that divine righteousness. When that happens, we must not demand explanations, but rather trust.

This is not to say that we must trust God's goodness with blind faith, although it might sound like that from our discussion so far. We have seen only part of the biblical response to the problem of evil, and when we see the rest, it will not seem to be a blind-faith response that God wants from us. Indeed, we saw earlier in this book that trusting God on the basis of his Word is not blind faith at all. The Word includes its own rationale and points to extrabiblical facts that also rationally confirm its teaching. Nevertheless, although faith is not blind, it is different from sight. The heroes of Hebrews 11 endured terrible sufferings, not seeing the fulfillment of God's promises, the heavenly city. They walked by faith. They had God's word, and that word was reliable. But it did not answer all their questions or tell each one why his or her suffering was necessary. Yet their faith prevailed. The very nature of faith is to persevere despite unanswered questions. Thus does God's Word encourage sufferers to hold on tightly to God's promises and not to be overcome with doubt.

Scripture Gives Us a New Historical Perspective

In this section, I intend to go more deeply into Scripture's rationale. Why are the biblical writers so sure of God's justice and goodness? As we have seen, they were not unaware of the problem of evil! Around them were all sorts of voices challenging the goodness and justice of God. One answer, of course—essentially the answer of the last section—is: God says so, and that ought to be enough. That answer is perfectly proper, and it is important, for it keeps our hearts fixed on their proper presuppositions. But that is not the only biblical answer; or, rather, it is not the full biblical answer. Scripture also tells us some things about *how* God reveals, and therefore vindicates, his goodness. We may summarize by saying that God vindicates his justice by giving us a new historical perspective, by helping us to see history through his eyes. Let us consider how the past, the present, and the future look through the eyes of God.

The Past: The Wait and the Dialectic

I have always felt that a great many mysteries in theology boil down to the mystery of time. Why is it that our eternal God loves to draw things out in time?[10] After all, if God's purpose was simply to create a universe and a people to glorify his name (temporal, to be sure), he could have accomplished it in a time barely perceptible to us. Even a drama of sin and redemption might, at least so it seems, have been accomplished in a few moments: a moment of disobedient thinking, a moment of divine-human suffering, a moment of resurrection triumph, and a moment initiating eternal glory.

Certainly a great part of the problem of suffering lies in the fact that our suffering is drawn out in time. We cry out to God, and he does not seem to hear. Or, rather, he in effect tells us to wait and wait and wait.

Scripture tells us a great deal about this waiting process. It shows us how God's people are tested by the passage of time over and over again. But it also shows us, again and again, how God brings the waiting periods to an end, vindicating himself and ending the sufferings of his people.

In the early chapters of Exodus, the people of Israel are in bondage in Egypt. Joseph, who brought the family there, has been dead for generations. During all that time, so far as we know, there has been no message from God. But the people cry out to him in their slavery (2:23ff.). Moses,

10. In my discussion of Leibniz (chapter 7), I indicated that the question whether this is the best of all possible worlds looks rather different when you think of the world as a whole historical sequence from creation to consummation.

the eventual deliverer, must also wait. At age forty, he goes into exile for killing an Egyptian; not until age eighty does he meet God and receive his commission to lead Israel to her promised home.

When Moses meets God in the burning bush, God identifies himself as the God of the past—"I am the God of your father, the God of Abraham, the God of Isaac, and the God of Jacob" (Ex. 3:6). The God of the past, however, is also a God of the present. He is here now to deliver his people from bondage. The mysterious name *I AM* in verse 14 could have some reference to this "temporal problematic": God is not merely the God of the past, but the God who is now, and will always be, present to deliver his chosen people (cf. 3:12). Thus, *Yahweh* (from "I am" in Hebrew), the Lord, will be his name forever, the name by which he will be remembered from generation to generation (v. 15). Yahweh is the same yesterday, today, and forever (cf. Heb. 13:8)!

This pattern is repeated over and over. The wilderness journey is a long wait before the people enter their new home—indeed, a long series of waits and new beginnings. Over and over, the people forget about God's great works on their behalf. They complain about their lack of water, of meat, of leeks; they complain about Moses' leadership. Each time, God enters in judgment, but preserves the people in grace. And they continue waiting.

Finally, they (actually the next generation, since the parents were judged unfaithful) enter the Promised Land. The conquest goes relatively smoothly during the days of faithful Joshua, but after his death the people do what is right in their own eyes (cf. Judg. 21:25 KJV) and the cycle repeats itself several times. Israel forgets the Lord; the people fall under bondage to foreign powers; they cry out to God; God sends a deliverer. There is some temporary improvement under Samuel and the early kings (especially David), but with the division of the kingdom and the prevalence of wicked kings, the waiting and divine visitations continue.

The whole Old Testament period may be described as a period of waiting. It is evident that Israel's home in Canaan does not in itself fulfill the promise made to Abraham. The bulls and goats offered in sacrifice do not take away the sin of the people. Of all the deliverers, none of them crushes the head of Satan. Indeed, Israel's disobedience—punctuated, to be sure, by periods of revival—becomes worse and worse.

In perspective, the long wait of the Old Testament period accentuates the problem of evil—not just because of its length, but also because it produces a kind of dialectic between justice and mercy. The prophets proclaim justice: Israel will certainly be judged for her disobedience. But they also proclaim grace: God is coming to redeem his people. Judgment is coming, but the promises to Adam and Abraham will nevertheless be fulfilled. Yet how can this be? Israel's sins are worse than those of the pagan nations of Canaan, even of Sodom and Gomorrah, which God destroyed. How can a just God do anything less than wipe the nation out entirely? Yet the promise of grace comes again. God will surely redeem his people. But how can he wipe them out and redeem them at the same time? It seems as though God's justice violates his mercy and vice versa. God is, it seems, in a bind. If he redeems, he must wink at sin; if he judges, he must renege on his promise.[11] As to the manner of resolution, there are dark hints—the messianic passages. But in the Old Testament itself, our question receives scant satisfaction. Indeed, God seems to be wanting precisely to build the tension, and build, and build.

The problem here is not only that evil raises questions about God's justice or goodness. It is that God's justice and goodness raise questions about each other. That is, God's very nature appears to be self-contradictory. If we could prove his justice, we would thereby disprove his goodness, and vice versa. Here the problem of evil becomes even more opaque than it has usually been in history.

And then comes Jesus. The wait is over. We saw in an earlier chapter how Jesus draws together the strands of Old Testament expectation—not only the explicit predictions, but the narratives as well—indeed, the whole religious system of the Hebrew Scriptures. Now let us observe how he solves the problem of evil in its particularly virulent Old Testament form.

Christ is the theodicy of Romans 3:26. When God gave his Son as an atonement for sin, "it was to show his righteousness at the present time, so that he might be just and the justifier of the one who has faith in Jesus."

Notice that the atonement vindicates both God's justice and his mercy. It is just and it justifies the ungodly. In Christ, the just penalty for sin is paid once for all. And because Christ endures that penalty in the place of his people, they receive lavish mercy beyond our power to imagine. God demonstrates both his justice and his love (Rom. 5:8); neither is compromised, but each is demonstrated in virtually infinite degree. We see this pattern also in Paul's summary statement: "Now the law came in to increase the trespass, but where sin increased, grace abounded all the more, so that, as sin reigned in death, grace also might reign through righteousness leading

---

11. Interestingly, the Psalms and the Prophets tend to juxtapose passages on judgment with passages on grace, one after the other, without transition. It is often unclear what motivates the prophet to move from the one topic to the other.

to eternal life through Jesus Christ our Lord" (Rom. 5:20–21). Grace reigning through righteousness! The mind boggles!

The Bible revels in this interplay. In the gospel of grace, the righteousness of God is revealed (Rom. 1:17).[12] Psalm 51:14–15 is fulfilled: when God saves us, he does it in such a way as to motivate us to praise his righteousness. And 1 John 1:9 tells us that God is not only faithful, but also just to forgive our sins. The forgiveness of sins is just, because of Christ.

Now let us look at Old Testament history in perspective. As I have mentioned, that history presents the problem of evil both as a wearisome wait through suffering and temptation and as an exceptionally difficult problem of reconciling divine attributes. Had I been living in the Old Testament period, I would have had very little idea (despite the hints of the coming Messiah) of how God would resolve the problem. Were I of a skeptical bent, I might even have been tempted to say that God could not possibly solve the problem. The problem of waiting could have been solved easily enough by bringing it to an end (but why does God *make* us wait?). But the "dialectic of justice and mercy" seems almost like a problem of logical contradiction: justice, as defined by the prophets, cannot be merciful, or so it seems. But God does solve the problem, in a way that none of us would likely have expected, in a way that amazes us and provokes from us shouts of praise.

And as for the wait, well, in retrospect it almost seems necessary. The tension must be built up to the nth degree so that we can feel to the utmost the liberating power of salvation.

Now, I grant that this redemptive history does not solve the problem of evil in every sense. It does not explain genocide or the suffering of little children, nor does it explain our present waiting as we look forward to God's final vindication. But here is the lesson for us: If God could vindicate his justice and mercy in a situation in which such vindication seemed impossible, if he could vindicate them in a way that went far beyond our expectations and understanding, can we not trust him to vindicate himself again? If God is able to provide an answer to the exceptionally difficult Old Testament form of the problem of evil, does it not make sense to assume that he can and will answer our remaining difficulties? Does it not make sense to trust and obey, even in the midst of suffering?

We may admire all the more the heroes of the faith listed in Hebrews 11, for they suffered and endured, with faith and trust, not having received the

---

12. One of Luther's great discoveries was that the phrase "righteousness of God" in this passage need not refer to the terror of God's judgment, but could rather refer to God's gracious justification of the ungodly.

promised Christ. In many ways it was far harder for them than it has been for us. They suffered more than most of us ever will, and they faced more mystery, living before the incarnation, than we do. Yet they, however sinful in certain ways, trusted in God's promise. Can we, who have experienced the incredible riches of Jesus' redemption, excuse ourselves from doing anything less?

The Present: The Greater-Good Defense

Scripture's new historical perspective enables us to look at our own present experience in a new way. In short, God is even now using evil for his own good purposes. This is sometimes called the greater-good defense, and of all the classical defenses (see chapter 7), it is the only one with scriptural support. It does, however, require some clarification.

As Jay Adams[13] and Doug Erlandson[14] have pointed out, Scripture deals with the problem of evil in its typically theocentric, as opposed to anthropocentric, way. So many traditional treatments of the problem assume that God's ultimate purpose is to provide happiness for man, and of course that is not so. God's ultimate purpose is to glorify himself, and indeed man's own chief end "is to glorify God, and to enjoy him forever."[15] Greater-good defenses often fail to see this point, and thus they arrive at a doctrine hard to distinguish from pagan hedonism. Erlandson therefore rejects this defense. But his point can be made just as well (and other important points can be made more easily) if instead of rejecting the greater-good defense we simply understand it theocentrically. That is, one good is greater than another when it is more conducive to the glory of God.

At the same time, theocentricity does not require us to ignore the happiness of human beings.[16] The biblical God is not Moloch, the pagan deity who demanded human sacrifice. Although we deserve death at his hands, the true God sacrifices his own Son to bring us life, and to bring it abundantly (John 10:10). Obedience to God is a way of life and happiness (Deut. 5:33; 8:3; 11:13–15; 28:1–14; 30:11–20; Pss. 1; 119:7).

---

13. Jay Adams, *The Grand Demonstration: A Biblical Study of the So-Called Problem of Evil* (Santa Barbara, CA: East Gate Publishers, 1991).

14. Doug Erlandson, "A New Perspective on the Problem of Evil," *Antithesis* 2, 2 (March–April 1991): 10–16.

15. Westminster Shorter Catechism, Answer 1.

16. This is, of course, the central Edwardian point of John's Piper's Christian hedonism. As he puts it, "God is most glorified in us when we are most satisfied in him." *Desiring God* (Sisters, OR: Multnomah, 1986), 10.

Self-denial and persecution are, of course, part of the Christian life, but the passages that stress these also emphasize that they lead to the most enduring happiness (Matt. 6:24–34; 10:16–42; Mark 10:29–31). Suffering is for a while; glory is for eternity.[17] Let us not forget that even the Westminster Shorter Catechism adds "and to enjoy him forever" to its theocentric statement of man's chief end. Therefore, when God seeks a "greater good" for himself, he seeks at the same time a greater good for his whole creation, that good described so rapturously in Revelation 21 and 22.

But we need still more clarification. The paragraph above might suggest universalism, the doctrine that all human beings will be saved. Scripture does not teach that; indeed, it teaches that some will endure eternal punishment for their wickedness. For this group, history is not working toward a "greater good," but toward a "greater curse." Obviously, more needs to be said about this than I can say in this particular book.[18] I conclude, then, that God's greater glory does bring with it a "greater good" for creation in general, and for those who love God (Rom. 8:28), but not for every individual person or thing in the universe. So at points the glorification of God does conflict with the happiness of some human beings; when that happens, we must choose the theocentric view.

With those clarifications, it is possible to learn from Scripture some of the ways in which God is using evil to bring about greater good. We must be cautious here. Scripture doesn't give us exhaustive explanations for all evils, as we've seen. It often calls on us to be quiet and accept in faith what providence brings our way. But it does show how God has used some evils to advance his purposes. Those purposes include:

1. Displaying his grace and justice (Rom. 3:26; 5:8, 20–21; 9:17)—the point made so well by Adams and Erlandson.[19]
2. Judgment of evil (Matt. 23:35; John 5:14), now and in the future. Remember, however, that there is not a one-to-one correlation between the sins of a person and the evil that befalls him in this life (Job; Luke 13:1–5).

17. This is a major theme of the New Testament, especially Romans 8 and 1 Peter.
18. In general, I agree with the viewpoint of Robert A. Morey in *Death and the Afterlife* (Minneapolis: Bethany House, 1984) and of John H. Gerstner in *Repent or Perish* (Ligonier, PA: Soli Deo Gloria Publications, 1990).
19. This is, of course, a very general way in which God uses evil; it overlaps other categories mentioned below.

3. Redemption: Christ's sufferings are redemptive in an obvious way (1 Peter 3:18).[20] But Paul claims for his own sufferings a similar significance (Col. 1:24). He does not claim to atone for the sins of others, but he does see a continuity between Christ's sufferings and his own, because both have suffered to plant the church and to draw individuals into it for their salvation. Many of the sufferings of God's servants today can be accounted for in that way. Those who would witness for Christ will be resisted by Satan, and in that witness, therefore, is suffering (cf. 2 Tim. 3:12).[21]

4. Shock value to unbelievers, intended to gain their attention and promote a change of heart (Zech. 13:7–9; Luke 13:1–5; John 9).

5. Fatherly discipline of believers (Heb. 12).

6. Vindication of God (e.g., Rom. 3:26).

We cannot always understand why God has chosen evil events to accomplish these good purposes. We do know that God never foreordains an evil event without a good purpose (Rom. 8:28). There could be other reasons than the ones we have mentioned, either to be found in Scripture or to remain locked up in God's own mind. We know that God has a reason for everything he does. Everything he does reflects his wisdom. But he is under no obligation to give us his reasons.

Nevertheless, as we see evil used for good again and again in Scripture, can we not accept in faith that those evils that are as yet unexplained also have a purpose in the depths of God's mind?

Again, we do not have a complete theoretical answer to the problem of evil. What we do have is a strong encouragement to trust God even amid unexplained suffering. Indeed, the encouragement is so strong that one would be foolish not to accept it.

The Future: Some Scripture Songs

The third dimension of our new perspective on history has to do with the future. We are, after all, still waiting. We have not seen how all of God's purposes result in good. Thus, the passage of time still tries our patience. And for those who are suffering, the sheer length of the trial can be an occasion for complaint against God. Still, in Scripture, God promises us

---

20. Recall God's use of "lawless men" in this connection (Acts 2:23; see Luke 22:22; Acts 4:27–28).

21. In the Old Testament, I see Joseph's sufferings in this way (Gen. 50:20)—preserving the seed of the promise until Christ should come.

that in the future he will be totally vindicated and we will be fully delivered from all evil. As we have indicated, the pattern is that of suffering now and receiving glory later.

When glory comes, the wicked will no longer prosper and the righteous will no longer suffer. From the sanctuary of God (Ps. 73) we see the certainty of God's victory.[22] The valleys will be exalted, and the mountains brought low; the proud will be abased, and the humble raised to greatness (Isa. 40:1ff.; Matt. 25; Luke 1:51).

God tells the prophet Habakkuk, who has complained about the apparent injustice of God's ways, first to wait for God's judgment (Hab. 2:2–3) and second to remember God's past deeds (3:2–16). As we wait for the future, seeking to be patient, it is helpful to remember the ways in which God has vindicated his judgment in the past (see the preceding section).

When the future—the culmination of God's plan—arrives, a great throng of angels and glorified saints will be singing to God of the righteousness of his deeds:

> Great and amazing are your deeds,
>   O Lord God the Almighty!
> Just and true are your ways,
>   O King of the nations!
> Who will not fear, O Lord,
>   and glorify your name?
> For you alone are holy.
>   All nations will come
>   and worship you,
> for your righteous acts have been revealed. (Rev. 15:3–4; cf. 16:5–7; 19:1–2)

Notice that there is no more doubt among God's servants as to the justice of his ways. The rhetorical question in this quotation has the answer "no one"—no one will fail to fear and glorify God. Why? Because his righteous acts have been revealed. I take it that the consummation of history will somehow reveal enough that remaining doubts concerning God's goodness will be entirely taken away from us. Does this mean that in that day we will finally receive a definitive, exhaustive, theoretical, and practical answer to the problem of evil? Not necessarily. God might simply shut our mouths, as he shut Job's, and reopen them in praise. It could be that when we see God

---

22. Cf. also Ps. 37. The two psalms that are most sharply focused on the problem of evil can be easily recalled if we remember that one reverses the digits of the other.

face-to-face, we will see a face of such supreme trustworthiness that all our complaints will simply disappear. Or it could be that as we see the One who is greater than Solomon, judging the whole earth in perfect righteousness, we will be far less inclined to bring up the perplexities of past history.

At any rate, we may be assured that in the last day there will be no problem of evil. There will be no more doubt, no more complaint. If there is a residual theoretical problem, it will be one that we will be completely happy to live with. And if we believe now that that day will certainly come, can we not be content in the present?

Again, we find in Scripture not a philosophical solution to the problem, but a great reassurance, a powerful motivation to keep trusting and obeying, despite all the wickedness in the world.

Scripture Gives Us New Hearts

Finally, Scripture gives us faithful hearts. As indicated earlier, the Word of God is powerful to save (Rom. 1:16–17). As the Holy Spirit speaks in the Scriptures, he turns our skepticism into faith. Our hearts are warmed as we hear the gospel (Luke 24:32). In such a mood, we cannot speak from the high horse of proud autonomy. We can only be full of thanks that God has been merciful to us, despite our sin. The marvelous thing, as John Gerstner and others have pointed out, is not that there is evil in the world, but that God has forgiven the evil in our own hearts for the sake of Christ.

Without that new heart of faith, we are blind (1 Cor. 2:14; 2 Cor. 4:4). But Christ opens eyes that were blinded by sin and opens lips to sing his praise (Pss. 51:15; 73:16–17).

Believers, even with their new hearts, do continue to ask about the problem of evil. But there are so many reasons for giving thanks that we can never look at evil with the same passion as the unbeliever. The believer simply looks at the world with values different from those of the unbeliever. And the change in those values is perhaps the closest we can get, at this point in history, to a theodicy.

9

APOLOGETICS AS OFFENSE: CRITIQUE OF UNBELIEF

Apologetics is not only defense, but also offense, an attack by Christians against unbelieving thought and action.[1] As the apostle puts it, "We destroy arguments and every lofty opinion raised against the knowledge of God, and take every thought captive to obey Christ" (2 Cor. 10:4f.). Indeed, as is true in some other fields, "the best defense is a good offense": that is, it could be argued that offense is the *primary* function of apologetics. After all, God has nothing to defend, to "apologize" for. Jesus Christ is the mighty ruler of heaven and earth, the invincible warrior on the march to bring in his kingdom, putting down all powers and authorities opposed to him (Col. 2:15). Apologetics is one of his tools for putting his enemies under his feet.[2]

So it is not enough for the apologist to respond to the unbeliever's objections. He is called to turn the attack against God's enemies. This is the role taken by the Lord himself: the prosecuting attorney of the covenant lawsuit.[3] See Job 38; Isa. 1:18ff.; 3:13; Jer. 1:16; Hos. 4:1; John 16:8 (the Holy Spirit). When Satan or his human associates bring accusations against God, God regularly refuses to answer the charge and brings accusations against his attackers. See Gen. 3:17–24; Job 38–42; Matt. 20:1–15; Rom. 3:3f. Similarly, Jesus, after refuting several questions intended to entrap him, turns on his

---

1. Obviously, when I speak of *offense*, I am not urging the apologist to be "offensive," that is, nasty or rude. The apologist ought to avoid giving offense, except for the offense of the cross of Christ itself. I am using *offense* as it is used in sports and war: our attack on the enemy.

2. Cornelius Van Til was once criticized for using military imagery. Without forgetting what I said in the previous section about gentleness and love, I must reply as he did: That language is biblical.

3. Meredith G. Kline, *Images of the Spirit* (Grand Rapids, Baker, 1980), 127.

critics (Matt. 22:41–45), as does Paul, after an extended attempt at defensive apologetics (Acts 28:23–28). Note also the element of solemn warning found in so many divine utterances: 1 Sam. 8:9; Ps. 81:11f.; Isa. 28:17; 44:25; Jer. 1:10; Lam. 2:14; Hos. 2:9, particularly against false claims to wisdom in opposition to his word. Unlike many today, God is not afraid to be negative.

We have already done much by way of apologetic offense. In chapter 2, we indicated that the fundamental choice is between two alternatives: the absolute personality of Christianity and the ultimate impersonalism of every other system (the systems that we have collectively described as the "conventional wisdom"). We have seen that the conventional wisdom cannot do justice to values and therefore cannot account for the trustworthiness of reason. This inability corrupts impersonalist ideas in every field of human thought: science, philosophy, psychology, sociology, the arts, economics, business, government, or whatever. But it also corrupts practical living: in a chance universe, what is the point of brushing your teeth in the morning?

In discussing the problem of evil, we mentioned the ad hominem but nevertheless useful point that an impersonalist philosophy cannot distinguish good and evil sufficiently even to raise the problem against Christianity.

As we have mentioned before, it is impossible to rigidly separate offensive from defensive and constructive apologetics. Negative criticism will not do much good unless at the same time we cogently present a positive Christian alternative. All our defensive and constructive strategies have depended on offensive premises, namely, that there are only two alternatives, and that the unbelieving alternative is inadequate either to defend its own view or to raise objections against the Christian position. To that extent, surely, "the best defense is a good offense."

But it will be helpful to describe our offensive argument somewhat more systematically. Hence this chapter.

Offense is certainly essential to apologetics in the Bible. We see over and over again how Scripture goes on the attack against doubt and unbelief. Remember how Job wished to have an interview with God, but God surprised him by taking the role of the interviewer, the offensive position, and exposing Job's ignorance (Job 38ff.). This was also important in Jesus' presentation of the gospel. In John 3, when Nicodemus ("the" teacher of Israel, as is suggested by the original Greek of v. 10) comes to Jesus by night, evidently hoping to have a cordial theological discussion, Jesus sweeps away all the pleasantries and tells him that apart from the new birth, he cannot even see the kingdom of God (v. 3). Jesus dismisses

Nicodemus's whole way of thinking and demands that it be rebuilt on an entirely different foundation.

The same thing happens in John 4, although Jesus is gentler in his approach.[4] The woman at the well, too, has a theological question: should we worship at Mount Gerizim or at Jerusalem? Jesus answers quickly, but then proceeds to dismantle her Samaritan orthodoxy by telling her of the coming kingdom in which true worship will not be limited to one location at all—and by telling her that he is the Messiah.

And when the Jewish leaders of various parties try to trap him with trick questions (Matt. 22, esp. vv. 41–46), he first shuts their mouths and then goes on the attack. He does this by asking them how the Messiah could be both David's son and David's Lord, according to Psalm 110.

In his Pentecost sermon, Peter boldly attacks the assembled population as the murderers of the Messiah (Acts 2, esp. vv. 36–41). And Paul even calls Gentiles to account for their ignorant, idolatrous worship and declares that the resurrected Jesus will judge all mankind (17:22–34).

And let us not forget Paul's militant language in 2 Corinthians 5:1–10; Ephesians 6:10–20; 1 Timothy 6:12; 2 Timothy 2:1–7; 4:1–5.

The Unbeliever's Twin Strategies

If we are to go on the offensive against unbelief, we ought to know more about it. What is unbelief, from a biblical standpoint? What is the structure of what we have called the conventional wisdom?

Remember from previous discussions that the unbeliever, at some level of his consciousness, knows God and knows the truth about God (Rom. 1:21), but suppresses it. Nevertheless, his suppressed knowledge guides him in many of his daily decisions. He usually assumes that there is a point to brushing his teeth, having breakfast, working for a living. He assumes the validity of value judgments when he criticizes politicians or bureaucrats, and even when he attacks the Bible. He might even acknowledge God, as did the Pharisees. So he might be an "orthodox" church member, whose fundamental unbelief is known only to God.

Still, the main drift of his thinking, his dominant presuppositions, is unbelieving. He is trying his best to think and live as though the absolute

---

4. As I mentioned before, Jesus tended to be tough with those who considered themselves experts in spiritual matters and gentler with those who recognized their ignorance. But Jesus never compromised his message. Reflecting this pattern, Van Til was fond of the saying *suaviter in modo, fortiter in re*—"gentle in our presentation, powerful in the content or substance of what we say."

personal God of Scripture did not exist. In most cases, this ambition does not lead to pharisaic orthodoxy, but to ways of thinking that more obviously proclaim unbelief. There are essentially two such ways: rationalism and irrationalism—or, to put them in biblical categories, atheism and idolatry.[5] These can be mixed together, although that creates its own problems (as we will see), and they can be mixed with that true knowledge that the unbeliever unsuccessfully tries to suppress. Such mixtures create ambiguity; it is not always easy to separate the truth from the error in them. Nevertheless, the basic outlines of idolatry and atheism are usually visible behind the overall complexity.

Irrationalism and Rationalism

Cornelius Van Til argued that every unbelieving system of thought—because it reflects unregenerate hearts—is simultaneously rationalistic and irrationalistic. While claiming that their reason has ultimate authority (rationalism), unbelievers do not acknowledge anything that connects reason with objective truth (irrationalism).[6] Van Til pointed out that the rationalist-irrationalist tension began in the garden of Eden. Eve would not take God's word as her ultimate authority; she looked at God's speech, Satan's, and her own as though the three were equal. But that is to imply that there is no final truth about anything—irrationalism. Nevertheless, when required to choose, Eve claimed the right to decide for herself, over against God—autonomous rationalism. So in our own day, it is not unusual for modern secularists to claim that all truth is relative, while insisting that naturalistic evolution is a proven fact, never conscious of the contradiction into which they have fallen.

This kind of analysis of the history of non-Christian thought in terms of rationalism and irrationalism gives to the Christian a wonderful insight into the structure and dynamics of intellectual movements.[7] It is immensely

---

5. Agnosticism is usually a disguised atheism. See the discussion of this idea in chapter 5.

6. For more discussion of the rationalist-irrationalist dialectic in non-Christian thought, see Cornelius Van Til, *The Defense of the Faith*, ed. K. Scott Oliphint, 4th ed. (Phillipsburg, NJ: P&R Publishing, 2008), chaps. 3 and 7; *CVT*, chap. 17; *DKG*, 360–63. This form of analysis can also be helpful in understanding how unbelievers often perceive Christians. On this point, see *DCL*, chap. 4.

7. These ideas can be fruitfully applied, I think, to disciplines other than philosophy. Cf. Rousas J. Rushdoony, "The One and Many Problem," in *Jerusalem and Athens: Critical Discussions on the Philosophy and Apologetics of Cornelius Van Til*, ed. E. R. Geehan (Nutley, NJ: Presbyterian and Reformed, 1971), 339–48, on politics, and the various essays on mathematics, education, psychology, history, economics, and so forth in Gary North, ed., *Foundations of Christian Scholarship* (Vallecito, CA: Ross House, 1976).

important both to the task of interpretation and to the work of apologetics. As I've stated in *DCL*, the rationalist-irrationalist dialectic of non-Christian thought bears on ethical reasoning, as well as on thinking about other matters. Nonbiblical ethicists often oppose absolutes in general, but they forget their opposition to absolutes when they propose their own fundamental ethical principles, such as love and justice. Joseph Fletcher provides us with one egregious example. In his book *Situation Ethics*, he says that "for the situationist there are no rules—none at all," but in the same paragraph he proposes a "'general' proposition . . . namely, the commandment to love God through the neighbor." Is there a contradiction here between "no rules" and the rule of love? Fletcher replies enigmatically that the love commandment "is, be it noted, a normative ideal; it is *not* an operational directive."[8] Evidently he thinks that the love commandment is not a commandment, and therefore not a rule. But this distinction is quite implausible. Fletcher is a rationalist in rejecting all external ethical absolutes and an irrationalist in that he must cheat to make his approach intelligible (smuggling in a single ethical absolute in the guise of an "ideal").

In fact, the history of Western philosophy provides us with many examples of this dance between rationalism and irrationalism.[9] In ancient philosophy, the rationalistic motif seemed to dominate the scene; in modern times, the irrationalistic motif seems to be largely in control. Yet neither exists independently of the other.

Let's start with ancient Greek philosophy. There we find some figures, such as the sophists, who were predominantly irrationalistic; yet the sophists' insistence that "man is the measure of all things" shows their rationalistic side (making autonomous man the final standard of truth, beauty, and goodness), and Plato was able to show that their skepticism was itself a dogmatic assertion, offered as a sure, universal truth. Others, such as Parmenides, sought to understand everything in terms of timeless logic; but Parmenides needed to resort to mythology to explain the "illusions" that didn't cohere with his rationalistic worldview. Therefore, the irrationalistic sophists were also rationalists; the rationalistic Parmenides was also an irrationalist.

Plato combined these motifs explicitly. He was rationalistic about our knowledge of the world of forms or ideas, while irrationalistic about our

---

8. Joseph F. Fletcher, *Situation Ethics: The New Morality* (Philadelphia: Westminster Press, 1966), 55.

9. For further discussion on the philosophers mentioned here, see my *A History of Western Philosophy and Theology* (Phillipsburg, NJ: P&R Publishing, 2015), chap. 2, "Greek Philosophy."

knowledge of the world of sense-experience. His problem was in fitting the two worlds together. Van Til offers an interesting and, I think, profound analysis of Plato's vacillations between the two motifs.[10] The same critique bears upon Aristotle. For him, form and matter are not found in different worlds, as in Plato, but they are complementary aspects of the world in which we now live. But like Plato, Aristotle understands form and matter antithetically—as pure universality and pure particularity—so that their relationship is as problematic as that of Plato's two worlds.

The dance of rationalism and irrationalism has also caused problems for some Christian theology. The medieval theologian and philosopher Thomas Aquinas, whose thinking for many centuries had official status in the Roman Catholic Church, adopted an epistemology based in part on Neoplatonism and Aristotle. Van Til attributes to that compromise many of the doctrinal and apologetic errors of the Roman Catholic tradition.[11]

In the modern era, rationalism is emphasized in Descartes, Spinoza, and Leibniz, but from an irrationalistic basis. The opposite is true of Locke, Berkeley, and Hume. Immanuel Kant (1724–1804), like Plato, seeks to develop a viewpoint that does equal justice to both motifs and, again, seeks to accomplish that by a division between two realms: in Kant's case, the *noumenal* realm, of which nothing can be known by man, and the *phenomenal* realm, in which autonomous reason reigns supreme. Kant is, in other words, irrationalistic about the noumena, rationalistic about the phenomena. In attempting to reconcile the concerns of rationalism and irrationalism, he advocated human autonomy even more explicitly and consistently than his predecessors: the human mind became the source of the categories that supply the structure to the phenomenal world.

Again, this tool of analysis helps us to see the twists and turns of the history of thought in perspective. Every several years, one hears the claim that contemporary thought has become radically different from anything that has gone before. The latest claim of this sort, opposing objective norms, comes from what is called *postmodernism*.[12] The name comes from the view that "modern" thinking must be overcome. Modern thinking assumes

---

10. Cornelius Van Til, *A Survey of Christian Epistemology* (Philadelphia: Presbyterian and Reformed, 1969), 24–43.
11. Van Til discusses Roman Catholicism and its traditional scholastic philosophy often in his writings. See my discussions in *CVT*, chaps. 19 and 25.
12. An excellent introduction to postmodernism is William Edgar, "No News Is Good News: Modernity, the Postmodern, and Apologetics," *Westminster Theological Journal* 57, 2 (1995): 359–82.

the competence and goodness of secularized reason, technology, and the institutions of Western civilization. In turn, this confidence presupposes that there is a single objective truth accessible to human reason through logical and scientific methods. We are told that thirty years ago or so, our culture rejected the rationalistic assumptions of the Enlightenment and came to recognize that "linear, scientific, objective" thinking is largely an expression of bias. Therefore, contemporary, "postmodern" thought rejects all the assurances of the past and opens itself to various non-Western, non-linear influences, such as Eastern religions, occultism, and various kinds of mystical or symbolic ways of understanding.[13] But postmodernism denies any sort of objective truth. Indeed, there is not even an authoritative way of interpreting any piece of language. The author's intention is not authoritative, for the meaning of language is independent of any individual intention. It "deconstructs" language to lay bare its essential use—not as a means of rational communication from one mind to another, but as a means of social power, to control and oppress.

Postmodernism denies that there is any one set of rules (*grand récit*, "metanarrative") for finding truth. There is on this view a multitude of criteria, held by different people, different groups, in different settings, that may or may not be consistent with one another. The claim of objective truth, in their somewhat Marxian view, is an oppressive claim. It amounts to oppression: males dominating women, whites dominating blacks, Westerners dominating other cultures, rich dominating poor.

Certainly the postmodernists are right to protest the proud claims of modernist rationality. And as a presuppositionalist, I appreciate their observation that all claims to knowledge are governed by presuppositions, that nobody is simply "neutral." Postmodernists understand that things look different depending on where you sit. Literature looks different to women than to men, to poor than to rich, and so on. And certainly they are right to say that claims to objective truth can be means of oppression.[14] But to reject objective truth entirely is quite impossible. Postmodernists inevitably exempt their own writings from this kind of criticism. William Edgar points out that

13. Postmodernists are more or less allied with the neo-Gnostic New Age spiritualities described in Peter Jones, *Spirit Wars* (Escondido, CA: Main Entry, 1997). His discussions there are worth noting.

14. Some applications that postmodernists are not inclined to make: dogmatism about women's "reproductive rights" is oppressive to unborn children; dogmatism about evolution is oppressive to Christians; dogmatism about the "separation of church and state" oppresses public-school students who are trying to find truth.

Christopher Norris has shown how a scholar like Stanley Fish, in his vehement attacks on theory as a mere justification for personal preference, perpetuates the illusion that he is somehow outside of the confines of that personal preference. . . . The most serious flaw in [Jean-François] Lyotard's presentation, however, is the deep-rooted contradiction between his claims to do away with metanarrative and his own program, which is suspiciously like a metanarrative of another kind.[15]

If postmodernists want to be consistent in denying objective truth,[16] they should abandon the attempt to persuade others of the truth of their position. What could that "truth" be, if it is not objective truth? But if they want to set forth their position as objectively true, then their viewpoint must be substantially revised. Postmodernists emphasize the irrationalist pole of unbelief's rationalist-irrationalist dialectic.[17] We will therefore set this kind of postmodern relativism aside and assume, as most everyone does, the objectivity of logical and moral norms.[18]

We need to take "cultural sea-change" in stride, not to be terrified by every new ideology that comes down the pike. When the opinion-formers announce such radical changes in the intellectual climate, Christians often wonder in frustration, "How do we deal with this new challenge to our faith?" Many evangelical leaders argue that some utterly new approach is needed.[19]

Our age is really nothing drastically different from what has been going on since the garden of Eden. Essentially it is the rationalism-irrationalism

15. Edgar, "No News Is Good News," 379. He cites Christopher Norris, *What's Wrong with Postmodernism?* (Baltimore: Johns Hopkins University Press, 1990), chap. 2.

16. But what would *consistency* mean if objectivity were excluded?

17. But of course, they are rationalistic in the dogmatism by which they assert their view. The rationalist pole in our society is emphasized by naturalistic scientism. That naturalistic scientism is, however, irrationalist, in that it has no rational basis for its dogmatism.

18. The meanings of the terms *objective truth* and *objectivity* need to be underscored. A Christian understanding of these concepts emphasizes at least two things. First, God's creative and decretive control over reality is independent from our own desires, wishes, or whims. Second, the notion of objective truth highlights the truth of the final judgment. Our attitudes and actions toward God, his creation, and image-bearers—each careless thought, word, or action—will be judged by God despite the skeptic's doubt. Judgment *is* still coming. *Every* knee will bow, both those who denied the truth of Scripture and those who lovingly submit to it. One last point is this: Knowing objective truth is not to be confused with knowing the truth objectively. The former (in a biblical framework) is the humble submission of one's thoughts to the reality of God's world and Word. The latter is a denial of our Creator-creature distinction. For more reflections on Christian-theistic objectivity, see Joseph Emmanuel Torres, "Perspectives on Multiperspectivalism," chap. 5 in *STL*, 123–25.

19. One such proposal is Myron B. Penner, *The End of Apologetics* (Grand Rapids: Baker Academic, 2013).

dance all over again. Thus, in their essence, the latest contemporary ideas are no different from those of the ancient Greeks, the modern rationalists and empiricists, Kant, Hegel, and the others. Postmodernism, insofar as it is really a change from what has gone before, is a shift from a rationalistic to an irrationalistic impulse. Its rejection of "linear objectivity" is something that we have seen before: among the Greek sophists, in Hume's critique of objectivity, in Kant's critique of metaphysics, in Hegel's attempt to achieve truth through negation and synthesis.

Rationalists and irrationalists are not found only among professional philosophers. Ordinary unbelievers also demonstrate these commitments, though not in such epistemologically self-conscious ways. The rationalist could be the self-made businessman who sees himself as the master of his fate, or the local politician who thinks that by careful government planning we may overcome all our social woes, or the bartender who has an opinion on everything, or the neighbor who thinks that "modern science" has utterly disproved Christianity. He could also be the church elder who thinks that because of his good works or doctrinal knowledge he deserves God's favor, or the "black sheep" who thinks that he must become a much better person before he will have the right to seek God. The irrationalist could be the town drunk who couldn't care less about anything, or the happy milkman who lives on sentimentality and seems bewildered when anyone asks him his basis for living, or the angry teenager who hates all authority and seeks to destroy everything he sees. In a fundamental sense, there is nothing new under the sun. Students who learn presuppositional apologetics, if they learn it well, will be prepared for the next new development when it comes; they will not have to learn their apologetics all over again.

My only caveat is that we should avoid using this analysis in a wooden way, insensitive to the diversity among non-Christian thinkers. That would make it a procrustean bed rather than an example of critical analysis. Nor should we assume that *everything* in the works of a non-Christian thinker can be exhaustively explained by the rationalist-irrationalist dialectic. Indeed, there is a certain complication here: a thinker's words often reflect *both* revelational insight *and* suppression of the truth, at the same time. When Plato says that the real world is rationally apprehensible, he is expressing revealed truth. The world is rationally knowable, first to God, then to us by revelation. But he is at the same time expressing his own rational autonomy, for the process of "rational apprehension" to Plato is far different from that of biblical "analogical knowledge." It would be wrong to disagree with Plato merely because he is an unbeliever; to do so would be an instance of the "genetic fallacy," judging something on the basis of its origin. On the other hand, it would be equally wrong to think that this statement in no way expresses Plato's suppression of the truth.

Once we are aware of this apologetic tool, we might be tempted to mechanically categorize everything in a philosopher's thought under either the heading of rationalism or that of irrationalism. But some of his assertions could have a different character entirely. It is important to note that unbelievers do sometimes discover and acknowledge truth "in spite of themselves." Our analysis of their thought must not routinely negate everything they say. Rather, we must be sensitive to distinguish in their formulations between the ideas they have learned from God's revelation and the ideas they are using to suppress that revelation. After all, rationalism and irrationalism are parasitic on Christianity. Of course, rationalism and irrationalism are both radically opposed to Christianity. Yet they depend on Christianity in some ways for their plausibility. It is, after all, the Christian revelation that tells us that human reason has both powers and limitations. Rationalism and irrationalism build on those notions of powers and limitations, respectively, but neither is able to specify what those powers and limitations are, independently of God. Thus, they have no principle to keep them from the extremes of sheer irrationalism and sheer rationalism. In these ways, rationalism and irrationalism are vulnerable to Christian attack. None of these positions is really distinct from the others; thus, each is subject to all the difficulties mentioned. They would have no plausibility at all if it were not for their resemblance to Christianity.

But as noted earlier, it is also helpful to view the dynamics of unbelief from the perspective of more biblical categories: atheism and idolatry.

Atheism

Atheism can be either practical or theoretical, or both. The theoretical atheist denies God; the practical atheist simply lives as though God did not exist. I include under atheism various forms of deism and theism in which there is some kind of God who, because of his transcendence, modesty, or whatever, has nothing to do with human life.

The natural result of atheism is a loss of standards and values, for we saw earlier that these can be revealed and enforced only by the God of Scripture. Atheists tend to be relativists. Indeed, many find atheism attractive for just this reason. After all, people flee from God (as Adam did) because they don't want to be held responsible before him. Like all other forms of unbelief, atheism is essentially an escape from responsibility.

Of course, the natural connection between atheism and relativism is not always made, even by atheists themselves. There are atheists who maintain some value judgments very strongly. In fact, even the most relativistic among them are inconsistent on that score. Some might even wish to defend objective morality. They must be told that they have no basis for making such judgments.

Unbelievers tend to go to extremes, in this case the extreme of denying objective meaning altogether. The unbeliever might resist this extreme, for he knows it is implausible, but there is nothing in his adopted philosophy to guard against it. He rejects the one revelation that would provide a basis for a more balanced assessment of reason and value. The one-and-many God of Scripture makes it plain that there is no such thing as meaningless plurality, plurality not united into order and structure.

Among Christian critics of culture, the late Francis Schaeffer and his disciples have perhaps presented most vividly the implications and dangers of atheistic relativism.[20] They characterize the modern period as dominated by this type of thought, as opposed to the more rationalistic thought of earlier periods. They analyze modern art, music, films, philosophy, and politics along these lines, with fruitful apologetic conclusions.

Idolatry

The other major form of unbelief is idolatry, namely, giving one's ultimate allegiance to some being other than the God of Scripture. This allegiance might be to some primitive god or gods (e.g., Zeus, Baal, Moloch, or Astarte), to some abstract principle (e.g., Plato's Good), to a non-Christian religion (e.g., Islam or Buddhism),[21] to a modern cultural movement such as the New Age, to oneself, to human reason, or whatever.

The total loss of meaning implicit in atheism is too much for most people to stand. They need some values, some standard, some ways to orient their lives. Among these people, those who continue to resist belief in the true God become inconsistent in their atheism, or, to that extent, they become idolaters. If they don't want the true God, they must seek some other.

20. This group includes Schaeffer's wife Edith, his son Frank, his daughter Susan Macaulay, and their present and past associates at L'Abri Fellowship, such as Os Guinness, Donald Drew, Ranald Macaulay, Jerram Barrs, Udo Middelmann, and Jane Stuart Smith.
21. I realize that I am stretching the traditional definitions a bit to call Islam idolatrous. I am using the term to make a general point that I think is scriptural, however we may want to debate about the terminology.

Again, the unbeliever tends toward an extreme. If the idol is to fill the role of God, he must have some divine attributes and fill some divine roles.

Atheism and idolatry are the only alternatives to Christianity. In order to reject Christianity, one must either deny all gods or select some god to worship other than the God of Scripture. In reality, of course, they together form a single alternative, for even the atheist must, practically, allow for some absolute, usually his own reason. To say that there is no God is to say that the most ultimate reality in the universe is impersonal—but that in itself is idolatry. Similarly, idolatry relies on atheism and tends to revert back to it. Idolatry depends on would-be autonomous thinking and the rejection of divine revelation. Thus, the line between atheism and idolatry is not sharp.

Like atheism, idolatry can be either theoretical or practical. The "god" can be a theoretical entity such as human reason, evolution, dialectical materialism (Marxism), the state, or even the universe (pantheism). Or it can be a practical reality such as money (Mammon!), pleasure (Dionysius/ Bacchus), family, self, or a non-Christian religion.[22]

And like atheism, idolatry is an escape from responsibility to the true God. It seeks freedom and autonomy. Unfortunately, the natural result of it is slavery—bondage to the idol.

Epistemologically, idolatry tends to be less relativistic than atheism. Indeed, idolatry accounts for the rather dogmatic certainty that accompanies much unbelief. Consider the amazing certainty that many people have concerning the theory of evolution, at a time when the theory has been subjected to serious challenges, not only by Christians, but also by secular scientists and logicians. Why are they so certain and so determined to keep out of the schools any discussion of its only significant alternative, creation?[23] The answer is that evolution has become for many a religious presupposition, an idol. To lose that idol would, for many, be to lose their fundamental worldview, the framework on which they rely for order and rationality.

I reject the theory of evolution on the following grounds:

22. It is sad to think of how often Christians themselves are tempted to betray their Lord in the interest of such idols. How many Christians today keep the fourth of the Ten Commandments, to "remember the Sabbath day [by keeping] it holy" (Ex. 20:8)? Must the Sabbath be completely forgotten in our pursuit of money and pleasure? If so, will we not one day be ashamed when our Lord returns?

23. California's chief of education, Bill Honig, sought to deny the Creation Research Institute of San Diego the right to grant degrees because the Institute (which taught both views, but presented evolution with a Christian critique) refused to teach evolution as established fact. In answer to many prayers, God restrained Honig through the court system.

1. In Genesis 2:7, it is a special act of God (inbreathing) that makes Adam a "living creature" (*nefesh hayyah*). God did not take an already-existing living creature and make him specifically human, as in theistic evolution. Rather, he took dust and gave it life. Adam came to life by the same divine action by which he became man.[24]

2. The frequent repetition of "according to their kinds" in Genesis 1:11–12, 21, 24–25 indicates that there are divinely imposed limitations on what can result from reproduction. I do not know how broadly these "kinds" should be construed, or how they relate to modern biological classifications such as family, genus, and species. But whatever a kind is, these passages evidently imply that plants or animals of one kind do not produce plants or animals of another. But that is what must happen if the theory of evolution is to be true.

3. Although I am not well equipped to judge scientific evidence, I will simply add that, as a layman, I am not convinced by the evidence presented to me for evolution. Doubtless there has been what is sometimes called microevolution: variations in the distribution of genetic characteristics within a species, due to natural selection. So in some environments moths of a certain color become more preponderant, and in other environments those of a different color, as color proves in different ways to be an aid to survival and reproduction. But this amounts to variation within already-existing genetic possibilities, rather than a process that produces a new species, that is, a new set of genetic possibilities. Nor does it come anywhere near to proving the existence of a process that could derive all present living forms from a single cell. Evidence for macroevolution, the derivation of all living organisms from the simplest by mutation and natural selection, seems to me to be sketchy at best.

4. Further, I agree with Phillip Johnson that the real persuasive power of the theory of evolution is not the evidence adduced in its favor, but rather the fact that it is the only viable alternative to theism.[25] Of course, that consideration carries no weight with me, nor should it influence any other Christian to view the theory favorably. Rather, it should make us open to criticism of the theory.

24. This argument is condensed from John Murray, *Collected Writings of John Murray*, vol. 2 (Edinburgh: Banner of Truth Trust, 1977), 5–13.

25. Phillip Johnson, *Darwin on Trial* (Downers Grove, IL: InterVarsity Press, 1993); *Reason in the Balance* (Downers Grove, IL: InterVarsity Press, 1995).

Nobody can prove evolution. Evolution is a hypothesis held by faith, and all supposed facts must be made to fit into its framework. It is a "paradigm" in Thomas Kuhn's sense,[26] a criterion for judging other proposals, itself not subject to judgment. Indeed, evolution is necessary, once one rejects creation. For either the earth was produced supernaturally (i.e., created) or it was produced naturally, apart from God. Any naturalistic origin of the world will involve evolution, for it will be the result of natural laws operating on primitive matter, producing complexity over time. Thus, the concept of evolution did not begin with Darwin.[27] Rather, it has been characteristic of every non-Christian philosophy since that of Thales in the sixth century B.C.

I agree with Johnson and many others that the theory of evolution has brought great harm to society, leading it to deny the biblical view of human nature as the image of God, the awful nature and consequences of sin, and our need for redemption. I am encouraged that opponents of Darwinism have recently been given a better hearing in academic circles than would have been possible fifty years ago.[28] More than any other single figure, Johnson has led this new assault on evolutionary dogma, with careful argumentation and gentle prodding of the establishment, rather than with stridency and dubious hypotheses. We are all greatly in his debt.[29]

Like evolutionary theory, many other ideas are often presented today as undoubted fact, even though they do not have any serious justification. For example: corporal punishment of children is wrong; abortion is right; the state has the competence and obligation to provide education and welfare; all races, genders, religions, and sexual-preference groups are equal in every way, and the greatest sin is that of disparaging one of these groups (except for Anglo-Saxon Protestant males).

26. See Thomas Kuhn, *The Structure of Scientific Revolutions*, 2nd ed. (Chicago: University of Chicago Press, 1970).

27. Darwin's accomplishment was to suggest a plausible mechanism for evolution.

28. The voluminous work of the intelligent-design movement has leveled severe criticisms against the Darwinian model, arguing from evidence ranging from the very small (microbiology) to the very large (cosmology). For just a sampling, see William A. Dembski and Jonathan Wells, *The Design of Life: Discovering Signs of Intelligence in Biological Systems* (Dallas: Foundation for Thought and Ethics, 2008); Stephen C. Meyer, *Signature in the Cell: DNA and the Evidence for Intelligent Design* (New York: HarperCollins, 2009); Stephen C. Meyer, *Darwin's Doubt: The Explosive Origin of Animal Life and the Case for Intelligent Design* (New York: HarperOne, 2013); Guillermo Gonzalez and Jay Richards, *The Privileged Planet: How Our Place in the Cosmos Is Designed for Discovery* (Washington, DC: Regnery Publishing, 2004).

29. See William A. Dembski, ed., *Darwin's Nemesis: Phillip Johnson and the Intelligent Design Movement* (Downers Grove, IL: InterVarsity Press, 2006).

If the Schaeffer group has been the most effective in identifying and criticizing atheistic relativism in modern culture, perhaps the Dutch "Philosophy of the Idea of Law," following the Christian philosophers Herman Dooyeweerd and D. Th. Vollenhoven, has best dealt with idolatry. This group distinguishes fifteen different spheres of human interest in the world, including the numerical, the mechanical, the biotic, the economic, the linguistic, the aesthetic, the juridical, the ethical, and the pistical (faith). Each of these reflects the others in various ways, so that it is tempting to regard one of them as the absolute, the origin of the rest. Hence there is a tendency in philosophy to reduce everything to number or space or matter or motion or economics. But to do this is idolatry. God rules over all the spheres and is not limited to any one of them.[30]

The followers of Schaeffer tend to downplay modern idolatry, because they tend to be committed to a historical model in which ancient optimism concerning reason and order degenerates into modern irrationalism (atheistic relativism).[31] They are therefore so committed to seeing modern man in terms of irrationalism that they often miss his idolatry and dogmatism—his rationalism.

On the other hand, the Dooyeweerdians are less adequate on irrationalism and atheism than they are on idolatry. Dooyeweerd himself was a bit unclear on the role of reason in human thought. He insisted that God was not rational, for to say that God was rational would be to limit him to one of the fifteen spheres of creation. I doubt that it would; it seems to me that if we recognize the differences that Van Til does between the divine and the human mind, we can attribute to God an intelligence analogous to, but not identical with, human rationality. That the Dooyeweerdians consider Van Til himself a rationalist indicates to me that they have fundamental misunderstandings in this area.[32]

Idolatrous Atheism

As I have indicated, idolatry and atheism are not as distinct from each other (or as opposed to each other) as they might initially appear to be. Atheism needs idolatry: you cannot live consistently as a relativ-

---

30. I have a lot of questions about the details of the Dooyeweerdian model, but its main thesis is cogent and of great help to the apologist.

31. It would be interesting to see how much this is related to Schaeffer's original premillennialism.

32. Gordon Clark and his disciples have considered Van Til an irrationalist. The distribution of critics on either side of him suggests that perhaps Van Til was very close to the truth.

ist without some constant, absolute meaning in life. And relativists are always dogmatic about excluding nonrelativist ideas—for example, when they say that people "should not" impose their values on others. Also, idolatry needs atheism: the choice to worship a false god is ultimately irrational and rebellious.

Thus, most unbelievers combine these motifs in various ways. Plato and Aristotle taught that the universe is divided into one part that is rational and knowable and another part that is wildly irrational and unknowable. But how do you know the unknowable? To that question they failed to offer any cogent answer.

Plotinus began as a rationalistic idolater. He claimed to have discovered a god who could give us a perfect explanation for everything. But it turned out that this god was knowable only in a nonrational experience. Irrationalism triumphed in the end.

Marxism claims scientific status, but preaches ethical relativism. If ethics are relative, why should we value science?

Modern public schools claim religious neutrality. What this means in practice is that they are relativistic in their values, but dogmatic in excluding Christianity from all substantive discussions.

The modern media tend to convey the message that "anything goes," that values are relative, that it is cute to offend society's typical "prejudices" about sex, religion, and politics. On the other hand, they are highly dogmatic (often unwilling to argue at all, or even to acknowledge dissent) in promoting their own values of legal abortion, a centrally planned economy, high taxes and government spending, "rights" for all sorts of special-interest groups, and so on. The same is true of the arts and the entertainment field to a large extent.

Big business tends to be more conservative, more supportive of traditional values. But such conservative ethics are mocked by the "anything goes" attitude of advertisers (who, it seems, will say or portray almost anything to make a sale) and by the rush for government subsidies and protection from competition whenever those become available. "Anything goes" is the slogan of the atheistic relativist.[33] "I have a right to a subsidy" is the cry of an idolater to his idol.

Since Kant, scientists have recognized that their discipline is not purely objective, but reaches results that are considerably influenced by what scientists want to see. The epistemological barriers between the scientist and

33. Recall Dostoyevsky: "If God does not exist, all is permitted."

the real world are enormous, not least because scientific theories tend to take on a presuppositional status.[34] When a theory becomes a paradigm or presupposition, it comes to govern all future research, so that it is next to impossible to challenge the theory through scientific methods. Such paradigms tend to be held (very much like religious dogmas) with great tenacity, and those who raise fundamental questions risk ostracism from the community. Thus, we have in the scientific community an oscillation between relativism and dogmatism, atheism and idolatry. This is why, in the face of significant modern challenges to the dogma of evolution, secularists cling to it all the more tightly, even to the point of refusing to present any alternatives to schoolchildren.[35]

These attitudes are even more obvious in the social sciences. Sociologists insist dogmatically on their cultural relativism. Psychologists fight fierce "denominational" wars over what sort of therapy should be used (when none of the accepted forms has had much success). Educators dogmatically forbid "politically incorrect" speech while insisting that all viewpoints (in practice, all approved viewpoints!) receive equal respect.

The same is true of "mainstream" or liberal theologians. They reprove orthodox Christians for being dogmatic, but they themselves are highly dogmatic in the way they elevate philosophical, political, and social proposals to the level of gospel.

If the Schaeffer group has been strong in dealing with atheistic relativism, and the Dooyeweerd group has been strong in dealing with idolatry, it is in recognizing combinations of the two that Van Til has excelled.[36] He above all has seen that atheism and idolatry (he calls them irrationalism and rationalism, as I did in *DKG*) are really one position— apparently contradictory, but actually dependent on each other. He has seen the nuances, the way in which these dialectical motifs interweave, supporting each other while challenging each other down through the history of thought.

34. Again, Thomas Kuhn calls them "paradigms" in *The Structure of Scientific Revolutions.*
35. In the early 1990s, Christian members of the Vista, California, school board sought to encourage teachers to present the "weaknesses" of evolutionary theory. The teachers reacted in strong opposition to this suggestion. But don't all theories have weaknesses? And whatever happened to the liberal idea of presenting all sides of issues? That ideal would seem to be dispensable when the ultimate presuppositions of the secularist ideology are at stake.
36. See also Herbert Schlossberg's excellent *Idols for Destruction* (Nashville: Thomas Nelson, 1983). And see James B. Jordan, *Through New Eyes* (Brentwood, TN: Wolgemuth and Hyatt, 1988), also a response to idolatry and promoting a positive reconstruction of the world after Schlossberg's critique.

Christian Apologetic Responses

I cannot reproduce here all the critical insights of Van Til, Schlossberg, Dooyeweerd, Schaeffer, and the others, although I do recommend their writings to anyone interested in studying these matters further. But let me, in a very general way, suggest strategies that cover a great many actual cases.

Against Atheistic Relativism

When you find an unbeliever who stresses the atheistic relativist side of unbelief, be persistent in asking these questions: (1) How can you be sure that relativism is right, when it itself rules out all assurance? (2) How can you live as a relativist? Having no assurance of anything must be a terrible strain, rationally, emotionally, and volitionally. What basis do you have for making decisions? What basis do you have for criticizing the treatment you receive from others? How can you say that anything is wrong, unfair, or unjust? What basis do you have for trusting logic—or, for that matter, your own mind?

Against Idolatrous Rationalism

When you meet someone who tends to stress the powers, rather than the limits, of autonomous thought and action, you will likely be dealing with someone in the grip of an idol. Find out what his idol is and take aim by asking these questions: (1) What basis is there for thinking that this idol is absolute? (2) Does your god really do the job of a god? Did it create the world? Is it the ground of logic, mathematics, ethical value, and universal judgments in science? Is it adequate as a final standard of meaning, truth, and right?

We know that an impersonal god can do none of these things. So the unbeliever will be tempted either to lapse into relativism or to grant to his god some elements of personality. Once he does the latter, he is granting part of our case, and we can pursue him further, especially by asking him, "How do you know this person?"

Against Atheistic Idolatry

Press the fundamental contradiction in this rationalistic-irrationalistic combination: a proof that there are no proofs, an absolute statement that there are no absolute statements. Then attack the original rationalistic and irrationalistic elements, as above. It will not be easy. The unbeliever will slide from one position to another, from rationalism to irrationalism and back again. Argument itself will not be enough; God must intervene. Thus, prayer is the ultimate apologetic weapon.

10

TALKING TO A STRANGER

Introduction

Parts of this book have been fairly technical, but I do want to make it clear that the type of apologetics that I recommend can be used in practical situations. I trust that people looking for this sort of practical help will not be put off too much by the earlier discussions. Perhaps they will follow the advice in the Preface and begin with this chapter. I hope this chapter will whet their appetite to see what theory lies behind the apologetic expressed here.

I readily admit that this is not my own natural milieu. I am far better suited to technical discussions than to exchanges with "people on the street." Indeed, I rarely enter into such exchanges, since I think God has equipped me to carry out the Great Commission through the written medium much better than orally. Among other things, my mind is not nearly as quick, at least in unfamiliar surroundings, as is that of "John" in the dialogue below—how I wish it were. Still, I do feel a certain obligation not to leave the reader entirely up in the air. The following should give the reader at least some idea of how this apologetic would work out in real life.

One more thing by way of introduction: this is not a realistic dialogue. In most real conversations of this sort, much time is wasted through misunderstandings, impoliteness, digressions, incidental occurrences, failed attempts at humor, and so forth. To save time, I will keep them out of this dialogue.

Encounter on a Plane

AL (fuming): What a bummer!

JOHN: What's the trouble?

AL: Well, I bought my briefcase because it was just the right size to fit under an airplane seat. You know how they always tell you to stow your carry-on luggage under the seat ahead of you?

JOHN: Oh, yes.

AL: Well, I bought this briefcase specifically to meet their rules, and now I find that they've given me a seat without a seat ahead of me. So it has to be stowed in the overhead bin. And since all the overhead bins here are full, the flight attendant took it to the back of the plane.

JOHN: They'll bring it back to you after takeoff, if you ask.

AL: I shouldn't have to ask. I have a right to have my briefcase here with me, takeoff or no. Besides, it'll take them forever, if they remember at all. I can picture myself trying to get to the back of the plane, squeezing around the lunch wagon, three flight attendants, and everyone trying desperately to get to the bathroom before lunch.

JOHN: I can understand your annoyance.

AL: By the way, I'm Al. What's your name?

JOHN: John. Nice to meet you.

AL: I'm a securities analyst. What's your line?

JOHN: I'm a Presbyterian minister.

AL: Oh! Well, I used to go to church as a boy, but I haven't been back in many years. I guess you'd say I'm an agnostic.

JOHN: Oh, that's interesting. What kind of agnostic are you?

AL: What do you mean, what kind? Are there denominations of agnostics?

JOHN: No, but there are some agnostics who insist that nobody can know God at all, and then there are other agnostics who don't know God themselves, but leave the door open to the possibility that someone else might know him.

AL: I guess I'm in the second group. I really don't know whether God exists, and I really don't know whether it's possible to know him—if he does exist. I guess I'm a superagnostic.

JOHN: Well, let me invite you to attend my church in San Diego . . .

AL: Wait a minute! I said I was an agnostic!

JOHN: You go to church somewhere else?

AL: No; I told you I haven't been to church in years.

JOHN: Well, we'll have to fix that. Every agnostic should be in church once every two weeks.

AL: Every two weeks?

JOHN: Sure. Look, you really don't know whether or not God exists, right?

AL: Right.

JOHN: Then you ought to hedge your bets, right?

AL: Hedge my bets?

JOHN: Sure. If you were an atheist, you would feel confident in living as if God didn't exist. If you were a Christian, you would feel an obligation to live as a Christian: attending church, praying, loving your enemies, and so on. But how do you live as an agnostic? Shouldn't you adopt a lifestyle halfway between these extremes—maybe go to church every *other* week?

AL: Very clever; but, to be honest, I never go to church, and I never intend to. From a practical standpoint, I live just like an atheist.

JOHN: You never go to church, never pray, never test your conduct by the Bible?

AL: Right.

JOHN: Then you're an atheist.

AL: But I don't *know* whether or not . . .

JOHN: I can tell your beliefs only by your actions. If you claimed to believe that hamburgers were poison, but you kept eating them all the time (without any apparent suicidal impulse), I'd say you didn't really believe hamburgers were poison—or perhaps the truth would be that you held conflicting beliefs, with the pro-hamburger belief being dominant.

AL: Well, okay—let's say I'm an atheist. Prove to me that God exists.

JOHN: What would it take to prove that to you?

AL: Oh, I don't know. It would sure help if he would show himself to me.

JOHN: But he's invisible.

AL: But didn't he show himself in visible form to people in the Bible?

JOHN: Well, yes. But sometimes those forms, like the earthly body of Jesus, were quite ordinary in outward appearance. I can't imagine that such a thing would impress you.

AL: I want to see the bright shining light surrounded by angels and all that.

JOHN: What do you make of near-death experiences, where people return from clinical death and report a bright light, visitations from departed friends, and so on? These are quite well documented, you know; it seems to be a fairly common occurrence.

AL: It's evidently some sort of dream or other psychological phenomenon. Of course, I haven't had such an experience myself.

JOHN: Well, even if you had, you could write it off as a dream, couldn't you?

AL: Sure.

JOHN: Imagine an even stronger case: suppose God appeared to you at night, in a bright light, surrounded by angels, and said, "Al, I am the Lord, the God of Abraham, Isaac, and Jacob." How would you respond?

AL: I might be pretty overwhelmed, but in the end . . .

JOHN: You'd dismiss it as a dream.

AL: I'd dismiss it as a dream.

JOHN: What if the same thing happened to you in broad daylight?

AL: To be honest, I guess I'd dismiss it as a hallucination.

JOHN: But suppose you were driving past the Vice President's mansion in Washington and you saw Al Gore get out of a limousine in the driveway. Would you dismiss that as a hallucination?

AL: No, of course not.

JOHN: Why not?

AL: Well, that's the sort of thing I'd expect to see there. It would fit in with all my other beliefs.

JOHN: So you interpret alleged facts according to what you already believe. In other words, your beliefs control your judgments about facts. Your atheist presuppositions determine how you interpret what you observe, so that other interpretations are out of the question.

AL: I suppose so.

JOHN: You can understand, then, why I (and God) resist the idea of giving you some visible revelation of God. If you won't even *consider* a Christian interpretation of such an experience, why should God bother to give you one?

AL: I hadn't thought of it that way.

JOHN: Is there another kind of proof you would consider?

AL: How about some evidence among the facts of the world that God exists?

JOHN: Well, every fact in the world testifies to God, because God made them all and directs them to his purpose.

AL: Every fact, huh. My house has been overrun with cockroaches. How does that prove God's existence?

JOHN: Hmm . . . isn't that just the sort of thing you'd expect if the Bible is true? Scripture says that because man fell into sin, the earth produces thorns and thistles to make our work difficult and our existence wearisome. Cockroaches are part of that.

AL: Interesting, but that doesn't prove that God exists. I can interpret the cockroaches as pure accidents of evolution. The universe doesn't care whether they annoy me or not.

JOHN: But notice again that you are using your atheistic commitment to interpret the facts. You're ruling out a Christian interpretation because you're already committed to a different one. Can you prove your presupposition to me?

AL: I can't prove that God doesn't exist, if that's what you mean. You'd just give my facts a Christian interpretation.

JOHN: That's right, and we're both doing the same thing, up to that point. So in principle, you could reject any proof I could give you on the basis of your presupposition.

AL: OK. But then there's nothing more to say. You have your presupposition and I have mine. You interpret facts in a Christian way and I don't. You can't prove anything to me, and I can't prove anything to you.

JOHN: Not so fast! At least you now recognize that the matter of proof is more complicated than you had thought.

AL: I see that. But I'm wondering how you intend to continue this conversation.

JOHN: Can we go back to the cockroaches?

AL: How can that possibly help your case?

JOHN: I suppose you'd say that the overrunning of your house was a bad thing, right?

AL: Well, it sure was bad for me. But as I said, from the standpoint of the universe as a whole, it doesn't much matter.

JOHN: What about the flight attendant's taking your briefcase?

AL: That was wicked! Seriously, they should have notified me when I picked this seat that I would be deprived of my briefcase for a time. To me, that is a more serious matter than whether I get a window or aisle seat, or even whether I sit in first class or coach.

JOHN: Would you say, then, that the airline was wrong?

AL: Sure—not that I would make a federal case out of it, though.

JOHN: Now, tell me how an atheist or agnostic decides what is right and what is wrong.

AL: Conscience, I suppose.

JOHN: Conscience is a moral sense; it senses right and wrong as the eye senses light and color. But the eye doesn't *create* light and color. Would you say that your conscience *creates* right and wrong?

AL: Well, some people would. But I'm uncomfortable with that idea; I mean, if right and wrong are my own inventions, why should anyone else care about them?

JOHN: Exactly. And you think that others ought to care; that, too, is a moral judgment. But it's something more than just a feeling of yours. It's something objective that obligates you and them.

AL: Yes, I can see the importance of objective moral values.

JOHN: Then these values bind us; they impose obligations.

AL: Yes.

JOHN: But why? Why are we obligated to accept those values?

AL: I guess it's just part of the way the universe is. In the physical universe, what goes up must come down. So in the moral universe, he who hurts others incurs guilt.

JOHN: But physical laws don't *obligate* me to do anything. I can't imagine anything merely material that could impose an obligation. Can you?

AL: Well, I do sense that the obligation is there. Where else could it come from?

JOHN: Look at the alternatives: either the universe is ultimately impersonal (that is, everything reduces to matter, motion, space, time, and chance) or it is personal (an ultimate being creates and uses matter, motion, and so on for his own purposes). Which is the more likely origin of moral obligation?

AL: I don't see that either is likely. Even if a person tells me what to do—say, a policeman—I am not thereby obligated to do what he says.

JOHN: Sure. A policeman can be wrong. He can exceed his authority. And even when he is right, he doesn't create moral obligations any more than you or I do.

AL: I'm confused. I thought you were leading me in the direction of a personalistic account of morals.

JOHN: I am, but of course moral values cannot be entirely explained by finite personalities.

AL: Oh, of course! This is your proof for God!

JOHN: Well, think it through! Moral values are rather like loyalty, aren't they? In fact, loyalty is a moral value, and it obligates us to behave in certain ways. Now, how do we get into positions where we find ourselves loyal to someone or something?

AL: I suppose deep personal relationships are the strongest motivation. If you insult my mother, I'll punch your lights out, for she is the most loving, gentle, kind person on the face of the earth. I'll be loyal to her as long as I live.

JOHN: Sure. Loyalty to one's country is a bit different, but again it probably has much to do with the blessings a person experiences through fellowship with other people of that country.

AL: I suppose so. Loyalty to the people, even generally considered, seems more important than loyalty to a particular system of government; and when we are loyal to a system, it is largely based on our perceptions of what the people running that system are doing for the other people in the nation.

JOHN: Well, to make a long story short: moral values depend on personal relationships. Absolute and objective moral standards presuppose loyalty to an absolute person.

AL: Absolute person? Hold on a minute.

JOHN: What's the worst evil you can think of?

AL: Genocide.

JOHN: Is that always wrong?

AL: Always.

JOHN: What if there were a minority living in the U.S. that you just couldn't stand. Suppose they spent all their time robbing, mugging, raping, and molesting children, all the while sponging off the taxpayers by living on welfare. Wouldn't it make sense to do away with them?

AL: We might be tempted to do so, but it would be wrong. We should prosecute criminals, change the welfare laws, and so on; but we should never destroy a whole race of people.

JOHN: But you use the terms *always* and *never*. What kind of personal relationship is it that justifies that kind of consistency?

AL: I guess it's loyalty to the human race as such.

JOHN: But when has "the human race as such" ever voted against genocide? In the cases of Hitler, Stalin, and Pol Pot, the human race itself sat idly by.

AL: What I meant was that if I value people as people, as ends and not merely as means, I could never support genocide.

JOHN: But who taught you to value people as ends rather than means? That sort of ethic has actually been rather rare among the peoples of the world.

AL: Well, this ethic seems bound up with real love for one's fellow man. We ought to try to do what's best for everybody, right?

JOHN: But how do you know that an occasional genocide might not be good for the human race as a whole?

AL: It certainly wouldn't be best for the victims! And again, it wouldn't be treating people as ends.

JOHN: Your ethic is very lofty. But what makes you think that "humanity in general" deserves this kind of unconditional love? As you say, there is plenty of wickedness out there.

AL: I know what you're saying. I sure spend enough time complaining about nincompoops and moral idiots. People are so thoughtless, like the bureaucrats that make up the airline travel rules.

JOHN: How, then, can a world of idiots and nincompoops motivate unconditional love?

AL: When you put it that way, I guess I have to concede that it doesn't. But I still maintain my convictions against genocide.

JOHN: Fine! But can you honestly find any cogent basis for those convictions other than the God of the Bible? After all, here is a God who is perfectly holy, righteous, and loving. Is there anyone else who deserves that loyalty, with no exceptions?

AL: I can see there's much to be said for theism if you confine yourself to talk of moral values. But morals are so slippery. Who, really, knows where they come from? I find it safer to base my life on human reason than to entrust myself to some supernatural being.

JOHN: Reason is a great faculty. But why follow its dictates?

AL: Because living irrationally brings failure, pain, and suffering.

JOHN: Not always. Don't you know some irrational politicians who are living high on the hog? Don't you know some rational people who are suffering miserably because of their commitment to the truth?

AL: Are you advocating irrationalism?

JOHN: No; I am asking *why* I should live according to reason.

AL: Well, you're committed to moral justice; you ought to be committed to truth as well, because that is also a moral value. When your reason shows you a truth, you *ought* to recognize it and confess it.

JOHN: Exactly! Reasoning itself presupposes the objective moral standard of truth.

AL: And . . .

JOHN: And that moral standard in turn presupposes loyalty to an absolute person.

AL: To God.

JOHN: To God.

AL: You're going too fast. Maybe there's a person up there who serves as a criterion of morality. But why call him God? How can you show that he is all-powerful, all-knowing, and all the rest?

JOHN: That's where the "absolute" part comes in. If God has weaknesses, then he cannot be the absolute final Judge of good and evil. If he is ignorant in any measure, then he cannot rightly judge the good and evil that we do. If he has a beginning or an end, then it is possible to give a rational account of a world without God. But we have seen that that is impossible.

AL: But what God are you talking about? Allah? Zeus? Jehovah? Jesus? Buddha? Brahma?

JOHN: I'm talking about the biblical God, who is Jehovah and Jesus and the Holy Spirit as well.

AL: Why not the others?

JOHN: Well, to make a very long story short: Zeus is not an absolute being; he's finite, though a bit larger and more powerful than we are. Certainly he is not a moral paragon. Buddha never claimed to be god, and his original teaching is arguably atheistic. Brahma approaches the idea of absoluteness, but "he" is essentially impersonal, one of many gods in Hinduism, and "beyond good and evil," thus not capable of serving as a moral standard.

AL: What about Allah?

JOHN: Allah is a kind of revised version of the biblical God. Muhammad, the founder of Islam, regarded the Bible as the Word of God; but with some inconsistency he revised its more difficult teachings, like the Trinity, and produced his own religious book, the Qur'an. Indeed, he turned the biblical God into an arbitrary source of fate, seriously compromising biblical personalism. The chief argument between Christians and Muslims is over whether the Bible itself permits this sort of tinkering. The Muslims say that the Bible predicts the coming of Muhammad to fulfill God's purposes. Christians deny it.

AL: So you're telling me that only the Bible advocates a God with absolute personality?

JOHN: Exactly.

AL: But what of the Mormons and the Jehovah's Witnesses?

JOHN: The Mormons are polytheists. And the Jehovah's Witnesses deny the Trinity.

AL: What's so important about the Trinity?

JOHN: Well, the Bible teaches it, and the Bible is God's Holy Book. Scripture says there is one God, but then it points us to three beings who have divine status. They are not just one person playing three roles: Jesus prays to the Father; the Father and Son send the Spirit into the world. The Father speaks from heaven, while the Son is being baptized in the Jordan River and the Spirit is falling on him in the shape of a dove.

AL: How do we know that the Bible is God's Holy Book?

JOHN: Well, as we've seen, the biblical tradition alone teaches that God is an absolute personality. That same tradition makes it clear that God intends to rule his people in the very personal way of using language. And that language is to be written down in book form. The Ten Commandments were written by the finger of God, and the apostle Paul said that Scripture was "breathed out by God." Throughout the book—see especially Psalm 119—there are praises and superlatives directed to the written words of God.

AL: But you're using the Bible to prove the Bible.

JOHN: Yes, but just as you used reason to prove reason, or just as you earlier used your atheistic presuppositions to prove atheistic conclusions. We all have our presuppositions!

AL: But can't one believe in a God of absolute personality without accepting any single religious tradition?

JOHN: I suppose we could, if it weren't for Jesus.

AL: What difference does Jesus make?

JOHN: Al, how do you think the absolute person looks at you? Since he is a person, and he is the very standard of morality, he must have an opinion. What does he think of your moral behavior?

AL: Well, on a curve, I guess I'm better than a lot of people; of course, I'm no plaster saint.

JOHN: How would you feel if you were called right now to stand before a holy, absolutely righteous God?

AL: Terrified.

JOHN: But what if God loved you so much that he didn't want to destroy you for your sins, but wanted to save you? Wouldn't it be worth your while to find out about that?

AL: Sure! But where do I go to find out?

JOHN: Again, there is only one alternative—Jesus. All the other religions, even the "theistic" ones, claim that you can win favor with God by your good behavior. That claim produces pride in those who think they measure up to the standard, but despair in those who think they can never measure up to perfection.

AL: To be honest, I'd have to say that I belong to the second category.

JOHN: Me, too.

AL: But how is Jesus different?

JOHN: The Scriptures tell us that Jesus is the eternal Son of God, who came to earth to pay the penalty for our sins and thus to provide salvation as a free gift to anyone who believes. Read especially John 3:16; Romans 5:8; 6:23; Ephesians 2:8–9; 2 Timothy 1:9; Titus 3:5–6; and 1 Peter 3:18.

AL: Then he wasn't just a human religious teacher.

JOHN: If he were, you would be doomed to a life of despair.

AL: But look, granted all the evil in the world—and, I must admit, in my own heart—how could this world have come from a good God?

JOHN: The best answer to that question is: I don't know.

AL: I thought you knew everything.

JOHN: In spiritual matters, I know only what Scripture tells me; and it doesn't fully answer that question.

AL: I noticed you said "fully." What *does* it tell us?

JOHN: Well, it does say that God works everything together for good (Rom. 8:28), and it says that everything God does follows a wise plan (Ps. 104:24; Jer. 10:12; 51:15). This implies that God has a good purpose for all the evil that he admits into the world. But what those good purposes are, he has not chosen to tell us fully, and he has no obligation to explain it all to us.

AL: But how can I trust him if I don't have such an explanation? Maybe he is a wicked being, rather than a good one. In that case, I can't allow him to be my moral criterion.

JOHN: Well, what you allow has very little to do with what is the case. He *is* the moral criterion, whether you like it or not. But to answer your question, there are many reasons to trust him, despite unresolved problems.

AL: What reasons?

JOHN: Chiefly, Jesus.

AL: Jesus again?

JOHN: Yes. He shows us that God will not compromise one inch on justice. God requires death for sin, even if his own Son must be the victim. And Jesus also shows that God is willing to give his Son (in an important sense, to give himself) to save us from that awful death. That is not a God of moral wickedness or indifference. We may be sure that a God like that must have had some very good reasons for including evil within his eternal plan, even if we do not know what those reasons are.

AL: I know what I'll do. I'll promise to become a Christian if he reveals himself to me and tells me why evil came into the world.

JOHN: Be careful! Job made that same request, and he got his interview with God.

AL: Good! There is precedent, then.

JOHN: Remember, though, a while ago, how you said you would feel face-to-face with a holy and righteous God?

AL: Hmm, yes. I forgot about that. I guess I didn't think the question of my own sin would come up in the interview. I was hoping God would follow my agenda.

JOHN: Ha! But that's not how he does things. When God met Job, *God* asked the questions, reminding Job of his finitude and his moral inferiority. The outcome was that Job hung his head in shame.

AL: Maybe asking for an interview was not such a good idea.

JOHN: Actually, the best remedy for your concern about the problem of evil is to get to know Jesus better. Jesus is a mirror of God's goodness and righteousness. Indeed, in all of Scripture we learn about the truly good things God has done. So those who know the Bible best tend to be less troubled by the problem of evil—though, to be sure, even Christians agonize over it at times.

AL: Maybe so.

JOHN: John 17:6–8 promises that if you desire to do the will of God, you can know whether Jesus' claims are true. Are you willing to spend some time studying those claims?

AL: I think I would like to.

JOHN: Just read through, say, the Gospels. Maybe Mark first (it's the shortest), then John (it answers our questions most simply and clearly). Pay special attention to the story of the resurrection. Ask what could account for that story other than the reality of the supernatural event.

AL: And if Jesus is risen?

JOHN: If Jesus is risen, then God has vindicated his teaching and work, and we—his people—are raised with him to newness of life. If Jesus is risen, then he really is God. And if Jesus is risen, then he is right in saying that "Scripture cannot be broken" (John 10:35; cf. Matt. 5:17ff.).

AL: Where can I go to get help in understanding the Bible?

JOHN: My invitation to come to church still stands.

AL: I'll take you up on it. But what about when I get home?

JOHN: Let's stay in touch. I'll try to recommend a church near your home. It is important that you find a fellowship where you can learn more about Christ. That is God's purpose for the church and for you.

AL: Hey, we're about to land! I didn't even need my briefcase.

JOHN: Perhaps God had a good purpose in removing it from you.

AL: Perhaps so.

APPENDIX A:
VAN TIL AND THE LIGONIER APOLOGETIC

(Note: This review was originally published in *Westminster Theological Journal* 47, 2 [Fall 1985]: 279–99. It is reprinted here in the belief that it will help the reader to better understand the differences between presuppositional or Van Tillian apologetics on the one hand and traditional or classical apologetics on the other. Since writing this review, I have become a bit more favorable to the use of probability in apologetics [thus differing both with Cornelius Van Til and with the Ligonier version of the tradition], and I have become a bit more guarded in my defense of circularity. In general, however, the review continues to speak for me as I interact with the rival approach to apologetics.—JF)

Introduction

Classical Apologetics, by R. C. Sproul, John H. Gerstner, and Arthur W. Lindsley (Grand Rapids: Zondervan, 1984), has been eagerly awaited. This book puts into systematic (and at least somewhat technical) form an apologetic approach of considerable interest, which up until now has been primarily expressed in popular writings and taped lectures. It is also notable for its critique of "presuppositionalism" (mainly in its Van Tillian form). This book is one of the most extensive critiques of Cornelius Van Til to date,[1] and I think of all the critiques of Van Til this one shows the most thorough research and the most accurate interpretation.[2] In saying this, I should

---

1. Its only rival in this respect is James Daane, *A Theology of Grace* (Grand Rapids: Eerdmans, 1954); but that book is limited in its focus to Van Til's doctrine of common grace, and it shows much less understanding of Van Til's thought than the volume under review.

2. I will indicate that in this book also there is much, and serious, misunderstanding of Van Til; but these authors are much closer to the truth about him than his earlier critics, such

acknowledge a possible conflict of interest: the authors express indebtedness to me for correspondence between myself and Gerstner that "significantly sharpened our understanding of Vantillian apologetics."[3] In commending these authors for their understanding of Van Til, however, I am not intending to commend myself. My contribution to their formulations was relatively small (and, as it turns out, not always understood or accepted). But Gerstner himself is a former student of Van Til and has (as I know from personal discussions) been mulling over Van Til's position for many years, with an intense interest and scholarly care not matched, in my view, by other critics of Van Til.[4] Thus, the credit for the book's high critical standards must go to the authors themselves.

I will not discuss the details of the book's historical studies, though these are interesting and are among the book's best features. Gerstner was a professor of church history for many years, and this is his chief area of expertise. In general, the historical sections argue that a kind of "evidentialism" similar to the Ligonier type[5] has been the common view of orthodox Christians through most of church history; hence it deserves to be called the "classical" or "traditional" view. This argument is supported by studies of Augustine, Luther, Calvin, seventeenth-century orthodoxy, and Eastern and Roman orthodoxy.[6] The authors believe, however, that classical apologetics today is "sick and ailing," though not dead.[7] "Presup-positionalism," they tell us, "has become the majority report today among Reformed theologians, although it cannot even be called a minority report of church history."[8] Other reviewers more historically inclined than I will doubtless seek to evaluate this thesis. Substantial arguments, I think, can be presented on either side. Of course, the issue is not terribly impor-tant in evaluating the relative validity of the two approaches. If Van Til's view is relatively new, it is not on that account false; Protestants are not

---

as the Calvin Forum group (see Cornelius Van Til, *The Defense of the Faith* [Philadelphia: Presbyterian and Reformed, 1955], 4ff.) or the critics in E. R. Geehan, ed., *Jerusalem and Athens* (Nutley, NJ: Presbyterian and Reformed, 1971).

3. R. C. Sproul, John H. Gerstner, and Arthur W. Lindsley, *Classical Apologetics* (Grand Rapids: Zondervan, 1984), x. Cf. also the slightly extravagant comment on 299.

4. The book is *dedicated* to Van Til, "who has taught a generation that Christ is the Alpha and Omega of thought and life" (ibid., v). I do not doubt the genuineness of the authors' admiration and affection for Van Til: see ibid., 183f.

5. "Ligonier" is a convenient shorthand for "Sproul-Gerstner-Lindsley," since all three authors have been associated with the Ligonier Valley Study Center in western Pennsylvania.

6. Ibid., 89–211.

7. Ibid., 34.

8. Ibid., 183.

traditionalists.[9] In general, it seems to me that the history of apologetics before our century is ambiguous on these questions. Orthodox Christian apologists have always believed in the supreme authority of Scripture over all human reasoning—the essence of the Van Tillian position. On the other hand, they have also spoken of various kinds of reasoning that in some sense legitimately "precede" faith.[10] The apparent contradiction here was, in general, not perceived as a problem until after Kant's "Copernican revolution," which greatly increased the epistemological sophistication of theologians and philosophers. Only after Kant could the logic of presuppositions be systematically investigated (as it was, even before Van Til, by thinkers such as Hegel, Marx, Kierkegaard, and Wittgenstein, and by Christian apologists such as James Orr). Thus, to ask whether Calvin was a "presuppositionalist" or an "evidentialist"[11] is a bit like asking whether Augustine was a Protestant or a Catholic.[12]

As to the modern situation, many of us will be surprised to hear that presuppositionalism is the "majority report" among current apologists. It all depends, of course, on how you define presuppositionalism. I suppose that a case can be made that in this age, following Kant, Hegel, Marx, Einstein, pragmatism, phenomenology, existentialism, Wittgenstein, Kuhn, Polanyi, Hanson, Dooyeweerd, and many others, most apologists have taken seriously the issue of presuppositions. In our time, it is exceedingly difficult to deny that human thought (whether scientific, logical, historical, philosophical, religious, or whatever) is influenced by our "pretheoretical" attitudes and commitments.[13] Perhaps this fact is what suggests to our authors that presuppositionalism is ascendant presently; they do not document their assertion, so it is hard to say. In my view, this openness to considering the influence of pretheoretical commitments on thought is a long way from a full-fledged

9. Van Til himself finds relatively little of value in his apologetic predecessors. See his *A Christian Theory of Knowledge* (Nutley, NJ: Presbyterian and Reformed, 1969) and his syllabus "Christianity in Conflict" (unpublished, 1962).

10. "Precede" adds to the ambiguity. Few concepts in theology are as unclear as that of "priority." More comments on this issue will follow.

11. I use these terms to accommodate the authors under review, but really I think they are quite misleading, suggesting that Van Til is opposed to the use of evidence or that the traditionalists have no presuppositions to examine. On the contrary: all parties to the discussion must deal with both presuppositions and evidences, and they differ only on the *roles* to be played by these.

12. I am not saying that such questions are unanswerable, but rather that they are subtler than often supposed, and difficult to answer in any useful way.

13. Contra Dooyeweerd, however, I maintain that the reverse is also true and that no *sharp* distinction can be drawn between "pretheoretical" and "theoretical." See John M. Frame, *The Amsterdam Philosophy* (Phillipsburg, NJ: Harmony Press, 1972).

presuppositionalism. Still, it is a positive development in the dialogue. One of my great disappointments about the current volume is its failure to deal in any serious way with these powerful philosophical currents that create, for many, considerable presumption against the Ligonier type of apologetic.

Ligonier and Van Til

I will now try to analyze the authors' critique of Van Til, before discussing their positive apologetic. In the book itself this order is reversed, but I feel that in this review questions of methodology and epistemology ought to precede discussion of the authors' arguments for Christianity; and the former questions are inseparably bound up with the critique of "presuppositionalism."

Van Til's apologetics is essentially simple, however complicated its elaborations. It makes two basic assertions: (1) that human beings are obligated to presuppose God in all their thinking, and (2) that unbelievers resist this obligation in every aspect of thought and life. The first assertion leads Van Til to criticize the notion of intellectual autonomy; the second leads him to discuss the noetic effects of sin. The Ligonier group criticizes Van Til in both areas, which we will consider in that order.

Autonomy, Reason, and Circularity

The initial description of presuppositionalism shows insight in the prominent place given to Van Til's critique of autonomy:[14] this is, I think, the foundation of Van Til's system and its most persuasive principle.[15] We must not do apologetics as if we were a law unto ourselves, as if we were the measure of all things. Christian thinking, like all the Christian life, is subject to God's lordship.

But the book's *analysis* of the autonomy question reveals unclarity or misunderstanding. The authors deduce from Van Til's statements about autonomy that he wants us to "start with" God, rather than with ourselves.[16] Now, "start with" is (like "precede" and "priority") an extremely slippery

14. Sproul, Gerstner, and Lindsley, *Classical Apologetics*, 185.

15. In my view, this point is both more important and more cogent than, e.g., Van Til's view of the noetic effects of sin. The latter is often singled out as being central to Van Til's thought, but it is one doctrine that Van Til himself admitted to have difficulty formulating: see "An Introduction to Systematic Theology" (unpublished class syllabus, 1961), 26f. Autonomy is the more crucial issue, for Van Til's analysis of it indicates that *even if man had not fallen*, he would still have been obligated to reason presuppositionally.

16. Sproul, Gerstner, and Lindsley, *Classical Apologetics*, 185, 212ff.

phrase in theology and apologetics. It can indicate a pedagogical order of topics, an emphasis, a method of study, a conviction about prominence or importance, a relation of necessary or sufficient conditionality, or a criterion of truth. I believe that Van Til almost always has the last alternative in mind, though there is occasionally some ambiguity. At any rate, one would expect the Ligonier authors to offer some analysis of this concept, to make some attempt to define it (both for Van Til and for their own system). But no such analysis is forthcoming. The authors write as if the meaning of the idea were perfectly self-evident.

So they insist that we must, in coming to know God, "begin with ourselves," and therefore reason autonomously in some sense. "One simply cannot start outside himself. To begin outside oneself, one would first have to depart from himself."[17] Now, certainly, in one sense this is true, and Van Til quite readily admits it. Our authors even quote him to this effect,[18] but they claim that it represents an inconsistency in his thought, a kind of embarrassing admission.[19] Anyhow, on Van Til's view, the self is the "proximate," but not the "ultimate," starting point.[20] What this means, I think, is that it is the self that makes its decisions both in thought and in practical life: every judgment we make, we make because we ourselves think it is right. But this fact does not entail that the self is its own ultimate criterion of truth. We are regularly faced with the decision whether we should trust our own unaided judgment or rely on someone else. There is nothing odd or strange (let alone logically impossible) about such a question; it is entirely normal.

Therefore, there are two questions to be resolved: (1) the metaphysical (actually tautological!) question whether all decisions are decisions of the self, and (2) the epistemological-ethical question of what standard the self ought to use in coming to its decisions.[21] Van Til and the Ligonier group agree, I think, on the first question, though it is not of much interest to Van Til; but that agreement does not prejudice the answer to the

17. Ibid., 212.

18. Ibid., 214f.; cf. 316f.

19. Unfortunately, this is rather typical of the volume. The authors make statements about Van Til that can be contradicted from his writings; but instead of reconsidering the accuracy of their interpretation in these cases, they simply accuse Van Til of inconsistency. Thus, their accounts of Van Til's positions are almost always oversimplified at best.

20. Van Til, "Introduction to Systematic Theology," 203.

21. Our authors charge Van Til with confusing the order of being with the order of knowing (Sproul, Gerstner, and Lindsley, *Classical Apologetics*, 229). At this point, however, it is they who confuse metaphysics with epistemology.

second question. That one still needs to be posed and resolved. And it is the second question that Van Til—and Scripture—is concerned about. Scripture regularly calls God's creatures to submit their judgment to that of their Creator. If someone objects that even a choice to serve God is a choice made by the self and therefore "starting with" the self in one sense, Van Til can simply grant the point, while reminding his questioner that in another sense, in a far more important sense, this choice does *not* "start with" the self.[22]

The same sorts of distinctions need to be made in the discussion of human reason, another topic prominent in this book. *Classical Apologetics* is rationalistic with a vengeance. The authors attack the anti-intellectual trends of our time,[23] laud signs of a "retreat from this anti-intellectual binge,"[24] and show at length from Scripture our obligation to reason with unbelievers.[25] "Fideism" is the great enemy.[26] Van Til, however, they say, abandons apologetics,[27] refusing to reason with unbelievers. He doesn't believe in proofs[28] or evidences.[29] He denies that you can find God at the end of a syllogism.[30] The present reviewer, that notorious Van Tillian, cannot engage in rational argument with anyone:

> [The Arminian] can argue with Frame, but Frame will not argue with him. Frame can only tell him that he is in error and that he must change his mind because he, Frame, has been illumined by God to see otherwise.[31]

On the contrary, say our authors: Just as we cannot avoid "starting with ourselves," so we cannot avoid the use of reason (in any area of life, particularly apologetics). Any attempt to persuade an unbeliever of Christian truth requires reasoning; indeed, rational argument is necessary if

22. If "autonomy" in the first sense necessitates "autonomy" in the second sense, then, of course, it necessitates autonomy for Christians and non-Christians alike. Therefore, if our authors' argument were sound, it would prove too much. It would legislate autonomy for everyone, not just for those who are "beginning" their path toward Christianity, as on the Ligonier view (ibid., 231f.). Human reason, then, would be the "ultimate" criterion, not merely the "penultimate" or "provisionally ultimate" as our authors would have it (301, 331).

23. Ibid., 12ff.
24. Ibid., 15.
25. Ibid., 18ff.
26. Ibid., 24ff.
27. Ibid., 188.
28. Ibid., 253ff.
29. Ibid., 276ff.
30. Ibid., 287.
31. Ibid., 301.

we are going to show the "rational necessity of presupposing God."[32] And in fact, presuppositionalists *do* give reasons.[33] In practice, "there is no real difference on the matter of autonomy."[34]

Buttressing all of this is the familiar argument that some basic principles of reason (such as the law of noncontradiction) must be presupposed in any intelligible discourse; indeed, "*The Law of Noncontradiction [Is] a Universal Prerequisite for Life.*"[35] You can't question logic without presupposing it; you can't argue against the primacy of logic without presupposing it as primary.

So our authors support the "principle of the primacy of the intellect." This does not mean that the intellect is more excellent than the God whom the intellect discovers; rather, "primacy of intellect means that we must think about God before we can actually know him."[36] Thus, when Van Til speaks of a "primacy of the intellect based on the creator-creature distinction," he seems to be talking nonsense. If the intellect is primary, its primacy is not "based on" anything. And if God is somehow known before intellectual activity, then how do we know him at all?

But here, as with "starting point," some distinctions must be made. "Intellect" or "reason" can mean various things: laws of logic, the psychological faculty by which we make judgments and draw inferences, the judgments and inferences themselves, systems of thought.[37] It is certainly true that reason as a psychological faculty is involved in any rational activity. Thus, putting it tautologically emphasizes the obviousness of the point. It is the same sort of obviousness we saw earlier in the proposition that one must "start with the self." But just as "starting with the self" leaves open the question of what criterion of truth the self should acknowledge, so "starting with reason" leaves open the question of what criterion of truth human reason ought to recognize. As a psychological faculty, reason has the choice of operating according to a number of different principles: different systems of logic, different philosophical schemes, different religious commitments. Van Til, therefore, may (and does!) grant that reason is involved in all human thought and life. But for him the important question is: What criteria of truth ought our reason to acknowledge?

32. Ibid., 224.
33. Ibid., 238f.
34. Ibid., 239; cf. 324f.
35. Ibid., 80 (emphasis theirs); see 72–82.
36. Ibid., 227.
37. Philosophers, such as Hegel, have sometimes defined rationality in terms of their systems so that, for example, rationality = Hegelianism.

Our authors would answer this question by saying, first of all, that reason ought to acknowledge the law of noncontradiction. (Perhaps they even define reason in terms of the laws of logic, so that for them the "primacy of reason" means not the primacy of a psychological faculty, but the primacy of logic; that, again, isn't clear.) Again, however, the main point is true in a sense. The law of noncontradiction denies that p and not-p can both be true at the same time and in the same respect. That is a Christian principle, presupposed by Scripture itself. But it is, of course, also highly abstract. Nothing more concrete can be derived from the law of noncontradiction alone. To derive concrete conclusions, we need additional principles—principles that are religiously, as well as philosophically, problematic.[38] Hence the tendency for various philosophers to define rationality in terms of their particular systems. It is at this point that Van Til enters the discussion and demands that God's voice be heard in the selection of rational principles. It is at this level, with this sort of concern, that he talks about "a primacy of the intellect based on the creator-creature distinction." He refers here to a reasoning process that recognizes God's standards as supreme. Perhaps for clarity's sake he would have been wiser not to speak of the "primacy of the intellect" at all;[39] but it isn't difficult to understand what he means. Reason is always involved in the human search for knowledge; but reason must always choose its standards, and that choice is fundamentally a religious one.

Our authors reply, however, that we must, after all, "think about God before we can know him."[40] And if we are trying to think about God *before* we know him, then obviously, at that stage of our inquiry, we cannot presuppose God. We cannot make God our supreme standard until we know that he exists. Therefore, we must adopt some other standard, at least "provisionally."[41] But this analysis (1) denies the clear teaching of Romans 1 that everyone knows God already (vv. 20–21), (2) posits an exception to 1 Corinthians 10:31: that when you are just beginning your quest for knowledge, you do not need to think "to the glory of God"; you can justifiably think to the glory of something/someone else. Such notions fall by their own weight. They are intolerable to the Bible-believer.

38. Cf. Vern S. Poythress, "A Biblical View of Mathematics," in *Foundations of Christian Scholarship*, ed. Gary North (Vallecito, CA: Ross House, 1976), 159–88; John M. Frame, "Rationality and Scripture," in *Rationality in the Calvinian Tradition*, ed. Hendrik Hart et al. (Lanham, MD: University Press of America, 1983), 293–317.

39. There are several other reasons why this phrase is misleading. See *DKG*, 331–32.

40. Sproul, Gerstner, and Lindsley, *Classical Apologetics*, 227.

41. Ibid., 301, 331.

Our authors have therefore failed to show that Van Til abandons rational argument, proofs, evidences. He does abandon neutral or autonomous reasoning; that is all. And nothing in *Classical Apologetics* shows that he is wrong in rejecting these. For the record, let me emphasize that Van Til does *not* reject proofs, arguments, evidences; on the contrary, he endorses them in the strongest terms.[42] The Ligonier authors are quite aware of this, but they dismiss it as inconsistency or insist that Van Til's arguments aren't really arguments at all.

Yet it is quite impossible to argue for Christianity, or anything else for that matter, without making a presuppositional choice. One cannot reason without criteria of truth. And criteria of truth come from a wide variety of sources, ultimately religious commitment.[43] Those criteria will be either Christian or non-Christian.[44] If they are non-Christian, they will be self-defeating and subject to divine judgment.

To say this is to say that argument for Christianity will always be in one sense circular. Arguments for Christianity must be based on Christian criteria, which in turn presuppose the truth of Christianity. You can't prove God without presupposing him. This is one of the principles of Van Til's apologetics that most irritate our authors.[45] To them, circular reasoning is a logical fallacy, pure and simple.[46] But what is the alternative? Again, the alternative seems to be that an unbeliever begins his quest either with no criterion at all or with a "provisional" criterion of a non-Christian (or perhaps "neutral") sort; then by linear, noncircular reasoning, he learns that he must adopt the Christian criterion.[47] But as we noted earlier, this construction violates Romans 1 and 1 Corinthians 10:31. According to Scripture, there is no one in this position—no one without a knowledge of God's criteria. Those who seek to adopt non-Christian standards (and there are no "neutral" ones) are simply disobedient to the revelation they have received. If one could proceed from neutrality to truth, then noncircular

42. See Van Til, *Defense of the Faith*, 120, 196; "Introduction to Systematic Theology," 102ff., 114f., 196; *Christian Theory of Knowledge*, 292; *Common Grace and the Gospel* (Nutley, NJ: Presbyterian and Reformed, 1969), 179ff., 190ff. See also Thom Notaro, *Van Til and the Use of Evidence* (Phillipsburg, NJ: Presbyterian and Reformed, 1980).

43. Again, it would have been helpful if the Ligonier authors had offered some response to the rather broad range of philosophical opinion (even outside Christianity) to this effect. *Classical Apologetics* seems to be written in a curiously pre-Kantian, pre-Kuhnian context, and thus it strains credibility. The authors have not dealt with the most serious criticisms of their position.

44. Listen to the law of noncontradiction!

45. See Sproul, Gerstner, and Lindsley, *Classical Apologetics*, 318ff.; cf. 137ff., 144ff.

46. Ibid., 322.

47. Ibid., 325.

argument would be possible. But of course, it is not possible, because Scripture condemns autonomy.[48]

Does this circularity entail the death of all reasoning, as the Ligonier authors fear? No: (1) All reasoning—Christian, non-Christian, presuppositional, "classical"—is in this sense circular. There is no alternative. This is not a challenge to the validity of reason; it is simply the way in which reason works. (2) There are distinctions to be made between "narrow circles" (e.g., "The Bible is God's Word because it says it is God's Word.") and "broad circles" (e.g., "Evidence interpreted according to Christian criteria demonstrates the divine authority of Scripture. Here it is: . . ."). Not every circular argument is equally desirable. Some circular arguments, indeed, should rightly be dismissed as fallacious. (3) Reasoning on Christian criteria is persuasive because (a) it is God's approved way to reason, (b) it leads to true conclusions, and (c) everyone, at some level, *already knows* that such reasoning leads to truth (Romans 1 again).

The Noetic Effects of Sin

Why is it necessary to presuppose God, according to Van Til? The Ligonier authors have a theory about that. They attribute to Van Til the notion that "the fundamental fallacy of the traditional approach is in not recognizing that without knowing everything one cannot know anything."[49] (Without the double negatives: what they are saying is that for Van Til we cannot know anything unless we know everything.) This point comes up elsewhere in the book,[50] and the authors think it is important enough to embellish poetically: "one cannot know the flower in the crannied wall unless he knows the world and all."[51] On this account, Van Til would be teaching that we need to presuppose God in order to have, somehow, that omniscient perspective on reality. But the authors never give any references in Van Til's writings to show that he believes any such thing; and of course they cannot, for this is not his position. Van Til does sometimes argue, in terms reminiscent of idealism, that true human knowledge presupposes the existence of a comprehensive system of knowledge; but unlike the idealist, Van Til finds this comprehensive

48. Again, even many non-Christian authors (see earlier note) concede this sort of point about circularity. It simply is not responsible, in the present intellectual context, to dismiss all circularity as a mere logical fallacy.

49. Ibid., 186.

50. Ibid., 306, 313.

51. Ibid., 186.

system in the God of Scripture. He explicitly denies the similar-sounding proposition that *we human beings* must have comprehensive knowledge in order to know anything:

> One of the points about which there has been much confusion when we speak of the objectivity of human knowledge is whether human knowledge of the world must be comprehensive in order to be true.... But we believe that just for the reason that we cannot hope to obtain comprehensive knowledge of God we cannot hope to obtain comprehensive knowledge of anything in the world.[52]

Van Til, in fact, explicitly denies the principle that we must know everything in order to know anything. He attributes this principle to "the non-Christian methodology in general, and that of modern phenomenalism in particular."[53]

On the contrary: to Van Til, our need to presuppose God has nothing to do with such idealist epistemological speculations. Rather, we presuppose God because in the nature of the case that is the right way to reason, and because, therefore, we are obligated to reason that way. The necessity is an *ethical* necessity.

Which brings us to the question of the noetic effects of sin. At this point, I find a surprising amount of agreement between the Ligonier authors and Van Til. "The pagan's problem," they say, "is not that he does not know that God is, but that he does not like the God who is."[54] The nature Psalms and Romans 1 tell us that God is clearly revealed in the world and that all human beings know God through this revelation.[55] Thus the unbeliever is without excuse. This "natural theology," they argue, is mediated through the creation.[56] (I agree that this is the teaching of Romans 1, but I would add that this fact does not preclude other forms of revelation in addition to the mediate form described in Romans 1.) Why, then, do people need complex arguments in order to believe? The answer is that they repress the truth revealed in creation.[57]

52. Van Til, *Defense of the Faith*, 60.

53. Ibid., 136. In the immediate context, he discusses idealist epistemology, from which this notion comes.

54. Sproul, Gerstner, and Lindsley, *Classical Apologetics*, 39.

55. When our authors say that for presuppositionalists God "reveals Himself exclusively in Holy Scripture" (ibid., 287) (presumably in contrast with natural revelation), they are evidently getting carried away with themselves. Van Til's belief in natural revelation needs no documentation.

56. Ibid., 43ff.

57. Ibid., 47.

They are not morons, but foolish.[58] Their problem is not intellectual weakness, but moral refusal to accept what is clearly revealed. Or, to put it more precisely, they do have intellectual problems, but "the intellectual problem is produced by the moral problem, not the moral problem by an intellectual one."[59] They know God, but they do not know him savingly. Honestly, in all of this (and in their summary[60]), I have not found anything that I or Van Til would disagree with! The Ligonier men seem to think that Van Til holds a very different position—that he thinks sin destroyed the unbeliever's reasoning power[61]—but as usual they fail to adequately document their interpretation and they ignore statements in Van Til to the contrary.

I will surprise them even more by saying that I agree, in general, with their account of the testimony of the Holy Spirit.[62] The utterly fideistic view that they attribute to me[63] is their own creation, made up out of thin air. They present no documentation of it from my writings. Apparently they believe that my other positions necessitate such a view. I find that hard to believe! They say that for me "the internal testimony of the Holy Spirit must be utterly apart from and prior to speculative knowledge and evidence of the inspiration of the word."[64] Nonsense. I quite agree with them that the Spirit witnesses to the Word through witnessing to evidences (along with other ways, to be sure). As for the Spirit's being "prior to speculative knowledge," I think I have sufficiently expounded the ambiguities of "priority" language in theology. In any case, I grant what I think they want me to, that people sometimes reach true conclusions about God without the witness of the Spirit.

Van Til's writings do pose some difficulty here. He does clearly recognize that unbelievers know the truth (Rom. 1:21) and that they sometimes reach true conclusions "in spite of themselves," that is, in spite of their unbelieving presuppositions. Yet there are points at which he seems to say that unbelief always leads to intellectual error and that no propositional truth is possible apart from the Spirit's witness. His representations, I think, are not fully consistent. What's more, he has admitted some dif-

---

58. Ibid., 52.
59. Ibid.
60. Ibid., 62.
61. Ibid., 241ff., esp. 245.
62. Ibid., 137ff., 162ff. See my article "The Spirit and the Scriptures," in *Hermeneutics, Authority, and Canon*, ed. D. A. Carson and John D. Woodbridge (Grand Rapids: Zondervan, 1986), which also appears as Appendix Q in *DWG*.
63. Sproul, Gerstner, and Lindsley, *Classical Apologetics*, 299ff.
64. Ibid., 299.

ficulty in this area.[65] The problems stem from Van Til's realization that even though unbelievers do know the truth, their rebellion often infests their intellectual activity. Much pagan philosophy can be explained precisely as attempts to evade the truth of God's revelation. Therefore, it is not sufficient to say (as the Ligonier writers seem to *want* to say; but see below) that the unbeliever's problems are moral rather than intellectual. Morality influences intellectual judgments.[66] At times, indeed, the authors of our volume recognize this fact: they write, "The intellectual problem is caused by the moral problem, not the moral problem by the intellectual one."[67] I agree, and I note that here they at least recognize that there *is* an intellectual problem as well as a moral one, though they don't stress that fact very much in their discussion.

The interesting net result is that *on paper* there is very little difference between the Ligonier group and Van Til on the noetic effects of sin and the testimony of the Spirit. Both maintain that depravity is total, that it causes repression of the truth, that the unbeliever has intellectual difficulties because of his moral rebellion, that he has knowledge of God but not saving knowledge. To both, the testimony of the Spirit works with and through our apologetic arguments to break down that rebellion and lead the unbeliever to acknowledge the truth that he already knows. Part of the reason for this agreement is that the Ligonier form of the traditional apologetic (as opposed, e.g., to that of Clark Pinnock) is self-consciously Calvinistic.

But the Ligonier authors are not very consistent in their confession of total depravity. Note here what they say about people who are not yet Christians, but seeking the truth:

> [Van Til] always assumes that the person who begins to examine the universe without presupposing the existence of the divine Lawgiver necessarily presupposes his own status as a lawgiver. That is by no means a necessary assumption of the person who begins by examining the data which he has at hand. . . . They do not necessarily deny the divine being as Van Til insists that they do. People do not assert their autonomy against an initially known God as Van Til insists that they do. They simply operate according to human nature.[68]

65. Van Til, "Introduction to Systematic Theology," 26f.
66. More than that, all intellectual judgments are morally determined. A right judgment is a judgment that we *ought* to make (the *ought* being a moral *ought*).
67. Sproul, Gerstner, and Lindsley, *Classical Apologetics*, 52.
68. Ibid., 232f.

Here, note that they deny what they earlier affirmed on the basis of Romans 1, that the unbeliever knows God. Further, they deny that all unbelievers are hostile to God, repressors of the truth. At least some unbelievers, in their opinion, are sincere seekers after truth, operating merely according to the necessities of created human nature. Seriously, now: is this a doctrine of depravity worthy of Calvinists?

So though on paper the differences in this area are not great, there is in the Ligonier authors a lack of seriousness in the application of the doctrine of depravity to apologetics. Similarly, on the question of "common ground," our authors state a position that is precisely identical with Van Til's:

> If we consider common ground to mean a common perception and perspective of reality, then obviously no such common ground for discussion exists between believer and unbeliever. From the believer's vantage point every aspect of life, every bit of experience, every dimension of reality, is understood and interpreted from a theological perspective. . . . It would appear that both [believer and unbeliever] enjoy a univocal understanding of the daffodil . . . [but] the believer acknowledges the *significance* of that daffodil, not as a cosmic accident, but as something that in itself bears witness to the majesty and beauty of the Creator God. This the unbeliever does not acknowledge, positing, instead, a completely opposite and antithetical understanding of the daffodil's significance.
>
> From a different perspective, however, there is common ground, namely the whole of creation. Believer and unbeliever live in the same universe. Each sees the same phenomena. The unbeliever and the believer can agree that two and two are four, and that certain principles of deduction are valid while others are invalid. Thus a kind of common ground is established.[69]

In my opinion, Van Til himself could have written this formulation, except for the bit about a "univocal" understanding, which raises a few (in my view minor) problems.[70] In fact, paragraphs nearly identical to these might be pasted together from Van Til's writings. But both Van Til and the Ligonier authors have had trouble maintaining consistency here, Van Til tending to forget the areas of agreement between believer and unbeliever ("in spite of themselves"), and the Ligoniers tending (as we have seen) to

69. Ibid., 70f.
70. Van Til seems to resist any positive use of the term "univocal" in regard to our knowledge of God. But if as in this context it simply means "literal," I know of no principle in Van Til's thought that would be violated by such a "univocal" knowledge of God. See my "The Problem of Theological Paradox," in *Foundations of Christian Scholarship*, 310f.

compromise their concept of "a completely opposite and antithetical understanding" between believer and unbeliever.[71]

One last comment in this area: It is unfortunate that a demonstrable misreading of Van Til at one point leads the authors to a serious misrepresentation of Van Til's position. On page 214 they quote Van Til as saying that the Christian "has no *point of contact* with the non-Christian."[72] They take this as a statement of Van Til's own view, but in context it is actually a paraphrase of Stuart Hackett's critique of Calvinism. I could write this off as a minor mistake, except that it shows, in its way, an extraordinary ignorance of Van Til's position. Van Til would *never* say that the Christian has no point of contact with the non-Christian; in fact, he has said the opposite innumerable times. Mistakes such as this make one wonder how seriously these authors have tried to understand Van Til. Could they have simply dismissed as inconsistencies the countless positive references in Van Til to "point of contact," focusing on this one reference as his definitive formulation, without even trying to explain the others? Or did the author of this section have such a poor knowledge of Van Til that he actually thought this was a representative formulation? It is hard to account for this sort of blunder except as a serious lapse of scholarship stemming from ignorance and intense prejudice, a desire to make Van Til say something that he does not actually say, in order to make him more vulnerable to criticism.

The Ligonier Apologetic

I must needs be briefer in dealing with the book's positive argument for Christianity, because of the demands of time and space and because the argument itself is not as novel or interesting (to me!) as the critique of Van Til. Still, there are a few new wrinkles.

The Ligonier authors believe, as we have seen, that traditionalist apologetics is sick and ailing, though not dead. One of the reasons for the malaise, in their view, is that other modern classicists have abandoned the traditional claim that the truth of Christianity can be demonstrated, settling for arguments that merely claim probability.[73] Here, interestingly, is another point of agreement between the Ligonier group and Van Til. Our

---

71. Is some of this inconsistency related to the book's triple authorship?

72. Sproul, Gerstner, and Lindsley, *Classical Apologetics*, 214, quoting Van Til in *Jerusalem and Athens*, 16.

73. Ibid., 100f., 125, 148, 276.

authors here frequently sound Van Tillian notes: that if Christianity is not *certainly* true, then we have, to some extent, an excuse for unbelief.

But how can we reach the level of demonstrative certainty? On the Ligonier view, decisive appeal to special revelation is excluded; that would be "presuppositionalism." But that means that the argument must be wholly based on human sensation and reason, unaided by special revelation. Everyone agrees that human reason and sensation are fallible. So whence the desired certainty?

The Ligonier authors believe such certainty can be attained by appeal to certain "universal and necessary assumptions." These are assumptions that, though sometimes challenged, cannot be regularly and consistently denied. Thus, they are prerequisites of science and, indeed, of all human life.[74] These are the law of noncontradiction, the "law of causality," and "the basic reliability of sense perception." Since these principles cannot be regularly and consistently denied, the book argues, they must be regarded as certain, along with any of their implications. Thus the authors try to show that Christianity is one of those implications: to deny Christianity is to deny one or more of those "universal and necessary assumptions." Since we cannot deny those, Christianity must also be regarded as certain.

The argument is "transcendental,"[75] even presuppositional in a sense. The authors are asking, "What are the assumptions necessary for life and knowledge to be possible?"[76] Van Til asks the same question and concludes that the whole content of God's revelation is such a necessary assumption! In one sense, the Ligonier authors are saying the same thing, but less directly. To deny Christianity, they say, is indeed to deny truths that we cannot consistently and regularly deny. Van Til, similarly, says that unbelievers cannot consistently and regularly deny Christianity, that they can exist only on "borrowed capital," inconsistently making use of Christian ideas that they wish to reject. I am tempted, therefore, to read the Ligonier argument as a kind of "indirect presuppositionalism," an attempt to show (more concretely than Van Til) the *ways* in which Christian assumptions are unavoidable. On such an approach, the authors would be asking the non-Christian to presuppose Christian concepts (concepts compatible with Scripture) of logic, cause, sense-experience, since denying these concepts leads to chaos. Van Til and the Ligonier group, on that interpretation, would again be very close. In my view, the

74. Ibid., 71f.
75. Ibid., 71.
76. Ibid.

cogency of the Ligonier argument arises from the fact that something like this is going on. But on the other hand, we have to remember all the talk in this book about autonomy, the inconsistencies on depravity, and so on. Whatever might actually be the case, these authors at least *think* that they are reasoning on a neutral basis, with concepts of cause and so on that are not distinctively Christian, even though they imply a distinctively Christian worldview.[77]

A brief look now at the authors' theistic proofs. Their ontological argument, following Jonathan Edwards, is virtually Parmenidean: We have an idea of being; in fact, we can think of nothing else than being. Nonbeing is unthinkable. Thus, being must be eternal, omnipresent, limitless in all perfections—in other words, God. There is an obvious objection to this, however, which the book doesn't even mention. However infinite being may be, our idea of being extends to finite being as well. Therefore, if "being" is divine, then finite beings are part of that divine being. In other words, without some modifications, the argument proves pantheism. And the argument fails to draw any distinction between the kind of "infinity," "eternity," "omnipresence," and so on attributable to a pantheistic god, and the very different (but similar-sounding) attributes revealed concerning the God of Scripture.[78]

The cosmological argument: Our authors state the "law of causality" first in what they admit to be tautological fashion: "Every effect has a cause."[79] Since the world is contingent, they argue, it must be an effect. What, then, is its cause? The world is not a mere illusion (nonbeing—see above), nor is it self-created, which is nonsense. If it is self-existent, then it is in effect transcendent and divine, so God's existence is proved. If it is created by a self-existent being, then again, God is proved. An infinite number of contingent beings cannot be the world-cause: if no one of them is sufficient to cause the world, then the whole series will not be sufficient either. Much could be said (and has been said) about this sort of argument. What is most notable to me is that, as in the Ligonier version of the ontological argument, the authors fail to clearly rule out the pantheistic alternative, namely, that the universe is its own god. About all I can find in the book responding to this objection is one sentence: "[God] is personal because He is the pervasive cause of all things including the purpose and

---

77. How is it possible for a concept to logically imply a Christian worldview if that concept is not itself in an important sense distinctively Christian?

78. Ibid., 93ff.

79. Ibid., 82f., 111.

the personal."[80] But it is by no means obvious that a being must itself be personal in order to be the cause of personality.

The ontological and cosmological arguments together suggest that on the Ligonier view, being is unlimited and therefore possesses all excellencies in infinite degree.[81] These excellencies include all the traditional attributes of the Christian God, including personality. Therefore, God exists. But the concept of an "excellency," a perfection, is religiously problematic. What is excellent to one person is a defect in the eyes of another. Personality is a perfection to a Westerner imbued with Christian teaching. To a Buddhist, that would not necessarily be the case. Therefore, the sort of proof offered in our book presupposes a particular set of values, or else it is simply invalid. In other words, either it is a presuppositional argument or else it is a failure.

I will pass over the teleological argument to look at the authors' presentation of Christian evidences. Here the authors follow the pattern of other books of this kind. They begin with the premise that the Gospels are "reliable historical sources."[82] (It would not do, of course, to presuppose more than this, that these books are the Word of God. That would be circular and presuppositional.) In these reliable historical sources, we learn about Jesus: that he worked miracles and that he claimed to be God.[83] Jesus' miracles prove divine attestation of his claim; therefore, he is God, and his testimony that Scripture is God's Word is to be believed. At that point, we conclude that Scripture is our ultimate standard. Thenceforth, we argue on the basis of biblical authority—that is, like presuppositionalists![84]

A few comments on this argument: (1) The authors overestimate, I think, the current scholarly consensus on the reliability of the Gospels. They assume that almost every New Testament scholar will concede that the Gospels are "generally reliable." I doubt it. (2) Even if we grant that some very unusual events took place in the ministry of Jesus,[85] how can we be sure that these can be explained *only* as a divine attestation to Jesus' authority? It is extremely difficult to prove (apart from Christian presuppositions) the

80. Ibid., 123.
81. Ibid.
82. Ibid., 141.
83. Interestingly, at this point, our authors sound another Van Tillian note: miracles are of no evidential value without a theistic presupposition (ibid., 146ff.).They believe that they have established the existence of God by means of theistic proof, and therefore have decisively refuted any notion that miracles are impossible. Of course, Van Til would go beyond this and say that the cogency of miracle requires not a barely theistic but a full-blown Christian worldview.
84. Except, presumably, when we are doing apologetics. But why should that be an exception?
85. And of course, the question must be raised as to *how* unusual an event must be before we call it a miracle.

negative proposition that no other cause could have produced these events. The authors need to prove this proposition in order to make their case, but nothing in the book amounts to such a proof. (3) Recall that these authors boasted earlier that they were offering not just a probable argument, but a demonstration, warranting certainty. Now, I can understand how they can make this claim for the earlier part of their argument: the "universal and necessary assumptions," the theistic proofs. (I do not think they succeed in making good this claim, but I can understand why they *think* they have made it good.) But when they get to the historical evidences, I do not find even the slightest plausibility in their claim to demonstration. The assumption of the Gospels' reliability is highly debatable; the argument that miracles always testify to a divinely appointed messenger is also weak. And some have questioned whether Jesus did warrant belief in the Scriptures. Of course, on these matters I think the Ligonier authors are right and the liberal critics wrong. But if they look at these questions without the full range of Christian presuppositions, I do not see how they can responsibly claim anything more for their argument than a high degree of probability.

Some Formal Matters

At the risk of losing the reader's attention, I think I should point out some editorial problems in the book that ought to be corrected in future editions. There are a great many of these, possibly in part because of the triple authorship. (1) I do not understand the need, in context, for three pages dealing with theological creativity (pp. 64ff.). (2) The excursus on probabilism in theology (pp. 125ff.) seems also to belong somewhere else. It breaks up the discussion of dysteleology. (3) On page 185, the third point does not make much sense to me; at least it does not seem clearly distinguishable from the second point. (4) Note the typographical error on page 187—the "poetic influence of sin" (!). (5) On page 220, the authors give the impression that Van Til's *Survey of Christian Epistemology* is a different book from his *Metaphysics of Apologetics*. Actually, the two books are one and the same, the former being a more recent printing of the latter.[86] (6) Recall our earlier point about the misreading of the Van Til reference on page 214. (7) I agree with the authors' assessment of Runner's

---

86. I must say that I am also somewhat disturbed by the large number of references to this title and the relatively small number of references to Van Til's more recent writings. It hardly seems fair to judge Van Til to such a large extent on the basis of his first, relatively unnuanced, class syllabus, dating back to 1929.

concept of "republication" (pp. 251f.), but it fits rather awkwardly into the context. (8) On page 254, second paragraph, who is speaking? Van Til, Sullivan, or the Ligoniers? (9) The material on Duns Scotus (p. 260) also seems out of place.

Conclusions

There is much here to make us think. I was surprised at how close these authors were to Van Til at various places. There are, I think, some areas here for further dialogue between Van Tillian and Ligonier apologists. There is much similarity in regard to general revelation and the noetic effects of sin. There is recognition of the need for more than mere probability in grounding our faith. The authors also recognize that evidential arguments presuppose some elements of a Christian worldview. The chief difference is in the evaluation of autonomy. There is also room for further debates as to who is the most consistent with the shared Calvinistic premises.

Surely there is plenty of room for mutual support and encouragement in the Lord. Speaking personally, I owe a great deal to John Gerstner, who for several decades was the most cogent and tireless defender of the Reformed faith in western Pennsylvania. Sproul and Lindsley, through the Ligonier Valley Study Center, continue Gerstner's ministry, sending this Reformed message all over the world by lectures and tapes: excellent communications, on the whole, of the gospel of Christ. We Van Tillians have much to learn from these valiant men; and I dare say they have much to learn from us as well.

APPENDIX B:
JAY E. ADAMS'S REPLY TO FRAME

(Note: Jay Adams was gracious to reply to my critique of him in chapter 7. I'm happy to thank him for this contribution and to announce that we are still friends! As for me, I'm sticking by what I wrote in the text. The reader may decide who is closer to the truth. In any case, I am quite willing to let him have the last word; in that respect, I am hoping to set an example for other theological controversialists.—JF)

What John Frame, in his kindly, somewhat jocular fashion, is saying is that Adams can't stand loose ends and must always try to find an answer to problems; he is a problem-solver. That's why Adams wants to find an answer to what he calls the "so-called problem of evil." Now, this inclination to find solutions to everything might be a good thing in counseling, but in theology it doesn't always work. Indeed, in the issue before us, it is clear that Adams has gone too far. There is no solution to the problem of evil (not the "so-called" problem, as Adams puts it), perhaps even in eternity. After all, if Augustine couldn't solve it, who does Adams think he is to do so?

Well, let's look at those thoughts for a moment. First, let me dispose of the Augustine argument. While I must applaud Augustine for his rigorously biblical theological formulations in some areas, I cannot go along with him in others. For instance, he believed that baptism washes away sin. Augustine is not the final answer—Scripture is!

But enough of that. What of Frame's real objections? Well, on one score he certainly is right: I do like to tie up loose ends. On the wall of my study is an inscription that reads: "Problems Are for Solving." I have no difficulty in confessing that I am eager to tie up as many loose ends as I can—that is to say, as many as can be tied up biblically. But I want you to know that I understand and try to follow the admonition of Deuteronomy 29:29. And I hope you understand that I want to speculate about nothing that that verse prohibits. I am convinced that in my book *The Grand Demonstration*, I have set forth nothing about the so-called problem of evil that the Scripture has not first revealed. That, then, is the issue: have I or haven't I?

Romans 9 is clear. It gives a reason why evil exists. God says that he wanted to demonstrate his nature. He wanted to demonstrate his wrath and power, and so he endured with long-suffering the vessels of wrath that he designed for that purpose. Unless evil existed, it would be impossible for a good God to exhibit wrath, judgment, and power. The same is true for the other side of his nature. Wishing to exhibit his mercy and grace, God designed the vessels of mercy for that purpose. There would be no need for mercy if evil did not exist. And of course, God determined to bring this about not through automatons, but through responsible creatures.

Now, I maintain that that is a solution and answer to the problem raised by the so-called problem of evil. The problem may be stated as follows: How can there be evil in a good God's world? The answer? God decreed it in order to demonstrate his nature.

Of course, Frame can play the child's game of asking why, if he wishes. You know how that goes, don't you? The child asks his mommy why in response to every answer she gives. If Frame does not think that the answer revealed in Romans 9 is sufficient, he can go on asking why. "Why did God want to demonstrate his nature?" is the next in line, I suppose. But God has not revealed that to us.

Yet God has told us why evil men exist. And that should be enough. Indeed, it is far more than most will admit. In my opinion, in Romans 9 God provides the ultimate answer that we need: he determined to demonstrate his nature in this way according to his own good reasons for his glory.

If that is not a solution to the problem, then there is none—at least with revelation as it stands at the moment. Perhaps God, in eternity, will reveal more of his mind to us, but for now he has not. Yet there is no mystery in all of this; God tells you why he has raised up and fitted men for wrath: for the purpose of demonstrating his nature. Come on, John, what more do you want? Do you want to get into God's mind and ask why?

APPENDIX C:
FAITH VS. FAITH:
COVENANT EPISTEMOLOGY
AND AUTONOMOUS FIDEISM

Joseph E. Torres

Introduction

The following dialogue is adapted from an actual online discussion I had on God's existence. I was having a conversation on the transcendental argument (TAG) until I was interrupted by a fellow we'll call Richard. It didn't take long to realize that Richard was quite hostile to Christianity. What is presented here, unlike what is found in chapter 10, is a real discussion with an unbeliever, albeit somewhat cleaned up.

Dialogue

JOE: What I offer for your consideration, Sam, is known as the transcendental argument for the existence of God (TAG). TAG is more than a simple argument concluding that "God exists." Instead, it aims to demonstrate that Christianity as a whole is true. In contrast to the traditional arguments—which tend to focus on God's being the first cause, the grand designer, or the most perfect being—TAG argues that it is the God of the Bible who makes cause, purpose, design, morality, science, and even logic intelligible in the first place. Without *this* God, nothing is intelligible, meaningful, or valuable.

[I then explain the general contours of TAG from rationality, morality, and the uniformity of nature as found in chapter 4.]

. . . I hope you'll see the overall transcendental thrust of my argumentation.

[In enters Richard. Sam doesn't stick around much after this.]

RICHARD: . . . I must praise the eloquence of your presentation. I read a small amount of your writing before I realized that it was all taken from the Bible and put into semi-scientific language, presenting a model for the history of the universe and the physical world. From your earlier discussion with Sam, I see you're under the impression that without God, there can be no basis for science, or morals. If this is correct, you're mistaken. Science is derived from observation based on thorough mathematic deduction. . . . The idea that morals cannot exist without God seems to me to be very problematic as well. As I understand it, your argument is like parents who mistakenly believe that if they didn't teach their children right from wrong, their children would never have learned it. But morality is intuitive. If one simply lives his life by the law of reciprocity, he'd lead a truly moral life without the need for a deity. Likewise, the Ten Commandments were not the the origin of moral reasoning. These laws were commonly known and believed in the ancient world. . . . The Israelites just codified them and claimed that they came in the form of a "command" from God. This was done so that they would receive more reverence and acceptance.

Let me be honest with you. The only book I've read on Christianity is the Bible itself. And it was anguishing to work through. The Bible is marginally factual at best. To believe Jesus is the Son of God—the Lord and Savior of the world—takes more than *blind faith*; it takes a *blind eye* to the process of logical deduction and the scientific process. . . . There's no logical way, through direct or indirect observation, or using sound scientific method, to deduce that Jesus Christ was in any way divine. It has no basis in fact; it is a *belief*.

JOE: Thanks, Richard, for your comments and compliments. If you don't mind, I would like to point some things out. You seem to miss the transcendental thrust of my origin argument. I'm not saying that non-Christians do not live morally, do science, or think rationally. What I'm saying is that their *worldview* cannot account for it. A non-Christian philosophy cannot make sense out of why it is that we can do science; it cannot explain the laws of logic, human dignity, or the authority of moral obligations. What I'm saying is this: Non-Christians know, in their heart of hearts, that God exists. Non-Christians must borrow Christian principles in order to argue against Christianity. This is conceptual plagiarism.

Your reasons for rejecting Christianity are not specific. You make many assumptions that you are unable to justify. You seem to assume that evolutionary theory has discredited the scientific respectability of Christianity. But as I've mentioned earlier, science depends on the inductive principle, that the future will be like the past. Scientists must assume the uniformity of nature in order for it to proceed with repeatable observation. But they *cannot* prove induction (because it's not observable). It must be established on philosophical or religious grounds. So on what grounds do you justify induction? According to Darwinism, the universe has a determinative blueprint, one that governs exactly how things will unfold. In a reality of chance, why expect the future to be like the past? Anything is possible given time! After all, that is the Darwinists' origin story.

May I ask you another question? Are you a materialist? Do you believe that all that is real is physical? If so, can you explain either the existence or epistemologically binding nature of laws of logic? After all, you've claimed that Christian belief is subrational. But how do you explain an abstract thing like *reason*? Are laws of logic just rules established by majority opinion? If they are, why *ought* we to follow them? If they're not absolute, what's the big deal if we don't follow them? On the other hand, if they're universally binding, how do you account for them in a materialist framework? Are they physical objects? Do they exist in space somewhere? Do they exist in a world of Platonic forms?

My challenge to you is to account for the uniformity of nature, the authoritative quality of moral absolutes, and laws of thoughts on a materialistic account. Unless you can justify these things, then it is you, not I, that is operating on blind faith.

RICHARD: Morality really has nothing to do with God. After all, I knew right from wrong long before I had any concept of God, and I continued (and will continue) to hold true to my moral ideals long after I rejected belief in God.

Logic likewise has nothing to do with God. Here I'll lean on Michael Martin's transcendental argument for the nonexistence of God (TANG).[1]

---

1. Atheist philosopher Michael Martin has formulated a photo-negative version of TAG, which he calls the transcendental argument for the nonexistence of God (TANG). According to Martin, the laws of logic, the nature of science, and the like all presuppose the nonexistence of God in order to be intelligible. For Martin's argument in his own words, see his "The Transcendental Argument for the Nonexistence of God" (1996), at http://www.infidels.org/library/modern/michael_martin/martin-frame/tang.html. Several of Frame's responses to Martin have been worked into the main text of this new edition. For one particularly poignant rebuttal, see Michael Butler, "TAG vs. TANG," *Penpoint* (August 1996), available at http://www.reformed.org.

According to the brand of Christianity assumed by TAG, God created everything, including logic; or at least everything, including logic, is contingent on God. Moreover, if principles of logic are contingent on God, God could change them. Thus, God could make the law of noncontradiction false; in other words, God could arrange matters so that a proposition and its negation were true at the same time. But this is absurd. How could God arrange matters so that New Zealand is south of China and that New Zealand is not south of it? So one must conclude that logic is not dependent on God, and insofar as the Christian worldview assumes that logic is dependent, it is false. Logic is simply a by-product of the observable and deductible universe.

JOE: Richard, I'm beginning to think that at *some* level we're speaking past each other. As I read your replies, I continue to think that you're missing my point. I am *not* saying that non-Christians do not lead moral lives. You explain that you learned morality apart from a conscious belief in God. Fine; I never said, nor do I believe, the opposite. I'm not asking about how we came to learn the details of morality. Rather, I'm asking what is the ultimate *authority* behind moral injunctions. I am arguing that it cannot be reduced to personal preferences or societal consensus. You've mentioned examples of people having a moral sense apart from theistic belief, as if this were a refutation of my position. But Richard, it is not. I am *not* saying that non-Christians do not think rationally. I'm asking the question, "What would have to be true of the world in order to justify our everyday assumption regarding morality, logic, science, values, etc.?"

The TANG argument misunderstands the Christian doctrine of God. God cannot violate his character or change his essential nature.[2] When logic is properly conceived and applied, it reflects the consistency that has already characterized God's thoughts. We, as creatures created in his image, can thus reflect his thinking on a finite scale. Thus, the example that Dr. Martin provides of God's possibly changing things around arbitrarily is a straw man. One cannot go about arguing against a *generic* concept of God. I defend the *biblical* God. Thus, arguments against such a God must be familiar with the nature of *this* God.

RICHARD: The uniformity of nature has nothing to do with God. . . . I don't believe we can have certainty by any singular deduction, but when many deductions—from differing perspectives—converge on the same conclusion, the certainty becomes undeniable. The uniformity of natural law certainly falls under this sort of irrefutable deduction.

---

2. Num. 23:19; Mal. 3:6; Titus 1:2; Heb. 1:11–12; 6:18; James 1:17.

JOE: In order for your comments on scientific "deduction" to make sense to me, I'll have to reread it while inserting the word "induction" where you write "deduction."

[I present an extended argument to demonstrate that science works according to the inductive principle. Deductive conclusions are not absolutely certain if built from inductively constructed premises.]

Now, once this is done, your comments become viciously circular. We can justify belief in induction because induction has never failed us before? That's an inductive argument! That's the same as saying that we can ground the uniformity of nature in the uniformity of nature. "We believe that the future is going to be like the past because it's always been like the past before!" This is not a scientific statement; you've made a bold declaration of faith! Your comments are circular in two senses: first, in the sense that I've noted above, and second, because they assume that miracles have never occurred in history. But isn't that part of the very thing we're arguing over? You're boldly assuming naturalism in order to establish naturalism.

I submit to you that you indeed, in your heart, know God. *No*, this doesn't necessarily mean that you're blatantly lying to me, only that there's a strong possibility that you are self-deceived. You are created in the image of God, and his stamp of his Creatorhood is clearly impressed into your very nature.

I have attempted to demonstrate that your reason for denying God's right as your King is not rooted in intellectual difficulties. The ultimate issue here is not that you cannot believe in God, but that you *will not* believe in him.

RICHARD [*Closing statements*]: Your TAG . . . is just another more clever and harder-to-refute explanation for Christianity. I would have to concede that your gift of the word and skills in field of debate don't permit me any reasonable chance of influencing you in any way. . . . All I've got is *something in my heart* that tells every fabric of my being that Christianity stinks. Something at its core is false.

Why all the mystery? All it would take to make a believer out of me—and all the world—is one more global divine intervention. I hope soon to better articulate my *instincts* into the form of a more intelligent argument than what I've presented so far. The key to humanity's future lies in the progress of human thought, and Christianity hinders this very progress. Christianity has all "the answers" and leaves no room for questions.

Earlier, you asked me if I'm a materialist. I guess you could say that. . . . I think everything has a physical explanation. But I don't believe all physical explanations have been accounted for, *nor do I believe they will be anytime soon.* There's simply too much in our universe and to the human mind to have it all explained in the mere blip of time that represents the duration of the human species. Again, your skill with the written word is too cunning for me to compete with. All I have is what you would call *faith*: *faith* that your worldview is complete, and wrong, and mine is very much incomplete, but at least heading in the right direction. Thanks for a good discussion.

JOE [*Closing statements to readers of the original conversation online*]: To the readers of this post, I ask a series of questions. Were Richard's objections to Christianity *really* based on logic, reason, and superior moral reasoning? Was the real issue at hand that we Christians operate on "blind faith," but atheists reason from "the facts"? Or, perhaps, is it one type of faith against another type of faith? I submit to you that in this conversation what you've read is the collision between two antithetical worldviews. This is the difference between blind faith and faith in the objective revelation of God's Word.

I have argued that unless the triune God of the Bible lives, there are no such things as objective moral values, no uniformity to nature (making the start of science impossible), no human dignity, no laws of rationality to be violated in intelligent debate. Richard, on the other hand, has brought to the facts a philosophy that he would have us believe he derived from the facts. But this is not so. Have we attempted to argue consistently from within our worldviews? Yes, I believe that we both have. But I assert that Richard has had to borrow from my worldview in order to launch an attack against it. I, on the other hand, argue that unless my worldview is already true, then rational discourse doesn't even make sense; it is not intelligible. I've tried to present arguments that prove the truth of the Christian worldview from the impossibility of the contrary. This is what is called a transcendental negative argument.

I would, in closing, like to make one thing perfectly clear. I do not claim to be wiser, more intelligent, or more righteous than any of those with whom I speak. I did not cleverly work my way up the philosophical ladder to figure out the existence of God. No, God has revealed himself in Scripture. In light of this Word, I humbly examine my world and myself. I, too, once rejected God's Word, and thus am no better than anyone else. If anything, I have been humbled because of his gracious and sovereign love for me though I did not (and still do not) deserve it. God, through his Spirit, has given me new eyes to see the world with the lenses of Scripture.

I thank you for your time, and Richard for his cooperation.

Closing Comments to Current Readers

My hopes for my current readers regarding this dialogue are (1) that the confusion and repetition of concepts will not turn off close analysis of what's happened here, and (2) that the jargon used will not hinder understanding. Now I'd like to interpret what's happened in these last few pages.

The transcendental apologetic formulated by Cornelius Van Til is largely unheard of by most unbelievers. Those of the evidentialist camp are far better at popularizing their arguments than are presuppositionalists. Because of this ignorance, most unbelievers don't know what to do with a transcendentally oriented apologetic argument. It offends their sensibilities, but a cogent or informed refutation is difficult to construe. I believe that evidentialists have too often argued what I call "second-order" arguments. I define these as arguments that work from common-grace benefits (beliefs in design, morality, science, logic, etc.). Now, there's nothing wrong with building on shared premises, that is, until the unbeliever argues epistemologically self-consciously. When this happens, a first-order argument is needed (an argument that challenges the unbeliever to account for the intelligibility of such notions).

First-order arguments can easily expose the rationalist-irrationalist dialectical tension in non-Christian thought. Richard sought to construct a worldview based on naturalism. He states, "I think *everything* has a physical explanation." This is rationalism in the Van Tillian sense; Richard explicitly says "everything." But exposing his irrationalist streak, he adds, "But I don't believe all physical explanations have been accounted for, *nor do I believe they will be anytime soon*." Here Richard engages what Francis Schaeffer called an "upper story leap." Though without proof, or any rational explanation on his own basis, he insists that such necessary concepts (love, justice, rationality, the uniformity of nature, morality, etc.) must, *and one day will*, be explained naturalistically. This is irrational belief, also known as *fideism*. What is most ironic about this situation is that normally it is Christians who are labeled fideists. But this is just plain wrong; after all, rationality presupposes the God who has revealed himself in Scripture.

In closing, I offer you the words of the apostle Paul in his first letter to the Corinthian church:

Where is the one who is wise? Where is the scribe? Where is the debater of this age? Has not God made foolish the wisdom of the world? For since, in the wisdom of God, the world did not know God through wisdom, it pleased God through the folly of what we preach to save those who believe. For Jews demand signs and Greeks seek wisdom, but we preach Christ crucified, a stumbling block to Jews and folly to Gentiles, but to those who are called, both Jews and Greeks, Christ the power of God and the wisdom of God. (1 Cor. 1:20–24)

APPENDIX D:
BETWEEN SCYLLA AND CHARYBDIS: PRESUPPOSITIONALISM, CIRCULAR REASONING, AND THE CHARGE OF FIDEISM REVISITED

Joseph E. Torres

Ali vs. Fraser. Lakers vs. Celtics. Continental rationalism vs. British empiricism. For almost as long as humankind has been around, there has been competition; and for as long as there's been thought, there have been schools of thought, competing for the right to claim the proper interpretation of reality. The intellectual terrain of Christian apologetics is no different. All agree that the Bible is God's true Word to an ethically hostile creation. But how the claims of Scripture bear on our standards of truth, rationality, proof, and a host of related topics in measure depends on whether your approach to apologetics is classical, evidentialist, presuppositional, or something else.

Perhaps the single most common argument against the apologetic method of Cornelius Van Til (1895–1987) is the charge of fideism. One doesn't have to look far in the relevant literature to find Van Tillians disregarded or said to hold to a position that undermines Christian apologetics.[1] Though the term *fideism* is being rehabilitated in some circles,[2] fideism is

---

1. For the remainder of this work, I will use the term *presuppositionalism* (*presuppositionalists*, etc.) as synonymous with a Van Tillian apologetic methodology.

2. Cf. Kevin J. Vanhoozer, *First Theology: God, Scripture and Hermeneutics* (Downers Grove, IL: InterVarsity Press, 2002), 358.

antiapologetic and widely understood as a dogmatic proclamation of one's view irrespective of rational argument. Nothing seems to better demonstrate the fideism of presuppositionalism, so it is believed, as Van Tillians' rejection of linear reasoning. Van Tillians are said to embrace, as a fundamental rule of their approach, the fallacy of begging the question. If this is true, presuppositionalists fail to adequately give "a reason for [their] hope" in Christ (1 Peter 3:15). Van Til is painted as an authoritarian who makes bare authority claims without appeal to the content of Christian faith.[3] If argumentation is flouted, then all that remains is a shouting match between competing authority claims. This brings to mind the argumentative stalemate in the "apologetic parable" of the "Shadoks" and the "Gibis" by John Warwick Montgomery in Van Til's festschrift *Jerusalem and Athens*.[4]

The Purpose of This Article

Too often in the literature, Van Tillians are dismissed by the twin charges of circularity and fideism. In fact, I would dare to say that most objections to Van Til's approach are rooted in these apparent bogeymen. The fideism-circularity objection to Van Til's method has been around nearly as long as the method itself. For reasons that surpass the guesswork of this author, there is a widespread misunderstanding on what Van Til believed about faith, reasoning, and argument.[5] This charge would almost be offensive if it weren't so readily demonstrable. As a result, Van Til has become another example of how *not* to do apologetics. In contrast, over the past twenty-five years an increasing number of apologetic works have been released that aim to integrate the best insights of both the traditional method (consisting of the classicist and evidentialist schools) and presuppositionalism.[6] That these camps are growing closer through dialogue is

3. See also Gordon R. Lewis, "The Biblical Authoritarianism of Cornelius Van Til," chap. 5 in *Testing Christianity's Truth Claims* (Chicago: Moody Press, 1976).

4. See John Warwick Montgomery, "Once upon an A Priori," in *Jerusalem and Athens: Critical Discussions on the Philosophy and Apologetics of Cornelius Van Til*, ed. E. R. Geehan (Nutley, NJ: Presbyterian and Reformed, 1971). John M. Frame refers to the account as an "apologetic parable" in *CVT*, 307.

5. James Anderson suspects that "this confusion arises from superficial interpretations of his criticisms of 'natural theology' and his opposition to certain methodologies adopted in the formulation and presentation of theistic arguments." "If Knowledge Then God: The Epistemological Theistic Arguments of Plantinga and Van Til" (2005), available at http://www.proginosko.com/docs/If_Knowledge_Then_God.pdf.

6. Cf. Ronald B. Mayers, *Balanced Apologetics: Using Evidences and Presuppositions in Defense of the Faith* (Chicago: Moody Press, 1984); Richard B. Ramsay, *The Certainty of the Faith: Apologetics in an Uncertain World* (Phillipsburg, NJ: P&R Publishing, 2008); Kenneth D. Boa and Robert

promising indeed, and the present work is geared toward further removing obstacles to integration.

The objective of this essay is twofold. First, we will examine the charge of question-begging by distinguishing between vicious and virtuous circles. I argue that presuppositionalists embrace the latter but eschew the former, just as their critics do. Second, I will show that the charge of fideism is both imprecise and inaccurate.

The "Problem" of Presuppositional Methodology

I should acknowledge here that presuppositionalists have in fact made statements embracing circularity, seemingly strengthening the charge of fideism. Cornelius Van Til himself confessed, "The Reformed apologist will frankly admit that his own methodology presupposes the truth of Christian theism."[7] For some, such comments seem to close the book on presuppositionalism as a valid method. Since apologetics aims at demonstrating the rational credibility of Christianity, any approach that renounces argumentation is beyond the pale.

The Link between Fideism and Circularity

And so it seems that Van Tillian presuppositionalism is caught between Scylla and Charybdis. Van Tillians face a unique double danger: either they are charged with refusing to reason at all (fideism) or they are charged with arguing poorly by begging the question. Perhaps *Scylla and Charybdis* is best switched to *Cerberus*, the name of the multiheaded beast of Greek and Roman mythology. This is because these twin objections are not separate and discrete as is often presented. Nevertheless, conjuring up the imagery of the two guardians of the Strait of Messina is helpful. Once presuppositionalists are exonerated from the allegation of fallacious circularity, much of the bite of the fideism charge is lost. If Van Tillians are to be considered serious partners in apologetic dialogue, these two beasts must be slain. In addressing these twin objections to presuppositionalism, I will first examine the charge of fideism, followed by the issue of circularity.

M. Bowman Jr., *Faith Has Its Reasons: Integrative Approaches to Defending the Christian Faith*, 2nd ed. (Waynesboro, GA: Paternoster, 2006). Note also how acknowledging the determinative power of philosophical presuppositions strengthens the argument against the Jesus Seminar in Michael J. Wilkins and J. P. Moreland, eds., *Jesus under Fire: Modern Scholarship Reinvents the Historical Jesus* (Grand Rapids: Zondervan, 1996), introduction.

7. Cornelius Van Til, *The Defense of the Faith*, 3rd ed. (Philadelphia: Presbyterian and Reformed, 1967), 99–100.

The Scylla of Fideism

The charge of fideism can be made in two interdependent ways. Negatively, one can be labeled a fideist if one denies the need for, or existence of, logical reasons for maintaining Christian theism. Surely Van Tillian thinker Rousas Rushdoony goes too far when he says, "It is blasphemy therefore to attempt to 'prove' God; God is the necessary presupposition of all proof."[8] Positively, the charge can be made of someone who claims that arational or irrational faith is the only acceptable ground for assenting to Christianity. The relation between these two forms should be apparent: if all rational grounds for Christianity are denied, we are left with faith alone. While this is vital to a Protestant doctrine of justification, it is deadly to apologetics. Van Til and his followers have been accused of both positive and negative fideism.

In *Faith beyond Reason*, C. Stephen Evans provides an example of the negative charge. In his words:

> Van Til . . . vigorously reject[s] the claim that apologetic arguments can be mounted that appeal to facts or logical principles that the unregenerate mind can grasp. Such an apologetic argument ignores the non-neutrality of human reason and implicitly concedes that sinful human reason can operate reliably. Van Til argues, for example, that *one should not try to give rational arguments that the Bible is the inspired word of God.*[9]

Likewise, in the entry on "Faith and Reason" in *101 Key Terms in Philosophy and Their Importance for Theology*, the author characterizes Van Til as a "chastened" fideist. This is because Van Til affirms "a certain antithesis between faith and 'reason.' "[10] Finally, Alister McGrath suggests that Van Til belongs to a school of thought that "disavow[s] a rational apologetic."[11]

8. Rousas J. Rushdoony, *The Institutes of Biblical Law* (Nutley, NJ: Presbyterian and Reformed, 1973), 127.

9. C. Stephen Evans, *Faith beyond Reason: A Kierkegaardian Account* (Grand Rapids: Eerdmans, 1998), 19 (emphasis added). John G. Stackhouse Jr. also comes very close to making the same claim in his *Humble Apologetics: Defending the Faith Today* (New York: Oxford University Press, 2002), 157.

10. Kelly James Clark, Richard Lints, and James K. A. Smith, *101 Key Terms in Philosophy and Their Importance for Theology* (Louisville, KY: Westminster John Knox, 2004), 28. It should be noted that saying that Van Til posits a "certain antithesis" between faith and reason is much too vague to justify calling anyone a fideist when, as we see below, granting antithetical definitions, any Christian can affirm a "certain" antithesis between the two.

11. *Intellectuals Don't Need God & Other Modern Myths* (Grand Rapids: Zondervan, 1993), 221. J. P. Moreland also makes the connection between presuppositionalism and the negative charge of fideism: "One's response to this objection will turn, in part, on one's approach to apologetics.

The positive charge of fideism is seen in the work of John Warwick Montgomery, who writes that Van Til gives "the impression that our gospel is as aprioristically, fideistically irrational as the presuppositional claims of its competitors."[12] Clark Pinnock advances that Van Til calls for "a total and *ungrounded* commitment" to Christianity, one that "*assumes* the theistic clue to ultimate reality."[13] Unbelievers, says Pinnock, are exhorted to voluntaristically "decide to become Christians and not think about it first. The basis of the choice cannot be known until after the axiom has been espoused."[14] Finally, Pinnock makes the accusation explicit: "[Van Til] cannot escape the charge of fideism, the view that truth in religion is ultimately based on faith rather than on reasoning or evidence."[15]

The Charybdis of Circular Reasoning

If faith is the singular basis for Christian commitment, the only way to do justice to this fact is calling for faith based on the Bible's own testimony. William Lane Craig comments, "As commonly understood, presuppositionalism is guilty of a logical howler: it commits the informal fallacy of *petitio principii*, or begging the question, for it advocates presupposing the truth of Christian theism in order to prove Christian theism."[16] So inimical to apologetics is circularity that he further states, "It is difficult to imagine how anyone could with a straight face think to show theism to be true by reasoning, 'God exists. Therefore, God exists.'"[17]

Problem Statements

As noted earlier, the accusation of fallacious circularity is fanned by statements that Van Til and others have made. Here are a few examples from Van Til himself:

If one is a fideist or a presuppositionalist (roughly, the view that *rational argumentation and evidence cannot be offered as epistemic support* for Christian theism from some neutral starting point), then one may say that begging the question is not a problem here." *Christianity and the Nature of Science* (Grand Rapids: Baker, 1989), 205n42 (emphasis added).

12. Montgomery, "Once upon an A Priori," as quoted in Greg L. Bahnsen, *Van Til's Apologetic: Readings and Analysis* (Phillipsburg, NJ: P&R Publishing, 1998), 638.

13. Clark Pinnock, "The Philosophy of Christian Evidences," in *Jerusalem and Athens*, 423 (emphasis added).

14. Ibid.

15. Ibid. While Montgomery calls Van Til's approach "fideistically irrational," Pinnock calls it "irrational fideism." So both bases are covered! See ibid., 425.

16. William Lane Craig, "A Classical Apologist's Response," in *Five Views on Apologetics*, ed. Steven B. Cowan (Grand Rapids: Zondervan, 2000), 232.

17. Ibid., 233.

- To admit one's own presuppositions and to point out the presuppositions of others is therefore to maintain that all reasoning is, in the nature of the case, *circular reasoning*.[18]
- The only alternative to "circular reasoning" as engaged in by Christians, no matter on what point they speak, is that of reasoning on the basis of isolated facts and isolated minds with the result that there is no possibility of reasoning at all.[19]
- We hold it to be true that circular reasoning is the only reasoning that is possible to finite man. The method of implication as outlined above is circular reasoning.[20]

Now I turn to statements embracing circularity from Van Tillians:

- Instead of trying to prove the truth of Christianity to the unregenerate, [the presuppositionalist] assumes at the outset and then challenges the natural man by demonstrating that on his presuppositions nothing is true, nothing can be accounted for, and his own thinking is invalid.[21]
- Christians should always refer back to God's word—his self-revelation in words in the Bible—as our final authority. Why do I believe something? Because *God* says so. How do I know that God says so? Because God says he says so![22]

Now, why is circular reasoning fallacious? Begging the question is marked by two traits. First, a viciously circular argument *assumes* its stance rather than providing support for it. In doing this, it avoids the burden of proof. According to Douglas N. Walton, author of the only full-length monograph entirely devoted to this topic,[23] "The requirement here is one of *evidential priority*. Arguing in a circle becomes a fallacy by basing it on prior acceptance of the conclusion to be proved. So the fallacy of begging the

18. Van Til, *Defense of the Faith*, 3rd ed., 101.

19. Cornelius Van Til, *An Introduction to Systematic Theology: Prolegomena and the Doctrine of Revelation, Scripture, and God*, ed. William Edgar, 2nd ed. (Phillipsburg, NJ: P&R Publishing, 2007), 243.

20. Cornelius Van Til, *A Survey of Christian Epistemology* (Philadelphia: Presbyterian and Reformed, 1969), 12. This last quotation hints at what Van Til is getting at, but more on that below.

21. Rousas J. Rushdoony, *By What Standard? An Analysis of the Philosophy of Cornelius Van Til* (Birmingham, AL: Cornerstone Publishers, 1974), 100.

22. Ramsay, *Certainty of the Faith*, 98.

23. Douglas N. Walton, *Begging the Question: Circular Reasoning as a Tactic of Argumentation* (New York: Greenwood Press, 1991).

question is a systematic tactic to evade fulfillment of a legitimate *burden of proof.*"[24] Second, viciously circular arguments merely restate the conclusion in one of the premises. According to S. Morris Engel, "if the supporting premises merely repeat or rephrase what is stated in the conclusion, as in all cases of begging the question, *the argument contains no premises* and is therefore fallacious."[25] The authors of *Classical Apologetics*, the largest critique of presuppositional methodology in print, assert that "presuppositionalists frankly admit to the use of circular reasoning in precisely this sense."[26]

Circularity

If question-begging is embraced, fideism is implied. Fideism is the rejection of a rational apologetic, and vicious argumentative circularity is one way to escape providing reasons, through argumentation, for one's religious convictions. If it is successfully demonstrated that presuppositionalists embrace fallacious circularity, then a major blow has been dealt to their methodology.

Vicious and Virtuous Circles

Here it is vital to distinguish between two types of circularity: vicious and virtuous. In the majority of the literature, circular reasoning and begging the question are presented as synonymous, with no distinctions made regarding different types of circularity. Among analytical philosophers and epistemologists there is a lively discussion[27] over (1) the validity of epistemic circularity and (2) whether all forms of circular reasoning should be equated

24. Douglas N. Walton, "Circular Reasoning," in *Blackwell Companion to Epistemology*, ed. Jonathan Dancy and Ernest Sosa (Cambridge, MA: Blackwell Reference, 1992), 66 (emphasis added).

25. S. Morris Engel, *With Good Reason: An Introduction to Informal Fallacies*, 5th ed. (New York: St. Martin's Press, 1994), 147 (emphasis added). J. P. Moreland provides an example of what it means to merely repeat or rephrase what is stated in the conclusion: "Capital punishment is *wrong* because it is an example of something we have *no business doing*, namely, taking a person's life." *Love Your God with All Your Mind* (Colorado Springs: NavPress, 1997), 123–24. "Wrong" and "something we have no business doing" are synonymous, a mere repetition of the same thought in different words.

26. R. C. Sproul, John H. Gerstner, and Arthur W. Lindsley, *Classical Apologetics* (Grand Rapids: Zondervan, 1984), 322.

27. Cf. William P. Alston, "Epistemic Circularity," *Philosophy and Phenomenological Research* 47 (1986): 1–30; Roy Sorenson, "P Therefore P, Without Circularity," *Journal of Philosophy* 88 (1991): 245–66; Michael Bergmann, "Epistemic Circularity: Malignant and Benign" (n.d.), available at http://web.ics.purdue.edu/~bergmann/epistemic%20circularity.htm.

with the fallacy of *petitio principii*. Walton notes that question-begging is a fallacy because it "prevent[s] the raising of further critical questions by an opponent in relation to one's argument in persuasion dialogue."[28] But not all circles are fallacious, nor are they all vicious. Circular arguments are, as Walton puts it, "often quite correct and useful—not fallacious, as traditionally portrayed in the logic textbooks."[29] I speak of nonvicious circles as virtuous circles. Virtuous circularity occurs when consistency is maintained from the fundamental principles of one's method, through to the presentation and examination of supporting evidence, down to the concluding point. This I term *circular coherence*. Nicholas Rescher clarifies:

> The justificatory procedure at issue is then indeed circular—the validated logic we achieve in the end should ideally turn out to encompass the very logic of which we have been making presystematic use. But there is nothing vicious or vitiating at work here; it is a matter of retrospective wisdom-of-hindsight reassessment, of revisiting something familiar to reconsider it from a different point of view. . . . In this way the validation of the modes of argumentation that constitute our logic is a process that is—to reemphasize—*virtuously circular*. We would not—should not—want it otherwise. Circularity in this domain is not just unavoidable but actually desirable. . . . In the validation of modes of argumentation, circularity is not something vicious or vitiating; it is a rational *sine qua non*.[30]

This from a Roman Catholic with no stake in the ongoing discussions over apologetic method.

Having differentiated between vicious and virtuous circularity, we can ask whether presuppositionalists embrace question-begging. Van Til and his followers have endorsed a brand of circularity. But do they endorse the fallacy of *petitio principii*? Recall that vicious circles "evade [fulfilling] a legitimate burden of proof." Traditional apologists often believe that presuppositionalists do precisely this largely because of a misreading of the *pre* in *presuppositionalism*, taking it to mean an arbitrarily posited axiom[31] rather than an epistemological precondition for intelligible discourse.

28. Walton, *Begging the Question*, 311.

29. Walton, "Circular Reasoning," 66.

30. Nicholas Rescher, *Cognitive Pragmatism: The Theory of Knowledge in Pragmatic Perspective* (Pittsburgh: University of Pittsburgh Press, 2001), 143 (emphasis in original). My thanks to James Anderson for bringing this reference to my attention.

31. Cf. ibid., 326, 328–29. There seems to be confusion here between the presuppositionalism of Cornelius Van Til (for whom this objection does not apply) and that of Gordon Clark (for whom it does). For a correction of this error, see *CVT*, 136–39.

Clarifying Statements

The statements provided earlier can lead one to think Van Tillians encourage question-begging. While they do not do so explicitly, taken in isolation, one can understand such widespread confusion and misunderstanding. As these statements are worded, it seems as though the authors take a presuppositional stance in order to avoid evidential priority. Here I distinguish between statements of qualified and unqualified embracing of circularity. As the distinction implies, the latter are statements made by Van Til and others that embrace circularity but do not distinguish between the fallacious and the felicitous. The former do provide such clarifying qualifications. The following quotes provide what I believe to be the proper interpretive matrix for such unqualified statements:

- We hold it to be true that circular reasoning is the only reasoning that is possible to finite man. The method of implication as outlined above is circular reasoning. Or we may call it spiral reasoning. We must go round and round a thing to see of its dimensions and to know more about it, in general, unless we are larger than that which we are investigating. Unless we are larger than God we cannot reason about Him by any other way, than by a transcendental or circular argument. The refusal to admit the necessity of circular reasoning is itself an evident token of Antitheism. *Reasoning in a vicious circle is the only alternative to reasoning in a circle.*[32]
- Van Til never suggested that anyone should commit the logical fallacy of begging the question (e.g., "A is true because A is true."). That would be strange indeed. In reality, he frequently called attention to the failure of such arguments. It is true that Van Til spoke positively of "circular reasoning," but he had something other than begging the question in mind. He was not talking so much about argumentation, setting down a convincing case that leads to a conclusion. *In argumentation, reasoning should be linear.* Instead, Van Til spoke of circularity in terms of the inescapable process by which finite minds attain knowledge to be used in arguments. . . . *This is the kind of circularity or spiraling that Van Til pointed out in all human reasoning. It has nothing to do with begging the question.*[33]

32. Cornelius Van Til, "The Metaphysics of Apologetics" (unpublished class syllabus, 1932), 24 (emphasis added).

33. Richard L. Pratt Jr., "Common Misunderstandings of Van Til's Apologetics," part 2, available at http://www.thirdmill.org/newfiles/ric_pratt/TH.Pratt.VanTil.2.html (emphasis added).

- The "circularity" of a transcendental argument is not at all the same as the *fallacious* "circularity" of an argument in which the conclusion is a restatement (in one form or another) of one of the premises. Rather, it is the circularity involved in a coherent theory (where all the parts are consistent with or assume each other) and which is required when one reasons about a precondition for reasoning.[34]

Van Tillians, at least implicitly, distinguish between circular coherence and begging the question, embracing the former and rejecting the latter. R. C. Sproul himself, one of the three authors of *Classical Apologetics*, sees no problem with Van Til's point. Sproul says, "That all reasoning is ultimately circular in the sense that conclusions are inseparably related to presuppositions is not in dispute."[35] John Frame sheds further light on the type of circularity embraced.[36] First, theologically, Christians have no alternative than to reason under the lordship of Christ, "in whom are hidden all the treasures of wisdom and knowledge" (Col. 2:3). Second, circularity "in a system is properly justified *only* at one point: in an argument for the ultimate criterion of the system."[37] Finally, Frame makes the distinction between broad and narrow circles. An example of a narrow circle is "Scripture is the Word of God because Scripture is the Word of God." Narrow circularity is nonpersuasive in apologetic dialogue. Broad circularity offers more data, including archaeology, history, and philosophy, but still interprets these data in ways consistent with the biblical worldview. With these considerations in mind, we may raise the following questions: Should we consider an argument viciously circular if it incorporates premises that comport only with its ultimate criterion of veracity? If so, what is the alternative? If we were to argue in some other way, would not such arguments be inconsistent and therefore destroy their claims to validity?

34. Bahnsen, *Van Til's Apologetic*, 518n122 (emphasis added).
35. R. C. Sproul, *Scripture Alone: The Evangelical Doctrine* (Phillipsburg, NJ: P&R Publishing, 2005), 70.
36. This discussion, along with other comments by Frame, can be found in *DKG*, 130–31. Clarifying the logic behind the Van Tillian embrace of circular coherence, Frame proposed an explicitly linear relationship between faith and reason. As he states it: God's rationality → human faith → human rationality (where the arrow means "is the grounds for"). See his article "Presuppositional Apologetics," in Cowan, *Five Views on Apologetics*, 216. There is progress here, not a series of circles while standing in place. Unfortunately, the contributors to *Five Views on Apologetics*, critical reviewers, and recent apologetic works from the traditional camp have not reformulated their critiques to take Frame's presentation into account.
37. *DKG*, 130.

Van Til equates circular argument with presuppositional, indirect, or *transcendental*[38] reasoning. A transcendental argument is, as Craig defines it, "an argument for a reality based on that reality's being the very conditions even of a denial of that reality."[39] Van Til defines a transcendental argument as one that "takes any fact of experience which it wishes to investigate, and tries to determine what the presuppositions of such a fact must be, in order to make it what it is."[40] In fact, when we grasp the centrality of transcendental reasoning to Van Til's approach, both Scylla and Charybdis are laid to rest. First, Van Til advocated the transcendental *argument* and the truth of Christianity. This fact rules out fideism. Second, "transcendental reasoning [focuses] on necessary enabling conditions either of coherent experience or the possession or employment of some kind of knowledge or cognitive ability, where the opponent is not in a position to question the fact of this experience [or] knowledge . . . and where the revealed preconditions include what the opponent questions."[41]

Here an example may serve us well. According to presuppositionalism, the existence of God is the necessary "enabling condition" for coherent experience. The apologist, if he is speaking to a materialist, may point out that the laws of logic are essential to rational interchange, are universally applicable, and are not mere social conventions (since a denial of the law of noncontradiction would imply that there is no difference between atheism and Christianity). Likewise, these laws are immaterial, are constant, and reflect a thinking mind more than nonthinking matter. The antitheist opponent is "not in a position to question the validity" of logical argumentation (granted that a debate has been entered into). Now it is the job of the presuppositionalist to demonstrate that the "revealed preconditions" of discourse include what the antitheist questions,[42] namely, the existence

38. K. Scott Oliphint notes that "Van Til's indirect method moves one out of the context of a direct argument and into the context of the *rationale* of any fact or law assumed to be, or to be true. Thus, circularity is inextricably linked to the transcendental approach and is not meant to be in reference, strictly speaking, to direct argumentation." Cornelius Van Til, *The Defense of the Faith*, ed. K. Scott Oliphint, 4th ed. (Phillipsburg, NJ: P&R Publishing, 2008), 123n8 (emphasis in original).

39. Craig, "A Classical Apologist's Response," in Cowan, *Five Views on Apologetics*, 232.

40. Van Til, quoted in *CVT*, 311–12.

41. *The Internet Encyclopedia of Philosophy*, s.v. "Transcendental Arguments," http://www.iep.utm.edu/trans-ar/.

42. This is the method adopted by Greg Bahnsen in his debate with Gordon Stein over the existence of God, available at http://www.bellevuechristian.org/faculty/dribera/htdocs/PDFs/Apol_Bahnsen_Stein_Debate_Transcript.pdf, accessed 11/10/09. Note especially the exchange on pages 10–11.

of God. This approach is taken not to avoid bearing the weight of eviden-tial priority, but to make the surprising claim that Christian theism, and *only Christian theism*, is able to sufficiently shoulder the burden of proof, escaping the accusation of begging the question.

Van Til's rejection of the presentation of natural-theology arguments should not be construed to mean that he rejected all uses of them. One of his central points is that all such arguments can and should "be taken together and reduced to the one argument of the possibility of human predication."[43] Perhaps, for the sake of clarity, it may be better to use the language of John Frame in saying that Van Til aimed to fundamentally reorient the traditional arguments in a transcendental direction.[44]

Fideism

I will now specifically address the charge of fideism in two ways: first by way of rebuttal, and then by way of refutation. Rebuttal is needed to demonstrate that the case against presuppositionalism fails to prove its point successfully. The refutation demonstrates the allegation as false.

Earlier I mentioned that the allegation of fideism is both imprecise and inaccurate. Starting with the imprecision of the allegations, several notions may be assigned to the terms *faith* and *reason*. *Reason* can be defined in one of at least four ways.[45] *Reason* may be defined as the human capac-ity for evaluating concepts (R1), as a human faculty independent of other faculties—such as the will and the emotions (R2), or as a faculty independent of presuppositional commitments (R3). The second and third definitions are related. While R2 sees reason as autonomous from other human faculties, R3 is autonomous from an individual's worldview. Fourth, reason (R4) may be thought of as man's ability to think, *simpliciter*. Similarly, *faith* may be defined in a number of ways. It may be defined as trust in the person, work, and words of Jesus Christ and his apostles (F1), as the capacity to believe something based on insufficient or no evidence (F2), or as a synonym for *intellectual assent* (F3).

---

43. Van Til, *Introduction to Systematic Theology*, 180.

44. *AGG*, 71.

45. Paul Helm in *Faith and Reason* (New York: Oxford University Press, 1999), 4–10, makes a similar point by distinguishing between several definitions of these terms. He notes that *reason* can be defined as (1) the rules of logical inference, (2) the accumulated wisdom of a tradition, and (3) shorthand for what is reasonable. Likewise, he points out that *faith* may be conceived as evidence-sensitive, evidence-insensitive (i.e., faith as something not open to investigation, a leap, and a risk), cognitive, and noncognitive.

R1	The human capacity for evaluating concepts	F1	Personal trust in the person, work, and words of Jesus Christ and his apostles
R2	A human faculty independent of other faculties—such as the will and the emotions	F2	The capacity to believe something based on insufficient or no evidence
R3	A faculty independent of presuppositional (worldview) commitments	F3	Intellectual assent
R4	Man's ability to think, simpliciter		

What should be observed is that fideism[46] results only when *incompatible* conceptions of faith and reason are paired. Presuppositionalists and most other Christian apologists dismiss the definition of *reason* in terms of R4, since it is simplistic. Likewise, R2 and R3 seem to fall short of the holism presented in Scripture[47] and are reminiscent of a Platonic anthropology. As we turn to the definitions of *faith*, F2 becomes immediately suspect. While many opponents of Christianity define *faith* this way, it seems more like credulity than anything the Bible presents as faith.[48]

Not only are *faith* and *reason* defined in a multiplicity of ways, so also is the central term of our discussion, *fideism*. Some understand the term to refer to a subjectivist theory of justification, while others maintain that it is a "negation of rational constructions."[49] C. Stephen Evans defines *fideism*

46. Here I am adopting the definition of *fideism* as irrational or arational belief.

47. Cf. *DCL*, 361–82.

48. This is the common definition of religious faith presented in the works of the New Atheists. By way of contrast, the historic threefold definition of faith against reason leaves us nothing to reconcile, since no tension is presented between faith and reason. J. P. Moreland notes, "Throughout church history, theologians have expressed three different aspects of biblical faith: *notitia* (knowledge), *fiducia* (trust), and *assensus* (assent). *Notitia* refers to the data or doctrinal content of the Christian faith (see Jude 1:3). *Assensus* denotes the assent of the intellect to the truth of the content of Christian teaching. Note that each of these aspects of faith requires a careful exercise of reason, both in understanding what the teachings of Christianity are and in judging their truthfulness. In this way, reason is indispensable for the third aspect of faith—*fiducia*—which captures the personal application of trust involved in faith, an act that primarily involves the will but includes the affection and intellect too." *Love God with All Your Mind* (Colorado Springs: NavPress, 1997), 60.

49. R. C. Sproul, "Fideism," in *The Encyclopedia of Christianity*, vol. 4, ed. Philip E. Hughes and George R. Jaffray (Marshallton, DE: National Foundation for Christian Education, 1972), quoted in Bahnsen, *Van Til's Apologetic*, 72–73.

as "the idea . . . that faith should not be governed or regulated by reason, where reason is understood to be an autonomous, relatively competent human faculty. The fideist says rather that faith must be accepted as at least partly autonomous or independent of reason, or even that reason must in some ways be corrected by or be made subservient to faith."[50] Given the qualifications provided, I am curious as to the identity of those who would disagree with this definition. If no examples can be produced, then the bar is set too high, and notable classical apologists such as Norman Geisler, William Lane Craig, and J. P. Moreland could well be reckoned as fideists! Craig, for example, follows Martin Luther in his distinction between the ministerial and magisterial uses of reason,[51] defining the latter in a way that seems very close to what a Van Tillian would call "autonomous." Thus, the fact that presuppositionalists reject a spurious definition of *reason*, as does Craig, is no grounds for labeling them fideists.

When *reason* is defined as independent of other human faculties, presuppositions, and spiritual appetites, Van Til objects. Likewise, he protests when *faith* is thought of in terms of credulity or irrational-arational belief. When the relation between faith and reason is conceived in terms of human beings' applying their God-given cognitive equipment to the message of the Bible, examining its propositions,[52] and believing its promises, he sees no tension between the two. Yet without specifying their definitions of *faith* and *reason*, objectors to presuppositionalism unwittingly appeal to vague connotation, rather than substantial argument. Van Til cannot rightly be called a fideist on the ground that he opposes faith and reason. Rather, he rejects a *particular combination* of several possible definitions for these terms.

Second, other than being imprecise, the charge of fideism is simply false. *Van Til was in diametric opposition to fideism.* In contrasting Abraham Kuyper's rejection of apologetics with B. B. Warfield's insistence on the rational defensibility of Christian theism, Van Til concludes, "To the extent that Warfield differs on this point with Kuyper . . . , he has done great service for Christian apologetics."[53] Moreover, he states that "there is absolutely certain proof for the existence of God and the truth of Christian

50. Evans, *Faith beyond Reason*, 9.
51. William Lane Craig, "Classical Apologetics," in Cowan, *Five Views on Apologetics*, 36–37. Craig makes this distinction in regard to "knowing Christianity is true," not "showing" it to be true. I doubt that in "showing" (as opposed to "knowing") Craig would approve of the magisterial use of reason.
52. Cf. Van Til, *Introduction to Systematic Theology*, chap. 4.
53. Cornelius Van Til, *A Christian Theory of Knowledge* (Nutley, NJ: Presbyterian and Reformed, 1969), 243.

theism." Furthermore, "the Reformed apologist maintains that there is an absolutely valid argument for the existence of God and for the truth of Christian theism." One may question the validity of these statements, but the point remains that the "proof" for Christianity is "absolutely certain," and the "argument" for Christian theism is "absolutely valid." For Van Til, "faith is not blind faith."[54] In an ironic twist, according to the *New Catholic Encyclopedia*, *semifideism* is the belief "which holds that man reaches truth by reason, but with probability only and not with certitude." According to this definition, those in the traditional camp are closer to fideists than Van Tillians![55]

The traditional method asserts that Christianity is the *best* handling of the relevant evidence, but Van Til insists that it is the *only* acceptable conclusion. "The Christian's position is not merely just as good as the non-Christian's position. Christianity is the *only* position that does not per se take away the very foundation for intelligible scientific and philosophical procedure. Christianity is the only rational faith!"[56] While I'm not defending this claim here, I am highlighting the fact that Van Til's position is the opposite of what is commonly charged. One may accuse Van Til of possibly overvaluing the rational credentials of Christianity, but it cannot fairly be said that he *under*valued them.[57]

Conclusion

In summary, we have noted the twin challenges to a presuppositional method. I have reviewed Van Til's position as presented in opposing literature, in the words of sympathetic interpreters, and in his own. Opponents have portrayed him as opposing the application of reason to divine revelation by eschewing rational discourse and evidential appeals. Likewise, presuppositionalists are often charged with holding to a methodology that is based

---

54. Ibid., 32.

55. Cf. Bahnsen, *Van Til's Apologetic*, 76–77.

56. Cornelius Van Til, quoted in ibid., 116.

57. Greg Bahnsen's words further refute the fideism charge: "God wishes for us to be rational: *to exercise and improve our reasoning ability* in understanding, propounding and defending the truths of Scripture.... The kind of rationality or reasoning that we will employ in defending the Christian faith involves not only study of formal logic (patterns or abstract forms of inference), but also attention to informal fallacies in ordinary language, the use of inductive reasoning, the handling of empirical evidence in history, science, linguistics, etc., and especially reflection upon the demands of an adequate worldview in terms of which all such thinking makes sense." *Always Ready: Directions for Defending the Faith* (Nacogdoches, TX: Covenant Media Press, 1996), 134–35 (emphasis in original).

on an elementary error in critical thinking. If fallacious circularity were built into the methodological DNA of presuppositionalism, this would aid in establishing the claim that it is fideistic. In response, we have examined the record and found both claims unsubstantiated. My contention is that these caricatures are based on either a lack of reading of Van Til's overall project or a misreading of it.

I made the distinction between vicious (fallacious) and virtuous (non-fallacious) forms of epistemic circularity, calling the latter *circular coherence*. The main distinguishing mark between these two forms of circularity is how one handles the burden of proof, or evidential priority. Since neither Van Til nor his disciples advocate the fallacy of *petitio principii*, or arguments such as "God exists because God exists," and instead equate presuppositional inquiry with transcendental reasoning, it is hard to understand why the charge of circularity persists.

Van Til *insisted* on the rational demonstration of Christianity. He explicitly rejected fideism, with its problematic conceptions of faith and reason. In contrast, Van Til posits an "absolutely certain proof" for Christian theism. As Thom Notaro puts it, "The frequency with which Van Til defends the notion of proof is alarming compared to what one might expect."[58] He might have been mistaken, confused, or otherwise wrongheaded, but he was not a fideist. We've seen that these objections to his method fail both semantically and substantially. The refutation of the first allegation is strong grounds for the refutation of the second. In the spirit of Christian charity and academic responsibility, we must recognize that the correlation between presuppositionalism and fideism cannot fairly be laid at Van Til's feet. Neither Van Til nor his disciples endorse question-begging or blind faith.

---

58. Thom Notaro, *Van Til and the Use of Evidence* (Phillipsburg, NJ: Presbyterian and Reformed, 1980), 65.

APPENDIX E:
DIVINE ASEITY AND APOLOGETICS[1]

The term *aseity* comes from the Latin phrase *a se*, meaning "from or by oneself." In the theological literature, the term designates a divine attribute by which God is "whatever he is by his own self or of his own self."[2] Since God is *a se*, he does not owe his existence to anything or anyone outside himself, nor does he need anything beyond himself to maintain his existence. He is not like the idols that depend for their existence on select materials, skilled craftsmen, and ritual offerings (Ps. 50:8–15; Isa. 40:19–20; 44:15–17). Indeed, he has no needs at all (Acts 17:25).[3] So the terms *self-contained*, *self-existent*, *self-sufficient*, and *independent* are often used as synonyms for *a se*.

God's attributes are not abstract qualities that God happens to exemplify. They are, rather, identical to God himself. That concept is sometimes called the doctrine of divine simplicity. For example, God's goodness is not a standard above him, to which he conforms. Rather, his goodness is everything he is and does. It is God himself who serves as the standard of goodness for himself and for the world. He is, therefore, his own goodness. But he is also his own being, wisdom, power, holiness, justice, and truth. These attributes, therefore, are concrete, not abstract, personal, not impersonal. Each describes the whole nature of God.[4] So to talk of God's attributes is simply to talk about God himself, from various perspectives.[5]

---

1. This article was originally published in K. Scott Oliphint and Lane G. Tipton, eds., *Revelation and Reason: New Essays in Reformed Apologetics* (Phillipsburg, NJ: P&R Publishing, 2007).

2. Herman Bavinck, *Reformed Dogmatics: God and Creation*, ed. John Bolt, trans. John Vriend (Grand Rapids: Baker, 2004), 151.

3. I here summarize my exegetical case for this divine attribute. The word *aseity* is not found in Scripture, but Scripture clearly teaches that God has no need of creatures. For a more elaborate discussion, see my *DG*, 603–8.

4. For more discussion of divine simplicity as an affirmation of personalism, see ibid., 225–30.

5. Ibid., 387–92.

God's attributes, therefore, apply to one another: God's justice is holy, and his holiness just. His goodness is eternal, and his eternality is not an abstract concept, but rather the eternal life of a good person. So God's aseity, too, is the aseity of a person, one who is infinite, eternal, unchangeable, and so on. And all of God's attributes are *a se*. His infinity, goodness, wisdom, and justice are all self-existent and self-sufficient.

Aseity also applies in one sense to God's relationships with the creation, particularly his lordship, which I have defined as his control over the world, his authority over the world, and his presence in the world.[6] Of course, to be Lord, one must have servants. In that sense, God cannot be Lord without his having servants to rule. Nevertheless, his power and right to rule as Lord are not derived from the creation. As King, he is not the beneficiary of a social contract, nor is he bound to terms imposed on him by creatures.[7] His lordship derives from his own being alone. God is such a God that he is necessarily Lord over anything and everything he creates.

So, considering the three attributes of lordship noted above, we may describe God's control as self-sufficient, his authority as self-justifying. His presence in the world is an implication of his universal power and authority. Wherever we go, we cannot escape from him (Ps. 139:7–12; Jer. 23:24). God's presence is inescapable, unavoidable, and therefore not dependent on the will of creatures. This is to say that God's lordship is *a se*.

In this paper, I will discuss the relation of divine aseity to apologetics, the defense of the Christian faith. No one has integrated these as fully as Cornelius Van Til, professor of apologetics at Westminster Theological Seminary from 1929 to 1972. So I will explore Van Til's teaching, drawing some inferences and applications for the work of apologetics today. I will suggest that the doctrine of aseity is helpful to the apologist in three ways: (1) it helps define the distinctive content of the Christian faith, which the apologist is called to defend; (2) it determines the epistemology of apologetics, how the apologist should seek to lead people to the knowledge of God; and (3) it suggests an important practical apologetic strategy.[8]

---

6. Ibid., 1–115.

7. God does, of course, voluntarily enter covenants with creatures, and in these covenants he binds himself to fulfill promises and threats. He is obligated to keep these covenants. But the obligations are self-imposed, not imposed by creatures.

8. For those who might be interested in the "three perspectives" that I've expounded elsewhere, (1) is situational: the facts of the gospel; (2) is normative: the rules of apologetic thought; and (3) is existential: the actual process of apologetic dialogue.

Aseity and the Distinctiveness of the Christian Worldview

For Cornelius Van Til, the doctrine of divine aseity is the key to a sound theology and apologetics. As he begins his discussion of the divine attributes, he says, "First and foremost among the attributes, we therefore mention the independence or self-existence of God (*autarkia, omnisufficientia*)."[9] He quotes Herman Bavinck's statement that

> in this aseity of God, thought of not merely as being by itself but as the fullness of being, all other virtues are included; they are but the setting forth of the fullness of God's being.[10]

Van Til typically refers to aseity by the term *self-contained*.[11] So he writes, "Basic to all the doctrines of Christian theism is that of the self-contained God, or, if we wish, that of the ontological Trinity."[12] And "we must take the notion of the self-contained, self-sufficient God as the most basic notion of all our interpretative efforts."[13]

Although Van Til puts aseity first among the doctrines of Christian theism, he finds it closely linked to other doctrines:[14] (1) In one of the quotations above, and in many other places, he links God's aseity to his ontological Trinity. These two concepts go together, for *ontological* here means that God's triunity is not derived from creatures, but is self-contained. God is a Trinity, not only in history, but in and of himself. God's triune character also implies that he cannot be construed merely as the aspect of unity within the world, correlative to the world's plurality. Rather, he has his own unity and plurality, which is distinct from the unity and plurality of the universe. (2) Van Til reasons, then, from God's aseity and triunity

9. Cornelius Van Til, *An Introduction to Systematic Theology* (Nutley, NJ: Presbyterian and Reformed, 1974), 206.

10. Ibid. He quotes Herman Bavinck, *The Doctrine of God* (Grand Rapids: Baker, 1951), 145.

11. A search for *self-contained* on the CD-ROM *The Works of Cornelius Van Til* (Labels Army Corp.) yielded 395 hits. He also uses as synonyms *self-sufficient, self-existent, self-referential, self-interpreting, self-determining*.

12. Cornelius Van Til, *The Defense of the Faith*, 3rd rev. ed. (Philadelphia: Presbyterian and Reformed, 1975), 100.

13. Cornelius Van Til, *Christianity and Idealism* (Philadelphia: Presbyterian and Reformed, 1955), 85; cf. 88: "A truly Christian philosophy should, it seems to us, begin with the notion of God as self-contained." G. C. Berkouwer criticizes Van Til's emphasis on this concept in his *The Triumph of Grace in the Theology of Karl Barth* (Grand Rapids: Eerdmans, 1956), 390–91, but he is very vague as to how precisely he differs from Van Til's position.

14. I prefer not to regard any doctrine or divine attribute as "most basic." For the dangers in such proposals, see *DG*, 392–94. I agree, however, that God's aseity is especially important for the work of formulating a Christian worldview in contrast with non-Christian alternatives.

to his all-controlling counsel: "Based upon this notion of the ontological trinity and consistent with it, is the concept of the counsel of God according to which all things in the created world are regulated."[15] If God is *a se*, then he has the resources within himself to carry out his purposes for history. His eternal plan does not depend on creatures for its formulation or implementation.

(3) Van Til also reasons from God's aseity to creation out of nothing:

> If God is fully self-contained then there was no sort of half existence and no sort of non-being that had any power over against him . . . and there was no sort of stuff that had as much even as refractory power over against God when he decided to create the world.[16]

And he reasons also from creation to aseity:

> The creation doctrine maintains that finite existence is wholly dependent upon God's rationality. And this is possible only if God is first self-contained.[17]

(4) In a summary of Christian metaphysics, Van Til enumerates the doctrines above—the self-contained God, the ontological Trinity, and "the fact of temporal creation"—and adds two others: "the fact of God's providential control over all created reality," and (5) "the miraculous work of the redemption of the world through Christ."[18]

Van Til often says that the apologist should argue for Christianity "as a unit."[19] That is, in his view we must not defend a general theism first and then later defend Christianity. Rather, the apologist must defend only the distinctive theism of Christianity. As Van Til often put it, we should not try to prove *that* God exists without considering *what kind* of God we are proving. And that means, in turn, that we should not try to prove that God exists without defining God in terms of the doctrines of Scripture.

15. Van Til, *Defense of the Faith*, 100.

16. Ibid., 188.

17. Cornelius Van Til, *The New Modernism*, 3rd ed. (Nutley, NJ: Presbyterian and Reformed, 1973), 373.

18. Cornelius Van Til, *The Defense of the Faith* (Philadelphia: Presbyterian and Reformed, 1955), 235. In these notes, *Defense of the Faith*, without further specification, will refer not to this first edition, but to the revised and abridged edition previously cited.

19. Cornelius Van Til, *Apologetics* (no publication data), 72. This is another of Van Til's favorite terms. A search for *unit* on the Van Til *Works* CD-ROM yielded eighty-eight hits.

Does this principle imply that we must prove all the doctrines of Christianity in every apologetic argument we employ? Critics are sometimes tempted to understand Van Til this way, and Van Til's own expressions sometimes encouraged that misunderstanding.[20] But Van Til was too thoughtful to teach anything so absurd. Rather, I think what he meant was that (1) the apologist must "presuppose" the full revelation of the Bible in defending the faith. (2) He must not tone down any biblical distinctives in order to make the faith credible. (3) His goal should be to defend (by one argument or many) the whole of biblical theism, including the authority of Scripture, Trinity, predestination, incarnation, blood atonement, resurrection, and consummation. And (4) the apologist should seek to show that compromise in any of these doctrines leads to incoherence in all human knowledge.

But beyond these general principles, Van Til also had in mind a focus on divine aseity, the "self-contained ontological Trinity." For aseity designates what most clearly distinguishes the biblical worldview from its alternatives.[21] Thus, it makes clear in what way Christian teachings are a system of truth, one "unit," and not just a fortuitous collection of ideas.

Only the Bible teaches that the universe is created and controlled by a personal[22] God who is *a se*, not dependent on the world in any way. Polytheistic religions teach the existence of personal gods, but those gods are not *a se*. Monistic worldviews, such as Hinduism, Taoism, and the philosophies of Parmenides, Plotinus, Spinoza, and Hegel, teach the existence of an absolute being, and indeed most polytheisms place a principle of absolute fate beyond the realm of the gods. But these "absolute" beings and fates are impersonal, so they do not have personal control over the world. Indeed, as Van Til emphasizes, these absolutes are *correlative* to the nonabsolute sectors of the world. They could not exist without the world. They cannot be defined or described except as aspects of the universe. They serve as the element of unity in the world, correlative to the world's plurality, contrary to the biblical doctrine of

---

20. See my *CVT*, 264–68.

21. Van Til says in *The Triumph of Grace* (Philadelphia: Westminster Theological Seminary, 1958), 28, "There is no speculative system that entertains the idea of such a self-contained God. It is only the Scriptures which teach us about this God."

22. Van Til correlates *personal* with *self-contained* in *The Reformed Pastor and Modern Thought* (Nutley, NJ: Presbyterian and Reformed, 1971), 74: "This reference point [for human thought—JF] must be taken as *self-contained*, or ultimate, that is, self-sufficient and self-interpretative; in the nature of the case it cannot be impersonal." His point is that an impersonal principle cannot *speak* to bear witness to itself or interpret itself.

the ontological Trinity. They serve as the unchanging aspect of the world, correlative to the changes of the world of our experience. So these supposed absolutes depend on the world as much as the world depends on them. They are not truly *a se*.[23]

In this way, the doctrine of divine aseity defines what is distinctive about the biblical worldview. To defend the faith is to defend its distinctives. So the phrase "self-contained ontological Trinity" summarizes the content that the apologist is called to defend.

Aseity and Biblical Epistemology

The second service that the doctrine of divine aseity renders to apologetics is that it determines what sort of knowledge we may have of God—or, indeed, of anything else. I noted earlier that Van Til uses terms such as *self-interpreting* and *self-referential* in apposition to *self-contained*, and that he regards God as self-contained not only in his being, but also in his "knowledge and will."[24] For Van Til, then, God's aseity has definite epistemological implications.

First, God knows himself and the world, both by knowing himself. He knows himself intuitively and perfectly. He knows the world also by knowing himself: He knows what is possible in the world by knowing his own powers; and he knows what is actual in the world (at all times) by knowing his own eternal plan, as well as by his perfect awareness of the temporal accomplishment of that plan. In other words, he does not depend on the creation for his knowledge even of the creation. His knowledge is exhaustive and perfect, because it is *a se*. Van Til says:

> God is absolute rationality. He was and is the only self-contained whole, the system of absolute truth. God's knowledge is, therefore, exclusively *analytic*, that is, self-dependent. There never were any facts existing

23. There are traces of the doctrine of aseity in Judaism, in Islam, and in heresies such as the views of the Jehovah's Witnesses. On this fact, two remarks: (1) To the extent that they ascribe aseity to God, they do it because at that point they are influenced by the Bible. (2) Their divergence from Bible teachings leads them to compromise the aseity of God: Islam makes God unknowable and remote, fearing that his direct involvement in the world will relativize him. If its God were truly *a se*, he would not lose his transcendent glory by entering history. Islam also turns predestination into fatalism, thus veering toward an impersonal concept of God. Judaism today (whatever recent scholarship might conclude about first-century Judaism) is a religion of works, rather than of an *a se* God who gives what we cannot repay. And Judaism, like the Jehovah's Witnesses and other cults, rejects the Trinity, which, as we've seen, is closely related to God's aseity.

24. Van Til, *Apologetics*, 7.

independent of God which he had to investigate. God is the one and only ultimate Fact. In him, i.e., with respect to his own Being, apart from the world, fact and interpretation of fact are coterminous.[25]

This view of God has implications for human knowledge. Van Til says that only on the presupposition of the self-contained God "can man know himself or anything else."[26] First, "from the Christian point of view, it is impossible to think of the non-existence of God."[27] If God alone provides the rational structure of all reality, then we cannot understand anything without presupposing him, even though we may verbally deny his existence. So all people know God, as Paul says in Romans 1:21, though apart from grace they repress this knowledge. Yet God is also *incomprehensible*. This term

> does not mean that God is incomprehensible to himself. On the contrary, man's inability to comprehend God is founded on the very fact that God is *completely self-determinative*.[28]

A self-contained God is necessarily beyond our complete understanding:

> If God does actually exist as a self-contained and eternally self-conscious being, it is natural that we, his creatures, should not be able to comprehend, that is, understand him exhaustively.[29]

So our knowledge of God is, in Van Til's terms, *analogical* rather than *univocal*. He defines this distinction as follows:

> Christians must also believe in two levels of knowledge, the level of God's knowledge which is absolutely comprehensive and self-contained, and the

25. Van Til, *Introduction to Systematic Theology*, 10. Note also Cornelius Van Til, *The Protestant Doctrine of Scripture* (Philadelphia: Presbyterian and Reformed, 1967), 19: "The Christian religion says that God is self-contained; that he can say 'I' without needing to relate himself to anything over against himself while doing so." And in his *Apologetics*, 7, he says, "God is self-sufficient or self-contained in his being. He therefore knows himself and all created existence by a single internal act of intuition."

26. Cornelius Van Til, *Christian Philosophy* (Phillipsburg, NJ: Grotenhuis, 1956). (I could access this pamphlet only from the *Works* CD-ROM, which does not provide page numbers.)

27. Van Til, *Introduction to Systematic Theology*, 9–10.

28. Ibid., 10.

29. Ibid. I will not enter into the discussion of divine incomprehensibility of God in the controversy of the 1940s between Van Til and Gordon H. Clark, a controversy in which the Van Til party defined incomprehensibility rather differently, as the lack of any identity between any human thought and any divine thought. See my *CVT*, 97–113. As a definition of incomprehensibility, I prefer the simpler definition used in the present quotation.

level of man's knowledge which is not comprehensive but is derivative and re-interpretative. Hence we say as Christians we believe that man's knowledge is analogical of God's knowledge.[30]

So our knowledge of God depends on God's original knowledge of himself. How do we gain access to that original divine self-knowledge? We can never know God as he knows himself. But we do have access to his thoughts in the revelation that he has chosen to give us, his thoughts given to us through created media. Van Til, as the Reformed tradition generally, distinguishes special revelation (God's words to us in human language), general revelation (God's self-manifestation in the created world), and a divine revelation in ourselves as the image of God. Thus, we receive knowledge of God from God, from the world, and from ourselves; knowledge of the world from the world, God, and ourselves; and knowledge of ourselves from ourselves, God, and the world.[31]

Van Til focuses especially on God's written revelation, Holy Scripture. For him, the authority of Scripture and God's aseity are related as follows:

> It is this God, as self-contained, who has spoken clearly while on earth in Jesus the Christ and who speaks clearly to men now in the Scriptures. The idea of the Scriptures as the Word of God is both the source and the result of knowledge of the self-contained triune God. To appeal to the one without appealing to the other is impossible.[32]

> The [message of Christianity] comes, in the nature of the case, by authority. The God of the Bible, as self-contained, cannot speak in any other way than by authority.[33]

---

30. Van Til, *Introduction to Systematic Theology*, 12. In *CVT*, 89–95, I argue that this terminology is misleading. Thomas Aquinas used these terms to distinguish between literal (*univocal*) and figurative (*analogical*) uses of language to refer to God. Van Til's distinction concerns a different, though related, issue. He does not deny, as Aquinas does, the possibility of literal language about God. Nor does Van Til use these terms to suggest any form of agnosticism, though that has sometimes been inferred from Aquinas's distinction. Van Til does say, as did Calvin, that God's revelation is "anthropomorphic," that is, "an adaptation by God to the limitations of the human creature," in *A Christian Theory of Knowledge* (Nutley, NJ: Presbyterian and Reformed, 1969), 41, and therefore that the confessions of the church are "approximated statements" (ibid.). But although he regards revelation as anthropomorphic and approximated, he does not deny that we can confess it as true: true anthropomorphisms and true approximations.

31. Van Til, *Introduction to Systematic Theology*, 62–109.

32. Cornelius Van Til, *The Great Debate Today* (Nutley, NJ: Presbyterian and Reformed, 1971), 33.

33. Cornelius Van Til, *The Case for Calvinism* (Philadelphia: Presbyterian and Reformed, 1964), 104–5.

Not only is God self-contained, but the Word of God is also self-contained.[34] So the Scripture does not depend for its truth on anything other than itself. It is true not because it accords with some higher standard; it is true because it is God's Word, and God's Word is true because he says it. And God "alone can identify himself."[35] Therefore, Scripture's testimony, even about itself, must be accepted on its own authority.

That we must accept the Bible on the Bible's own testimony raises the most standard objection to Van Til's apologetic, namely, that it is circular. In reply, Van Til insists that (1) all systems of thought are circular when it comes to establishing their most basic principles: e.g., rationalists must assume reason in order to prove reason; (2) unless one presupposes biblical theism, all human thinking, including non-Christian thought, becomes incoherent.[36]

To summarize: Scripture is God's Word, and therefore it is self-attesting. There is no higher authority than Scripture by which we can verify it, for there is no authority higher than God. God's Word is self-attesting because he is self-contained. He has within himself all the resources he needs to justify his Word to us.

So apologetics seeks to bring to unbelievers that self-attesting message. Apologetics also seeks to present reasons for believing that message. But the reasons may not contradict the message itself. So our ultimate appeal may not be to human reason, sense expression, feeling, or any merely human authority. Ultimately the apologist must appeal to Scripture in order to defend Scripture. To say this doesn't mean that we must simply say, "Believe Scripture because Scripture says so." As Van Til emphasizes elsewhere, we may use all sorts of rational arguments and evidences.[37] But we must allow Scripture to determine what evidences and arguments are appropriate. In

34. Van Til, *Christian Theory of Knowledge*, 41. Van Til has much to say about the self-contained God and the consequent self-contained character of Scripture in his "Introduction" to B. B. Warfield, *The Inspiration and Authority of the Bible* (Philadelphia: Presbyterian and Reformed, 1948), 3–68. On page 23, for example, he says, "The self-contained circle of the ontological trinity is not broken up by the fact that there is an economical relation of this triune God with respect to man. No more is the self-contained character of Scripture broken up by the fact that there is an economy of transmission and acceptance of the word of God it contains."

35. Van Til, *Christian Theory of Knowledge*, 41.

36. For more discussion, see my *DKG*, 130–33; *AGG*, 9–14; *CVT*, 299–309; and "Presuppositional Apologetics," in *Five Views on Apologetics*, ed. Steven B. Cowan (Grand Rapids: Zondervan, 2000), 208–10.

37. See Van Til, *Christian Theory of Knowledge*, 293. For discussion, see Thom Notaro, *Van Til and the Use of Evidence* (Phillipsburg, NJ: Presbyterian and Reformed, 1980), and my *CVT*, 177–84.

this sense, the apologist must "presuppose" Scripture, not only in his own worldview, but also when defending that worldview before unbelievers.

Aseity and Apologetic Strategy

The third emphasis of Van Til's doctrine of divine aseity is that it shows us the most radical defect in non-Christian thought. Of course, non-Christian thought often errs in its statements of fact, and it often presents invalid arguments. These are fair game for apologists, though the apologist must be willing to admit it when unbelievers discover such flaws in his own thought and witness. But the main issue between Christians and non-Christians is not incidental facts and occasional logical mistakes. Rather, the issue is the self-contained ontological Trinity. And it is always important for the apologist to be properly focused on that big picture.

Let us see how that big picture is relevant to two areas of philosophical debate.

Non-Christian Metaphysics

Many non-Christian thinkers have sensed the need to find something in the world that is *a se*. That *a se* being may be the universe as a whole (Parmenides, Spinoza, Hegel) or something within the universe (Plotinus, Hinduism) that somehow encompasses the whole. It is the *a se* being that accounts for everything else. Others have been skeptical about the existence of such a being. But Van Til points out that those who affirm an *a se* being are not terribly different from the skeptics. For either what is *a se* in non-Christian thought is the universe itself or it is relative to the other aspects of the universe. The *a se* being is "correlative" to the rest of the world.

When Thales said that "all is water," for instance, he took water to be *a se*, the cause and explanation of all else. But on this view, the water that explains is no different from the water that needs explanation. The water that causes is the water that is caused. The mind that seeks to understand water is itself water, and therefore no more fit to analyze water than water itself is.

Plato considered his Forms[38] to be *a se* and therefore to be a sufficient explanation for the changing world. But the Forms could not cause the world, or be intelligibly defined, without the aid of the changing world. The Forms cannot account for all reality, because some of that reality is

---

38. I.e., perfect, unchangeable archetypes of the things and qualities in our changing world.

by nature unformed matter and therefore irrational. So the Forms are *correlative* to the world. As such, they are correlative to the irrational aspects of the world, the aspects that are not Forms. So they cannot serve as the standard of rationality.

Aristotle's divine Prime Mover is supposed to be the cause of motion in the world. But it, like Plato's Forms, is impersonal, and it can be defined only by contrast with the finite world. It, too, is limited by the irrationality of Prime Matter, which is just as eternal and immortal as the Prime Mover.

Hinduism regards Brahma as the explanation for the world. But Brahma is an impersonal principle, not a person. He cannot be known, except as the opposite of the changing world, or as the content of human mystical experience that transcends reason.

In Plotinus, Spinoza, and Hegel also, the *a se* absolute is similarly relative to the temporal, irrational world. So in Van Til's terms, the rational principle is correlative to an irrational principle.

So skepticism and its opponents ultimately come to agreement. The proposed *a se* rational principles are not really *a se* because they are correlative to the realities that they try to explain. Therefore, they themselves need explanation. Indeed, there is no way to rationally account for the world apart from the self-contained God of Scripture.

Nor is skepticism, however, a legitimate option. For skepticism is itself a rational metaphysical statement, that the world is such that no sure knowledge is possible. Being a negative position, skepticism is even harder to prove than a positive principle would be. If one affirms it nevertheless, he affirms irrationalism by way of an arrogant rationalism. To be a skeptic, one must make, as Van Til says, a "universal negative statement."

The most radical attack on divine aseity in our day comes from the so-called open theists: Clark Pinnock, John Sanders, Gregory Boyd, William Hasker, and others. For these, God was once *a se*, but he somehow renounced his aseity so that now he cannot accomplish his goals without the free[39] choices of creatures. So in the present world, nothing is *a se*. In one sense, open theism wants to attribute aseity to the human free will. On the open theists' libertarian concept of freedom, human free decisions have no cause: not God, not the natural order, not even their own desires. But if my decision is not caused by my desire, then it is something I don't want to do. So even I do not cause my free decisions. They are random, arbitrary, irrational events, like the realm of Prime Matter among the Greeks. Not

---

39. In open theism, *free* is always to be taken in the libertarian sense, defined below.

only does this view fail to give a rational account of free choice, it makes any such account impossible. The rationalism of the open theists (seeking a definitive explanation of divine sovereignty and human responsibility) results in their positing a principle of sheer irrationality.[40]

Non-Christian Epistemology

So far, we have mainly looked at metaphysical issues: philosophers' trying to give an account of the nature of reality. But the same issues exist in epistemology. We saw earlier that aseity is both a metaphysical and an epistemological category. God, who is metaphysically self-contained, is epistemologically self-attesting. In non-Christian thought, it is man himself who becomes epistemologically *a se*. It is, of course, implausible to regard man as *metaphysically a se*, though mystics have frequently tried to identify themselves with the ultimate. But many others have claimed *epistemological* autonomy, which is epistemological aseity. When a thinker claims that human reason, experience, or feeling is the ultimate criterion of truth, he is claiming epistemological aseity. So Van Til says:

> The natural man virtually attributes to himself that which a true Christian theology attributes to the self-contained God. The battle is therefore between the absolutely self-contained God of Christianity and the would-be wholly self-contained mind of the natural man. Between them there can be no compromise.[41]

The doctrine of epistemological autonomy can be made to seem plausible: mustn't we think for ourselves, even in deciding what authority to submit to? Even if we embrace the God of the Bible, must we not do so on the basis of our own judgment? So Van Til refers to A. E. Taylor, who "cannot believe that any man could receive any revelation from such a [self-contained—JF] God without to some extent, in the very act of reception, confusing it with his own experiences that operate independently of this God."[42] On this basis, even the act of submitting to revelation is an act of our autonomous rationality, for revelation can never be clearly distinguished from our rationality.

---

40. For more discussion of open theism, see Bruce A. Ware, *God's Lesser Glory* (Wheaton, IL: Crossway, 2000); John Piper, Justin Taylor, and Paul Kjoss Helseth, eds., *Beyond the Bounds* (Wheaton, IL: Crossway, 2003); Douglas Wilson, ed., *Bound Only Once* (Moscow, ID: Canon Press, 2001); and *NOG*.
41. Van Til, *Apologetics*, 97.
42. Ibid., 93.

But Van Til points out that Taylor's argument assumes the nonexistence of the self-contained God of Scripture. If that God does exist, he can reveal himself clearly in history. He is the Lord of history and the Lord of our experience. He can control not only the initial revelatory events, but also our reception of that revelation, so that we can receive it with confidence. He has not chosen to make our subjective reception of that revelation infallible. But he has given us sufficient justification to affirm the infallibility of the revelation itself.

Of course, we cannot appropriate God's revelation without making use of our own thought, our "epistemic apparatus," which is part of our subjectivity. The question is whether, as Taylor thinks, that subjectivity necessarily distorts the revelation or renders it uncertain. The Bible itself teaches that this is not the case.

A General Strategy

The aseity of God, therefore, suggests this general strategy for apologetic argument: We should make clear to the non-Christian that his substitutes for divine aseity (in biblical terms, idols) cannot do their job. A principle within the world can never account for the world. For such principles are "correlative," as dependent on the rest of the world as the rest of the world is dependent on them.

Epistemologically, we must challenge the necessity of assuming intellectual autonomy. And we should show that such autonomy offers no adequate criterion of truth and falsity. At most, it can come up with a standard of rationality that turns out, upon inspection, to be correlative to irrationality. On the contrary, only on the assumption that the self-contained God exists and has revealed himself can we have any basis for claiming knowledge.

This kind of apologetic argument is not only cogent and persuasive (if the Spirit opens the heart of our opponent). It also focuses the apologetic encounter on what is most important. Apologetic discussions are easily encumbered with complex syllogisms and factual detail. But the ultimate issue is the self-contained ontological Trinity. This is the doctrine that is most clearly distinctive of the Christian faith.

Let us remember, too, that apologetics is evangelistic, a communication of the gospel of Jesus Christ. Of course, apologetics is valuable in dealing with the doubts of believers. But in dealing with believers, as with unbelievers, apologetics should help them to look to Jesus as the answer to their questions. Van Til's argument from aseity has the virtue of leading people to Jesus, for these reasons: (1) It exposes the pretensions of unbelief as delusions, lies, and idols. (2) It convicts people of the sin of claiming intellectual autonomy, and thus provokes intellectual repentance. (3) It presents Jesus as Lord, for, as a member of the ontological Trinity, Jesus is himself *a se*, and therefore in control of all things in heaven and earth. (4) It presents a God who does not need our good works in order to bless us, who therefore offers grace most freely. (5) It presents God's Word as self-attesting, warranting assurance that the gospel is true. (6) It shows that salvation is by grace, not only in the atoning work of Christ, but even in the illumination of mind necessary to believe in that atoning work. (7) It presents Christ as Savior of the mind as well as all other aspects of human life.

With many kinds of apologetics, it is exceedingly difficult to make a transition between the apologetic argument and the gospel. In Van Til's argument, the argument is already the gospel, *suaviter in modo*,[43] and it naturally leads to a more explicit presentation of the gospel. Of course, even Van Til's presuppositional argument can go off track, as when the apologist takes pride in presenting his transcendental refutations of Plato, Kant, and so forth. Satan tempts apologists of all schools to display their own intellectual achievements rather than saying what is evangelistically helpful. Scripture urges us here, as in all other situations, to speak the truth in love. But Van Til's model is useful even here, for it rebukes our pride and magnifies the power, wisdom, and grace of God.

---

43. Van Til often expressed appreciation for the Latin slogan *suaviter in modo, fortiter in re*, which in a discussion of apologetics can be rendered "gentle [or subtle] in the mode of presentation, but strong in content."

APPENDIX F:
EPISTEMOLOGICAL PERSPECTIVES
AND EVANGELICAL APOLOGETICS

(Note—2015: I delivered this paper at the Far West Regional Meeting of the Evangelical Theological Society in 1982. In 1984, it was published in the *Bulletin of the Evangelical Philosophical Society* 7 [1984]: 1–7. So this is one of my earliest contributions to the apologetic conversation among evangelicals— later than *Van Til the Theologian* but five years earlier than *DKG*. It was also my first significant publication in the twenty years [1980–2000] that I lived on the West Coast. So as a newcomer to the West, to ETS, and to apologetics, I intended here to begin from zero, assuming in my audience and readership some philosophical sophistication but no knowledge of Van Til or of past debates about presuppositionalism. I hoped to rise above those debates and present presuppositionalism afresh, without buzzwords and prejudices. I hoped this approach might rise above the partisan debates that had existed in past years. I would not claim to have accomplished that task well. But perhaps some readers will still benefit from this elementary, yet philosophical presentation. This paper also introduced for the first time the triperspectival program that has informed all my writings since this time. It is probably my clearest summary of how triperspectivalism relates to the debate over apologetic method.—JF)

I have sensed that in recent years the debate within evangelicalism over apologetic method has degenerated into a series of partisan shouting matches. The different parties ("presuppositionalists," "evidentialists," "Van Tillians," "Montgomeryites," "Gerstnerites," and the like) seem more and more to be talking past one another. In such a situation, there ought to be some value in all of us backing away a bit from our particular partisan commitments and in asking why we tend to misunderstand one another in this area. People with a common commitment to the Christ of Scripture ought to be able to achieve greater unity than we have now (and not only in the area of apologetics). The prospect for meta-apologetic discussion, then, should be considered promising. In this paper, I will seek to make some contribution toward clarifying our differences: first, by viewing them in historical perspective, and second, by a fresh evaluation of that historical development in the light of Scripture.

Historical Roots of the Issue

I would like to distinguish three general types of epistemology appearing through the history of philosophy. It is not important to my argument that this enumeration be the best possible classification, or the only possible classification, or an exhaustive classification. It is sufficient for us to recognize that these three tendencies have existed and have exerted influence on Christian and non-Christian thinking alike. The first tendency is *rationalism* or *a priorism*, which I will define as the view that human knowledge presupposes certain principles known independently of sense-experience, principles by which, indeed, our knowledge of sense-experience is governed. The second tendency is *empiricism*, the view that human knowledge is based on the data of sense-experience. Third, there is *subjectivism*, the view that there is no "objective" truth, but only truth "for" the knowing subject, verified by criteria internal to the subject.

No philosopher has succeeded in being a consistent rationalist, empiricist, or subjectivist. A few, at least, have tried: Parmenides comes close to being a consistent rationalist, John Stuart Mill a consistent empiricist, Protagoras and the other sophists consistent subjectivists. But the failures of such attempts have become well known in the philosophical literature. The greatest philosophers, such as Plato, Aristotle, Aquinas, and Kant, have not even tried to achieve epistemological purity in terms of our categories. Rather, they have sought to do justice to divergent epistemological concerns. But that, too, has proved to be a difficult task. The nature of the difficulty can be summarized with the observation that rationalism, empiricism, and subjectivism as defined above are simply inconsistent with one another. They cannot all be affirmed simultaneously.

Still, it is not too surprising that philosophers have tried to combine these inconsistent views. For each seems to arise out of legitimate concerns. The rationalist notes that without criteria of truth and falsity, no conclusions whatever can be drawn from sense-experience or from subjective states. Sense-experience is always problematic: How do I know whether a stick in the water is really bent or whether it only appears that way? The visual image, taken by itself, can be interpreted in either way. All sense-experiences, it would seem, can be interpreted in various ways; and if the criteria for proper interpretation are drawn from sense-experience, then they would also be problematic and incapable of yielding a conclusion. Thus, the rationalist argues, the criteria that determine the true interpretation of sense-experience must come from some source other than sense-experience. The rationalist takes a similar view of subjective states. Our feelings, desires, decisions do not in themselves tell us what is true; rather, they are, like sense-experience, problematic data that must be interpreted and evaluated by the application of a priori criteria. But what if the subjectivist tries to argue that no such objective truth is possible? The rationalist replies that to deny objective truth is inevitably self-defeating. If there is no objective truth, then the subjectivist has no right even to assert the truth of his own subjectivism. And if the subjectivist is willing to give up even that right, then he is simply declining to engage in rational discourse. His is not an epistemology, but an antiepistemology. Since he has no truth to assert, he has nothing to say to us.

The rationalist recognizes, of course, that appeals to sense-experience and to subjective states are often plausible. I know that a certain apple will fall to the ground if I drop it. How do I know this? It is plausible to say that I know this on the basis of past experience: other apples have always fallen when dropped. But the rationalist asks: how do I know that the future will resemble the past? Is it because such resemblance has always occurred in the past? But that merely shifts the problem to another level. How do I know that such resemblances between past and future will continue into the future? Clearly, I cannot derive such a principle from past or present experience. If it is true, says the rationalist, it must be derived from some source other than sense-experience. Similar arguments can be raised in regard to subjective states. Someone says, for example, that war is wrong because he subjectively perceives it to be wrong. The rationalist replies that if this judgment is a rational judgment, it must be based on something more than a mere feeling, since feelings often mislead us.

A strong case, then, can be made for rationalism. But strong cases can also be made for empiricism and subjectivism. The empiricist stresses the need for publicly observable facts as a basis for knowledge. He recognizes that sense-experience is problematic, but he points out that claims to a priori truth are also problematic. Philosophers have contradicted one another on the question of what can be known a priori; Parmenides claimed to know a priori that all motion was illusory; Plato denied this claim. Descartes claimed an a priori knowledge of his own existence as a thinking substance; Hume denied that claim. Surely, then, says the empiricist, claims to a priori knowledge are fallible: some of the historical claims must be wrong. How do we judge the truth of such claims? Certainly, says the empiricist, we cannot simply take someone's word for it. There must be checking procedures available to all, not just to the individual making the claim. To speak of publicly available checking procedures is to speak about sense-experience. But is sense-experience a truly public point of reference? Or is it, perhaps, something that varies greatly from person to person, a merely subjective phenomenon? The empiricist response to subjectivism parallels that of rationalism: if sense-experience is not a universally shared access to reality, then there is no such access, and knowledge is impossible. Thus, the empiricist argues that sense-experience is the ultimate test of alleged a priori principles and of all subjective convictions. For the consistent empiricist such as Mill, such argumentation virtually eliminates a priori principles altogether.

The empiricist can also argue against the rationalist that even if one can become assured of an a priori principle—say, the law of noncontradiction or the existence of the self—such a principle is quite useless without sense-experience. Nothing can be deduced from the law of noncontradiction alone. Logic becomes useful only when applied to nontrivial premises of arguments. But no one would argue that all premises of all valid arguments are known a priori or are deducible from premises known a priori. But if some premises are known a posteriori, then it would seem that logic yields truth only in dependence on a posteriori knowledge, most likely sense-experience.

What about subjectivism? Is it possible to make a case for that, too, after the apparently devastating attacks on it by the rationalists and empiricists? Certainly. If one accepts the rationalist argument for the fallibility of sense-experience and the empiricist argument for the fallibility of claims to a priori knowledge, then subjectivism seems unavoidable. Further, do not all claims to a priori knowledge and empirical fact boil down to subjective judgments? Take the law of noncontradiction, for example. Why should I affirm it? Is it not because I am personally convinced of its truth? No, reply the rationalist and the empiricist: whether you are subjectively persuaded is irrelevant; you should not affirm a principle unless it is objectively true. But, the subjectivist replies, I must be persuaded of that objective truth. The others insist: You must be persuaded on principle. The subjectivist reiterates: Yes, but I must also be *persuaded* that the principle is true. Any principle you propose, I must investigate and evaluate. I accept only those principles that I consider worthy of acceptance. Therefore, any appeal to principle would seem to depend on a subjective act by which that principle is adopted. We saw earlier that subjectivism can be made to seem impossible. But it can also be made to seem inescapable.

Now, Christian apologetics reflects the epistemological tendencies I have described. Gordon Clark is the clearest example among evangelical apologists of the rationalist tendency, but many have used the traditional rationalist arguments in refutation of skepticism and in defense of the objectivity of truth. Empiricism is evident in the work of John W. Montgomery and others. Subjectivism is relatively absent from evangelical apologetics, because of the evangelical emphasis on the truth-falsehood antithesis. But Edward J. Carnell's book *The Kingdom of Love and the Pride of Life*[1] does present what might be called a Christian subjectivism. In that book, Carnell appeals to feelings and intuitions that he considers universally human, without much (if any) reference to the objective grounding of these feelings or intuitions via a priori principles or empirical fact. Such objective grounding is, of course, presented in Carnell's other books, but if one had only this one book, he might be led to think that Carnell was an epistemological subjectivist. And that fact suggests what may be a significant observation: there may be a kind of subjectivism that is compatible with other epistemological principles, about which more at a later point.

Other evangelicals also combine motifs from various epistemological options. Norman Geisler preserves in large measure the balance between rationalism and empiricism characteristic of the Thomistic-Aristotelian tradition. Cornelius Van Til, in my view, should not be grouped with Gordon Clark as a "presuppositionalist," as is often done. Van Til, rather, presents us with a complex epistemology involving motifs from all three tendencies and more. My own construction, to which we will turn next, is indebted to Van Til, though I take full responsibility for the formulation.

Some Biblical Considerations

It is interesting to note that the three epistemological tendencies discussed above correlate roughly with the three sources of divine revelation affirmed in Scripture and Christian theology: Scripture, nature, and human personhood (the image of God). I say that the correlation is "rough"; I must add a few refinements. The precise biblical correlate of the "a priori principle" is divine law. Just as in secular rationalism the a priori principle supplies the criterion for truth and falsity, thus controlling the interpretation of sense-experience and subjective states, so in Christianity, God's law (or, equivalently, God's Word) serves as the ultimate criterion of truth and falsity, right and wrong. It is God's Word that governs the Christian's interpretation of experience and of himself. Scripture epitomizes God's law-Word; it is the covenant

1. Grand Rapids: Eerdmans, 1960.

constitution of the people of God, the only written human language that is also divine language. But the law of God is also available through other sources. Romans 1:18–32 makes it clear that even Gentiles who have no access to the written law nevertheless know what God requires of them and the penalty for disobedience. In Romans 1, the source of this knowledge seems to be the creation in general (vv. 18–20); in Romans 2:15 and elsewhere, the source may be human conscience. To my knowledge, Scripture does not trace the mechanism by which this knowledge from nature and the human self reaches us. That mechanism would be of interest for a number of reasons; one is the problem of understanding how the facts of nature could yield moral knowledge contrary to Hume's strictures against deriving *ought* from *is*. Whatever the mechanism, however, God gets his message through.

So although only Scripture is the law of God written, the law of God can be found everywhere. And equally comprehensive is the second form of revelation—"natural" or "general" revelation, the category that correlates naturally with the philosophical notion of "empirical fact." Nature includes everything in creation. It includes even the Bible as a created book; and it contains us human beings in the image of God.

Nature and *law*, then, are inseparable. The logical distinction between them is that nature is the environment in which we are called to live obediently to the law. The law calls us to replenish and subdue the earth (Gen. l:27ff.). The Word of God thus governs all our activity in this world. But what does the Word of God require of us concretely? How, specifically, do we go about "subduing" the earth? To find out, we must study not only God's command, but the earth itself as well. The nature of the earth will determine to some extent how it is to be subdued. Subduing a lion is one thing; subduing a river quite another. In an odd sense, we must study the world in order to properly exegete God's Word, or else we will not know the concrete meaning of the Word. And if we don't know its concrete meaning, then we don't know its meaning at all. Thus do general and special revelation work together in the believer's life. The Word directs us to the world; and in the world we find more of the meaning of the Word.

Then comes the third member of the triad, human nature, which correlates with philosophical *subjectivity*. Self-knowledge has always been philosophically difficult. As Hume and Wittgenstein especially have pointed out, the self is not one of the things we see as we look on the world. Yet it is through ourselves that we come to know everything else. All we know, we know through our own senses, reason, feelings, through what we are. And it is thus in knowing other things that we come to know the self. The self seems to be everywhere and nowhere. We know it, but only as we know other things. Hence the strange opening pages of Calvin's *Institutes* where he notes that we know God in knowing ourselves and vice versa and adds (casting some doubt on the purity of his presuppositionalism) that he does not know which "comes first." From a biblical standpoint, however, this is not so strange after all. Scripture tells us over and over that God-knowledge and self-knowledge are inseparable. What we *are* is "image of God." Knowing ourselves is knowing our resemblance to God, and indeed the defacement of that resemblance. The self is by its very nature a reflection of something else—a reflection of its ultimate environment. On the other hand, knowing God always involves attention to ourselves. "Knowledge of God" is an ethical concept in Scripture. Knowing God, in the most profound sense, involves obedience. Obedience is the fruit of the knowledge of God, and it is also the way to deeper knowledge of him (Rom. 12:1f.; Eph. 5:8–10; Phil. 1:10; Heb. 5:11–14).

In Christianity, then, law, object, and subject are distinguishable, but not discovered separately. In every act of knowledge, we simultaneously come to know God's law, his world, and ourselves. These are not three separable "parts" of our experience, but three "aspects" of every experience, or (perhaps better) three "perspectives" on experience. Thus I speak of *normative, situational*, and *existential* perspectives on experience. The normative perspective views our experience as a means of determining what God requires of us. It focuses especially on Scripture as the one written Word of God, but also on creation and the self as means of understanding and applying the norms of Scripture. The situational perspective views our experience as an organic collection of facts to be known and understood. The existential perspective views our experience as a means to self-knowledge and personal growth.

The resulting epistemology is complex, but illuminating. It is not rationalist, empiricist, or subjectivist in the senses defined earlier, but it appreciates the concerns that have generated these three positions. It recognizes, with the rationalist, that sense-experience and subjective impressions are fallible; but it also agrees with the empiricist and the subjectivist that the same fallibility attaches to the reasoning process and to all claims of a priori truth. Scripture alone is infallible. The search for some infallible element in human thinking as such is idolatrous. Similarly idolatrous, in my view, is the attempt to give any one perspective a "priority" over the others, that is, to claim that one perspective rather than the others furnishes the "ultimate" ground for belief in something. Only God's Word furnishes such an ultimate ground, and God's Word is available to us in all three perspectives. Why, for instance, do we believe that $2 + 2 = 4$? Is it because mathematical relations of this sort are presupposed by the very nature of thought itself (rationalism)? Is it because past experience has gotten me into the habit of expecting 2 + 2 to result in 4 (empiricism)? Or is it because that sum seems psychologically inescapable (subjectivism)? I find all three explanations persuasive, and I see no particular need to choose between them. I think I recognize all three sorts of mental processes taking place. But which is ultimate? On which of them do the others depend? Are my views about "the nature of thought itself" dictated by habits of mind developed through experience, or do those views dictate what my mental habits ought to be? (The same sort of question can be asked about any two of the three perspectives.) The answer is again that I see no need to choose. I see no reason to assume that any of the three perspectives is "prior" to the others; there is dependence, but mutual dependence. It is a system of "checks and balances."

Such checks and balances tend to be lacking in non-Christian thought. Without the Christian God to coordinate the law, the world, and the self, there is little reason to suppose that the three will cohere. Thus, one must simply choose the one that he considers most trustworthy and give it "primacy" over the others.

Now, the difficulties traditionally noted in rationalism, empiricism, and subjectivism result, I would say, precisely from the attempts made in these epistemologies to absolutize one perspective over against the others. The rationalist errs precisely in his claim to an infallible knowledge of a priori truths, not subject to any empirical or subjective tests. His method fails to yield such infallible knowledge, and the truths for which it claims infallibility are too few to establish a comprehensive framework for human knowledge. The empiricist and the subjectivist, on the contrary, fail to see the need of law, the need of principles by which to sort out and evaluate empirical and subjective data.

To say as I have that none of the perspectives is infallible and that none is ultimate has relativistic overtones. Indeed, my position would be relativistic if it were not for my presupposition, derived from Scripture, that each perspective brings us into contact with God's truth. And that truth *is* infallible, absolute, and ultimate. Therefore, though our thinking is fallible at every point, it is not *so* fallible that any of us has an excuse for failing to know God (Rom. 1:20) or for failing to live obediently before him.

Some Apologetic Implications

Earlier I distinguished three types of evangelical apologetics influenced by rationalistic, empiricist, and subjectivist epistemological tendencies, respectively. We may now describe these as normative, situational, and existential types of apologetics. Our earlier discussion would lead us to believe that all three types have biblical warrant if they are qualified in the ways demanded by a biblical epistemology. And so they do. Not only are all three general types of apologetic warranted in Scripture by inference from a biblical epistemology, but they are each found in Scripture explicitly.

Normative apologetics is found in the explicit appeals by the prophets, Jesus, and the apostles to the law of God in Scripture, but not only there. It is implicit in the way Scripture responds to doubting questions with rebuke (Job 38–42; Ezek. 18:25; Matt. 20:1–15; Rom. 3:3ff.; 6:1f.; 6:15; 7:7; etc.). The force of such passages is that *we have no right* to doubt God's truth, love, faithfulness; that such doubt is simply contrary to his law, a law of which we may not claim ignorance. Even those ignorant of Scripture are aware of that law (Rom. 1). One might even say that all biblical apologetics is normative; for even when the immediate appeal is not to law but to empirical fact or subjective awareness, the law is never absent. Scripture never leaves it an open question as to how the empirical or subjective data are to be interpreted and responded to. Such data do not lead merely to probable or optional conclusions; they lead to certainty, because indeed they are law-laden. Thus, Paul in Acts 17, though speaking to people without knowledge of Scripture, and though basing his apologetic on the facts of nature and history, puts his conclusion in the form of a demand for repentance (v. 30).

Just as certainly, Scripture contains situational apologetics. That should be the most obvious of the three. Continually Scripture refers to the mighty acts of God in nature and redemptive history, preeminently the resurrection of Christ, to validate the truth of the proclamation. Since the gospel itself is a proclamation of historical fact, one might say that all biblical apologetics is situational (not forgetting what we also said earlier, that all biblical apologetics is normative). The two do not exclude each other; they are perspectives on each other.

And there is biblical precedent for existential apologetics. The disciples on the road to Emmaus were surely impressed by the force of divine law as Jesus expounded the Scriptures to them, and by the correlation of this law with the events of Jesus' life (here we find both normative and situational perspectives); but it was also significant, and epistemologically significant, that when Jesus taught, their hearts burned within them (Luke 24:32). The point of an apologetic is never merely to convince the mind, but to influence the unbeliever's whole outlook, so that he not only accepts the truth, but loves it, treasures it, seeks earnestly to act on it. Only then can we say that people are truly "persuaded," truly converted. Thus, the Psalms, the sermons of Jesus, the letters of Paul are not academic treatises, not collections of definitions and syllogisms, but appeals to the "whole person," filled with poetry, figures of speech, expression of emotions, pleadings, weepings. The gospel is law, it is historical fact, but it is also something that people can live with, joyfully. The gospel speaks to our anxieties, our fears, our sorrows, our lusts, to the whole range of human subjectivity. Can we say that all biblical apologetics is existential, as we said earlier that it was all normative and all situational? Yes. For Scripture *always* addresses the full range of human subjectivity; it *always* seeks comprehensive inner change, "heart-change." Thus, although the existential approach is sometimes more, sometimes less prominent in biblical apologetics, it is a perspective on all biblical apologetics.

Thus, all three methods are biblically legitimate, as long as none seeks to claim ultimate priority or to exclude another as a complementary perspective. In the current debate over apologetics, we must recognize the claim of the presuppositionalists that knowledge is impossible without law and that the ultimate law is the Scripture. We must also grant the claim of the evidentialists that the truth is found through the publicly observable events of nature and history. And we must grant the point made by many that no one will think rightly unless he is psychologically qualified to do so (there is much to be said here about the noetic effects of sin and the illumination of the Holy Spirit). Any of these approaches may be prominent in any particular apologetic encounter, but none will be successful unless the other approaches are also implicitly present. If we seek to present God's requirements without relating them in any way to the individual's experience and consciousness, our apologetic is unintelligible. If we seek to examine the events of nature and history without organizing and interpreting these facts in a divinely acceptable way, and without addressing the unbeliever's capacity for doing such a thing, we achieve nothing. And if we seek to address an individual's subjectivity without giving him a legal and historical basis for inner change, then we are being manipulative and are not presenting the gospel at all.

Yet these strictures leave a wide scope for creativity, for using different methods, different starting points, depending on the area to be discussed, the gifts of the apologist, and the felt needs of the non-Christian. Scripture itself is wonderfully rich in the methods it uses to lead us to repentance and faith. It is a shame, indeed, that modern apologetics has fallen so largely into stereotyped patterns. I am hoping that the multiperspectival approach suggested in this paper may unleash our creative energies to show the world that indeed every fact of experience, every valid principle of reason, every burden of the human heart, has God's name upon it.

APPENDIX G:
APOLOGETICS GLOSSARY

Note (February 2012): I wrote up this Glossary for inclusion in my festschrift, *STL*. It is not a standard apologetics dictionary, but a dictionary of my peculiar technical terms and their definitions. I thought some readers might want some help with the somewhat idiosyncratic terminology of presuppositional apologetics.

One of the fun things about being a theologian (or any other kind of academic) is that you get to invent new words and sometimes attach new meanings to old ones. I try not to do this too often, but over the years I have done some of it. In the Glossary below, I do not, for the most part, define standard theological terms (such as *holiness* and *justification*). These definitions can be obtained from standard theologies, theological dictionaries, and online sources. But I include terms that I have invented, or that I have attached unusual definitions to, or that have a special prominence in my writings (even though the definitions may be standard).

absolute personality. Van Til's basic characterization of God. Unlike any non-Christian view, the biblical God is both absolute (*a se*, self-existent, self-sufficient, self-contained) and personal (thinking, speaking, acting, loving, judging).

ad hominem. Argument that exposes deficiencies in the arguer rather than deficiencies in the proposition under discussion—thus, a logical fallacy. But ad hominem argument is often appropriate.

antithesis. The opposition between Christian and non-Christian thought.

apologetics. (1) The application of Scripture to unbelief (including the unbelief remaining in the Christian). (2) The study of how to give to inquirers a reason for the hope that is in us (1 Peter 3:15). Van Til saw it as involving proof, defense, and offense.

apologetics as defense. Giving answers to objections, "defense and confirmation of the gospel" (Phil. 1:7).

apologetics as offense. Attacking the foolishness of unbelieving thought (Ps. 14:1; 1 Cor. 1:18–2:16).

apologetics as proof. Presenting a rational basis for faith; demonstrating Christianity to be true.

a priori knowledge. Knowledge acquired prior to experience, used to interpret and evaluate experience. Contrasted with *a posteriori knowledge,* knowledge arising out of experience.

argument by presupposition. Showing that Christianity is the necessary **presupposition** of meaning and rationality, and that the denial of Christianity destroys all meaning and rationality. Synonym for **transcendental argument.**

authority. God's right to demand unqualified obedience from his creatures. A **lordship attribute.**

authority of the expert. The principle that submission to the knowledge of someone better informed, rather than absolute submission to God, is the best way to truth. To Van Til, this is the only kind of authority that the unbeliever will accept.

autonomy. The claim that one is competent to serve as the final criterion of truth and right; the attempt to live apart from any law external to the self. To Van Til, this is the paradigm attitude of unbelief.

blockhouse methodology. An **apologetic** approach that begins with beliefs supposedly held in common between believers and unbelievers, and then tries to supplement that **common ground** with additional truth. Van Til finds this methodology in Aquinas's distinction between natural reason and faith, and in other forms of traditional **apologetics.**

borrowed capital. The truth known and acknowledged by the unbeliever. He has no right to believe or assert truth based on his own **presuppositions,** but only on Christian ones. So his assertions of truth are based on borrowed capital.

broad circularity. A **circular argument** enriched by evidence. For example: "Scripture is true because evidences X, Y, and Z imply its truth," when X, Y, and Z themselves are warranted by Scripture.

certainty. (1) Assurance of one's beliefs (also termed *certitude*). (2) The impossibility of a proposition's being false. Van Til emphasized that Christian truth is certain and should be presented as a certainty, not a mere **probability.**

chance. The condition of events' occurring without cause or reason.

Christian "irrationalism." The renunciation of rational **autonomy**.

Christian "rationalism." The belief that divine revelation gives us access to truth.

circular argument. (1) Argument in which the conclusion of an argument is one of its premises. (2) Argument assuming something that would ordinarily not be assumed by someone who didn't believe the conclusion.

circularity. An argument in which the conclusion **justifies** itself. All arguments seeking to prove the existence of an ultimate or final authority are circular in this sense.

cognitive rest. A godly sense of satisfaction, which is the goal of **existential justification.**

common grace. Nonsaving grace, which leads to many good things even in fallen culture.

common ground. That which believer and unbeliever have in common, making it possible for them to engage in **apologetic** discussion. See **point of contact.** Van Til sometimes denied that Christians and non-Christians had any beliefs in common. But his actual view was that they *would* not have such common beliefs if each were fully consistent with his **presuppositions.**

competing circularities. Arguments in which each party appeals to an authority that he considers to be self-attesting.

contingency. (1) Dependence on something else for origin and/or continued being; the opposite of necessity. (2) **Chance.**

control. God's power over the world, a **lordship attribute.**

correlative. Mutually dependent. For Van Til, the unbeliever holds that God and the world are correlative.

cosmological argument. The argument that if we try to discuss "cause" without God, our reasoning degenerates into **rationalism, irrationalism,** or both.

covenant. Relation between the Lord and his servants. In divine-human covenants, God as covenant Lord selects a certain people from among all the nations of the earth to be his own. He rules over them by his law, in terms of which all who obey are blessed and all who disobey are cursed. But there is grace as well as law. God's grace establishes the covenant, and since all men are sinners, it's only by grace that God sends any covenant blessing. God's creation and government of the world is analogous to covenant: he rules all things as the Lord.

determinism. (1) The view that every event in the world has a cause. (2) The view that every event in the world has a *finite* cause. Van Til might be considered a determinist in sense 1, but not in sense 2. Determinisms of both kinds, however, often presuppose *impersonal* causation as ultimate. In that sense, Van Til rejected determinism and pointed out that it is equivalent to **chance.**

epistemological argument. The argument that human reasoning is futile without moral standards, and that those standards in turn presuppose God. See **moral argument.**

epistemology. Theory of knowledge. With **metaphysics** and **value theory,** one of the major divisions of **philosophy.**

ethics. Theory of behavior.

evidence. (1) The **facts** used in an argument to establish a conclusion. (2) Statements of such **facts.**

existential justification. Justifying a belief according to the **existential perspective,** by showing that it brings true subjective satisfaction.

existential perspective. Dealing with a subject, emphasizing its character as a part of human experience, an aspect of human subjectivity. Derived from the **lordship attribute** of **presence,** for God is present to our innermost heart and mind.

fact. What is the case; a state of affairs in the real world, governed by law. Inseparable from **interpretation.**

faculties of the mind. Intellect, will, emotions, imagination, perception, intuition, etc., all perspectives on the heart, for human beings know and experience the world as whole persons.

fideism. Belief that God is known by faith and not by reason. Van Til is sometimes accused of fideism, but he repudiated it frequently.

God-is-his-own-standard defense. The defense against the problem of evil that because of who God is, human beings have no right to bring accusations against him (Job 38–42; Rom. 9:14–15, 19–21). I sometimes call this the "shut-up" defense, as in the gag line " 'Shut up,' he explained." This is the **normative perspective.**

greater-good defense. The defense against the problem of evil that God promises us that he will bring good out of evil (Rom. 8:28). This is the **situational perspective.**

immanence (biblical). The **lordship attribute** of **covenant presence.**

immanence (nonbiblical). God's being so near to us that he cannot be distinguished from finite persons and objects. Thus, when he draws near, he becomes a creature, or the creatures become God. In this sense, modern theologians sometimes say that God is "wholly revealed."

incomprehensibility of God. The doctrine that although we can genuinely know God, we cannot know him exhaustively or know him as he knows himself.

indirect argument. A synonym for *reductio.*

interpretation. A person's understanding of what the facts are. Inseparable from **fact.**

irrationalism. The view that human reason has no reliable access to truth.

justification (in epistemology). An account of why someone should believe a proposition to be true.

knowledge of God. A relationship of friendship or enmity with God, involving a covenantal response of the whole person to God's **lordship,** in obedience or disobedience.

lordship. God's relation to his **covenant** people, involving his **control** and **authority** over them and his **presence** with them; analogously, God's relationship to the whole creation.

lordship attributes. Qualities that appear prominently in biblical descriptions of God's **lordship:** his **control, authority,** and **presence.**

metaphysics; ontology. Theory of being, dealing with (1) a general view of the world, a world-and-life view; (2) the fundamental realities that exist. With **epistemology** and **value theory,** one of the major divisions of **philosophy.**

miracle. An extraordinary demonstration of God's **covenant lordship.**

monism. Belief that reality is all of one kind; hence, denial of the Creator-creature distinction.

moral argument. The argument that all meaning and reasoning presupposes moral principles. But moral principles in turn presuppose God as **absolute personality.**

multiperspectival. Of or relating to an account of something that considers more than one **perspective.**

narrow circularity. A **circular argument** that directly asserts the self-justification of a conclusion without additional premises: for example, "God exists because God exists."

naturalistic fallacy. Inferring what ought to be from what is.

neutrality. Trying to think or live without making a religious commitment or ultimate **presupposition** (which is impossible). Attempting it presupposes a commitment against the true God.

new-heart defense. The defense against the problem of evil that regeneration and our eventual glorification change our values and **presuppositions** so that we lose the inclination to charge God with wrongdoing. This is the **existential perspective.**

noetic effects of sin. The effects of sin on human thought, reasoning, knowledge. In Van Til, the sinner knows God, but represses that knowledge (Rom. 1).

non-Christian irrationalism. Skepticism.

non-Christian rationalism. Grounding human reason in some mundane authority.

normative justification. Justifying a belief according to the **normative perspective,** by showing that it conforms to the norms of thought.

normative perspective. Dealing with a subject, emphasizing its character as divine revelation. Derived from the **lordship attribute** of divine **authority.**

objective knowledge; truth. Knowledge or truth whose truth does not depend on what man thinks.

one-and-many problem. The issue that knowledge involves uniting particulars into universal categories. But if every particular is exhaustively described by universal categories, then it is no longer particular. But if some particularities cannot be described by universal categories, then they can't be known, or they have no nature. The same problem can be described in terms of the relation of logic to **fact,** and of that of subject to object.

ontological argument. The argument that a definition of God (a being with all perfections) implies his existence. Works only as a **presuppositional** argument that assumes a distinctively biblical concept of perfection.

ontology. In my work, a synonym for **metaphysics.**

person-variable. Of or relating to the fact that a particular person's response to an **apologetic** argument may differ from that of another person. Because an argument that will persuade one person will not necessarily persuade another, arguments should be formulated with a particular audience in mind.

perspective. A view or study of an object from a particular angle. When a tree is viewed from the north, the south, the east, and the west, these views constitute four perspectives.

persuasion. Convincing a person that your belief is true (as a goal of **apologetics**). An **apologetic** argument, therefore, should be valid (employing right logic), sound (incorporating true premises), and persuasive. Persuasion is the **existential perspective** of **apologetic** argument.

philosophy. An attempt to understand the world in its broadest, most general features; the exposition and defense of a **worldview.** Its constituents are **metaphysics, epistemology,** and **value theory** (or *axiology*). Philosophy is a subdivision of theology.

point of contact. (1) A belief held in common between two people that enables them to reason toward further agreement. In Van Til, particularly the point of contact between believer and unbeliever. For Van Til it is found not in a common **worldview,** but in the true knowledge of God that the believer has, and the unbeliever also has but suppresses. (2) A common interest between two people that can serve as the beginning of an evangelistic or apologetic conversation.

predication. Attaching a predicate to a subject; hence, making an assertion. Van Til says that only the Christian **worldview** makes predication possible.

presence. Also termed *covenant solidarity.* God's taking a people from among the other peoples to be his own exclusive possession. He commits himself to being with them ("Immanuel, God with us"), to be their God and for them to be his people. Often his presence is literal, as in the burning bush, the tabernacle, the temple, the person of Jesus (John 1:14), and the bodies of believers. A **lordship attribute.**

presupposition. (1) A belief that precedes other beliefs. (2) A belief that governs other beliefs. (3) Ultimate presupposition: the belief that governs *all* other beliefs, or the most fundamental commitment of the heart.

presuppositionalism of the heart. A basic commitment of the heart to bring all reasoning under the **lordship** of Christ. In my judgment, it is impossible to distinguish presuppositional from traditional **apologetics** merely by the form of their arguments, claims to **certainty** or **probability,** etc.

probability. The degree to which a proposition approaches **certainty.** Van Til believed that Christianity was certain, not merely probable, and that for an apologist to claim mere probability is to deny the clarity of God's revelation.

proof. An argument that establishes the truth of a conclusion. Van Til believed that there was "absolutely certain proof" of Christian theism by way of his **transcendental argument.**

rational autonomy. Reason, apart from tradition or revelation, as the final standard of knowledge.

rationalism. (1) The view that human reason is the final judge of truth and falsity, right and wrong. (2) The philosophical position that human reason is to be trusted above human sense-experience.

rationalist-irrationalist dialectic. The view that would-be autonomous thought is **rationalistic** in that it believes itself to be the final judge of truth and right; but that it is **irrationalistic** in that it believes the universe has no intrinsic order beyond the human person himself. So autonomous thought vacillates from optimistic to pessimistic views of reason, and back again.

reductio ad absurdum. A form of argument in which, rather than directly proving a conclusion, the arguer reduces the contrary conclusion to an absurdity. Hence it is also termed *indirect argument* or *argument from the impossibility of the contrary.* Van Til believed that all **transcendental arguments** must take this form. I disagree.

self-authenticating; self-attesting. Of or relating to the principle that since God's Word is the highest authority for us, it cannot be validated by anything higher than itself. So the ultimate source of Scripture's authority is its own word, validated to our hearts and minds by the Holy Spirit.

sense of deity, divinity. Also termed *sensus deitatis, divinitatis, semen religionis.* Calvin's way of describing the knowledge that the unbeliever has, but suppresses.

situational justification. Justifying a belief according to the **situational perspective,** by showing that it is in accord with the **facts.**

situational perspective. Dealing with a subject, emphasizing its character as a fact of nature, history, or both. Derived from the **lordship attribute** of **control,** for God's control governs all the facts of nature and history.

suaviter in modo, fortiter in re. Gentle in manner, strong in substance. Van Til's description of an ideal **apologetic** presentation.

teleological argument. The argument that one cannot even speak of "purpose" or "design" apart from moral values (see **moral argument**), which in turn presuppose God.

transcendence (biblical). God's exaltation as King, involving the **lordship attributes** of **control** and **authority.**

transcendence (nonbiblical). The idea that God is so far from us that we cannot know him or truly speak of him. In this sense, modern theologians sometimes say that God is "wholly other" or "wholly hidden."

transcendental argument. An argument that seeks to show the necessary conditions for the possibility of rational thought or meaningful discourse. Van Til believed this was the only kind of argument appropriate to a Christian **apologetic,** since the biblical God is the author of all meaning and rationality.

triperspectival. Of or relating to considering a subject from three **perspectives** connected with the **lordship attributes: normative, situational,** and **existential.**

value theory. Chiefly **ethics** and aesthetics. With **metaphysics** and **epistemology,** one of the major divisions of **philosophy.**

worldview. A way of understanding reality that governs all thought and life. The biblical worldview is unique in its view of (1) the Supreme Being as **absolute personality,** (2) the **lordship** of God, and (3) the Creator-creature distinction.

BIBLIOGRAPHY

Adams, Jay. *The Grand Demonstration: A Biblical Study of the So-Called Problem of Evil*. Santa Barbara, CA: East Gate Publishers, 1991.

Adams, Robert. *The Virtue of Faith*. Oxford: Oxford University Press, 1987.

Allis, Oswald T. *The Five Books of Moses*. 2nd ed. Philadelphia: Presbyterian and Reformed, 1949.

———. *The Old Testament: Its Claims and Its Critics*. Nutley, NJ: Presbyterian and Reformed, 1972; Grand Rapids: Baker, 1972.

———. *The Unity of Isaiah*. Philadelphia: Presbyterian and Reformed, 1950.

Alston, William P. "Epistemic Circularity." *Philosophy and Phenomenological Research* 47 (1986): 1–30.

Anderson, James N. "If Knowledge Then God: The Epistemological Theistic Arguments of Plantinga and Van Til." 2005. Available at http://www.proginosko.com/docs.

Anderson, James N., and Greg Welty. "The Lord of Non-Contradiction: An Argument for God from Logic." *Philosophia Christi* 13, 2 (2011).

Aquinas, Thomas. *Summa Contra Gentiles*.

Bahnsen, Greg L. *Always Ready: Directions for Defending the Faith*. Nacogdoches, TX: Covenant Media Press, 1996.

———. *An Answer to Frame's Critique of Van Til: Profound Differences between the Traditional and Presuppositional Methods*. Willow Grove, PA: Kirkland Printing, 1988.

———. *Van Til's Apologetic: Readings and Analysis*. Phillipsburg, NJ: P&R Publishing, 1998.

Bahnsen, Greg L., and Gordon Stein. "The Great Debate: Does God Exist?" Debate at University of California, Irvine, 1985. Available at http://www.bellevuechristian.org/faculty/dribera/htdocs/PDFs/Apol_Bahnsen_Stein_Debate_Transcript.pdf.

Bavinck, Herman. *The Doctrine of God*. Grand Rapids: Baker, 1951.

———. *Reformed Dogmatics: God and Creation*. Edited by John Bolt. Translated by John Vriend. Grand Rapids: Baker, 2004.

Beilby, James K. *Thinking about Christian Apologetics: What It Is and Why We Do It*. Downers Grove, IL: InterVarsity Press, 2011.

Bergmann, Michael. "Epistemic Circularity: Malignant and Benign." N.d. Available at http://web.ics.purdue.edu/~bergmann/epistemic%20 circularity.htm.

Berkouwer, G. C. *The Providence of God*. Grand Rapids: Eerdmans, 1952.

———. *The Triumph of Grace in the Theology of Karl Barth*. Grand Rapids: Eerdmans, 1956.

Boa, Kenneth D., and Robert M. Bowman Jr. *Faith Has Its Reasons: Integrative Approaches to Defending the Christian Faith*. 2nd ed. Waynesboro, GA: Paternoster, 2006.

Bratt, James D., ed. *Abraham Kuyper: A Centennial Reader*. Grand Rapids: Eerdmans, 1998.

Bultmann, Rudolf. *Existence and Faith*. Edited by Schubert M. Ogden. New York: Meridian Books, 1960.

Butler, Bishop Joseph. *Analogy of Religion*. New York: Harper and Brothers, 1898.

Butler, Michael. "TAG vs. TANG." *Penpoint* (August 1996). Available at http://www.reformed.org.

Calvin, John. *Institutes of the Christian Religion*. Edited by John T. McNeill. Translated by Ford Lewis Battles. 2 vols. Philadelphia: Westminster Press, 1960.

Carnell, Edward J. *An Introduction to Christian Apologetics*. Grand Rapids: Eerdmans, 1948.

———. *The Kingdom of Love and the Pride of Life*. Grand Rapids: Eerdmans, 1960.

Carson, D. A., and John D. Woodbridge, eds. *Hermeneutics, Authority, and Canon*. Grand Rapids: Zondervan, 1986.

Clark, Gordon. *The Johannine Logos*. Nutley, NJ: Presbyterian and Reformed, 1972.

———. *Religion, Reason, and Revelation*. Philadelphia: Presbyterian and Reformed, 1961.

Clark, Kelly James, Richard Lints, and James K. A. Smith. *101 Key Terms in Philosophy and Their Importance for Theology*. Louisville, KY: Westminster John Knox, 2004.

Clowney, Edmund P. *The Unfolding Mystery: Discovering Christ in the Old Testament*. 2nd ed. Phillipsburg, NJ: P&R Publishing, 2013.

Cooper, Derek. *Christianity and World Religions: An Introduction to the World's Major Faiths*. Phillipsburg, NJ: P&R Publishing, 2013.

Copan, Paul. "Questioning Presuppositionalism." March 12, 2012. http://thegospel coalition.org/blogs/tgc/2012/03/12/questioning-presuppositionalism/.

Cowan, Steven B., ed. *Five Views on Apologetics*. Grand Rapids: Zondervan, 2000.

Craig, William Lane. "A Classical Apologist's Response." In *Five Views on Apologetics*, edited by Steven B. Cowan, 232–35. Grand Rapids: Zondervan, 2000.

———. *Reasonable Faith: Christian Truth and Apologetics*. 3rd ed. Wheaton, IL: Crossway, 2008.

Daane, James. *A Theology of Grace*. Grand Rapids: Eerdmans, 1954.

Dancy, Jonathan, and Ernest Sosa, eds. *Blackwell Companion to Epistemology*. Cambridge, MA: Blackwell Reference, 1992.

Dembski, William A., ed. *Darwin's Nemesis: Phillip Johnson and the Intelligent Design Movement*. Downers Grove, IL: InterVarsity Press, 2006.

Dembski, William A., and Jonathan Wells. *The Design of Life: Discovering Signs of Intelligence in Biological Systems*. Dallas: Foundation for Thought and Ethics, 2008.

Edgar, William. "No News Is Good News: Modernity, the Postmodern, and Apologetics." *Westminster Theological Journal* 57, 2 (1995): 359–82.

Engel, S. Morris. *With Good Reason: An Introduction to Informal Fallacies*. 5th ed. New York: St. Martin's Press, 1994.

Erlandson, Doug. "A New Perspective on the Problem of Evil." *Antithesis* 2, 2 (March–April 1991): 10–16.

Evans, C. Stephen. *Faith beyond Reason: A Kierkegaardian Account*. Grand Rapids: Eerdmans, 1998.

———. *Philosophy of Religion*. Downers Grove, IL: InterVarsity Press, 1985.

Feinberg, John S. *Can You Believe It's True? Christian Apologetics in a Modern and Postmodern Era*. Wheaton, IL: Crossway, 2013.

Fletcher, Joseph F. *Situation Ethics: The New Morality*. Philadelphia: Westminster Press, 1966.

Flew, Antony, and Alasdair C. MacIntyre, eds. *New Essays in Philosophical Theology*. London: SCM, 1955.

Frame, John M. *The Amsterdam Philosophy*. Phillipsburg, NJ: Harmony Press, 1972.

———. *Apologetics to the Glory of God: An Introduction*. Phillipsburg, NJ: P&R Publishing, 1994.

———. "Christianity and Contemporary Epistemology." *Westminster Theological Journal* 52, 1 (Spring 1990): 131–41.

———. *Cornelius Van Til: An Analysis of His Thought*. Phillipsburg, NJ: P&R Publishing, 1995.

———. *The Doctrine of God*. Phillipsburg, NJ: P&R Publishing, 2002.

———. *The Doctrine of the Christian Life*. Phillipsburg, NJ: P&R Publishing, 2008.

———. *The Doctrine of the Knowledge of God*. Phillipsburg, NJ: Presbyterian and Reformed, 1987.

———. *The Doctrine of the Word of God*. Phillipsburg, NJ: P&R Publishing, 2010.

———. *Evangelical Reunion*. Grand Rapids: Baker, 1991.

———. *A History of Western Philosophy and Theology*. Phillipsburg, NJ: P&R Publishing, 2015.

———. *No Other God*. Phillipsburg, NJ: P&R Publishing, 2001.

———. *Perspectives on the Word of God*. Phillipsburg, NJ: Presbyterian and Reformed, 1990.

———. "Presuppositional Apologetics." In *Five Views on Apologetics*, edited by Steven B. Cowan, 207–31. Grand Rapids: Zondervan, 2000.

———. "The Problem of Theological Paradox." In *Foundations of Christian Scholarship*, edited by Gary North, 295–330. Vallecito, CA: Ross House, 1976.

———. "Rationality and Scripture." In *Rationality in the Calvinian Tradition*, edited by Hendrik Hart et al., 293–317. Lanham, MD: University Press of America, 1983.

———. "Reply to Don Collett on Transcendental Argument." *Westminster Theological Journal* 65, 2 (2003): 307–9. Available at http://www.frame-poythress.org/frame_articles/2003ReplytoCollett.htm.

———. "The Spirit and the Scriptures." In *Hermeneutics, Authority, and Canon*, edited by D. A. Carson and John D. Woodbridge, 217–35. Grand Rapids: Zondervan, 1986.

———. *Systematic Theology*. Phillipsburg, NJ: P&R Publishing, 2013.

Frame, John M., and Steve Hays. "Johnson on Van Til: A Rejoinder." 2005. Available at http://www.vantil.info/articles/johnson_on_vt.html.

Gaffin, Richard B., Jr. *Resurrection and Redemption*. Phillipsburg: NJ: Presbyterian and Reformed, 1987.

Geehan, E. R. *Jerusalem and Athens: Critical Discussions on the Philosophy and Apologetics of Cornelius Van Til*. Nutley, NJ: Presbyterian and Reformed, 1971.

Geisler, Norman L. *Baker Encyclopedia of Christian Apologetics*. Grand Rapids: Baker Academic, 1999.

Gerstner, John H. *Repent or Perish*. Ligonier, PA: Soli Deo Gloria Publications, 1990.

Goheen, Michael, and Craig Bartholomew. *Living at the Crossroads: An Introduction to Christian Worldview*. Grand Rapids: Baker Academic, 2008.

Gonzalez, Guillermo, and Jay Richards. *The Privileged Planet: How Our Place in the Cosmos Is Designed for Discovery*. Washington, DC: Regnery Publishing, 2004.

Griffin, David Ray. *Evil Revisited*. Albany, NY: State University of New York Press, 1991.

———. *God, Power, and Evil*. Philadelphia: Westminster Press, 1976.

Hart, Hendrik, et al. *Rationality in the Calvinian Tradition*. Lanham, MD: University Press of America, 1983.

Helm, Paul, ed. *Divine Commands and Morality*. Oxford: Oxford University Press, 1981.

———. *Faith and Reason*. New York: Oxford University Press, 1999.

Hepburn, R. W. *Christianity and Paradox*. New York: Pegasus, 1958.

Hick, John. *Evil and the God of Love*. New York: Harper & Row, 1966.

Hughes, John J., ed. *Speaking the Truth in Love: The Theology of John M. Frame*. Phillipsburg, NJ: P&R Publishing, 2009.

Hume, David. *Dialogues concerning Natural Religion*. Various eds.

———. *An Inquiry concerning Human Understanding*. New York: Liberal Arts Press, 1955, 1957.

Johnson, John. "Is Cornelius Van Til's Apologetic Method Christian or Merely Theistic?" *Evangelical Quarterly* 75, 3 (2003): 257–68.

Johnson, Phillip. *Darwin on Trial*. Downers Grove, IL: InterVarsity Press, 1993.

———. *Reason in the Balance*. Downers Grove, IL: InterVarsity Press, 1995.

Jones, Peter. *Spirit Wars*. Escondido, CA: Main Entry, 1997.

Jordan, James B. *Through New Eyes*. Brentwood, TN: Wolgemuth and Hyatt, 1988.

Kant, Immanuel. *Critique of Pure Reason*. Abridged, edited, translated, and with an introduction by Norman Kemp Smith. New York: Random House, 1958.

Kaufmann, Walter. *Critique of Religion and Philosophy*. New York: Harper and Brothers, 1958.

Kline, Meredith G. *Images of the Spirit*. Grand Rapids: Baker, 1980.

———. *The Structure of Biblical Authority*. Grand Rapids: Eerdmans, 1972.

Kuhn, Thomas. *The Structure of Scientific Revolutions*. 2nd ed. Chicago: University of Chicago Press, 1970.

Kushner, Harold S. *When Bad Things Happen to Good People*. New York: Schocken Books, 1981.

Lewis, C. S. *Christian Reflections*. Edited by Walter Hooper. Grand Rapids: Eerdmans, 1967.

———. *The Problem of Pain*. London: Geoffrey Bles, 1940.

Lewis, Gordon R. *Testing Christianity's Truth Claims*. Chicago: Moody Press, 1976.

Linnemann, Eta. *Historical Criticism of the Bible: Methodology or Ideology?* Translated by Robert W. Yarbrough. Grand Rapids: Baker, 1990.

Machen, J. Gresham. *Christianity and Liberalism*. Grand Rapids: Eerdmans, 1923.

———. *The Origin of Paul's Religion*. New York: Macmillan, 1921; Grand Rapids: Eerdmans, 1965.

———. *The Virgin Birth of Christ*. New York: Harper, 1930.

———. *The Virgin Birth of Christ*. 2nd ed. Grand Rapids: Baker, 1967.

Martin, C. B. "The Perfect Good." In *New Essays in Philosophical Theology*, edited by Antony Flew and Alasdair C. MacIntyre, 212–26. London: SCM, 1955.

Martin, Michael. "The Transcendental Argument for the Nonexistence of God." Available at http://www.infidels.org/library/modern/michael _martin/martin-frame/tang.html.

Martyr, Justin. *First Apology*.

Mayers, Ronald B. *Balanced Apologetics: Using Evidences and Presuppositions in Defense of the Faith*. Chicago: Moody Press, 1984.

McGrath, Alister. *Intellectuals Don't Need God & Other Modern Myths.* Grand Rapids: Zondervan, 1993.

McGrath, Gavin, W. C. Campbell-Jack, and C. Stephen Evans, eds. *The New Dictionary of Christian Apologetics.* Downers Grove, IL: InterVarsity Press, 2006.

Meyer, Stephen C. *Darwin's Doubt: The Explosive Origin of Animal Life and the Case for Intelligent Design.* New York: HarperOne, 2013.

———. *Signature in the Cell: DNA and the Evidence for Intelligent Design.* New York: HarperCollins, 2009.

Montgomery, John Warwick. "Once upon an A Priori." In *Jerusalem and Athens: Critical Discussions on the Philosophy and Apologetics of Cornelius Van Til,* edited by E. R. Geehan, 380–92. Nutley, NJ: Presbyterian and Reformed, 1971.

Moreland, J. P. *Christianity and the Nature of Science.* Grand Rapids: Baker, 1989.

———. *Love Your God with All Your Mind.* Colorado Springs: NavPress, 1997.

Morey, Robert A. *Death and the Afterlife.* Minneapolis: Bethany House, 1984.

Murray, John. *Collected Writings of John Murray.* Vol. 2. Edinburgh: Banner of Truth Trust, 1977.

Netland, Harold. "Apologetics, Worldviews, and the Problem of Neutral Criteria." *Trinity Journal* 12 (1991): 39–58.

———. *Dissonant Voices.* Grand Rapids: Eerdmans, 1991.

Norris, Christopher. *What's Wrong with Postmodernism?* Baltimore: Johns Hopkins University Press, 1990.

North, Gary, ed. *Foundations of Christian Scholarship.* Vallecito, CA: Ross House, 1976.

Notaro, Thom. *Van Til and the Use of Evidence.* Phillipsburg, NJ: Presbyterian and Reformed, 1980.

Oliphint, K. Scott, and Lane G. Tipton, eds. *Revelation and Reason: New Essays in Reformed Apologetics.* Phillipsburg, NJ: P&R Publishing, 2007.

Penner, Myron B. *The End of Apologetics.* Grand Rapids: Baker Academic, 2013.

Phillips, Timothy R., and Dennis L. Okholm, eds. *Christian Apologetics in the Postmodern World.* Downers Grove, IL: InterVarsity Press, 1995.

Pinnock, Clark. "The Philosophy of Christian Evidences." In *Jerusalem and Athens: Critical Discussions on the Philosophy and Apologetics of*

Cornelius Van Til, edited by E. R. Geehan, 420–25. Nutley, NJ: Presbyterian and Reformed, 1971.

Piper, John. *Desiring God*. Sisters, OR: Multnomah, 1986.

Piper, John, Justin Taylor, and Paul Kjoss Helseth, eds. *Beyond the Bounds*. Wheaton, IL: Crossway, 2003.

Plantinga, Alvin. *God, Freedom, and Evil*. Grand Rapids: Eerdmans, 1977.

Plantinga, Alvin, and Nicholas Wolterstorff, eds. *Faith and Rationality*. Notre Dame, IN: University of Notre Dame Press, 1983.

Poythress, Vern S. "A Biblical View of Mathematics." In *Foundations of Christian Scholarship*, edited by Gary North, 159–88. Vallecito, CA: Ross House, 1976.

———. *Redeeming Science*. Wheaton, IL: Crossway, 2006.

Pratt, Richard L., Jr. "Common Misunderstandings of Van Til's Apologetics." Part 2. *IIIM Magazine Online* 1, 42 (1999), http://www.thirdmill.org /newfiles/ric_pratt/TH.Pratt.VanTil.2.html.

Ramsay, Richard B. *The Certainty of the Faith: Apologetics in an Uncertain World*. Phillipsburg, NJ: P&R Publishing, 2008.

Rescher, Nicholas. *Cognitive Pragmatism: The Theory of Knowledge in Pragmatic Perspective*. Pittsburgh: University of Pittsburgh Press, 2001.

Robinson, A. T. *Honest to God*. Philadelphia: Westminster Press, 1963.

———. *Redating the New Testament*. London: SCM Press, 1976.

Rushdoony, Rousas J. *By What Standard? An Analysis of the Philosophy of Cornelius Van Til*. Birmingham, AL: Cornerstone Publishers, 1974.

———. *The Institutes of Biblical Law*. Nutley, NJ: Presbyterian and Reformed, 1973.

———. "The One and Many Problem." In *Jerusalem and Athens: Critical Discussions on the Philosophy and Apologetics of Cornelius Van Til*, edited by E. R. Geehan, 339–48. Nutley, NJ: Presbyterian and Reformed, 1971.

Russell, Bertrand. *Why I Am Not a Christian*. Edited by Paul Edwards. New York: Simon and Schuster, 1957.

Schlossberg, Herbert. *Idols for Destruction*. Nashville: Thomas Nelson, 1983.

Sire, James W. "On Being a Fool for Christ and an Idiot for Nobody." In *Christian Apologetics in the Postmodern World*, edited by Timothy R. Phillips and Dennis L. Okholm, 101–30. Downers Grove, IL: InterVarsity Press, 1995.

Sorenson, Roy. "P Therefore P, Without Circularity." *Journal of Philosophy* 88 (1991): 245–66.

Sproul, R. C. *Scripture Alone: The Evangelical Doctrine*. Phillipsburg, NJ: P&R Publishing, 2005.

Sproul, R. C., John H. Gerstner, and Arthur W. Lindsley. *Classical Apologetics*. Grand Rapids: Zondervan, 1984.

Stackhouse, John G., Jr. *Humble Apologetics: Defending the Faith Today*. New York: Oxford University Press, 2002.

Strobel, Lee. *The Case for Christ: A Journalist's Personal Investigation of the Evidence for Jesus*. Grand Rapids: Zondervan, 1998.

Torres, Joseph E. "Perspectives on Multiperspectivalism." In *Speaking the Truth in Love: The Theology of John M. Frame*, edited by John J. Hughes, 111–36. Phillipsburg, NJ: P&R Publishing, 2009.

———. "Presuppositionalism and Circularity . . . Again?" March 15, 2012. http://apolojet.wordpress.com/2012/03/15/presuppositionalism-and-circularity-again/.

Vanhoozer, Kevin J. *First Theology: God, Scripture and Hermeneutics*. Downers Grove, IL: InterVarsity Press, 2002.

Van Til, Cornelius. *The Case for Calvinism*. Philadelphia: Presbyterian and Reformed, 1964.

———. *Christianity and Idealism*. Philadelphia: Presbyterian and Reformed, 1955.

———. "Christianity in Conflict." Unpublished class syllabus, 1962.

———. *Christian Philosophy*. Phillipsburg, NJ: Grotenhuis, 1956.

———. *Christian-Theistic Evidences*. Philadelphia: Presbyterian and Reformed, 1961.

———. *A Christian Theory of Knowledge*. Nutley, NJ: Presbyterian and Reformed, 1969.

———. *Common Grace and the Gospel*. Nutley, NJ: Presbyterian and Reformed, 1972.

———. *The Defense of the Faith*. Philadelphia: Presbyterian and Reformed, 1955.

———. *The Defense of the Faith*. 3rd ed. Philadelphia: Presbyterian and Reformed, 1967.

———. *The Defense of the Faith*. 3rd rev. ed. Philadelphia: Presbyterian and Reformed, 1975.

———. *The Defense of the Faith*. Edited by K. Scott Oliphint. 4th ed. Phillipsburg, NJ: P&R Publishing, 2008.

———. *The Great Debate Today*. Nutley, NJ: Presbyterian and Reformed, 1971.

———. *An Introduction to Systematic Theology*. Philadelphia: Presbyterian and Reformed, 1955.

———. *An Introduction to Systematic Theology*. Nutley, NJ: Presbyterian and Reformed, 1974.

———. *An Introduction to Systematic Theology: Prolegomena and the Doctrine of Revelation, Scripture, and God*. Edited by William Edgar. 2nd ed. Phillipsburg, NJ: P&R Publishing, 2007.

———. "The Metaphysics of Apologetics." Unpublished class syllabus, 1932.

———. *The New Modernism*. 3rd ed. Nutley, NJ: Presbyterian and Reformed, 1973.

———. *The Protestant Doctrine of Scripture*. Philadelphia: Presbyterian and Reformed, 1967.

———. *The Reformed Pastor and Modern Thought*. Nutley, NJ: Presbyterian and Reformed, 1971.

———. *A Survey of Christian Epistemology*. Philadelphia: Presbyterian and Reformed, 1969.

———. *The Triumph of Grace*. Philadelphia: Westminster Theological Seminary, 1958.

———. *Why I Believe in God*. Philadelphia: Committee on Christian Education, Orthodox Presbyterian Church, n.d.

Walton, Douglas N. *Begging the Question: Circular Reasoning as a Tactic of Argumentation*. New York: Greenwood Press, 1991.

———. "Circular Reasoning." In *Blackwell Companion to Epistemology*, edited by Jonathan Dancy and Ernest Sosa, 66. Cambridge, MA: Blackwell Reference, 1992.

Ware, Bruce A. *God's Lesser Glory*. Wheaton, IL: Crossway, 2000.

Warfield, B. B. *The Inspiration and Authority of the Bible*. Philadelphia: Presbyterian and Reformed, 1948.

Wilkins, Michael J., and J. P. Moreland, eds. *Jesus under Fire: Modern Scholarship Reinvents the Historical Jesus*. Grand Rapids: Zondervan, 1996.

Wilson, Douglas, ed. *Bound Only Once*. Moscow, ID: Canon Press, 2001.

Wright, N. T. *The Resurrection of the Son of God*. Minneapolis: Fortress, 2003.

INDEX OF SCRIPTURE

INDEX OF SUBJECTS AND NAMES

ALSO BY JOHN M. FRAME

This magisterial opus—at once biblical, clear, cogent, readable, accessible, and practical—summarizes the mature thought of one of the most important and original Reformed theologians of the last hundred years. It will enable you to see clearly how the Bible explains God's great, sweeping plan for mankind.

"*Systematic Theology* brings together, slims down, sums up, and augments all the wisdom contained in Frame's four-volume Lordship series. It is a worthy climax to the life's work of one who has only ever sought to be a faithful servant of Christ, teaching in his church. . . . Thank you, John Frame, for this superb gift."

> —**J. I. Packer,** Board of Governors' Professor of Theology, Regent College, Vancouver, British Columbia

ALSO BY JOHN M. FRAME

A History of Western Philosophy and Theology: Spiritual Warfare in the Life of the Mind

To be published in 2015

Christians should evaluate philosophy by biblical criteria. The fall of Adam brought intellectual as well as moral corruption on the human race. The effects of the fall can be seen in the work of philosophers, most of whom try to understand the world autonomously—reasoning apart from God's revelation. But revelation should inform reason, and not the other way around. Frame evaluates the history of philosophy and theology from a thoroughgoing *Christian* worldview, thereby making a unique contribution to the history of Western thought.

"I have never read a history of Western thought quite like John Frame's. Professor Frame unabashedly tries to think through sources and movements out of the framework (bad pun intended) of deep-seated Christian commitments, and invites his readers to do the same. These commitments, combined with the format of a seminary or college textbook, will make this work invaluable to students and pastors who tire of ostensible neutrality that is no more neutral than the next volume. Agree or disagree with some of his arguments, but John Frame will teach you how to *think* in theological and philosophical categories."
 —**D. A. Carson**, Research Professor, Trinity Evangelical Divinity School

"John Frame has done it again! In the lucid and comprehensive style of his Lordship Theology volumes, he here presents a full overview of Western thought about knowledge of God. . . . The book deserves wide use as a textbook, and I hope it will achieve that. My admiration for John's work grows and grows."
 —**J. I. Packer**, Board of Governors' Professor of Theology, Regent College, Vancouver, British Columbia

JOHN FRAME'S HIGHLY ACCLAIMED THEOLOGY OF LORDSHIP SERIES EXPLORES GOD'S RELATIONSHIP TO US IN ALL ASPECTS OF OUR LIVES

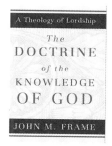 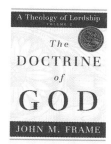 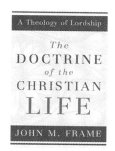 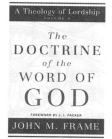

THE DOCTRINE OF THE KNOWLEDGE OF GOD

Our relationship with God is a knowing relationship. Often in Scripture God performs his mighty acts so that men will "know" that he is Lord.

THE DOCTRINE OF GOD

An Evangelical Christian Publishers Association Gold Medallion Award winner that examines the attributes, acts, and names of God in connection with relevant theological, ethical, and spiritual truths.

THE DOCTRINE OF THE CHRISTIAN LIFE

Surveys non-Christian ethical traditions before setting forth a solidly Christian ethical method. He presents a model for decision-making that honors God in all aspects of life.

THE DOCTRINE OF THE WORD OF GOD

Frame discusses God's word in modern theology and how God's word comes to us as his controlling power, meaningful authority, and personal presence.

JOHN FRAME'S SELECTED SHORTER WRITINGS, VOLUMES 1 AND 2

These pointed essays challenge fashionable arguments in theology and encourage us to abhor easy answers.

"John wrote this book so that the average person could understand it, which is a concept introduced by the apostle Paul but little employed ever since. John could do a number on us intellectually, but he prefers to communicate for the sake of the kingdom of God."
  —**Andrée Seu Peterson**, Senior Writer, *WORLD* magazine

"John Frame is certainly one of those 'dangerous theologians.' Of course, that means he is mild and loving even as he confronts error boldly and builds the necessary biblical theological frameworks for our times."
  —**Andrew J. Peterson,** President, Reformed Theological Seminary, Global Education

"This excellent book is a must-read for anyone who seeks to be challenged in understanding the biblical and theological issues that face the church of Jesus Christ today."
  —**Kenneth Gary Talbot**, President, Whitefield Theological Seminary

MORE FROM P&R ACADEMIC

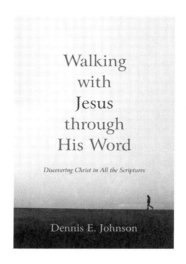

Dennis Johnson takes readers of the Bible on a journey of discovery through the Old and New Testaments, pointing out a network of trails—recurring themes that link events, individuals, institutions, and offices—connecting biblical texts and times to Jesus the Christ, the fulfiller of God's promises, the redeemer of God's people, and the founder of our covenant with him.

"Johnson shows us how we can read the Bible ourselves in a Christ-centered way and how this approach enriches our understanding of the Word of God."
—**John M. Frame**, J. D. Trimble Professor of Systematic Theology and Philosophy, Reformed Theological Seminary, Orlando